The Principle of Contradiction in Aristotle

The Principle of Contradiction in Aristotle

A Critical Study

Jan Łukasiewicz

Translated with an Introduction and Commentary
by Holger R. Heine

Published by Topos Books
An imprint of Topos Productions
1050 Queen Street, Suite 100, Honolulu, HI 96814
toposbooks.com

Originally published in Polish in 1910 as *O zasadzie sprzeczności u Arystotelesa. Studium krytyczne.*

Library of Congress Cataloging-in-Publication Data Available

ISBN 978-1-943354-06-1 (Paperback)
ISBN 978-1-943354-07-8 (Ebook)

Table of Contents

Foreword

Graham Priest

In 1910 the young Jan Łukasiewicz published a remarkable book, *The Principle of Contradiction in Aristotle.*

Something over 2000 years earlier, Aristotle, in book Γ of his *Meaphysics*, had taken the views of some of his Presocratic predecessors in his sights and defended the claim that no contradiction can possibly be true. The text is somewhat tangled—even by Aristotelian standards; but its success was undeniable. It fixed the Principle of (Non-)Contradiction into high orthodoxy in Western Philosophy—so much so, that virtually no Western philosopher for the next 2000 years felt the need to defend the Principle at any length. True, there have been a few dissenters. Hegel is the most obvious. However, such was the power of orthodoxy, that most commentators on Hegel—though certainly not Łukasiewicz—have gone out of their way to argue that when he said that the world was contradictory, he didn't really mean it.

In the first part of his book, Łukasiewicz takes Aristotle's text and, with clinical precision, demolishes its arguments. Why it had taken over two millennia for someone to do this is an interesting question, which I won't pursue here. But I think it fair to say that most commentators on *Metaphysics* Γ now take Łukasiewicz' critique to be substantially correct, and have had to work hard to try to salvage anything from Aristotle's arguments.[1]

Having demolished Aristotle's case for the Principle, the question then remains as to whether one should hold it to be true, and if so, why. That issue takes up the rest of Łukasiewicz' book. The

[1] For my own attempts in this direction, see 'To be and Not to Be—That is the Answer. On Aristotle on the Law of Non-Contradiction', *Philosophiegeschichte und Logische Analyse* 1 (1998), 91-130. Reprinted as ch. 1 of *Doubt Truth to be a Liar*, Oxford University Press, 2006.

outcome of this is not as impressive as that of the first part of the book, but the discussion is intellectually and psychologically fascinating. What we see is Łukasiewicz wrestling to defend a principle he obviously wishes to endorse, despite the evidence to the contrary he discusses. He is clear that there appear to be counter-examples to the Principle, such as the set-theoretic paradoxes, non-existent contradictory objects, and paradoxes of motion; and he is unable to defang them. Indeed, in places he even appears to endorse some of them them. Moreover, his final case for the Principle is disappointingly weak, even going against some insightful comments he makes earlier about reasoning under inconsistency. Łukasiewicz is clearly torn between reason and desire.[2]

Łukasiewicz' discussion is fascinating for another reason. As he is well aware, it is located at a crucial moment in the history of logic. He knows that new mathematical methods are coming to play a central role in logic. He is familiar with some of the writings of Frege and Russell (though presumably not *Principia Mathematica*, Volume 1 of which appeared only in November of the same year), and he makes explicit use of Couturat's 1905 *L'algèbre de la logique.* Moreover, his discussion of Aristotle is clearly informed by distinctions which the new symbolic techniques make clear. Modern readers will not be surprised by this.

What they may be surprised by is the extent to which Łukasiewicz draws on ideas in logic that—at least for most of the 20th Century—were out of fashion. The relevant intellectual climate in which Łukasiewicz is working is dominated by Hegel, on the one hand, and the phenomenological tradition of Brentano—who taught Łukasiewicz' own teacher, Twardowski—on the other. In particular, the ideas of Meinong—another student of Brentano—whose lectures Łukasiewicz attended in Graz, loom large in his discussion. What we have here, then, is an absorbing study of logic in flux.

Of course, Łukasiewicz was himself to go on to make significant contributions to the new area of mathematical logic, especially by inventing many-valued logic. In this, he was to take on, not the Principle of Non-Contradiction, but the other principle de-

[2] The case for these claims is made in detail in my 'Torn by Reason: Łukasiewicz on the Principle of Non-Contradiction', ch. 18 of S. Costreie (ed.), *Early Analytic Philosophy: Some New Perspectives on the Tradition,* Springer, 2016.

fended by Aristotle in the same book of the *Metaphysics:* the Principle of Excluded Middle (though Aristotle himself notoriously appears to backtrack on this in *De Interpretatione*). Why did Łukasiewicz switch his interest from the one principle to the other between 1910 and 1920? (As is now well known, many-valued logics may be used to challenge both principles.) Perhaps we will never know the answer, but Jan Woleński suggested to me that it was because of the criticism of his book which Łukasiewicz received in person from Stanislaw Leśniewski, eight years his junior.

Moreover, given his interest in the Principle of Non-Contradiction, Łukasiewicz could very easily have produced the first modern paraconsistent logic. In Appendix A of his book, he first specifies a positive propositional logic (drawn from Couturat). To this he then adds axioms for Boolean negation. It would have been simple for him to add axioms for a paraconsistent negation instead. He does not. The construction of the first modern paraconsistent logic was left for his student, Stanislaw Jaśkowski, only in 1948.

In the same year that he wrote his book, Łukasiewicz wrote a short paper in German, 'On the Principle of Contradiction in Aristotle', which contained his analysis of Aristotle's arguments. That paper was translated—somewhat belatedly—into English in 1970 and again in 1979. Hence, the content of this part of Łukasiewicz' book is now well known by Aristotle scholars—and should perhaps be better known by contemporary defenders of the Principle of Non-Contradiction. However, the contents of the rest of the book—which is the part which will probably be of more interest to logicians—was not canvassed in that paper.

The book itself was translated into German in 1993, and French in 2000. But it has never been translated into English before. Hence, it has been inaccessible to English-speaking logicians who are linguistically challenged (such as myself) until now. A great debt is therefore owed to Holger Heine for the present book, which contains not only his careful translation but a knowledgeable scholarly introduction and a perceptive commentary.

This book opens a window on a crucial period in the history of logic. It should be read by anyone interested in that history.

Graham Priest April 2021

Acknowledgments

This work was made possible through the generous support of many individuals and organizations. First and foremost, I want to thank my teacher and mentor, Graham Priest, who provided invaluable guidance and advice in addition to many patient and insightful discussions of the history of early paraconsistent thought, the principle of contradiction, and the significance of Łukasiewicz' early critical effort.

Greg Restall's constructive criticisms and comments benefitted my translation and commentary on Łukasiewicz' pioneering discussions. Participants of the Melbourne Logic Group meetings and Postgraduate Colloquia presented helpful commentary and questions about the research results that are presented here in the Introduction and Commentary.

An international research travel grant from the University of Melbourne allowed me to meet Jan Woleński, Sebastian Kolodziejczyk and Maja Kittel at Jagellonian University in Krakow, Poland. The discussions and comments of these three scholars greatly contributed to my understanding of the young Łukasiewicz and the history of Polish analytic philosophy, not to mention their helpful responses regarding the translation of Łukasiewicz' book. Peter Simons helped me untangle the philosophical connections between Meinong and the young Łukasiewicz. Finally, Arianna Betti provided valuable insights into the historical and philosophical connections between Twardowski, Łukasiewicz, and the beginnings of Polish analytic philosophy. My thanks to all of them for their kind support and interest in this research project.

Fellow postgrads at the University of Melbourne raised many constructive questions about the topics that are addressed in this work. I want to thank Rickie Bliss, Che Ping, David Sweeney, Kerstin Knight, Toby Meadows, Elena Walsh, Clare McCausland, Toby Mendelson, Zach Weber, and Mark Ressler. My office mate, Anya Daly, has been a constructive critic and steady supporter over the years.

The research for the initial presentation of this work was supported by an International Research Scholarship. My heartfelt thanks to the The University of Melbourne and everyone involved in providing this essential foundation for this research.

Additional support was provided by close friends and family members. Todd Manley, Carolyn Koo, Stephanie Lincoln, Heike Baars and Tim Holmes helped along the way. Armando and Gloria Savet, Lee Nasso, Tina Foster, Chris and Vicky Ingalls, all supported this effort. My mother, Wilma Heine, supported the work on this project with great patience from start to finish. My son Malcolm was an inspiration throughout.

Finally, I want to thank Suzanne, my life partner and companion on this unexpected journey. Without her cheerful determination, this project would not have been possible.

Holger Heine, March 2021

Introduction: Jan Łukasiewicz and the Principle of Contradiction

In 1910, at age thirty-two, Jan Łukasiewicz published his first major philosophical work, a monograph titled *O zasadzie sprzeczności u Arystotelesa. Studium krytyczne (On the Principle of Contradiction in Aristotle. A Critical Study).* In this work, he develops a pioneering critique of the logical and metaphysical foundations of the Aristotelian principle of non-contradiction—and its modern descendants—by applying the newly gained analytic tools of early twentieth century formal logic and mathematics. Łukasiewicz' aim is to develop a new type of logic, a non-Aristotelian[1] logic, which he envisioned as a formally constructed logic that does not include or endorse the principle of contradiction in its Aristotelian conception.

Łukasiewicz is clearly aware of the historical significance of his undertaking. In the opening pages of his work (Introduction, 77 ff. below),[2] he presents his readers with a provocative historical thesis: The history of the principle of contradiction, Łukasiewicz proposes, can be characterized by three crucial moments. The first two moments—inextricably connected with the names of Aristotle and Hegel—have left the issues and questions surrounding the principle unresolved. However, a third moment, a moment that has its beginning at the onset of the twentieth century, will bring a resolution to the seemingly insoluble aporia between Aristotle and Hegel's views.

This third moment coincides with a renewed, mathematically informed investigation of the fundamental principles of logic and mathematics, and—with respect to the principle of contradiction—this moment, as Łukasiewicz envisions it, will culminate in a new and more complete understanding of the principle, a scientifically grounded understanding of its relevance and significance as a logical principle in axiomatic systems of inference. It will become clear, Łukasiewicz writes,

> which rank the principle of contradiction takes among the other logical rules, what the justifications are for its validity

> and value, how far its applicability reaches; then it will become clear whether this principle is really the highest of all and can be considered the keystone of our entire logic, or if it can also be altered or, even further, if it is possible to develop a system of a non-Aristotelian logic, without taking it into account at all (Introduction, on page 80).

Łukasiewicz' call for an investigation of the possibility of a non-Aristotelian logic at the onset of the twentieth century is both remarkable and astonishing. In 1910, the validity and truth of the principle of contradiction was not the subject of serious debate. Nevertheless, today, a hundred years later, it is an indisputable historical fact that Łukasiewicz' prediction at the beginning of the twentieth century was accurate. The twentieth century saw a radical transformation of the understanding of the principle of contradiction, a mathematically informed understanding that brought new and—at times—unexpected answers to the questions raised by Łukasiewicz in 1910.

The discovery of non-classical logics to which Łukasiewicz himself made some of the earliest and highly influential contributions in the nineteen-twenties and thirties, and—even more important—the subsequent discovery of paraconsistent logics during the second half of the twentieth century, established that the Aristotelian principle of contradiction is not the ultimate and indispensable foundation of logic and rational deliberation that it traditionally had been. Instead, the interpretation and significance of the principle varies dramatically depending on the logic in which it is formulated. Furthermore, given the multitude of competing and often incompatible logics, there is *prima facie* no longer a single logic that is the exclusive and unassailable arbiter of valid inference and truth. Consequently, there also is no longer a single formulation and interpretation of the principle of contradiction. Finally, the question which one of these logics (and their formulations of the principle of contradiction) supports the most accurate and comprehensive description of reality is still the topic of an intense and—so far—inconclusive debate.

It is a curious historical fact that the opening charge of this far-reaching transformation of the classical, Aristotelian based understanding of logic and its fundamental principles took place at the beginning of the twentieth century, at the same time in which the new mathematical interpretations of logic and logical relations as pioneered by George Boole (1815–1864), Augustus De Morgan

(1806–1871) and William Stanley Jevons (1835–1882), were just beginning to gain broad recognition as core tenets of early analytic philosophy. In the early mathematical approaches to logic, charted by these pioneers and further developed and refined in the work of Gottlob Frege (1848–1925), Ernst Schroeder (1842–1902), Hugh MacColl (1837–1909), Charles Sanders Peirce (1839–1914), Giuseppe Peano (1858–1932), Bertrand Russell (1872–1970) and Alfred North Whitehead (1861–1947), the validity of the principle of contradiction is never put into serious question. Instead, the Aristotelian paradigm of consistency and non-contradiction is endorsed without reservations and incorporated as one of the core principles of the classical, bivalent systems of logic that were developed and formalized by this group of philosophers and logicians.

However, at the same time in which modern Frege/Russell logic was beginning to gain broad recognition as *the* standard account of logic, a cluster of writings emerged that challenged the Aristotelian principle of contradiction in new and unprecedented ways. Łukasiewicz' monograph is one of the most important of these writings, but Łukasiewicz was not the only voice critical of a blind acceptance of the principle of contradiction. Other philosophers also argued for the possibility that the principle of contradiction may not be universally valid. Two of Łukasiewicz' contemporaries, the Austrian Alexius Meinong (1853–1920) and the Russian Nicolas A. Vasil'év (1880–1940) are of particular importance as early challengers of the traditional understanding of the principle of contradiction. During the first two decades of the twentieth century, both philosophers independently published works that rejected the universal validity of the principle.[3] Even more intriguing, in addition to Łukasiewicz, both Meinong and Vasil'év published crucial works in 1910, adding to the significance of the year with respect to the history of modern logic.[4]

The philosophical and logical investigations of these philosophers led them to hold, respectively, that there are decisive logical and metalogical reasons (Łukasiewicz), certain kinds of objects (Meinong), and conceptions of radically different worlds with correspondingly different logical and ontological principles (Vasil'év), which establish that the principle of contradiction is not a universally valid principle. Each of these philosophers developed an account of logical and ontological relations that included the claim that there are certain conditions under which the principle of contradiction fails and, consequently, that the validity of the principle is limited to certain domains.

By thinking and articulating what was unthinkable at the time, namely, that the principle of contradiction is not a universally valid *a priori* principle at all, this group of philosophers opened a space for the emergence of earliest modern conceptions of non-Aristotelian logic and philosophy. However, they arrived at their positions within a historical and philosophical setting that was less than receptive to such revolutionary ideas. Even today, more than a century later, their pioneering work and historically important contributions to the development of paraconsistent logic and related philosophical positions have remained in relative obscurity. And among these pioneering efforts towards emancipation from the rigidity of the Aristotelian metaphysical dogma of non-contradiction, the work of the young Łukasiewicz is of unparalleled importance and significance.

In his metalogical analysis and critique of the Aristotelian principle of contradiction and its modern descendants, Łukasiewicz, endorses and practices a mathematically informed style of philosophical and logical analysis, and aligns himself with the basic conceptions of logic as advocated by Frege and Russell. However, other than Frege and Russell and the majority of their followers, Łukasiewicz does not share their confidence in the validity of certain core logical principles, most importantly, the principle of contradiction.[5] Applying the conceptual tools that arise from a mathematical analysis of logical relations, Łukasiewicz—in 1910—aims to show that the principle of contradiction is not as secure and reliable as the traditional view will have it, but that the Aristotelian principle of contradiction is "a thesis that demands proof" (Introduction, 82).

Aristotle, in his seminal account and defense of the principle in *Book Γ* of the *Metaphysics* claimed that the principle cannot be proven by a direct demonstration because it is a first principle or *arche* and no other, simpler principles exist that would be prior to it and from which the principle of contradiction could be proven. Aristotle, in his effort to convince his audience that the principle is indeed universally valid, offers a cluster of arguments and reasons, including an indirect demonstration or proof by refutation, which aim to show that the principle is true or, at the very least, that a denial of the principle has unacceptable and absurd consequences. In Łukasiewicz' analysis, none of Aristotle's arguments succeeds in proving the principle, leaving the principle without justification apart from Aristotle's assertion that it is a first principle.

In demanding that the principle of contradiction requires proof before it can be accepted as a scientific truth, Łukasiewicz adopts the position advocated by Richard Dedekind (1831–1916), who insisted on rigorous proofs as the indispensable foundation for any scientific claim (Dedekind 1888, 1995). But Łukasiewicz does not stop here. In a direct challenge to Aristotle's account, he asserts that a proof of the principle of contradiction is possible and, furthermore, that "this proof can be found" (Introduction, 82).

Prima facie, the claim that there is a proof of the principle appears to foreclose any possibility for Łukasiewicz to succeed in his declared goal to challenge the universal validity of the principle and to develop a logic that does not include or endorse the principle. However, for Łukasiewicz, a proof of the principle reveals the specific premises and assumptions from which the principle is directly derived (a proof by *reductio* would involve a *petitio principii*, since it would rely on and apply the principle). Thus, a formal, direct derivation of the principle not only satisfies Dedekind's demand that for a claim to be accepted in scientific discourse, it must have proof, but it also determines the conceptual and logical foundations of the principle. In turn, the analysis of the foundations from which the principle is derived sets the stage for an exploration of different, alternative foundations, foundations that no longer entail the principle in its Aristotelian interpretation.

Łukasiewicz' introductory remarks show, on one hand, that his critical investigation of the principle of contradiction proceeds within the framework of the emerging tradition of modern analytic philosophy and relies on the newly developed analytic tools afforded by a mathematical understanding of formal logic. On the other hand, Łukasiewicz also describes his investigations explicitly as an attempt to lay the foundation for a logic that does not include the principle of contradiction as one of its axioms (Introduction, 81).

Łukasiewicz' early work marks a significant turning point both in the history of philosophy and the history of logic. It raises important issues for the understanding of the philosophical background and motivations that led to one of the first articulations of a conception of a non-classical logic that is based on a formal, mathematical understanding of logical systems of inference.

Hegel and the Logische Frage

Łukasiewicz discusses Hegel and Hegel's legacy of a dialectical philosophy based on a metaphysical logic that asserts the fundamental importance of real contradictions at considerable length. He revisits questions that Hegel himself left unanswered and questions that—due to the state of logic at the time—Hegel could not even begin to formulate. Łukasiewicz' critical engagement with Hegel's metaphysical logic raises many intriguing questions. Łukasiewicz appears to be one of the first early analytic philosophers to take Hegel's challenge to the Aristotelian dogma seriously, but he is also highly critical of the philosophical views articulated by the German Idealist tradition. The key question pursued in this introduction is whether Łukasiewicz's critical investigation of the principle of contradiction constitutes an attempt to resolve the so-called *Logische Frage* that engaged German speaking philosophers in the wake of Hegel's legacy during second half of the nineteenth century.

Non-Euclidean Geometry

Next to the problems posed by Hegel's project of a dialectical science, the discovery of non-Euclidean geometry exerted a major influence on Łukasiewicz' thinking. Łukasiewicz entertained the hypothesis that if a new model of spatial relations could be generated by a change to Euclid's parallel postulate (or its modern equivalents), then it may be possible to generate a new logic in an analogous fashion by a change to the principle of contradiction. In Łukasiewicz' view, a careful analysis of the steps that led to the discovery of non-Euclidean geometry may lead the way to the discovery of non-Aristotelian logic. However, given that Łukasiewicz' failed in the development of a non-Aristotelian logic in 1910, the question as to the aptness of the analogy between non-Euclidean geometry and non-Aristotelian logic furnishes a further, important field of research for an understanding of Łukasiewicz' early attempt to develop a non-Aristotelian logic.

Formal Logic and Set-Theoretic Paradoxes

Even in the emerging field of formal or mathematical logic, as exemplified in the work of Frege and Russell, questions about the principle of contradiction emerged unexpectedly but with serious and far-reaching implications. Łukasiewicz took great interest in the set-theoretic paradox that Russell discovered at the foundation of Frege's project as well as the paradoxes that arise in the theory of transfinite numbers and infinite sets advanced by Georg Cantor (1845–1918). These paradoxes are different from the traditional paradoxes that generated much controversy and debate in ancient Greece. The new, formal paradoxes emerge at the very foundations of logic and mathematics, at the foundation of *a priori* knowledge as such. The main question investigated in the current context is the relation between the discovery of these new paradoxes and Łukasiewicz' analysis of the principle of contradiction.

Meinong and Object Theory

Additional support for Łukasiewicz' search for a non-Aristotelian logic was found in Meinong's *Gegenstandstheorie* or theory of objects, which includes contradictory and non-existent objects as bona-fide objects that permit logical treatment and analysis. The principle of contradiction fails with respect to contradictory objects, which prompted Russell's severe criticisms of Meinong's theory. Łukasiewicz, on the other hand, includes Meinongian objects in his analysis of the principle of contradiction, which allows him to articulate some key conclusions about the truth-values of statements about such objects. The relation between Meinong and the young Łukasiewicz and their philosophical agreements and differences, present a further important area of research.

Determinism and Aristotelian Logic

Already in 1910, Łukasiewicz was critical of what he described as the rigidity of Aristotelian logic, the logical coercion exerted by its concept of necessity. He also sought new solutions to the problems surrounding the truth-value of future contingent statements and the principle of bivalence. One of the most interesting questions in this context is whether Łukasiewicz' attempt to develop a non-Aristotelian logic in 1910 was a first attempt to overcome the problem of logical determinism which, as Łukasiewicz himself reports, was one of his main motivations for his work towards three and many-valued logics less than a decade later.

The connections between Łukasiewicz' work and the discovery of non-Euclidean geometry, algebraic and formal logic, and Meinong's theory of objects is frequently recognized and discussed in the existing literature. However, the impact of Hegel's dialectical philosophy and the debate on the "*logische Frage*" by German philosophers and logicians on Łukasiewicz' early work has remained largely unexplored.[6] The responses to Hegel's legacy by Friedrich Adolf Trendelenburg (1802–1872), Friedrich Ueberweg (1826–1871) and Christoph von Sigwart (1830–1904), provided Łukasiewicz with crucial material for his own investigation of the fundamental principles of logic. The research for this introduction to Łukasiewicz' work on the principle of contradiction sheds new light on the historical context in which the work and its call for a non-Aristotelian logic emerged and, in particular, it brings out the full importance of the investigations into the foundations of logic by Trendelenburg, Ueberweg, and Sigwart to Łukasiewicz' analysis of the principle of contradiction.

The foundations of contemporary non-classical logic were developed by philosophers and logicians that took Hegel's challenge to the traditional understanding of the principle of contradiction seriously. However, to consider Hegel's arguments and reasons for a dialectical logic carefully does not mean swallowing Hegel's account hook, line, and sinker. Rather, at the onset of the twentieth century, it meant that—for analytic philosophers—the challenge of Hegel's arguments, his metaphysical logic, and the debate about Aristotle's principle of non-contradiction, was still without a decisive, scientifically grounded resolution. In 1910, the young Łukasiewicz proposes that Hegel's metaphysical logic, and its opposition to the Aristotelian dogma of non-contradiction, needs its own *Aufhebung*. Łukasiewicz attempts to find such a resolution to Hegel's legacy by a renewed investigation of Aristotle's account of the principle of contradiction based on a formal, mathematically grounded conception of logic and an increasingly critical stance against traditional, metaphysical considerations.

Łukasiewicz' work on the principle of contradiction is an ingenious and pioneering effort to find a solution to the questions posed by Hegel's project of a dialectical logic and its opposition to the traditional Aristotelian conception of the principle of contradiction. Lukasiewicz' work is an attempt to resolve the debate of the "*Logische Frage*" within the philosophical framework of early analytic philosophy and a mathematical understanding of formal logic.

Lukasiewicz builds on the work of nineteenth century German speaking philosophers and their efforts to solve the problem of the "*Logische Frage*" but he deploys the techniques of the emerging tradition of modern analytic philosophy and mathematical logic to unravel the puzzles surrounding Aristotle's principle of contradiction.

Most importantly, the response to Hegel's work that led to the debate about *Die Logische Frage* (The Logical Question) is of crucial importance to Łukasiewicz' early work. The debate was initiated by Trendelenburg, Hegel's successor in Berlin, and exerted a strong influence on the work of German speaking logicians during the second half of the nineteenth century. The work of Ueberweg and Sigwart provided much of the groundwork that Łukasiewicz relies on and develops in his own analysis of the role and validity of logical principles.

Łukasiewicz' early work presents a continuation and expansion of the investigations charted by these philosophers. However, what sets Łukasiewicz apart from the just-mentioned philosophers is his involvement in the emerging field of formal logic and the new methods of logical analysis that a mathematical approach to the investigation of logical relations afforded. Spurred on by the discovery of Non-Euclidean geometry and equipped with the conceptual tools provided by Alexius Meinong's theory of objects, Łukasiewicz ingeniously combined resources and issues into one of the earliest, pioneering and visionary, metalogical investigation of the foundations of *a priori* sciences.

Biographical and Philosophical Background

Jan Łukasiewicz was in his early thirties when his work on Aristotle and the PC was published in Kraków in 1910. Born on the 21st of December 1878, in the city of Lwóv (Lemberg) in Galicia, Łukasiewicz grew up and completed high school in Lwóv. Following high school, he enrolled at the University of Lwóv, initially as a law student, but soon changed to philosophy which he studied under the direction of Kazimierz Twardowski (1866–1938).

Twardowski was the central figure in the history of the Lwóv-Warsaw School of Philosophy, which began with Twardowski's appointment to the Chair of Philosophy as professor extraordinarius at the University of Lwóv in 1895. The initial, formative period of the School spanned roughly the years from 1895 to 1902 and came to an end when the first doctoral students of Twardowski, including Łukasiewicz, completed their studies under his supervision. From this pool of young philosophers, a group emerged that continued to collaborate with Twardowski and shaped the philosophical outlook of the School (Woleński 1989, 1).

Twardowski's own philosophical views were strongly influenced by his teacher Franz Brentano (1838–1917), whose account of intentionality is clearly present in Twardowski's influential work *On the Content and Object of Presentations,* which was first published in 1894 (Twardowski 1977 [1894]).

In addition to Twardowski, Brentano's remarkable circle of students and followers included Carl Stumpf (1848–1936), Alois Höfler (1853–1922), Edmund Husserl (1859–1938), and Alexius Meinong. Other notable students of Brentano include Sigmund Freud (1856–1939) and Rudolf Steiner (1861–1925) (Albertazzi 1993, 11).

The work of Brentano, through the influence of Twardowski, forms a key philosophical nexus that connects Łukasiewicz with Meinong and Husserl. In particular, the already mentioned aspects of Meinong's work on object theory (Meinong 1904, 1907, 1910) and the conceptual foundations of possibility and probability (Meinong 1915), as well as the first part of Husserl's *Logische Untersuchungen* (Husserl 1900) came to play an important role in Łukasiewicz' work on the principle of contradiction.

The topic of Łukasiewicz' Ph.D. thesis (Łukasiewicz 1903) was the inverse theory of induction, that is, the idea that the process of inductive inference constitutes the inverse of the process by which deductive inferences are reached (Woleński 2010, 381). The topic matter of Łukasiewicz' thesis already shows a marked concern with the relation between science and logic. As Woleński notes, the idea of induction as the inverse process of deduction was previously articulated by Jevons and Sigwart (Woleński, 381). The work of both logicians continued to engage Łukasiewicz in his investigations into the foundations of the principle of contradiction.[7]

After receiving his PhD from Lwóv University in 1902, Łukasiewicz continued his studies while traveling in Europe, visiting universities in Germany and Belgium. In Germany, he attended lectures by Stumpf, who had founded the Berlin Laboratory of Experimental Psychology at the University of Berlin in 1893. In Belgium, he attended lectures by Deciré Mercier (1851–1926) at the Catholic University of Louvain (Raspa 1999; Woleński 2000). In 1906, Łukasiewicz returned to Lwóv where he began work as *Privatdozent* at Lwóv University. During the winter semester of 1908-9, he spent time in Graz, where he met and attended

Meinong's lectures on object theory and the object-theoretical modalities of possibility and probability (XVIII, 189), (Simons 1989, 257). Łukasiewicz' time in Graz and his engagement with Meinong's project of a general theory of objects was influential and productive. It is the time in which he began work on the logic of probability (Łukasiewicz 1912). It is also during his stay in Graz that Łukasiewicz began work on his monograph on the principle of contradiction.

In 1911, Łukasiewicz was appointed extraordinary professor at the University of Lwóv and in 1915, after the re-activation of the University of Warsaw, he was offered the Chair of Philosophy at Warsaw, a position he held until the German invasion of Poland in the fall of 1939.

In the years 1918–1920, Łukasiewicz took leave from his post at the University of Warsaw to serve in the Ministry for Religion and Public Education (*Ministerstwo Wyznań Religijnych I Oświecenia Publicznego*). In 1919, he joined the cabinet of the second Prime Minister of the newly formed Second Polish Republic, Ignacy Paderewski (1860–1941), as the head of the ministry (Woleński 2000). It was prior to joining the ministry, on the occasion of his "Farewell Lecture" at the University of Warsaw in March 1918, that Łukasiewicz first announced his discovery of a three-valued logic (Łukasiewicz 1970b [1918]). Two years later, after his return to the university, he published a brief summary of his findings in an article titled "On Three-Valued Logic" (Łukasiewicz 1970c [1920]). On two occasions during his tenure at Warsaw University, Łukasiewicz was elected Rector Magnus of the university and served in that capacity in 1922–23 and in 1931–32.

In the two decades between the world wars, the Lwóv-Warsaw School flourished and gained international recognition. The School received its first major international exposure when Łukasiewicz and Alfred Tarski (1901–1983) participated in the 8th International Congress of Mathematicians in Bologna, Italy, in 1928. Around the same time, in the late 1920's and early 30's, logicians and mathematicians like Karl Menger (1902–1985), Rudolf Carnap (1891–1970), Ernst Zermelo (1871–1953), Heinrich Scholz (1884–1956) and Willard van Orman Quine (1908–2000) visited Warsaw University to learn first-hand about the work that was being done there.

The international reputation of the Warsaw School grew even more during the 1930's when Łukasiewicz, together with Tarski and Adolf Lindenbaum (1904–1941), participated in the congresses of scientific philosophy organized by the Vienna Circle in 1934 in Prague and in 1935 in Paris (Woleński 2008, 40).

During the 1930's, Lukasiewicz was instrumental in fostering a strong relationship between the Warsaw School and the University of Münster, where the German philosopher Heinrich Scholz had succeeded in establishing the first department of mathematical logic in Germany in 1936. Four years earlier, in 1932, when German-Polish relations were already beginning to show considerable tensions, Łukasiewicz had invited Scholz to come to Poland and present lectures in Warsaw and Lwóv (Schmidt am Busch 2007, 68). Scholz gladly accepted and over the years his appreciation of the Warsaw School, and of Łukasiewicz' work in particular, grew profoundly. For example, as reported by Słupeki, Scholz greatly admired Łukasiewicz' paper "On the History of the Logic of Propositions" (Łukasiewicz 1970d [1934]), first published in Polish under the title "*Z historii logiki zdań*" (Łukasiewicz 1934) and published in a German translation the following year by the journal *Erkenntnis* (Łukasiewicz 1935), declaring that it offered "the most interesting thirty pages ever written on the history of logic" (cit. Słupeki 1970, x).

In 1938, Scholz traveled to Warsaw to present an honorary doctorate of the University of Münster to Jan Łukasiewicz on the occasion of his 60th birthday (Peckhaus 1998, 11; Schmidt am Busch 2007). During the same visit, Scholz was awarded an honorary doctorate by the University of Warsaw. Early the following year, in February 1939, Łukasiewicz traveled to Münster, at the invitation of the Faculty of Philosophy and Science, and presented four lectures (Schmidt am Busch 2007, 68). Tragically, only a few months later, the onset of World War II plunged Europe into utter chaos and work in philosophy and logic in Poland, as well as international scholarly exchanges, became extremely difficult if not altogether impossible.

Łukasiewicz stayed in Warsaw during the German occupation. He worked primarily in an administrative capacity at the University, but also took part in secret lectures that were organized by the University faculty (Woleński 2000, 2). During that time, he also gave private lectures on logic in which he maintained at least parts of his views on the principle of contradiction that he had first developed in his 1910 book (Woleński 2000, 20). The contents of one of these lecture series is documented in a book by M.Bizoń on the origin of logic (Bizoń 1942), which contains the summaries of ten lectures given by Łukasiewicz in 1942.

In August 1944, during the early stages of the Warsaw uprising, Łukasiewicz and his wife managed to leave Warsaw and made their way to Münster with the help of his old friend at the University of Münster, Heinrich Scholz. Łukasiewicz had originally planned to travel to Switzerland, but the deteriorating situation in Germany left him stranded and without proper papers in Münster until British and American forces occupied Münster at the beginning of April 1945. It is likely that Łukasiewicz experienced the heavy bombings of Münster at the end of March, which preceeded the Allied advance. It was during these bombings (or in their aftermath) that the posthumous writings of Frege and Schröder, which Scholz had managed to bring to Münster in the 1930's, were lost (Peckhaus 2008).

Shortly after the end of World War II, Łukasiewicz left Münster and spent some time in Belgium. In 1946, he accepted the chair of logic offered by the Irish Royal Academy of Dublin. He held this post until his death in 1956. During his final years in Dublin, Łukasiewicz worked on an English translation of his 1910 work on Aristotle and the PC. However, the manuscript of the translation remained at a draft stage and was not completed.

Bibliographic Notes

The first edition of Łukasiewicz' work was published in Kraków by the Polish Academy of the Arts (*Polska Akademia Umiejętności*). While greeted with great interest at the time of publication, the tumultuous history of Europe during the first half of the 20th century left the work difficult to obtain outside of Poland and—if a copy could be found—it was of course accessible only to readers of Polish. Finally, more than 75 years after the original publication, and more than 30 years after Łukasiewicz' death, a second edition of the book was published in Poland under the editorship of Jan Woleński (Łukasiewicz 1987). A German translation followed in 1993, published by Georg Olms (Łukasiewicz 1993); a French translation appeared in 2000, published in Paris by Éditions de L'Éclat (Łukasiewicz 2000).

In addition to the book, Łukasiewicz also published a companion article in German, which presents a summary of the main points of the book, including the critical analysis of Aristotle's arguments in defense of the principle of contradiction and the challenges posed to it by the analysis of the logical properties of Meinong's contradictory and incomplete objects (Łukasiewicz 1910). However, even this shorter work had to wait some 60 years until a first English translation by Vernon Wedin appeared in *The Review of Metaphysics* in 1971 and introduced a broader English speaking audience to Łukasiewicz' early work and thought (Łukasiewicz 1971 [1910]). In 1979, a second English translation of Łukasiewicz' article by Jonathan Barnes (Łukasiewicz 1979 [1910]) was published as part of an anthology of articles on Aristotle's metaphysics.

Finally, also in 1910, Łukasiewicz presented a talk to the Polish Philosophical Society in Lwóv on the Principle of the Excluded Third (PET) in which he offered an analysis of the PET. In the presentation, Łukasiewicz argued that the PET, just as the PC, is not nearly as certain and self-evident as traditionally believed. A summary of this talk was published the same year in the Polish journal *Przegląd Filozoficzny* (Łukasiewicz 1910) and in 1987, Jan Woleński and Peter Simons published an English translation of the article together with an additional brief introduction to the text (Łukasiewicz 1987 [1910]).

A Third Moment in the Understanding of the Principle of Contradiction

The Hegelian ring of some of Łukasiewicz' introductory remarks, in particular, his announcement of a *third* moment in the history of the principle of contradiction is certainly not accidental. Łukasiewicz intends to resolve the issues created by the second moment in the history of the principle, Hegel's analysis of contradictions and his dialectical logic. *Prima facie*, Łukasiewicz appears to think of the content and solutions, which this third moment will bring, specifically in Hegelian terms, as a moment of *Aufhebung*, of a simultaneous dissolution, resolution, and preservation of the apparently irreconcilable opposition between Aristotle and Hegel's views.

However, Łukasiewicz' work on the principle of contradiction is also an important part of Łukasiewicz' progressive emancipation from philosophical views of the German Idealist tradition, as it is a decidedly analytic attempt to resolve the questions that surround the principle. It is not at all Hegel's dialectic, that Łukasiewicz wants when he speaks of the possibility of a non-Aristotelian logic. His approach is guided by analytic and empiricist principles; he wants to use mathematics and a formal understanding of logic to dissolve the fog of metaphysics.

The principle of contradiction certainly holds a unique place in the history of philosophy. More than any other metaphysical principle, it has dominated the thought of the Western philosophical tradition since the days of Aristotle.

> It is impossible for anything at the same time to be and not to be (Met. 1006a 2).

Whether it was by strength and persuasiveness of Aristotle's argument, or by sociological and historical reasons, the Stagirite's pronouncement in defense of the principle became accepted as a secure and certain truth. For millennia to come, it was a certain truth that reality does not contain contradictions, that the real is a consistent whole – that whatever is, is, and whatever is cannot at the same time and in the same respect not be, whatever it is.

Aristotle's account and defense of the principle of contradiction in the *Metaphysics* marks the first of Łukasiewicz' three moments that shaped the history of the principle of contradiction. The second is Hegel and his dialectical philosophy and logic. The third begins with renewed attempts to find solutions to the unresolved questions that arise from the apparently irreconcilable differences between the philosophical positions articulated by Aristotle and Hegel.

Aristotle

In the *Metaphysics,* Aristotle introduces the principle of contradiction as the first principle or *arche* of a revolutionary new science. The task of this science is the investigation of being *qua* being. The first principle of this science is the principle that governs all being—all that is real. Being *qua* being does not (and cannot) contain contradictions.

Formulations of the Principle

Aristotle articulates the principle of contradiction at different locations and in different formulations. Łukasiewicz distinguishes three formulations of the principle:

1) *Ontological (Object-Theoretical)*—a claim about objects and their properties: "the same attribute cannot at the same time belong and not belong to the same subject in the same respect" (1005b 19-20).
2) *Psychological*—a claim about consciousness (psyche) and beliefs: "It is impossible for anyone to believe the same thing to be and not to be" (1005b 23).
3) *Logical*—a claim about propositions and truth-values: "contradictory statements are not at the same time true" (1011b 14).

Aristotle's formulations, while expressing what appears to be a single, underlying principle, differ with respect to the subject terms and predicates that are employed in the statements of the principle. The range and diversity of the formulations indicates a general difficulty in formulating the principle in its most general and universal form. The question arises, is there a single formulation of *the* Principle of Contradiction, a formulation that articulates the *target* or *core* principle as such? In Łukasiewicz' reading, Aristotle's ontological formulation is the primary formulation—it describes the fundamental characteristic of being *qua* being. "The *ontological* principle is the principle of contradiction *κατ' ἐξοχήν*" (I, 87).

The Arche of the Science of Metaphysics

Aristotle, in his introductory discussion of the purpose and justification of the new science of being *qua* being, does not begin his discussion of the PC with a statement of the principle itself. Instead, he offers a list of attributes of the principle. The PC is "the most certain principle of all." It is impossible to be in error about it. It is "the *best known*" principle and "*non-hypothetical.*" And, it is the one principle that "everyone must have who understands *anything that is*" (1005b 10-17, italics added). The principle is a necessary pre-condition of any knowledge as such, and any rational being that comes to know anything at all, must have a prior understanding of the principle.

Aristotle's qualifying remarks aim to establish that the PC is indeed the first principle of the science that investigates being *qua* being, the science of metaphysics. It is only *after* he has developed the criteria that any principle or *arche* must satisfy to be a first principle, that Aristotle proceeds to state the principle in its object-theoretical formulation: "the same attribute cannot at the same time belong and not belong to the same subject in the same respect" (1005b 19-20).

Aristotle presents the object-theoretical formulation as the formulation that best satisfies the criteria of a *first* principle. The object-theoretical formulation, Aristotle notes, does evoke the required degree of certainty and conviction regarding its truth and, most importantly, "it answers to the definition [of a first principle] given above" (1005b 22).

Unprovable and Indubitable

In Aristotle's account, the PC is not only *a priori*, certain, and indubitable but—as a first principle—it is also unprovable. A proof of the principle through direct argument or positive demonstration is impossible because a positive demonstration requires premises that are "the causes of the conclusion, better known than it, and prior to it." (*Post. An.* 71b 29). Thus, the PC, as a first principle, is a foundational truth that can only be articulated in the form of an immediate proposition and "an immediate proposition is one which has no other proposition prior to it" (*Post. An.* 72a 8). Consequently, the PC, as a first principle, cannot be derived as the conclusion of a demonstration since there are *eo ipso* no propositions available that are prior to it and could serve as premises in a demonstration. Furthermore, in Aristotle's view, any reasoned argument presupposes, asserts and applies the PC and, therefore, any positive demonstration of the PC would necessarily be begging the question.

Despite the improvability of the PC, which arises from its privileged position as a first principle, Aristotle nevertheless holds that it is possible to give what he calls a negative demonstration or '*elenchus*', which aims not only to show that a denial of the PC has utterly unacceptable consequences, but also that a denial of the PC cannot be articulated without an application of the principle and, thus, that any denial of the PC itself relies on the validity of the very principle that it aims to deny. At the center of Aristotle's negative demonstration lies the claim that meaningful speech requires unequivocal signification, i.e., that every word or term signifies exactly one thing (or is disambiguated to that end), and this is only possible if the PC is not violated. Aristotle's *elenchus* consists of a lengthy, complicated, and somewhat torturous conundrum of arguments and reasons, followed by several shorter arguments, all of which aim to establish the validity of the Aristotelian principle of non-contradiction in some form or other. However, apart from the question of the scope and validity of the principle as such, the success of Aristotle's arguments in support of the PC is controversial and continues to be the subject of intense debate.

Statements, Truth, and Contradiction—The Logical Formulation

In an Aristotelian universe, thought and symbolic representations of being may not contain contradictions. If a representation is to grasp what is real, that is, if it is to succeed in the articulation and representation of what is the case, then it cannot contain contradictions since contradictions are not part of being. Thus, it is impossible for any representation that contains a contradiction to be true. A contradiction always indicates a failure or error of some sort, be it perceptual or intellectual, but the contradiction itself can never be actual and true. It is a direct consequence of the core claim of Aristotle's science of being *qua* being, encapsulated in the principle of non-contradiction: reality is consistent. In its fundamental nature, being does not—and cannot—contain contradictions. Since contradictions do not exist in the actual world, it follows that it is impossible for a pair of contradictorily opposed assertions to be true at the same time (*Met.IV* 1011b 14).

It is important to note that Aristotle introduces the logical formulation of the principle, which he characterizes as the "the most indisputable of all beliefs" only towards the end of his discussion of the PC, long after he has addressed the issues that arise about the ontological (object-theoretical) and psychological formulations.

In his defense of the principle, Aristotle's concern is focused on the metaphysical, that is, the ontological and psychological dimensions of the principle. The consequences of this defense of the principle are finally—and almost like an afterthought—spelled out at the end of Aristotle's account, suggesting that Aristotle, at least, in the *Metaphysics*, was only incidentally concerned with the purely logical consequences of the principle of contradiction.

The Ancient Debate

Historically, Aristotle's account gained practically universal acceptance and dominated Western philosophical thought for more than two thousand years. However, Aristotle's seminal account and defense of the principle was articulated amidst a lively debate. Łukasiewicz reminds his readers that Aristotle's account emerged in response to views that did not recognize the principle of contradiction (PC) as a universally true principle or *arche*, views that denied the universal validity and truth of the PC. Several of Aristotle's predecessors, Heraclitus, Cratylus, and Protagoras, denied the truth of the principle. The views associated with the Megarian dialecticians and with many philosophers of nature, as Aristotle called them, also appear to violate Aristotle's principle of contradiction and argue for an account of reality that includes contradictions. Heraclitus' fragments suggest a view of the nature of the world that appears to be opposite to Aristotle's conception, a world characterized by continuous flux in which a stable moment of being—of non-contradiction—can never be realized. Protagoras, on the other hand, famously declared that 'man is the measure of all things' and that what appears to one man to be in a certain way, may appear differently to another man (resulting in contradictory but *primae facie* equally justified claims about one and the same thing). Even Plato, though for different reasons, suggests that the objects that are perceivable by the senses violate the PC and belong to "that which partakes of both, of *to be* and *not to be*" (*Republic* 478e).

Aristotle won the debate on the nature of being and contradiction that that lay at the heart of the efforts of his contemporaries and predecessors. The *arche* or first principle of his science of being *qua* being, the metaphysical claim that it is impossible for being to contain contradictions, did emerge as a universally accepted philosophical dogma that informed philosophical inquiry in the Western tradition for two millennia to come. However, beyond this historical fact, it is far from settled whether Aristotle's success is due to the strength of his arguments and the persuasiveness of his reasoning or whether it is primarily the result of other, mostly sociological and historical reasons. Historically, the outcome of Aristotle's defense of non-contradiction was decisive. Aristotle's theory became accepted as a fundamental insight into the structure of reality. Aristotle's first principle of his revolutionary new science that investigates being *qua* being acquired a status that elevated it beyond doubt and the controversy that engaged the Ancients about the issue lost its momentum. For centuries to follow, Aristotle's first principle of being, the principle of contradiction, was the ultimate foundation of philosophical inquiry and knowledge.

Hegel

The impact of Georg Wilhelm Friedrich Hegel (1770–1831) on modern philosophy is beyond question. What to make of his conception of dialectical philosophy and its impact on philosophical discourse is another question. Hegel's insistence on contradictions as the ontological foundation inherent in all being and the corresponding dialectical account of the nature of change and being continues to engage the minds of his followers and critics to the present day. In arguing that the simultaneous presence of contradictory moments is the essential feature of being as such, Hegel's philosophy directly contradicts Aristotle's central metaphysical claim, which—encapsulated in the principle of contradiction—declares that the one fundamental feature of being is that it does not contain contradictions.

A Fusion of Logic and Metaphysics

The issue of the contradictory aspects of being is taken up and developed in Hegel's "speculative" logic. This new conception of logic is radically distinct from the Aristotelian syllogistic, which was the traditional domain of logic at Hegel's time. Instead, Hegel returns to the connection (and distinction) between being and logos, which informed Aristotle's account of the PC in the *Metaphysics*, and claims a much broader range of inquiry as the subject matter for his dialectical logic: it "contains all previous Logic and Metaphysics: it preserves the same forms of thought, the same laws and objects, while at the same time remodeling and expanding them with wider categories" (Hegel 1892, 16). As a fusion (or *Aufhebung* of the distinction) between the traditional fields of logic and metaphysics, Hegel's "speculative" or "metaphysical" logic is neither of the two, but a completely new form of inquiry that sets out to trace the movement of pure thought, which begins with the most abstract (and empty) of all categories, pure being.

The Identity of Being and Nothingness

Hegel's "pure being" (*das reine Sein*) is being in its most abstract and empty form. It is positive in content but lacks all differentiation. Thus, in its immediate aspect, it has no distinct features or qualities of any kind. And here, with the negative characterization, which constitutes the only mode in which pure being can be grasped, the Hegelian dialectic begins: "this mere Being, as it is mere abstraction, is therefore the absolutely negative : which, in a similarly immediate aspect, is just Nothing" (Hegel 1892, 161).

Being, as an abstraction and considered in its negative characterization, is indistinguishable from non-being; it is nothing. The identity of the two notions is symmetrical: nothing, as pure non-being, is identical to being in its most abstract form. The traditional conception of metaphysics as the Aristotelian science of being *qua* being and the Hegelian analysis of the logical and conceptual content of these two most abstract and fundamental notions collide with explosive force in what appears to be an inescapable (and somewhat disorienting) contradiction.

As Hegel himself points out, the distinction of pure being from nothing "is a mere intention or meaning" (Hegel 1892, 162). Neither pure being nor nothingness has any features and, thus, no differentiating predicate can be attributed to either of the two in a positive manner. Both notions arise from and are constituted by a complete absence of features, that is, they arise from the negativity brought about by a completed process of radical abstraction, a process that can go no further, a process that has reached the terminus that is its own limit. Thus, the radical and exhaustive abstraction of Hegel's analysis generates not only the notion of pure being but also its limit, pure nothingness. Limits, however, as Priest has argued at length, are dialethic by their very nature, that is, they generate contradictions that are not simply false (cf. Priest 1987, 1995).

The contradiction that reveals itself in the identity and difference of pure being and non-being is the Hegelian *Urwiderspruch*, the original contradiction, which constitutes both the logical starting point and the source of tension that propels the dialectical progression of pure thought. And, in the Hegelian dialectic, this fundamental contradiction is *aufgehoben,* i.e., it is simultaneously resolved and preserved in all subsequent moments of the progression of thought.

In relation to the Kantian background of Hegel's analysis, the Hegelian notion of pure nothingness is conceivable while necessarily unknowable, that is, in its complete negativity, it is inaccessible both cognitively and empirically, and in this fashion, it resembles the Kantian thing-in-itself (noumenon). Pure being—in its positivity—constitutes ultimately the ground of all that is knowable, both subjectively and objectively, through the categories of the understanding. Thus, for Kant, noumena are forever beyond the limits of reason and remain intrinsically separated from phenomena whereas for Hegel, the realization of the identity of being and nothingness, while preserving their difference, constitutes the third moment of a dialectic that characterizes the nature of being.

Aufhebung in Motion

This third moment in the dialectic, which is the resolution (*Aufhebung*) of the contradiction engendered by the first two, i.e., the positing of pure being (first moment) and its negation, non-being (second moment), unites the two moments into a third and more complete notion, the notion of becoming. "The truth of Being and of Nothing is accordingly the unity of the two : and this unity is Becoming" (Hegel 1892, 163).

For Hegel, the notion of becoming, and its constitutive and contradictory aspects of being and non-being, informs and characterizes the essential features of all change and movement. As such, it is not limited to the progression of ideal notions of pure thought, but it also finds instantiation in the empirical realm. An important example is provided by Hegel in his analysis of physical movement. In his *Science of Logic*, Hegel offers the following account:

> External sensuous motion is contradiction's immediate existence. Something moves, not because at one moment it is here and at another there, but because at one and the same moment it is here and not here, because in this "here," it at once is and is not (Science of Logic, cit. Priest 1989, 389).[8]

If Hegel is right, then true empirical contradictions are to be found in the analysis of the physical phenomenon of motion. The analysis of an object in motion will result in a true conjunction of the form A & $\sim A$ (where, using Hegel's example in the citation above, A stands for "object x is at position p at moment t" and $\sim A$ for "object x is not at position p at moment t"). Thus, whereas Hegel's dialectic of the abstract notions of pure being and nothingness relies on an intensional interpretation, the dialectic of empirical motion, allows an extensional representation.

In the present context, it is important to note that in his work on Aristotle and the PC, Łukasiewicz refers to the above quoted passage not just once, but twice (V, 109; XIX, 200). Furthermore, the fact that the second citation is followed by a detailed discussion and analysis of a body in motion, a situation that for Hegel illustrates the presence of contradictions in the real (physical, material) world, is a clear indication that the problem of Hegel's dialectic with its denial of the principle of non-contradiction constitutes an important aspect of Łukasiewicz' work.

For Hegel, contradictions are a fundamental and constitutive aspect of all reality. Contradictions are the very fabric of being itself. In his 'metaphysical' logic, Hegel traces the movement of pure thought as it progresses from the dialectical connections between being and non-being through increasingly more complex moments of realization. Hegel's fusion of logic and ontology into an original and systematic dialectical science set the stage for a sustained philosophical debate that lasted for much of the nineteenth century and into the twentieth.

The Work that Hegel did not do – Łukasiewicz and "*Die Logische Frage*"

The relation between Łukasiewicz' early work on the principle of contradiction and Hegel's legacy has not received the attention it deserves. In fact, the mere mentioning of Łukasiewicz and a connection of his early work to Hegel may still raise eyebrows in places. But the connection is not as surprising as it may seem. To begin with, one important strand in Łukasiewicz' early philosophical development is a critical engagement with German idealism, which over time led to a gradual emancipation from doctrines associated with the German Idealist tradition. Clearly, Hegel and his dialectical philosophy mark a highpoint (and, to some, the culmination) of German Idealism.

Even Bertrand Russell, certainly one of the central figures in modern analytic philosophy, had an early Hegelian phase. In fact, Russell's rejection of Hegel around the beginning of the twentieth century and his turn to analytic philosophy and a logicist program in his *Principles of Mathematics* (Russell 1903) may very well mark one of the earliest indications of the beginning of that third moment in the history of the principle of contradiction that the young Łukasiewicz envisioned. This third moment, after all, is inextricably bound up with the emergence of early analytic philosophy and the development of formal logic.

Still, the association with Hegel creates a slightly odd picture. Łukasiewicz is far better known for his rather dim estimates of modern philosophy in general and, especially, his disdain for German Idealism. These views generally belong to his second, "logical" period, covering the years following WWI. On the other hand, Łukasiewicz' critical engagement with the logical and metaphysical issues of Hegel's dialectical philosophy clearly belongs to his early "philosophical" period, which—roughly— covers the years up to the outbreak of WWI.[9]

A first indication of Łukasiewicz' increasingly critical stance towards the "great philosophical systems" is found in his *Farewell Address* of 1918, where he comments that these systems, including Kant's project of a critical philosophy,

> "fall into nothingness when subjected to logical criticism. They become a collection of loose ideas, sometimes brilliant, but devoid of scientific value" (Łukasiewicz 1970b [1918], 85).

In contrast, Łukasiewicz' earlier views of his "philosophical" period show considerably more sympathy towards the work of Kant and Hegel. A comment in his article on *Creative Elements in Science* (Łukasiewicz 1970 [1912]) outlines the character and proposed method of Łukasiewicz' engagement with the unresolved issues left by German Idealism. This method is that of critical logical analysis, the same method Łukasiewicz developed and employed in his 1910 work on Aristotle and the principle of contradiction. Łukasiewicz comments that Kant's critique and, in particular,

> the Copernican idea of Kant, who tried to prove that objects follow cognition rather than cognition follows objects, includes views that favor the thesis of creative elements in science. But I have tried to demonstrate that thesis not on the basis of any special theory of cognition, but on the basis of common realism, by means of logical research (Łukasiewicz 1970 [1912], 13 n.21).

Two decades later, in 1936, at the height of Łukasiewicz' "logical" period, the mild sympathies towards Kant and German Idealism of his "philosophical" period have been replaced by a full-scale, scathing rejection:

> When we apply to it the requirements of scientific criticism, Kantian philosophy collapses like a house of cards. At every step, we find vague concepts, incomprehensible statements, unjustified assertions, contradictions, and logical errors. Nothing is left except a few perhaps inspired ideas, a raw material that awaits scientific elaboration. That is why that philosophy has not performed its task, although its influence has been great. After Kant, people have not started to philosophize more critically, more reasonably, more cautiously. Kant gave rise to German idealistic philosophy, whose flights of fancy and non-scientific character has surpassed all pre-Kantian systems (Łukasiewicz 1970e [1936], 227).

In 1910, however, Łukasiewicz' position was dramatically different. The unresolved issues brought forth by Hegel's conception of a dialectical logic are not merely "raw material that awaits scientific elaboration" but form a central concern in Łukasiewicz' investigation. Hegel's presence in his early work is unmistakable. Hegel's name appears in the very first sentence of the book, together with Aristotle's, and no other philosopher—except for Aristotle—is mentioned more frequently than Hegel. Łukasiewicz makes a total of 19 direct references to Hegel, followed by 12 references to Russell and 9 references each to Meinong and Couturat.

Of course, the statistical data only suggests what a close reading of the text reveals: Łukasiewicz articulates clearly and unambiguously the importance of the connections between his own work and the problems left by Hegel's dialectic. He positions his own attempt at a renewed critical and logical analysis of the PC and related principles as one of the "investigations that had not been considered by Hegel" (Introduction, 80). Historically, this renewed investigation marks—after the two major turning points in the understanding of the principle that were brought about by Aristotle and Hegel—the beginning of "a third moment in the history of the principle of contradiction … a moment that will remedy old shortcomings" (Introduction, 80). Finally, the critical and precise analysis and restructuring of the fundamental principles of logic—

the task that Łukasiewicz has set for himself in his work on Aristotle and the principle of contradiction—is precisely "the work that Hegel did not produce" (Introduction, 79).

Łukasiewicz is explicit about the fact that he takes Hegel to mean and believe precisely what he wrote: contradictions are present in everything. In response to the claims of some of Hegel's interpreters that Hegel did not really mean that contradictions could (really) be true, Łukasiewicz defends the position that "Hegel does claim *seriously* that the principle of contradiction is false" (XX, 207), not the least because it would be "much simpler to assume that Hegel really *believed* what he wrote" (V, 109).

It is precisely the questions that remained unresolved as part of the legacy of Hegel and his dialectical method, which provide the major impetus and motivations for Łukasiewicz to take on the issue of the PC once again. Łukasiewicz' attempt to solve these issues presents one of the first twentieth century efforts to develop an analytic response to Hegel's project. More than seventy-five years after Łukasiewicz' early attempt, Hegel's dialectic logic continued to be a major influence in the development of paraconsistent and dialethic logics. As Ayda Arruda (1989) points out,

> the handling of dialectical contradictions influenced the construction of paraconsistent logic. However, this influence was not in the sense of formalizing aspects of dialectical discourse, but rather in the sense of constructing logics which can be used as basis for inconsistent but non-trivial theories in general (Arruda 1989, 101).

At a unique point in history, roughly a century after Hegel, Łukasiewicz can employ new analytic tools—tools that were unavailable to Hegel—in his investigation of the logical features of contradictions: the methods and discoveries of the emerging new science of mathematical logic. Recent defenders of Hegelian dialectic, for example, Priest who outlined an account of how the Hegelian dialectic can be presented within a paraconsistent logic (cf. Priest 1989), also emphasize the importance of taking Hegel seriously. Paul Redding comments in his work on *Analytic Philosophy and the Return of Hegelian Thought* (Redding 2007) that

> Priest's approach has the advantage of taking Hegel at his word when he avows his 'law of contradiction'. Moreover, by linking Hegel's alleged 'dialetheism' to the issue of

> thought's limits, Priest locates Hegel's avowal of contradiction in just that part of the Hegelian programme where his complex relation to Kant is perhaps most significant (Redding 2007, 202).

Hegel's dialectical idealism is not merely compatible with contemporary dialetheism—it presents a crucial first articulation of a modern, dialetheist account. Contradictions not only exist in the conceptual and abstract structures contemplated by mind, but they do exist in the actual, empirically accessible world. Reality is inconsistent. This claim is endorsed by many contemporary dialetheists. The core Dialetheist position, apart from its increasing number of varieties,[10] is characterized by an endorsement of the claim that there are *some* contradictions that are true (and also false!)—dialetheism does not claim that *all* contradictions are true. Some contradictions are simply false (and not also true).[11]

Łukasiewicz clearly and unequivocally asserts a strong historical and philosophical lineage connecting his own work to that of both Aristotle and Hegel, but the details of his position are less clear. On the one hand, his work is not simply a continuation in the sense of a purely critical response to Aristotle and Hegel, but a continuation in the sense of a progressive movement towards "a third moment in the history of the PC" which aims at a greater completion in the understanding of the PC and related fundamental logical and ontological principles. On the other hand, Łukasiewicz is most certainly not Hegelian in his approach, methodology, or overall philosophical orientation.

In this sense, Łukasiewicz' investigation into the PC presents both a response and a contribution to the debate on the legacy of Hegel's dialectic logic that took place under the label of "*Die Logische Frage*" (The Question of Logic) in Germany during the middle of the 19th century. The origin of the debate goes back to Kant's introduction of his transcendental logic in the Critique of Pure Reason. The fundamental change in the understanding of logic introduced there by Kant and Hegel's subsequent development of a metaphysical logic set the stage for a sustained critical debate about the "correct" logic (and the logical treatment of contradictions) to support scientific investigations.

Trendelenburg

Roughly a decade after Hegel's death in 1831, Friedrich Adolf Trendelenburg (1802-–1872), Professor of Moral Philosophy at the University of Berlin, published two articles in the *Neue Jenaische Allgemeine Literaturzeitung* (Trendelenburg 1842, 1843) that raised the question of a scientific evaluation of Hegel's logic. Under the heading "*Die logische Frage in Hegel's System*" (*The Logic Question in Hegel's System*), the articles engaged a large readership and generated a substantial debate on the question of logic reform in Germany. The two articles were re-published as a monograph in 1843 (Trendelenburg 1843a) and present a summary of the main points of criticism of Hegel's system that were first developed in Trendelenburg's larger work, *Logische Untersuchungen* (Trendelenburg 1840), a work that Łukasiewicz cites in his own discussion, suggesting that he was familiar with the position advocated by Trendelenburg (cf. VII, 1 n.2)

In Trendelenburg's view, the fundamental question of Hegel's system is the question of logic, that is, the question about the suitability and effectiveness Hegel's dialectical logic as a scientific method. For Hegel, philosophy is the systematic production of knowledge; it is—literally—*Wissenschaft* ("knowledge making"). Philosophy is science; its task is to generate knowledge and, in Hegel's philosophy, the one and only method that successfully generates complete scientific knowledge is dialectical thought. Thus, the concept of dialectical movement is of fundamental value and importance to Hegel's entire philosophical work.

But Trendelenburg charges that Hegel's all-encompassing dialectic has become a new dogma that rigidly asserts that

> the dialectic method is the absolute method; and even those who held on to this great discovery—apparently the greatest that has ever been made on the field of philosophy—were not satisfied by the results (Trendelenburg 1843a, 6).[12]

According to Trendelenburg, Hegel's project fails to satisfy its own fundamental claim, namely to derive the concepts and determinations of being from within itself, without any presuppositions, in a pure form that does not rely on synthesis with empirical or sensible elements (Trendelenburg 1843a, 12).[13]

Trendelenburg argues that his critique of Hegel's dialectic leave but two courses of action: either to concede the difficulties raised in his exposition and therefore abandon the Hegelian project, or to defend Hegel's account and refute Trendelenburg's criticisms are unwarranted or mistaken. For Trendelenburg, however, the matter is resolved.

> The question to be decided is simply this: Is Hegel's dialectical method of pure thought a scientific procedure? . . . Following the concluded investigations, we have to purely and roundly deny this (Trendelenburg 1843a, 26).[14]

However, Trendelenburg's rejection of Hegel's dialectic method does not address what lies at the heart of the issue, the truth and validity of Aristotle's principle of contradiction. A rejection of Hegel's dialectic method because it does not satisfy its own demands and conditions—even if justified—does not settle the matter. The traditional acceptance and certainty associated with the principle had suffered tremendously under the weight of Hegel's philosophy and the need to ascertain its status by determining its conceptual and logical foundations arose with new urgency.

Ueberweg

The logician and historian of philosophy Friedrich Ueberweg investigated the questions and uncertainties regarding the truth and validity of the fundamental principles of logic, which fuelled the debate about the *Logische Frage,* in his *System der Logik und Geschichte der logischen Systeme* (Ueberweg 1857, 1871, 2001). Ueberweg, who had been a student of Herman Lotze (1817—1871) at Göttingen, where he attended Lotze's courses on logic and philosophy, and of Friedrich Beneke (1798—1854) and Trendelenburg in Berlin, held the view that the three core principles of logic, the principle of identity, contradiction, and excluded third, need proof and cannot be accepted by an appeal to the traditional authority of Aristotle or by an appeal to their allegedly immediate truth. Thus, in his approach to logic, Ueberweg raised Dedekind's demand for proof for all *a priori* claims some thirty years before Dedekind (cf. p.21 above) and like Łukasiewicz—but fifty years earlier—Ueberweg thought that such proofs and, most importantly, a proof of the principle of contradiction, can be produced.

Remarkably, Ueberweg attempts to show that the principle of contradiction can be derived from an analysis of the concepts of affirmation and denial, the concept of truth, and the concept of a judgment or statement and its meaning. Franz Brentano, who had been a student of Trendelenburg in Berlin whose own students came to include Edmund Husserl, Alexius Meinong, and Łukasiewicz' teacher Kazimierz Twardowski, discusses Ueberweg's attempt as part of his survey of the various analyses of *a priori* knowledge in his lecture notes on logic and epistemology (Brentano 1956). Pointing out that John Stuart Mill (1806–1873) and Herbert Spencer (1820–1903) considered the principle of contradiction not as an *a priori* claim but as an inductively derived principle, Brentano contrasts their accounts with Ueberweg's, who does hold that there are certain universal, *a priori* truths and that the traditional principles of logic are paradigmatic instances of such *a priori* statements. However, Ueberweg denies that the acceptance of the truth of these principles is warranted by an appeal to an immediate cognition of their truth, that is, he denies that the truth of such universal principles arises immediately and directly from the understanding of the concepts that are employed in their formulation. Instead, Ueberweg argues, the principles are derived from even more fundamental, logical and epistemological concepts, which are not an immediate part of the formulations of the principles, but which are necessary for the formulation of the principle. Thus, Brentano notes—and not without a certain amount of incredulity—Ueberweg makes the attempt to provide such a derivation, a proof of the principle of contradiction "based on an analysis of the concepts of truth, judgment, and the difference between affirmation and denial" (Brentano 1956, 163).[15]

Even though Brentano swiftly dismisses Ueberweg's attempt to prove the principle of contradiction as an error without serious consequences (Brentano 1956, 164),[16] his description of Ueberweg's attempt suggest striking similarities between parts of Łukasiewicz' investigation of the principle of contradiction and the approach taken by Ueberweg.[17] Ueberweg's attempt presents an important precursor to Łukasiewicz' investigations. Łukasiewicz' analysis of the possibility and conditions of a formal derivation of the principle of contradiction from simpler principles advances and corrects many of the shortcomings of Ueberweg's analysis. Unfortunately, (for Ueberweg, at any rate), Łukasiewicz' analysis also reveals that the attempt to prove the principle of contradiction in this approach is bound to fail.

Ueberweg begins his discussion of the principle of contradiction by emphasizing Aristotle's focus on the problems of ontology (instead of logical problems) that engage Aristotle in the *Metaphysics.* Aristotle does not explicitly position the fundamental principles of logic as axioms at the top of logic,

> but insofar as he articulates them in a scientific form at all, he introduces them on some occasions as norms for the construction of judgments and conclusions and, on other occasions and in the Metaphysics, in particular, he introduces them in regard to the ontological principle on which they are founded (Ueberweg 1857, 173).

Ueberweg argues that the conception of the three principles as normative or fundamental principles of logic is the result of the historical development of logical understanding since the days of Aristotle. He points out that it was Joachim Georg Darjes (1714–1791) and Hermann Samuel Reimarus (1694–1768), who first expressed the idea that the principles articulated by Aristotle as part of his ontological inquiries, including the principle of contradiction, constitute fundamental principles of logic. However, Ueberweg agrees with the criticism articulated by Hegel's contemporary and philosophical nemesis, Jakob Friedrich Fries (1773–1843). In *System der Logik* (Fries 1811), Fries argues that the principles do not belong at the top of a logical system (as axioms or fundamental principles) because they can only be understood in their full significance after the structure of concepts and the relation of subject and predicate in a statement are already developed (Ueberweg 1857, 174).

In Ueberweg's account, the first challenges to the privileged status of the principle of contradiction as a first principle were advanced by Scotist philosophers in the Middle Ages. In particular, Ueberweg mentions the Franciscan theologian Antonius Andreas (c.1280—1348), who had been a student of Duns Scotus (c.1265—1308), as one of the first to dispute the principle's position as an *arche* and the impossibility of a direct proof and "attempted to derive the principle of contradiction from the principle: *ens est ens*, which, as a positive principle, is prior to it" (Ueberweg 1857, 195).[18] It was Francisco Suarez (1548—1617), who later[19] defended Aristotle's claim that the PC is indeed a first principle (and thus impossible to prove directly) against Andreas' challenge by arguing that "the formula *ens est ens*, because of its emptiness and infertility, is unsuitable to be accepted as a first principle and ground of the principle of contradiction" (Ueberweg 1857, 195).[20]

At the time of Ueberweg's writing, doubts about the status of the principle of contradiction as an unprovable first principle had taken on new urgency. Hegel's challenge and Trendelenburg's critique generated a need to find new answers, scientifically grounded answers that would settle the matter. Ueberweg's solution is a proof of the principle. A proof will not only establish that the principle is not a first principle (which cannot be demonstrated), but it will also shed light on the logically most precise formulation of the principle, determine its underlying foundations and—with that—delimit the range and scope of its validity. In a striking passage, which anticipates key components of Łukasiewicz analysis some fifty years later, Ueberweg argues in 1857 that

> the principle of contradiction is not the supreme logical principle, but rather the idea of truth, i.e., the correspondence of the content of perception and thought with being. Today, it can hardly be disputed that a proof [of the principle of contradiction] is desirable since there is much discussion not only about the right formulation but also about the validity of the principle, its conditions, and the potential limitations on its application, so that these discussions will never find a generally accepted resolution without a proof, which also will have to illuminate the true significance of the principle (Ueberweg 1857, 181).[21]

Ueberweg believed that he had found a proof of the principle of contradiction. He begins his proof by specifying the target principle:

> The principle of (to be avoided) contradiction (*principium contradictionis*) is: contradictorily opposed statements (as: A is B, and: A is not B) cannot both be true but the one or the other of the same must be false; from the truth of one follows the falsity of the other. Or: a double answer, yes and no, with respect to one and the same question understood in the same sense, is inadmissible (Ueberweg 1857, 178).[22]

The core formulation of the principle corresponds to Aristotle's logical formulation: it is impossible for two contradictorily opposed statements to be both true (*Met. Γ* 6, 1011b 13-14).[23]

However, Ueberweg goes on to qualify this formulation with additional claims that first introduce a version the principle of bivalence, followed by an appeal to the principle of the excluded third. Ueberweg then presents his proof of the principle

> The proof of this statement is to be conducted through the definitions of truth (§3), statement (§67), and affirmation and denial. According to these definitions, truth means the agreement of the presentation-combination with reality and, consequently, the falsity of the denial, and the truth of the denial means the disagreement of the presentation-combination with reality and, consequently, the falsity of the affirmation, so that, if the affirmation is true, the denial is false, and if the denial is true, the affirmation is false, which was to be demonstrated (1857, 178).[24]

Ueberweg's proof most certainly falls short of its goal of demonstrating the principle of contradiction. At best, it establishes a conclusion about the logical behavior of negation within the framework of a correspondence theory of truth and the added assumption of bivalence. But Ueberweg's effort provides a blueprint of what a successful proof of the principle might look like.

Łukasiewicz, who agrees that the principle of contradiction is not a first and unprovable statement, also considers simpler principles that might provide the foundation for a proof. He investigates the possibility of a proof based on the principles of identity and double negation (VII, 118 ff.) However, Łukasiewicz concludes that none of these attempts can succeed because it is impossible to formulate the principle of contradiction without the concepts of logical multiplication and negation. The formulations of the principles of identity and double negation, on the other hand, are independent of the concept of logical multiplication and, in Łukasiewicz' analysis,

> it is impossible to formulate the principle of contradiction if two statements, of which one is the negation of the other, and which jointly constitute a logical multiplication, are not available (VII, 122).

But Łukasiewicz takes one of Ueberweg's core concepts and subjects it to further analysis: the theory of truth and, more specifically, the definition of a true statement. Thus, while Łukasiewicz is convinced that Ueberweg's attempt cannot succeed in the form in which it is constructed, he gives serious thought to the proposed approach of a direct derivation from simpler and more fundamental principles.[25]

Sigwart

Christoph von Sigwart (1830–1904) entered the debate about the *Logische Frage* with an influential account of systematic logic in his two volume work *Logik* (1873-78, 1895 [1873], 2001 [1873]). Łukasiewicz discusses three aspects of Sigwart's theory:

1) the analysis of the principle of contradiction as the most complete moment in a successive unfolding and development of the concept of negation
2) the distinction between contrary and exclusive relations, and
3) the logical analysis of universal categorical statements.[26]

Negation and the Principles of Logic

Sigwart presents an analysis of the fundamental principles of logic, that is, the PC, PI, PDN, and PET, and the relations between these principles in terms of their explicative power with respect to the concept of negation.

Negation, for Sigwart, is a subjective function of thought. He denies that there are negative facts that correspond to negations. Negations are "subjective expedients" which are needed "in order to know the world of reality in which no counterpart of our negating thought is contained" (Sigwart, 126). Sigwart follows Trendelenburg and argues that Hegel's mistake was to consider negation as a real relation.

> It is only by a constant confusion between negation in thought and those real relations in being which are very imperfectly expressed by mere negation that the Hegelian logic succeeds in presenting it as a real power, and as the nature of things; but unless we may admit this confusion once for all, as may well be done after Trendelenburg's penetrative criticism, it must pointed out at almost every step of the Logic (Sigwart, 126-7).

In Sigwart's analysis, the principle of contradiction articulates the final and most complete determination of the logical content of negation; it is the terminus of a series of increasingly comprehensive determinations of the concept of negation.

Łukasiewicz, however, rejects Sigwart's construction. The principle of contradiction cannot be developed based on the principle of identity and the definition of true statement, as Łukasiewicz' analysis has already shown and, furthermore, it cannot be developed on a definition of a false statement (XVII, 186).

Contrary and Incompatible Relations

Łukasiewicz agrees with Sigwart's account of contrary and exclusive relations. In his analysis of Aristotle's argument in support of the psychological formulation of the principle of contradiction, Łukasiewicz adopts Sigwart's position and shifts the issue of contrarily opposed beliefs to beliefs that are exclusive of each other. Sigwart rejected the notions of "opposition" and "opposed" as "almost useless" for logical purposes because of "the different meanings given to them and . . . the frequently vague relation between what was called opposition and negation on the one hand, and difference on the other" (Sigwart, 131).

Incompatibility, on the other hand, is logically useful because "incompatibility has no degrees" and, thus, it is the foundation of the relations of contrariety and opposition, which "merely refer to the magnitude of the difference, and are easily confused with it" (Sigwart, 133).

Łukasiewicz deploys Sigwart's distinction in his argument to show that in case of the psychological principle of contradiction, the mutual exclusion of convictions or beliefs is an empirical question, and cannot be proven *a priori* and, consequently, that the psychological principle of contradiction is, at best, an empirical hypothesis (V, 107; cf. Commentary, 310).

Analysis of Universal Categorical Statements

Łukasiewicz adopts one more analytic tool from Sigwart. In Chapter VII, Łukasiewicz presents the PI, PDN, and PC in the form of conditional statements, because the conditional form makes it easier to detect the differences between statements (VII, 120). The conditional statements are logically equivalent to their categorical counterparts, i.e., the pairs of categorical and conditional statements for each principle mutually entail each other. Further, the pairs of statements are not only logically equivalent, they also have the same meaning. This identity of meaning, Łukasiewicz argues, is a consequence of the correct rendering of the meaning of "all *x*" and "no *x*", which is hidden in the categorical formulations but explicated and revealed in its logical structure (as an inference relation) by the combination of antecedent and consequent in the conditional formulations.

> "All A are B" means that "if something is A, then it is also B", and "no A is B" means that "if something is A, then it is not B". The equivalence of these formulas cannot be doubted; their identical meaning, however, follows from the meaning of the words "all" and "no" (VII, 120).

At the beginning of the twentieth century, Sigwart's theory of the logical meaning of universal categorical statements was still the subject of intense debate. Thomas Case in his 1911 *Encyclopedia Britannica* entry on "Logic" (Case 2005 [1911]) points out that Sigwart "holds that the appropriate form of 'all M is P' is 'if anything is M it is P.'" Case goes on to acknowledge that Sigwart's view "influenced not only German but also English logicians, such as Venn, Bradley and Bosanquet," but Case is not prepared to endorse Sigwart's account because it "destroys the fabric of inference, and *reduces scientific laws to mere hypotheses*" (Case 2005 [1911], Italics added for emphasis).

Łukasiewicz, on the other hand, writing in 1910, adopts Sigwart's account of the logical equivalence between universal categorical and hypothetical statements. He rejects Sigwart's theory that grounds logical principles in the concept of negation. But Łukasiewicz also applies Sigwart's distinction between contrary and exclusive relations in his analysis of the psychological version of the principle of contradictions and its proofs (V, 107). Finally, in his article on "Creative Elements in Science", published in 1912, Łukasiewicz endorses the view that scientific laws are only probable hypotheses, as compared to the certainty afforded by *a priori* demonstrations. In Łukasiewicz' view, universal *a priori* claims, if applied to reality, become hypotheses that require their own proof and confirmation by empirical investigation (Łukasiewicz 1970 [1912], 122, 127).[27]

The way and extent to which a theory fits the world is not a matter than can be determined on *a priori* grounds. For Łukasiewicz, this also holds for systems of logic and inference—the extent to which a system of logic fits the world is not decidable on *a priori* grounds. Just as the discovery of non-Euclidean geometry shook the age-old faith in the truth and certainty of a Euclidean presentation of physical space, the discovery of a new, non-Aristotelian logic will demonstrate that the structure of a logical system and being-*qua*-being are distinct domains and the question whether a given logic has the best fit to the world is a separate—and empirical—question. And, for Łukasiewicz, nothing has brought the issue more to the fore than the discovery of non-Euclidean geometry.

Non-Euclidean Geometry

Lobachevsky's discovery of Non-Euclidean geometry in 1825 marks a crucial turning point in the understanding of mathematics and *a priori* truths. According to Nidditch, "the fact that one was able to have a system other than Euclid's came as a deep shock" (Nidditch, 29). The traditional view that mathematics provided completely certain knowledge, as for example, espoused by Plato, Spinoza, Leibniz, or Kant, was no longer tenable. The realization that instead of one single geometry, multiple and incompatible geometries were available, led to a view in which mathematical theories were no longer viewed as "natural knowledge, but as in themselves works of art, dependent for their value on their abstractions for the mind, though they may sometimes be judged to have another value in addition: that of being a help in the natural sciences" (Nidditch, 29-30). Echoing Dedekind's famous phrase about numbers, Nidditch writes: "Mathematics is the free invention of the mind, limited only by possible uses in natural science that may be desired and by rules of logic that one is willing or is forced, as a person of good sense, to be guided by" (Nidditch, 30).

The foundations of these "rules of logic" are at the center of Łukasiewicz' undertaking. For Łukasiewicz, the discovery of geometry promised to open new possibilities in the understanding of logical principles and their role in the scientific exploration of the physical world. The way in which it was discovered that Euclidean geometry is not the only possible representation of spatial relations offered Łukasiewicz a blue-print for his own project, the development of a non-Aristotelian logic in which the principle of contradiction would take the place of Euclid's parallel postulate. Łukasiewicz aims to find out whether

> if it is possible to develop a system of a non-Aristotelian logic, without taking it [the principle of contradiction] into account at all, just as a system of non-Euclidian geometry

> emerged through a change to the parallel axiom (Łukasiewicz, Introduction, 81).

By modeling his approach on the historical events that led to the discovery of non-Euclidean geometries, Łukasiewicz explores whether a non-Aristotelian logic might be developed by exploiting the structural similarities between axiomatic systems that describe logical and spatial relations. Non-Euclidean geometries were discovered as the result of attempts to prove the parallel postulate.

Many attempts to prove Euclid's postulate (or equivalent formulations) tried to derive a contradiction through a *reductio* argument. An attempted *reductio* proof begins with the assumption that the parallel postulate is false and then attempts to derive a contradiction from the negation of the postulate and all or some of the four simpler Euclidean postulates, which in Euclid's account are introduced prior to the parallel postulate. However, unexpected results ensued. First, there is not just one denial of the parallel postulate—both the claim that there are an infinite number of parallel lines that intersect and the claim that there are an infinite number of parallel lines that do not intersect form a negation of the Euclid's postulate of exactly one line—and, secondly, neither one of the two denials of Euclid's parallel postulate does entail a contradiction. Instead, the two denials characterize the two main types of non-Euclidean geometries, Hyperbolic and Elliptic geometry.

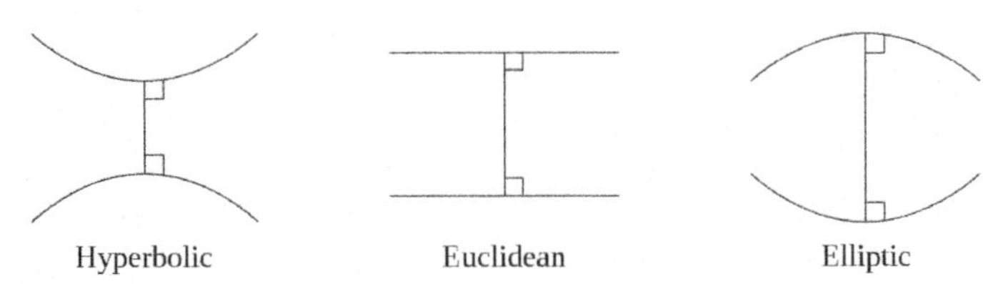

The two alternatives to a Euclidean geometry, Hyperbolic and Elliptic, do suggest a strikingly different analogy to a logical principle at the heart of a non-Aristotelian logic, but it is not the principle of contradiction. Both Łukasiewicz and Vasil'év consider the PC as the (logical) analog to Euclid's parallel postulate, but Łukasiewicz argues that the PC is dependent on other, simpler principles and, thus, a derived theorem that would change with a change in the principles that are adopted prior to it. But Euclid's parallel postulate cannot be demonstrated. That is, after all, what is shown by the construction of non-Euclidean geometries that deny the postulate in some form.

An interesting and, arguably, more fitting analogy is generated if the principle of bivalence is selected as the logical principle that corresponds most closely to Euclid's parallel. In this analogy, instead of a single truth-value (or its absence) corresponding to one parallel line in the Euclidean-Aristotelian model, there are an infinite number of parallel lines that in an Elliptic geometry intersect the original line at two points, analogous to a combination of two truth-values into gluts of true-and-false (as found in some paraconsistent logics like LP, for example), as well as a second alternative, again involving an infinite number of parallel lines, now in a Hyperbolic geometry with none of the lines intersecting the original line, analogous to an infinite number of truth-value gaps.

However, in 1910, Łukasiewicz did not have the principle of bivalence in his sights. His strategy towards a non-Aristotelian logic targets the principle of contradiction. In presenting a proof of the principle of contradiction, even if empty and purely formal, Łukasiewicz follows the history of the discovery of non-Euclidean geometry, but his result, a formal proof of the principle, appears to show that the construction of a non-Aristotelian logic is impossible. However, Łukasiewicz' proof shifts the focus of inquiry on the foundations of the principles of *a priori* reasoning, mathematical or logical, and—with respect to logic and geometry—on the role of *a priori* constructions in the scientific investigation of reality.

Mathematicians and Logicians

The history of the discovery of non-Euclidean geometry and the responses to this discovery are but one instance that illustrates how historical contingencies are real factors in the historical unfolding and development of *a priori* theories. According to José Ferreirós, even the emergence of modern formal logic, as exemplified by First Order Logic, is the outcome of a "combination of rational argument and historical contingencies" (Ferreirós 2001, 441). Ferreirós argues that First Order Logic "is not a 'natural unity', i.e., a system the scope and limits of which could be justified solely by rational argument" (Ferreirós 2001, 441). For Ferreirós, the influence of the mathematical approach to logic, pioneered by British mathematicians, provided the initial impetus for a complex interaction with existing, traditional conceptions of logic in terms of its scope, methods, and role within the disciplines of philosophy, psychology and mathematics.

A similar view is taken by Volker Peckhaus, who argues that the development of mathematical logic during the second half of the nineteenth century, and the corresponding radical transformation of the concept of logic, was primarily the work of mathematicians, not philosophers, and the "strange collaboration" between the disciplines (Peckhaus 1999, 435).

In his opening remarks, Łukasiewicz offers what was to become an early draft of the now familiar canon of logicians that shaped and created the paradigm classical Frege/Russell logic of early analytic philosophy: "Boole, De Morgan, Jevons, Peirce, Schröder, Russell, Peano—they are the outstanding founders of the new logic," he notes (Introduction, 80). This list of mathematicians and logicians clearly places Łukasiewicz in line with a mathematical approach to logic that led to the great advances in formal logic during the second half of the nineteenth century.

In a second list, Łukasiewicz mentions Russell, Couturat, Frege, Hilbert, and Peano; mathematicians "who investigated the foundations of arithmetic and geometry in connection with symbolic logic" and whose investigations support a logicist account of the relationship between logic and mathematics. As Łukasiewicz observes, their work appears to "prove that all of mathematics, both in terms of its form as well as its content, can be derived from a few fundamental logical concepts and presuppositions" (Introduction 81).

Łukasiewicz' two lists indicate the presence of an older rift that began to be bridged during the second half of the nineteenth century by a frequently uneasy collaboration between logicians and mathematicians, a collaboration that aimed to develop a scientific account of the foundations of mathematics and logic. De Morgan commented on the indifference between the two disciplines to each other.

> We know that mathematicians care no more for logic than logicians for mathematics. The two eyes of exact science are mathematics and logic; the mathematical sect puts out the logical eye, the logical sect puts out the mathematical eye; each believing that it see better with one eye than with two (de Morgan 1868).[28]

As Łukasiewicz' two lists show, some fifty years after de Morgan, Łukasiewicz is able to draw on the developments in both fields of research. However, it should be noted that, in 1910, the pioneers listed by Łukasiewicz did not enjoy the same standing and recognition that they do today. At the onset of the 20th century, the works of Frege, Peano, and Russell were known by only a relatively small group of philosophers and mathematicians and their discussions were remote to the contemporary 'mainstream' of philosophical interest and debate. A good illustration of this fact is provided by the entry on "Logic" in the 1911 edition of the Encyclopedia Britannica (cited earlier with reference to Sigwart), which does not mention Russell, Frege, Peano, Pierce, or anybody else that from today's perspective was among the more important contributors to the advancement of formal logic during that time (Case 2005 [1911]).

Łukasiewicz, on the other hand, was keenly aware of the great progress that had been made by these logicians and mathematicians. But the new conception of a formally constructed system of inference as pioneered by Frege and Russell, was still essentially an Aristotelian logic. Contemporary formal logic, Łukasiewicz notes,

> remains in a similar relation to Aristotelian logic as contemporary Euclidean geometry to the Elements of Euclid. It continues to be an Aristotelian logic because it takes over all the principles that Aristotle had already discovered and recognized (Łukasiewicz, Introduction, 80).

And, despite the success of the new understanding of logical principles, and the developments in the theory of numbers and set theory, questions regarding the principle of contradiction emerged—often unexpectedly—within these new disciplines.

Łukasiewicz discusses Cantor's theory of transfinite numbers and notes that, even though Cantor's theory seems to resolve contradictions at one part of the account, it merely ends up repositioning the contradictory moment at a different place within the system (XVIII, 194). No matter how Cantor's project is interpreted, some of the antimonies that develop on its foundation are, at the time Łukasiewicz is writing, still without a solution.

But, for Łukasiewicz, it was Russell's discovery of the set-theoretical contradiction at the foundation of Frege's *Grundgesetze*

(Russell 1903) that presented one of the most decisive and tremendously influential moments in the revolutionary, mathematical transformation of the understanding of logic and the structure of systems of inference. In Łukasiewicz' view,

> this contradiction is one of the strangest and the most interesting logical discoveries that have ever been made (XVIII, 194).

Łukasiewicz comments that, in his estimate, a solution to the paradox is not only possible but also of great importance. A solution must be found, because

> this contradiction is not merely a logical toy, but it is deeply connected with the foundations of mathematics and logic" (XVIII, 197).

Łukasiewicz perceived a further contradictory aspect, also at the foundation of logic, in the form of the logical zero. In Appendix I, where Łukasiewicz presents and discusses a classical, two-valued logic, he argues that this logic

> does employ a contradictory object in its formulas, namely, the logical zero. Thus, it appears that even in symbolic logic the principle of contradiction is not a universal law but a law that has exceptions (Appendix I, 257).

The new logic, the non-Aristotelian logic that Łukasiewicz envisioned, would preserve the achievements of formal, mathematical logic, but it would also no longer treat the principle of contradiction as a privileged, foundational claim.

Towards A Non-Aristotelian Logic

Creativity and Necessity in *A Priori* Reasoning

Łukasiewicz' attack on the principle of contradiction in 1910 takes place within the general framework of formal, classical Frege/Russell logic. But Łukasiewicz' efforts are characterized by a significant tension. On the one hand, Łukasiewicz embraces the findings of contemporary logical research, exemplified by Boole, de Morgan, Jeavons, Peano, Schröder, Couturat, Frege and Russell—all of which accepted consistency, non-contradiction, as an obvious and fundamental principle for their systems. But, on the other hand, Łukasiewicz also perceives a creative aspect at the core of formal reasoning. Science does not merely record "facts" that obtain in the world; it organizes this collection of facts within a logical structure. This logical structure, however, is the product of a creative interpretation of these facts and not by itself a reproduction of empirical facts. Łukasiewicz attributes a greater independence to *a priori* reasoning and it is in this independence that creativity in *a priori* reasoning can manifest itself.

The tension between these two opposing tendencies finds expression in Łukasiewicz' article on "Creative Elements in Science" (Łukasiewicz 1970 [1912]). The article presents Łukasiewicz' thoughts about the concepts of logic and science in the years prior to World War I and demonstrates the importance that Łukasiewicz attributed to a creative component in scientific work. Łukasiewicz' discussion provides vital background information about the motivations and direction of his search for a non-Aristotelian logic.

> Both scientists and those who are remote from science often deem that the goal of science is truth, and they understand truth as agreement between thought and existence. Hence they think that the scientist's work consists in reproducing facts in true judgments, similarly as a photographic plate reproduces light and shadow and a phonograph reproduces sound. The poet, the painter, and the composer work creatively; the scientist does not create anything, but merely discovers the truth (Opening paragraph, Łukasiewicz 1970 [1912], 1).

Łukasiewicz goes on to defend the thesis that this view is mistaken, that science is not a mere truthful recording of facts and, further, that there is an important creative aspect, which is inseparable from the reasoning that the scientist undertakes to justify the claims of his or her science. "In all reasoning there is inherent formal creative reasoning: a logical principle of reasoning" (Łukasiewicz 1970 [1912], 11).

In his argument, Łukasiewicz distinguishes between facts that are empirically ascertained and those that are provided by *a priori* reasoning and points out that the "principles of reasoning *do not reproduce* facts that are empirically given" (Łukasiewicz 1970 [1912], 11). Rather, the reproduction of facts in an abstract, symbolic form is generated by an interpretative act, like the way a painting presents a landscape. It is not bound to a single schema in which to translate the visual facts that make up a landscape. It is possible to invent new schemas of representation, because the criteria for the adequacy of a presentation rest internally in whichever schema is adopted, not in the (external) visual facts presented by an actual landscape.[29]

On the other hand, in logic and the *a priori* sciences, truth is grounded in the principles that govern their own construction. The axioms of logic "are true on the strength of definitions and axioms derived from reason and not from experience." (Łukasiewicz 1970 [1912], 11). The independence of *a priori* truths from empirically verifiable facts severs the two domains.

> Logical and mathematical judgments are truths only in the world of ideal entities. We shall probably never know whether these entities have counterparts in real objects (Łukasiewicz 1970 [1912], 12).

In a footnote, Łukasiewicz adds that in his earlier work on Aristotle and the principle of contradiction, he had "tried to demonstrate that we cannot even be sure that real objects are subject to the principle of contradiction" (Łukasiewicz 1970 [1912], 12 n.20). In Łukasiewicz' analysis in 1910, no conclusive answer can be given that would establish "with certainty whether seemingly contradiction-free objects really are such" (XVIII, 197).

The principle of contradiction is an *a priori* statement. Its truth depends on the axioms and rules adopted by a given logic. Whether this principle holds outside of a logical system is a second and independent question. Łukasiewicz distinguishes between statements that take ideal objects as their subject terms and statements that assert empirical facts. The latter are true if they correspond to the facts that exist, the former are true if the relations or properties asserted about an object are the case in correspondence to applicable definitions and rules of inference.[30]

Regarding the relation between *a priori* sciences, and specifically the relation between logic and mathematics, Łukasiewicz endorses the logicist program of Frege and Russell. If their arguments are correct, then "logic gives rise to mathematics" (Łukasiewicz 1970 [1912], 11). And, "if all mathematics is reducible to logic, then it is also a *pure mental product*" (Łukasiewicz 1970 [1912], 12). As a pure mental product, the *a priori* science of

> logic, with mathematics, might be compared to a fine net which is cast into the immense abyss of phenomena in order

> to catch the pearls that are scientific syntheses. It is a powerful instrument of research, but an instrument only (Łukasiewicz 1970 [1912], 12).

It is this contribution of creativity which is contained in "*the* a priori *mental constructions, which are contained in every synthesis*" and which in turn "*imbue the whole science with the ideal and creative element*" (Łukasiewicz 1970 [1912], 12). The ideal and the creative aspect are one and the same.

In 1910, Łukasiewicz adopts a classical, two-valued, sentential calculus modeled on Couturat's *L'Algebre de la logique* (Couturat 1905, 1914) for his investigation of the *a priori* claim that is articulated by the principle of contradiction. His attempt to develop a logic that emerges from a modification or omission of the principle of contradiction fails. But Łukasiewicz does succeed in showing that Aristotle's claim that the principle of contradiction is a first principle that cannot be derived from other, simpler principles, is false. In the logic that Łukasiewicz introduces in Appendix I to his monograph, the principle of contradiction is a derived theorem. Its proof is complex and relies on a long series of simpler principles, rules of inference, and definitions. Still, the principle of contradiction is a claim that has proof and this proof proceeds on purely *a priori* grounds.

According to the "mathematical" Łukasiewicz of the nineteen-thirties, Wittgenstein and Carnap erroneously considered *a priori* statements to be tautologies that "do not convey anything about reality" (Łukasiewicz 1970e [1936], 233). For Łukasiewicz, "all *a priori* systems, as soon as they are applied to reality, become natural science hypotheses which have to be verified by facts in a similar way as is done with physical hypotheses" (Łukasiewicz 1970e [1936], 233). The reason why *a priori* systems must be tested by empirical investigations is based on the following consideration:

> "we know today that not only do different systems of geometry exist, but different systems of logic as well, and they have, moreover, the property that one cannot be translated into another. I am convinced that one and only one of these logical systems is valid in the real world, that is, is real, in the same way as one and only one system of geometry is real. Today, it is true, we do not yet know which system that is, but I do not doubt that empirical research will sometime demonstrate whether the space of the uni-

verse is Euclidean or non-Euclidean, and whether the relationship between facts correspond to two-valued logic or to one of the many-valued logics" (Łukasiewicz 1970e [1936], 233).

Outline of a Non-Aristotelian Logic

Łukasiewicz embarks on a renewed investigation of the foundations of logic and ontology and the relation between the two disciplines. The focal point and testing ground for this investigation is the principle of non-contradiction and the possibility of the development of a non-Aristotelian logic by an alteration or omission of the principle. Łukasiewicz called these investigations "meta-logical" (Introduction, 81), a term now in common use and remarkably similar in meaning to Łukasiewicz' usage in 1910.[31]

Łukasiewicz' proposal of non-Aristotelian logic in 1910 is nothing but remarkable—and somewhat puzzling—given that at the beginning of the 20th century, the PC was generally unquestioned in its validity. An immediate question, then, arises regarding the motivations and inspirations that led Łukasiewicz to propose and engage in a project that ran contrary to the conventional logical wisdom of the time.

It is well known that Łukasiewicz' positioned his three-valued logics as a response to the problems raised by determinist arguments based on a strictly two-valued logic. Three-valued logic provided him with a logical foundation that was able to support an indeterminist position which preserves human freedom and creativity (Łukasiewicz 1970b [1918]). However, it is not clear to what extent the problem posed by a determinist interpretation of classical, two-valued logic provided an impetus for Łukasiewicz' work on Aristotle and the PC in 1910.

Jan Woleński argues that "Łukasiewicz, already in 1910, connected the validity of certain logical laws with the problem of indeterminism. But there are no reasons to think that Łukasiewicz already at that time questioned the principle of bivalence" (Woleński 2000, 23 n.15). Arianna Betti (2010) agrees with Woleński's point. However, she adds a note of caution:

> There are specific questions, especially regarding the first period of Łukasiewicz's activity, which have not yet found a clear and convincing answer in the critical literature. Łukasiewicz's rejection of the principle of the excluded

> middle in 1910, according to which the principle fails in application to general objects, as well as (probably) to future ones, has more than once been confused or deliberately assimilated with his later rejection of bivalence (Betti 2010, 21).

Apart from the question of Łukasiewicz' position on the principle of bivalence, his explicit aim of a non-Aristotelian logic raises further questions about the nature and structure of such a logic. Many of these questions still are debated in contemporary literature but, of course, with the advantage of today's knowledge of a multitude of non-classical logics. One distinction between logics is drawn in the question whether a given non-classical logic is intended as a *rival* or as a *supplement* to classical logic. Some are and some are not. As Susan Haack points out, "a rival system is . . . one the use of which is incompatible, and a supplementary system one the use of which is compatible, with the use of the standard system" (Haack 1974, 2).

For Haack, the main difference between the two approaches, between supplement and rival theories, is that

> the former tends to regard classical logic as *mistaken*, as including assertions which are not true, whereas the latter tends to regard classical logic as *inadequate*, as not including assertions which are true (Haack 1974, 2).

Łukasiewicz distinguishes two possibilities for the construction of a non-standard logic:

1) to alter the principle of non-contradiction in some form, that is, to introduce a modification to the existing logical apparatus, and

2) to omit it altogether from the axioms of a system.

Either approach would bring about a non-Aristotelian logic.

With respect to Haack's first option, which includes the position that classical logic contains assertions that are "not true", Łukasiewicz does not consider classical logic as mistaken in this sense. In the algebraic logic that he presents in Appendix I (224 ff.), the PC is a derived theorem, i.e., it is one demonstrated logical truth among the theorems associated with classical bivalent logic. However, Łukasiewicz considers that classical logic may be inadequate in that it fails to include assertions that should be recognized by logic, and that classical logic instead imposes too coarse a structure on its representations of the world and thus limits what can be cognized and reasoned about.

> Aristotelian logic, as useful as it may be for the cognition of facts, is perhaps too coarse a tool in order to be capable to discover the artful construction of the *essential* world behind the chaos of *appearances* (Introduction, 78).

In his conception of a non-Aristotelian logic, Łukasiewicz wants to preserve the truth and cognitive power of both Aristotelian and modern, formal logic, but he also wants a greater subtlety in distinction, a finer resolution, a logic that also includes propositions that are not strictly "true" (*simpliciter*) as within classical logic, but which are nevertheless true (or, at least, not false) in such a new, non-Aristotelian logic. The crucial points of attack for this new logic are the PC and PET, and the implicational consequences of their modification or adherence.

The axiomatic structure of algebraic representations of logical relations provided Łukasiewicz with the conceptual and analytic tools for a more precise and scientific investigation of both logical and ontological principles. And the discovery of non-Euclidean geometry suggested a promising parallel (pun intended) that showed how a critical analysis of the PC as an axiom of Aristotelian logic might open a path to a new, non-Aristotelian system of logic.

Contradictory and Incomplete Objects

Łukasiewicz visited Graz, Austria, during the winter semester 1908-9. He attended the lectures of Alexius Meinong on Object Theory [*Gegenstandstheorie*] and began work on his book on Aristotle and the Principle of Contradiction (Woleński 2000, 16-17, n.10). However, Łukasiewicz' work in Graz also included an investigation of probability theory and (modal) logic. At the time of Łukasiewicz' visit, Meinong was working on his *magnum opus*, published in 1915, *Über Möglichkeit und Wahrscheinlichkeit* (*On Possibility and Probability*). Meinong and Łukasiewicz' discussions about an object-theoretical account of modalities of possibility and probability led to Łukasiewicz' article "On the Logical Foundations of Probability Theory" (Łukasiewicz 1970 [1913]).[32]

At the time, Łukasiewicz reports, he was searching for a new conception of logic, a logic that would go beyond the "logical coercion" that "is most strongly manifested in *a priori* sciences" (Łukasiewicz 1970b [1918], 86). For Łukasiewicz, this logical coercion exercised by Aristotelian logic springs from Aristotle's notion of necessity. The new, non-Aristotelian and three-valued logic, which he had just discovered, "destroys the former concept of science," which is science based on necessity (Łukasiewicz 1970b [1918], 86).

Thus, already in 1909, Łukasiewicz sets out to develop what he called a non-Aristotelian logic at that time. The characteristic feature of such a non-Aristotelian logic is that it is either built with a modified version of the PC or—far more radical—a logic that disregards the principle altogether.

By including Meinongian objects in his analysis and—especially—incomplete and contradictory objects, Łukasiewicz arrives at conclusions about the logical properties of such objects that are inexpressible within the framework of formal, two-valued logic. With respect to contradictory objects, the PC fails and a consequence of the logical properties of a contradictory object is that there are propositions that are both true and false – a conclusion that Łukasiewicz is not prepared to accept in 1910. In the case of the PET and incomplete objects, the result is that there are propositions that are neither true nor false–again a conclusion Łukasiewicz is unable to accommodate within the framework of his analysis.

It is in the analysis of the logical properties of incomplete and contradictory objects that Łukasiewicz encounters the crucial structural limit of two-valued logic that prevents him from developing a non-Aristotelian logic in 1910, the principle of bivalence. It is the assumption of bivalence, that is, the presupposition and acceptance of the claim that every proposition has exactly one, and only one, of two truth values, i.e., that every proposition is exclusively either true or otherwise false, which left Łukasiewicz' analysis inconclusive at the time. As Graham Priest put it, Łukasiewicz "opens the way for paraconsistent enterprise, but does not follow the road opened" (Priest 1989, 25).

Paraconsistency and Bivalence: The Success and Failure of Łukasiewicz' Attempt

The main obstacle that prevented Łukasiewicz from developing a non-Aristotelian logic in 1910 is his acceptance of the principle of bivalence. His analysis of the principle of contradiction proceeds with the assumption of bivalence, that is, the assumption that a statement has exactly one of two truth values, it is either true or otherwise false. In the case of the principle of the excluded third, *A* or not-*A*, the solution that led to the first three-valued logic was the addition of a third truth-value (possible, in the sense of neither true nor false). In the case of the principle of contradiction, the corresponding solution is the admission of a truth-value that combines both true and false.

The non-classical valuations of statements that Łukasiewicz derives in his analysis of incomplete and contradictory objects are based on (and a direct consequence of) the classical conception of truth that Łukasiewicz adopts. A statement *p* is true iff *p* is the case. Or, in object-theoretical terms, the statement "object *x* contains property *F*" is true iff object *x* contains property *F*.

Łukasiewicz realizes that his analysis of the PC suggests this new truth-value, in particular in the case of contradictory objects. In arguing that the PC does not follow from the definitions of true and false statements, Łukasiewicz concludes that while it follows from his definitions that in case a statement is true, its negation must be false, this does not exclude the possibility that its negation can also at the same time be true as well (!)—as it is in the case of the contradictory properties of a contradictory object (XVII, 184).

However, he resists his own conclusion that a statement can have both truth-values, true *and* false, by two stipulations: First, under the pressure of his results with respect to the logical properties of contradictory objects, he reformulates his definition of a false statement so that it no longer forces a result in which certain statements about contradictory objects have to be accepted as both true and false (XVII, 185).

Secondly, after re-stating the consequences that follow from an acceptance of the principle of bivalence, i.e., by saying that affirmation and negation, truth and falsity, cannot exist next to each other, that they exclude and cancel each other (XVII, 186), he claims that there is only one way to avoid the problems caused by contradictory objects—they are not proper objects at all but nothing (XVII, 187). By defining an object as necessarily consistent, i.e., free of contradictory properties, he then arrives at a formal proof of the PC. While this move solves the problem caused by the insistence on bivalence, it is incommensurable with Meinong's theory of objects in which contradictory objects are bona fide proper objects. In the case of general and thus incomplete objects, however, he maintains Meinong's view that these objects are undetermined with respect to certain properties and predications of those properties result in statements that are neither true nor false. The reason for this appears to be Łukasiewicz' ontological outlook as reflected in his definition of truth and his acceptance of the Aristotelian position that (logical) truth follows (ontological) being.

The difference between an ontologically based construction of logic and a purely formal or mathematical one becomes clearer if we consider the situation from a purely formal position. Two truth-values, i.e., true and false, allow for a total of four combinations that exhaust all possibilities: true *simpliciter*, false *simpliciter*, true and false, and neither true nor false. Thus, from a purely formal position, the situation is such that a statement can take any one of these four values. The assumption of bivalence is prior to logic proper, so to say. It is an assumption that is (or is not) made prior to the development of a logical system. At the same time, the stipulation as to what truth-values a statement may take fundamentally shapes the character of the logic(s) that are subsequently constructed. It was one of the key achievements of Boole's algebraic logic that it was not based on any ontological or linguistic considerations, but instead is constructed from purely mathematical and formal point of view.

With respect to the issue raised by Betti (2010) and others, the picture that emerges is as follows: Łukasiewicz discovered that contradictory (and general) objects generate statements that violate the principle of bivalence. However, he did not explicitly recognize the principle of bivalence in 1910 and was thus prevented from rejecting the principle. The main reason for his adherence to bivalence stems from his largely Aristotelian ontological position on truth and the corresponding bivalence of statements (relation between logic and ontology).

In 1910, Łukasiewicz took aim at the principle of contradiction (and, to a lesser extent, the principle of the excluded third),[33] which Aristotle placed at the heart of his metaphysics. It was only later, after his discovery of multi-valued systems, that Łukasiewicz realized that it had not been the principle of contradiction, but the principle of bivalence, which was the defining feature of Aristotelian logic. However, as Łukasiewicz points out in his later writings, the strongest defender of strict bivalence in Antiquity was not Aristotle, who in *De Interpretatione* appears to at least consider the possibility that future contingent statements may not have a truth-value, but Chrysippias.

In 1910, Łukasiewicz efforts are concentrated on the principle of contradiction, the foundation of Aristotle's metaphysics. In his effort to clear the way towards a non-Aristotelian logic, Łukasiewicz sets out to demonstrate that the Principle of non-contradiction is not a "first" and "ultimate" principle in the Aristotelian sense. The PC "is neither a *final* nor an *unprovable* law" (Appendix I, 256). Even further, with respect to the PC as a core logical axiom and necessary condition of all logical thought, Łukasiewicz ultimately arrives at the conclusion that careful logical analysis shows that

> a large number of logical laws have no connection at all to the principle of contradiction; consequently, this principle is not only not final, but it also does not form an indispensable foundation of logical thinking (Appendix I, 256).

While Łukasiewicz presents a strong argument that this is the case, he did not accomplish his larger goal of a non-Aristotelian logic in 1910. Eight years later, in 1918, when he first announced his discovery of a three-valued logic in his "Farewell Lecture at Warsaw University", he offered some insights into the background and motivations of his discovery, connecting it with his earlier work on Aristotle and the principle of contradiction:

> I strove to demonstrate that that principle is not so self-evident as it is believed to be. Even then I strove to construct non-Aristotelian logic, but in vain (Łukasiewicz 1970b [1918], 86).

Today, a hundred years after its first publication, Łukasiewicz' early work on Aristotle and the PC is clearly recognizable as a significant moment in the history of logic and philosophy. It marks an important first step in the evolution of logic and the development of non-classical logics.

In 1910, Łukasiewicz did not break through the constraint of bivalence. He came close, but the possibility of a statement having both true and false as truth-values was too radical at the time. But Łukasiewicz' work on Aristotle and the principle of contradiction achieved many pioneering results. It marks the first time that the arguments and reasons that Aristotle presents in support of the principle of contradiction in the *Metaphysics* are subjected to a strict logical analysis and none of them is found to establish what it aims to establish. Aristotle fails to demonstrate that the first principle of the science of metaphysics is true. More recently, Priest arrived at the same conclusion. In his view, too, none of the arguments and reasons Aristotle presents succeed (Priest 2006).

In addition to the Aristotelian scholarship that Łukasiewicz demonstrates in his discussion of Aristotle's account, his analysis of the principle in terms of contemporary formal logic provides a striking example of a logical realist approach to the issues and questions. The combination of these two directions of research illustrates how the study of the history of philosophy and logic can contribute and advance the progress of contemporary logic research.

However, the main concern of this introduction to Łukasiewicz' work has been to emphasize the importance of Hegel and the debate about the *Logische Frage* on Łukasiewicz' investigation. The aim was to show that Łukasiewicz' work on the principle of contradiction is an attempt to answer the *Logische Frage*, which had engaged Trendelenburg, Ueberweg, and Sigwart.

Łukasiewicz' work presents the opening credo to the anticipated third moment in the history of the principle of contradiction, the moment in which the aporia between Aristotle and Hegel finds its *Aufhebung* with the aid of a formal, mathematical understanding of logic and philosophical analysis.

In his work, Łukasiewicz brings many controversial issues into sharper focus, among them the relation between logic and ontology, the nature of propositions or statements, paraconsistency, and the question of logical monism vs. logical pluralism. It is a clear indicator of the importance and significance of Łukasiewicz' early work on Aristotle and the PC that all these issues are still at the center of contemporary debate.

Notes on the Translation

Drafts of the translation have been reviewed and compared to the original Polish by Jan Wolenskí, Sebastian Kolodziejczyk, and Maja Kittel. During a visit to Jagellonian University, Krakov, Poland in 2009, I had the opportunity to consult and discuss my translation with each of these three scholars. I am deeply grateful for their many insightful comments and constructive criticisms, which greatly benefitted the translation. It is due to their kind assistance and support in the preparation of this translation that I am convinced that the translation presents not only an accurate reflection of Łukasiewicz' text, but also of the philosophical goals and interests that motivated his work. Of course, any shortcomings that may have remained undetected in the translation are solely my responsibility.

Łukasiewicz' Citations and Translations of Original Greek Texts

Łukasiewicz includes passages of Aristotle's texts in classical Greek in his work and provides his own translations to these passages. Łukasiewicz' translations of the Classical Greek texts have been preserved in this translation since they do provide important information about his interpretation of Aristotle's philosophical positions and form an integral part of his exposition and analysis. However, authoritative English translations of Aristotle's writings have been included to assist the reader. Also, Łukasiewicz cites various German philosophers and logicians throughout the monograph in the original German. The English translations of these citations are my own.

Sentences, Statements, Propositions

The Polish word *"sąd"* contains a range of meanings: a legal judgment issued by a judge or court, a statement of a declarative nature, a proposition, and simply a sentence.

While Łukasiewicz adopted the view that sentences are the proper truth-bearers in his later work, his position in 1910 is less clear. At times, he speaks as if he is employing "statement" in the sense of a Russellian proposition. At other times, his usage suggests a Meinongian conception of an *Objektiv*. And sometimes his usage comes close to a Fregean interpretation of meaning [*Bedeutung*] as one of two truth-values.

An additional influence on Łukasiewicz' use of 'statement' is the range of meanings for the German word *Satz*, which also encompasses a diverse set of senses ranging from grammatical sentence to logical or mathematical proposition, and from statement all the way to fundamental principle, as in *Der Satz vom Widerspruch*.

However, an inclination to stay close to the actual sentence is already perceptible in Łukasiewicz' 1910 work. He emphasizes the idea that sentences, declarative sentences or statements in the classic Aristotelian sense, are the bearers of truth, not propositions or *Objektive*, which posit an additional conceptual entity between sentence and meaning.

Initially, the translation used 'judgment', which seems appropriate given the historical context of the work. However, urged by Jan Wolenskí, the more modern term 'proposition' was adopted as the default translation. Finally, towards the final phase of editing and writing the commentary as well as the introduction to Łukasiewicz' work, the use of 'statement' seems to present the best choice and has been adopted throughout the translation.

The concept of what exactly constitutes the bearer of truth (and meaning) is of crucial importance to Łukasiewicz' analysis. He argues that the three formulations offered by Aristotle are three distinct statements. To support his claim, a close investigation into what it means for two sentences to have the same meaning as distinct from two sentences being logically equivalent is crucial. Łukasiewicz tackles the issue at various locations throughout the book, but in particular in Ch.II, III, and VII, where the issue of logical equivalence as compared to identity in meaning is of fundament importance to his argument (cf. also II, 291; and endnote 48).

Principle of Contradiction or Principle of Non-Contradiction

In the translation, the term "Principle of Contradiction" is used throughout. In modern usage, emphasis is frequently placed on the aspect of non-contradiction which is at the heart of the Aristotelian and traditional interpretation of the principle. However, the corresponding German expressions include variations that apply the accusative, "the principle about contradiction" or dative "the principle from contradiction" in addition to the genitive, which most closely corresponds to the ordinary English formulation as "the principle of contradiction". While subtle distinction like these often are not fully reflected in their English counterparts, the core meaning of the principle in its Aristotelian and traditional sense is that it is impossible for contradictory states to obtain simultaneously in actuality and, thus, that statements asserting that such states do obtain are necessarily false. Thus, the Aristotelian and traditional conception of the principle asserts the truth of universal consistency and it is this aspect which receives emphasis in the phrase "principle of non-contradiction". Łukasiewicz' views, articulated in the wake of the debate about Hegel's challenge to the Aristotelian conception and with the aim of critical investigation of the claim of consistency as the universal property of all being, are better reflected in the phrase "principle of contradiction", taken in the sense of "the principle governing contradiction". That is, the choice of expression does not emphasize consistency or inconsistency as a feature of being, but as an expression that emphasizes a focus on contradictions and their properties and implications that are subject to a renewed and scientific investigation.

Jan Łukasiewicz

The Principle of Contradiction in Aristotle

A Critical Study

Translated by Holger R. Heine

JAN ŁUKASIEWICZ

O ZASADZIE SPRZECZNOŚCI U ARYSTOTELESA

STUDYUM KRYTYCZNE

KRAKÓW
AKADEMIA UMIEJĘTNOŚCI — NAKŁADEM FUNDUSZU
WYDAWNICZEGO IMIENIA WIKTORA OSŁAWSKIEGO
SKŁAD GŁÓWNY W KSIĘGARNI SPÓŁKI WYDAWNICZEJ POLSKIEJ
1910.

Cover Page Original 1910 Edition

Λόγον ζητοῦμεν ὧν ἔστι λόγος[3]

Introduction

There are two moments in the history of philosophy in which the dispute over the principle of contradiction excited the minds of an age—one is bound up with Aristotle's name—the other with Hegel's. Aristotle formulated the principle of contradiction as the highest law of thought and being. He pursued everyone who would not recognize this principle with stubborn polemics in which, at times, anger and annoyance find a voice: Antisthenes and his school, Eristics from Megara, followers of Heraclitus, students of Protagoras. Aristotle won this fight. And, whether it was the persuasive force of his arguments or the correctness of the position that he defended—for centuries no one dared to contradict this highest of all laws. Only Hegel allowed the convictions that had been buried by Aristotle to come back to life and instructed us to believe that reality is simultaneously rational and contradictory. In this manner, he restored respect for the Greek sophists and included the teachings of Heraclitus in his system of logic. But this conception also generated passionate debate: the attempt was made to overcome Hegel, too, with the words of Aristotle.

Nowadays, these exchanges have faded away, and the *range of problems* surrounding the principle of contradiction is no longer part of today's interests. So much the better—it now can be investigated *sine ira*.

In such an investigation, the principle of contradiction needs to be subjected to a careful but also strict criticism. Earlier attempts were clearly unable to reach a decision on these problems—if one considers these efforts, one finds many unresolved beginnings that relate to the problem of the principle of contradiction. These first attempts touch upon the deepest foundations of all our knowledge—they form a bundle from which the threads emerge that are to guide and direct us in the methodical investigation of reality. The smallest discovery, which would solve even only one

[3] Translator's note: *λόγον ζητοῦμεν ὧν ἔστι λόγος*— we seek proof for which there is proof.

of the knots, could have far-reaching consequences for science. In a situation like this, it not only pays to investigate the problems connected with this principle, but one also must ask and wonder why so far this investigation has not been critically taken up by anybody?

The answer to this is found in the history of science. In the early fight about the principle of contradiction, Aristotelian logic won. Despite the challenges, which it was not spared, it persisted in an only slightly altered form for centuries. The scientific investigations, which followed it, did not appear to step over its bounds. Since then, both deduction and induction rely in principle on the logical guidelines of the *Organon*. This logic has proven itself extraordinarily useful for the cognition of objects and phenomena. After all, we should attribute the incredible progress of science in the West to this astonishing thought of Hellenic mind. It needs to be stated: in centuries, no problem has arisen in the individual sciences that would have forced us into a revision of the principles of Aristotelian logic and, with that, into a critical check and review of the principle of contradiction. This logic, like Euclidian geometry, has shown itself to correspond to the facts and its immeasurable utility as well as its continuing significance for the future, rests precisely on this correspondence.

Even though the individual sciences developed vigorously, the general science, which Aristotle had called "first philosophy", stayed far behind this development. "First philosophy" was supposed to investigate not particular being but being itself together with all its essential properties; beyond this, it was to explore the world in its entirety, its past and future, its origin and destination. It must be openly admitted, this "first philosophy", later called *metaphysics*, never went beyond the foundations that were already created by the Stagirite. And, since Kant, we hear again and again the opinion that the questions of metaphysics go beyond the cognitive abilities of the human understanding.

Of course, doubts have been raised that it is not our human understanding that is limited but our ability to deal with these questions. Clearly, subtle metaphysical problems require subtle methods of investigation. And Aristotelian logic, as useful as it may be for the cognition of facts, is perhaps too coarse a tool to be able to discover the artful construction of the *essential* world behind the chaos of *appearances*.

Hegel arrived at such a thought. He believed in the power of cognition; the skeptical results of Kantian criticism, however, put him off. Kant asserted that the human intellect, by investigating the world in its entirety, necessarily falls into antinomies and is caught in contradictions. Hegel accepted these assertions but did not draw the consequence from them that the essential nature of the world is not cognizable. He recognized the real existence of contradiction and perceived in it the fundamental element of movement and life. In this manner, he created a "metaphysical logic" that does not rely on the principle of contradiction. This attempt, however, was far too radical, not strict enough and not clear enough for it to be immediately grasped and accepted. One cannot be too careful, too strict and critical in the investigation and restructuring of the highest logical and ontological principles. More than that, it needs to be ascertained with the greatest precision: *What is the significance of these principles, how are they to be formulated, how can assurance for their certainty be given, what consequences result from each one of them, is it possible to give up some of them and replace them by others, are they useful for the investigation of facts, and so forth*. However, it is precisely this work that Hegel did not produce. He negated the principle of contradiction only verbally. Because of this, his idea had not enough scientific value to shatter faith in the validity of this principle or to contribute to the solution of metaphysical problems. Today, Hegel's struggle with contradiction is history; what is left to us after this struggle, as a precious memento, is the miraculously beautiful treatise of Father Gratry, in which he scolded the head of the pantheists with the words of Aristotle.[4]

Thus, the debate about the principle of contradiction came back to life for only a brief period during the time of Hegel's philosophy. Over the centuries, neither in the individual sciences nor in science in general, did the need arise to engage with this highest principle. We believe today as we did in the past that the principle of contradiction is the most certain law of thought and of being. Only a crazy person might deny it. The correctness of this law is impressed on everyone by direct evidence. It does not need justifi-

[4] Here, I am thinking of the second book on logic by Gratry, titled "*La Logique du Panthéisme*". (Cf. his *Logique*, 5th ed., Paris 1868, Vol.I, p. 256-415).

cation; indeed, it cannot even have one. Aristotle taught us to believe this. So why is it so strange that no one has bothered with something that is so clear, so beyond doubt and solved forever?

Of course, it is bad if philosophy includes principles that are *untouchable*; it is worse if they are *unfounded*; and it is the worst if these untouchable and unfounded principles had once been the subject of an intense *dispute*. In fact, how did it happen that a disputed principle, one that nobody knows how to prove, could come to be considered as so certain that it was no longer permissible to question it? What happened to scientific critique that we are so proud of in this epoch of criticism?

If I am not mistaken, the *third* moment in the history of the principle of contradiction is approaching now, a moment that will remedy old shortcomings. This point in time comes as necessarily in the development of logic as it came necessarily in the development of geometry with the revision of the parallel axiom. Aristotle created the *beginnings* of logic, but every beginning is incomplete. This charge does not diminish the value of his ingenious work; on the contrary, one ought to deplore the fact that he left us such a complete whole in a single stroke, which initially hindered the possibility of further development. Centuries went by while logic froze in its predefined forms. The logical system created by Aristotle still appeared to Kant as such a closed entity that it prevented him from advancing even by a single step. However, first Leibniz and later, in the second half of the 19th century, the English deepened and expanded traditional formal logic in ways never seen before. Boole, De Morgan, Jevons, Peirce, Schröder, Russell, Peano—they are the outstanding founders of the new logic. *Contemporary symbolic logic remains in a similar relation to Aristotelian logic as contemporary Euclidean geometry to the Elements of Euclid.* It continues to be an *Aristotelian* logic because it takes over all the principles that Aristotle had already discovered and recognized; furthermore, at the height of its current development, it also knows of logical laws that the Stagirite was not aware of or which he did not formulate clearly enough, as for example, the principle of identity, double negation, the law of logical multiplication and addition, the principle of tautology, absorption, simplification, and so forth. So, a time must come in which logicians begin to review the common relations of these principles and to dedicate themselves to those investigations that had not been considered by Hegel. Only then will it become clear which rank the principle of contradiction takes among the other logical rules, what the justifications are for its validity and value, how far its applicability reaches; then it will become clear whether this principle is really the highest of all and can be considered the keystone of our entire logic, or if it can also be altered or, even further, if it is possible to develop a system of a *non-Aristotelian* logic, without taking it into account at all, just as a system of *non-Euclidian* geometry emerged through a change to the parallel axiom. So far, no one has undertaken these investigations even though sections in Aristotle's *Metaphysics* and in his logical writings directly demand them!

These investigations could fittingly be called "meta-logical". They would not lose their value even if they were to demonstrate that a uniform and consequent system of non-Aristotelian logic is impossible in scientific practice. Whatever the results may be, they throw a light on the foundations of the traditional logic and in this light, the contours of those final principles that grow from the foundation of this, as of any other science, will be traced. The critical illumination of these principles would be the completion of a great task, because perhaps it not only could put logic on a more secure foundation, but also simultaneously refine its entire structure and in this same manner form a flexible and strong armor for a victorious battle for the cognition of the world.

In the past years, mathematicians (Russell, Couturat, Frege, Hilbert, Peano), who investigated the foundations of arithmetic and geometry and their connections to symbolic logic, started work on a similarly analytic-critical task. The results of this research lead already today to unexpected conceptions; they seem to prove that all of mathematics, both in terms of its form as well as its content, can be derived from a few fundamental logical concepts and assumptions.[5] The efforts by these mathematicians should be considered in every respect as a methodological example for a similar enterprise in logic.

It is not the aim of this treatise to present the "meta-logical" investigations in a comprehensive way or to deal with all aspects of the problem of the principle of contradiction with respect to contemporary logic. Before this can be done, one must first return to Aristotle himself; some unsolved problems (related to this principle), which nowadays have been forgotten, need to be recalled and

[5] Cf. B. Russell, *The Principles of Mathematics*, Vol.1, Cambridge 1903, Ch.1.

new investigations should then connect to them. I want to convince the reader that this principle is not as unshakable as one might suspect considering its general acceptance. I want to show that it presents a thesis that demands proof and that, despite the Stagirite's words: "they search for a proof for something that has none" (*λόγον ζητοῦσιν ὧν οὐκ ἔστι λόγος*)[6]— this proof can be found. If I can awaken this conviction in the reader and to create from an untouched and untouchable problem, that is, from a problem that today is already dead, a nevertheless living one of great importance, then this treatise will have accomplished its goal completely.

[6] *Metaph Γ* 6, 1011a 12.

Chapter I

Three Formulations of the Principle of Contradiction

Aristotle formulates the principle of contradiction in its ontological, logical, and psychological senses even though he nowhere explicitly distinguishes these senses.

a) He determines the ontological principle of contradiction in the following statement:

> *Met. Γ* 3, 1005b 19-20: *τὸ γὰρ αὐτὸ ἅμα ὑπάρχειν τε καὶ μὴ ὑπάρχειν ἀδύνατον τῷ αὐτῷ καὶ κατὰ τὸ αὐτό*
>
> It is impossible that one and the same, and in the same respect—simultaneously does and does not belong to the same.[7]

He expresses this principle even more briefly in the following words:

> *Met. B* 2, 996b 30: *ἀδύνατον (scil. τί) ἅμα εἶναι καὶ μὴ εἶναι.*

[7] Translator's note: Łukasiewicz provides his own translations together with the Greek texts. Furthermore, for certain key passages, Łukasiewicz offers a second set of translations in Appendix II. These additional translations tend to stay even closer to the original Greek. In order to illuminate the subtle differences in the interpretation of Aristotle's text, one or more existing English translations of the corresponding passages are included as footnotes. Łukasiewicz also occasionally cites passages in the original Greek in footnotes without providing a translation. In these cases, existing English translations have been added to the notes.

The passage cited above is translated by Ross (Aristotle 1992) as: "The same attribute cannot at the same time belong and not belong to the same subject in the same respect."

> It is impossible that something simultaneously is and is not.[8]

Aristotle uses the expressions: *ὑπάρχει πάρχει τι τινί*—"something belongs to something" and *μη* [*ούκ*] *ὑπάρχει τι τινί*—"something does not belong to something" as designation of a relation that is not further determined and which corresponds, in a logical statement, *ἀποφασίς*, to the relation of predicate to subject. I think this relation may be called an inherence relation and its members object and property. *By object, I understand any something whatever that is "something" and not "nothing"; by property—everything that can be asserted about any object.* The relation of inherence exists between an object and a property if the object possesses that property, that is, if it can be asserted about it; if it does not possess it, then there is also no inherence relation. Applying this terminology, I formulate the ontological principle of contradiction as follows:

No object can contain and simultaneously not contain the same property.

This formulation does not alter Aristotle's thought; it merely posits the nouns "object" and "property" instead of the stylistically awkward "the same" and "something".

The principle stated above is called *ontological* because it relates to all of being, *τὸ ὄν*, that is, to everything that is "something" and not "nothing". It relates to *ἅπασι γὰρ ὑπάρχει τοῖς οὖσιν.*[9]

b) Aristotle determines the logical principle of contradiction with the words:

> *Met. Γ* 6, 1011b 13-14: ... *βεβαιστάτη δόχα πασῶν τὸ μὴ εἶναι ἀληθεῖς ἅμα τὰς ἀντικειμένας φάσεις.*

[8] Ross (Aristotle 1992): "A thing cannot at the same time be and not be."

[9] *Metaph Γ* 3, 1005a 22-23. Ross (Aristotle 1992): "hold good for everything that is."

> The most certain of all principles is that contradictory statements are not simultaneously true [cf. Appendix II,[10] 262, 1].[11]

Aristotle understands by opposed statements, *ἀντιφατικῶς, ἀντικείμεναι φάσεις,* an affirmative, *κατάφασις,* and a negative statement, *απόφασις,* about the same object under the same point of view. For example: "Callias is just"—"Callias is not just". The relation of such statements is designated as contradiction, *ἀντιφασις*. We read:

> *De Interpretatione* 6, 17a 32-35: . . . *πάσῃ καταφάσει ἐστὶν ἀπόφασις ἀντικειμένη καὶ πάσῃ ἀποφάσει κατάφασις. καὶ ἔστω ἀντίφασις τοῦτο, κατάφασις καὶ ἀπόφασις αἱ ἀντικείμεναι. λέγω δὲ ἀντικεῖσθαι τῆς (scil. κατάφασιν καὶ ἀπόφασιν) τοῦ αὐτοῦ κατά τοῦ αὐτοῦ.*
>
> To each affirmative statement corresponds an opposite one that contradicts it and to each negative statement—an affirmative one. This is what a contradiction is—and opposite statements are to be affirmation and negation. Opposite statements are called the affirmation and the denial of the same property (*τοῦ αὐτοῦ*) of the same object (*κατά τοῦ αὐτοῦ*) [cf. Appendix II, 262, 2].[12]

Accordingly, two statements are contradictory if one attributes a property to an object that the other denies of it. Thus, the logical principle of contradiction can also be determined as follows:

[10] Translator's note: Łukasiewicz provides additional translations to certain key phrases in Appendix II. References include page and passage number.

[11] Ross (Aristotle 1992): "The most indisputable of all beliefs is that contradictory statements are not at the same time true." In comparison, Kirwan's translation of the same passage is (philosophically) more cautious and stays closer to the original Greek: "The opinion that opposite assertions are not simultaneously true is the firmest of all" (Kirwan 1993, 23).

[12] Ackrill (Aristotle 1992): "For every affirmation there is an opposite negation, and for every negation an opposite affirmation. Let us call an affirmation and a negation which are opposite a contradiction. I speak of statements as opposite when they affirm and deny the same thing of the same thing."

Two statements, of which one attributes precisely that property to an object that the other denies of it, cannot be simultaneously true.

This principle is called *logical* because it concerns the truth of these statements, that is, logical facts.

c) Aristotle expresses the psychological principle of contradiction with the following words:

> *Met. Γ* 3, 1005b 23-26: *ἀδύνατον γὰρ ὁντινοῦν ταὐτόν ὑπολαμβάνει εἶναι καὶ μὴ εἶναι, καθάπερ τινὲς οἴονται λέγειν Ἡράκλειτον. οὐκ ἔστι γὰρ ἀναγκαῖον, ἅ τις λέγει, ταῦτα καὶ ὑπολαμβάνειν.*
>
> No one can believe that one and the same (simultaneously) is and is not, as Heraclitus is supposed to have said as reported by others; the speaker, after all, does not have to believe what he is saying.[13]

Here, *ὑπολαμβάνειν*, does not mean "to accept", that is, "to presuppose", but (placed in opposition to *λέγειν*, "to speak", "to express an opinion") it expresses the psychical act that usually— even if not always— accompanies the expression of an opinion. This act is *conviction, belief.* Schwegler, too, translates *ὑπολαμβάνειν* in this passage with "to believe",[14] and Maier ascertains that this word, and—*in passim*—just as the noun *ὑπόληψις*, determines for Aristotle a mental condition of "conviction", of "holding something to be true", that is, a subjective decision that is connected with a moment of belief.[15]

Whenever we have any kind of conviction, we are convinced of something; believing, we always believe that something is or is not, that it is so or not so, that some object contains some property or does not contain it. *I call a string of words or other signs, which*

[13] Ross (Aristotle 1992): "It is impossible for any one to believe the same thing to be and not to be, as some think Heraclitus says; for what a man says he does not necessarily believe."

[14] Schwegler, Albert (1847). *Die Metaphysik des Aristoteles*, Vol. 2, 54.

[15] Maier, Heinrich (1896). *Die Syllogistik des Aristoteles*, Vol.1, 46.. Note: "The first sentence [in the above cited passage from *Met.Γ*] relates to the sphere of subjective conviction, considering to be true …"; p.104, note: "In *De an.* III, the synthetic activity (*διανοεῖσθαι*) and the *ὑπολαμβάνειν* (the subjective decision, connected to the moment of *πιστις*) come apart."

say that some object contains a property or does not contain it, a logical sentence or statement. To every *belief*, as a *mental* phenomenon, corresponds, as a *logical* fact, some affirmative or negative *statement* that is expressed in words or other signs. Thus, the Aristotelian principle, that "nobody can simultaneously believe that something is and also is not" can also be formulated as follows:

Two convictions, for which there are corresponding contradictory statements, cannot exist simultaneously in one and the same intellect.

Thus, this principle, in that it concerns mental phenomena, is a psychological one.

d) Even though Aristotle did not determine the differences that appear between the three principles, he certainly must have sensed them; his deliberations on the relations of these principles to each other witness that. However, he directed the greatest attention to the *ontological* formulation, which aims to grasp the entire principle in its most complete form. Because of this, he listed this formulation first and did not investigate the problem of contradiction in *De Interpretatione*, nor in the *Analytics*, nor in the treatise on the soul, but in *Book Γ* of the *Metaphysics*, which he opened with the unforgettable words:

> *Met*. 1003a 22: *Εστιν ἐπιστήμη τις ἣ θεωπεῖ τὸ ἦ ὂν καὶ τὰ τούτῳ ὑπαρχοντα καθ' αὑτό.*
>
> There is a science that investigates being as such and its essential properties [cf. Appendix II, 262, 3].[16]

The *ontological* principle is the principle of contradiction *κατ' ἐξοχήν*.

Note: I particularly place the greatest emphasis on the distinction that is to be made between a *statement* that is based on a *logical* fact and a *conviction* that is to be considered as a *psychical* phenomenon. This distinction is gaining an ever-increasing clarity in the minds of contemporary logicians and psychologists. For example, Meinong distinguishes in this manner convictions as

[16] Ross (Aristotle 1992): "There is a science which investigates being as being and the attributes which belong to this in virtue of its own nature."

judging acts from the objects of convictions, which in turn consist of facts, whether something is or is not, or respectively, whether something is so or different. Meinong called these facts "*Objektive*" [objectives] and assigned the investigation of them to a special science, the so-called "*Gegenstandstheorie*" [theory of objects]. "Pure logic" as well as mathematics is to belong to this science.[17] However, in this work I will not use the term "*Objektiv*" because "statement", in my usage, is not identical in sense with "*Objektiv*". A statement is an *Objektiv* that is *expressed in words or with other signs*. It further seems to me that this designation corresponds best to the concept of statement in Aristotle. He also distinguishes between statement and conviction, clearly emphasizing that conviction, *δόξα*, *ὑπόληψις*, which is located in the soul, *ἐν τῇ ψυχῇ*, has a correlate or sign, *σύμβολον*, in the *sounds of a language*, *ἐν τῇ ψυχῇ* [*sic*].[18] This sign, however, is an affirmative statement, *κατάφασις*, or a negative statement, *απόφασις*.[19] Accordingly, a statement is a sentence *stated in words* and, more specifically, it is a sentence that also means something. Every sentence *means* something, but not every sentence forms a statement—only a sentence that can be attributed the properties true or false does this.[20] But only a sentence, which asserts that something is or that something *is not*,[21] can exclusively

[17] See, for example, the treatise by Alexius Meinong (1907) *Über die Stellung der Gegenstandstheorie im System der Wissenschaften*.

[18] Translator's note: The corresponding expression is *ἐν τῇ φωνῇ*. See the passage from *De Interpretatione* 14 cited in note 16 below.

[19] Cf. De Interpretatione 14, 24b 1-3 (discussed in Ch.3): ὥστε εἴπερ ἐπὶ δόξης οὕτως ἔχει, εἰσὶ δὲ αἱ ἐν τῇ φωνῇ καταφάσεις καὶ ἀποφάσεις σύμβολα τῶν ἐν τῇ ψυχῇ, δῆλον ὅτι καὶ καταφάσει ἐναντία ... ἀπόφασις. "If then this is how it is with beliefs, and spoken affirmations and negations are symbols of things in the soul, clearly it is the universal negation about the same thing that is contrary to an affirmation" Ackrill (Aristotle 1992).

[20] *De Interpretatione* 4, 17a 1-3: *ἔστι δὲ λόγος ἅπας μὲν σημαντικός ... ἀποφαντικὸς δὲ πᾶς, ἀλλ' ἐν ᾧ τὸ ἀληθεύειν ἢ ψεύδεσθαι ὑπάρχει.* "Every sentence is significant ... but not every sentence is a statement-making sentence, but only those in which there is truth or falsity" Ackrill (Aristotle 1992).

[21] *De Interpretatione* 1, 16a 16-18 : *καὶ γὰρ ὁ τραγέλαφος σημαὶνει μὲν τι, οὔπω δὲ ἀληθὲς ἢ ψεῦδος, ἐὰν μή τὸ εἶναι ἢ μὴ εἶναι προστεθῇ.* "Even 'goat-stag' signifies something but not, as yet, anything true or false—unless 'is' or 'is not' is added" Ackrill (Aristotle 1992).

be designated as true or false. To summarize these remarks in a single concept, one could say that according to Aristotle, *a statement is a sequence of words, which state that something is or is not.* How much better is this designation than the usual definitions of statement that wander around logic text books and which see in a statement the combination of concepts or a psychical state of conviction! The “golden mountain” is also a combination of concepts, and the fact that “the sun is shining” is not a psychical phenomenon.

Chapter II

The Relation of the Ontological Principle of Contradiction to the Logical Principle

Someone might very well doubt that the above listed formulations in fact contain *three distinct principles* and suppose instead that they present only a *single* principle, which has only been expressed in different words. In order to remove this doubt, it needs to be determined in what cases two statements, composed of different words, express the same thought.

Every statement can be brought into one of two forms: "Object *x* contains property *F*" or "Object *x* does not contain property *F*".[22] *The two statements "x contains F" and "x' contains F'" express the same object in different words. They have the same meaning, if x designates the same object as x', and F designates the same property as F'*. For example, the following statements express the same thought with partially different words: "Aristotle was the founder of logic"—"The Stagirite was the founder of logic". Based on current convention, the word "Stagirite" designates the same person and, thus, the same object as the word "Aristotle".

No negative statement has the same meaning as its affirmative counterpart, because affirming has a different sense than denying. The one is just as simple as the other, and it is impossible to reduce one to the other.

If it is the case that the statements "*x* contains *F*" and "*x'* contains *F"* have the same meaning, then the truth of the second follows from the truth of the first and the truth of the first follows from the truth of the second. If, for example, it is true that "Aristotle was the founder of logic", then it is also true that "The Stagirite was the founder of logic"—and in reverse. *Two statements that stand in such a relation to each other that the second follows from the first and the first follows from the second, are equivalent*. Ac-

[22] Translator's note: instead of *p* (for *przedmiot*) and *c* (for *cecha*) in the Polish original, the following designations are used: *x* for object, *F* for property.

cordingly, two statements that have the same meaning are equivalent. From this, it follows *a contrario*: if two statements are not equivalent, then they do not have the same meaning. The lack of equivalence is the surest criterion for a difference of sense.

However, it is the case that two equivalent statements may not be identical in sense. For example, the statements: "Aristotle was a student of Plato" and "Plato was a teacher of Aristotle" are equivalent—the second follows from the first and the first follows from the second. But they are not statements that are identical in sense because the word "Aristotle" relates to a different object than the word "Plato", and the words "was a student of Plato" relate to a different property than the words "was a teacher of Aristotle."[23]

The formulations of the principle of contradiction listed in the first chapter are not statements that are identical in sense. In the ontological principle of contradiction, the topic is objects, in the logical principle it is statements, and in the psychological principle it is convictions. The words "object", "statement", "conviction" designate *different* things. Thus, statements in which these words are found do not present one principle expressed in different words, but form *three different statements*.

These statements, though different, may be equivalent. Indeed, it is possible to show that according to Aristotle, *the ontological and the logical principle of contradiction are equivalent statements*. Aristotle did not state this directly. However, it is contained in his conceptions about the relation of true statements to being.

a) The logical principle of contradiction follows from the ontological one. We read:

> *De Int.* 9, 18a 39 – b 1: *εἰ γὰρ ἀληθὲς εἰπεῖν ὅτι λευκὸν ἢ ὅτι οὐ λευκὸν ἐστιν, ἀνάγκη εἶναι λευκὸν ἢ οὐ λευκόν.*

[23] In my opinion, the distinction of statements that are identical in sense from equivalent statements that are not identical in sense belongs not only to the most difficult tasks of logic, but also to the most important ones. We seize all of the knowledge about the world in statements, that is, in signs and symbols. It is necessary to have some criterion to be able to decide in each instance whether the difference in signs is *real*, that is, whether it corresponds to actually existing, even if equivalent differences in the objects, or whether it is only *apparent*, that is, merely a difference in signs. The remarks in this text certainly do not solve this problem; but I do think that they should be sufficient for the aims of the present treatise (cf. Appendix § 9 γ).

> If a statement is true that something is white or is not white, then it must be white or not white [cf. Appendix II, 262, 4].[24]

In this context, it shows that this example is typical, that is, *λευκόν* (white) replaces any arbitrary property. A further consequence: if a statement, which attributes a property to an object, is true, then this object contains that property. If a statement, which denies a property of an object, is true, then it does not contain it. Accordingly, if two contradictory statements were to be true, then the same object would contain and simultaneously not contain a property. This, however, is not possible in virtue of the *ontological* principle of contradiction. Thus, two contradictory statements cannot simultaneously be true.

b) The ontological principle of contradiction follows from the logical one. We read:

> *De Int.* 9, 18b 1-2: *εἰ ἔστι λευκὸν ἢ οὐ λευκόν, ἀληθὲς ἦν φάναι ἢ ἀποφάναι.*
>
> If something is white or not white, then the affirmative or negative statement was true [cf. Appendix II, 262, 5].[25]
>
> *Met.* Θ 10, 1051b 3-4: *ἀληθεύει μὲν ὁ τὸ διῃρημένον οἰόμενος διῃρῆσθαι καὶ τὸ συγκειμενον συγκεῖσθαι.*
>
> He speaks the truth who holds what is separated to be what is separated and what is composite to be what is composite.[26]

Accordingly: If an object contains a property, that is, if it has been put together with it, then that statement is true that ascribes the property to the object. If it does not contain it, that is, if the object remains separate from the property, then that statement is

[24] Ackrill (Aristotle 1992): "For if it is true to say that it is white or is not white, it is necessary for it to be white or not white."

[25] Ackrill (Aristotle 1992): "If it is white or is not white, then it was true to say or deny this."

[26] Ross (Aristotle 1992): "He who thinks the separated to be separated and the combined to be combined has the truth."

true which denies the property of the object. Thus, should the same object contain and not contain a property, the two contradictory statements would be simultaneously true. However, this is impossible based on the *logical* principle of contradiction: thus, no object can simultaneously contain and not contain the same property.

Taken together, the proofs a) and b) confirm that the ontological and logical principle of contradiction present two equivalent statements.

I consider this result to be correct. It is the consequence of the correct conception that being and true statements correspond to each other. In turn, this conception relies on the definition of true statements: *True is that affirmative statement that attributes this property to an object that does contain it; true is that negative statement that denies the property of an object that it does not contain*. Similarly, in reverse fashion: *Every object contains that property that a true statement attributes to it; and no object contains the property that a true statement denies of it.* Aristotle would agree to these definitions since he says:

> *Met.* Γ 7, 1011b 26-27: *τὸ ... γὰρ λέγειν ... , τὸ ὂν εἶναι καὶ μὴ ὂν μὴ εἶναι ἀληθές.*
>
> To say that that, which is, is, and that that, which is not, is not, that is true.[27]

The equivalence of the ontological and logical principle of contradiction follows necessarily from these definitions.

However, Aristotle would call this equivalence merely logical, but not real. I read:

> Met. Θ 10, 1051b 6-9: *οὐ γὰρ διὰ τὸ ἡμᾶς οἴεσθαι ἀληθῶς σε λευκὸν εἶναι εἶ σὺ λευκός, ἀλλὰ διὰ τὸ σὲ εἶναι λευκὸν ἡμεῖς οἱ φάνες τοῦτο ἀληθεύομεν.*
>
> It is not that you are white because we, by calling you white, speak the truth, but it is because you are white, that we, calling you white, do speak the truth.[28]

[27] Ross (Aristotle 1992): "To say of what is that it is, and of what is not that it is not, is true."

[28] Ross (Aristotle 1992): "It is not because we think truly that you are white, that you *are* white, but because you are white we who say this have the truth."

Accordingly, then, being is the logical reason for the truth of statements, just as it is a real cause for their assertion. The truth of statements, on the other hand, is merely a logical reason, but not a real cause of being. I suspect that Aristotle would have formulated this difference in the same manner, if he had realized it clearly for himself.

Chapter III

The Relation of the Ontological and Logical Principle of Contradiction to the Psychological Principle

Aristotle deals with the psychological principle of contradiction differently than with the two previous ones. He quietly considers the ontological and logical principles to be equivalent and asserts emphatically that they—as ultimate principles—cannot be proven; on the other hand, he attempts to prove the psychological principle based on the logical and ontological principles. This proof is divided into two parts:

a) The first part is contained in the following sentence:

> *Met. Γ* 3, 1005b 26-32: *εἰ δὲ μὴ ἐνδέχεται ἅμα ὑπάρχειν τῷ αὐτῷ τἀναντία ... , ἐναντία δ' ἐστὶ δόξα δόξῃ ἡ τῆς ἀντιφάσεως, φανερὸν ὅτι ἀδύνατον ἅμα ὑπολαμβάνειν τὸν αὔτον εἶναι καὶ μὴ εἶναι τὸ αὐτό ἅμα γὰρ ἂν ἔχοι τὰς ἐναντίας δόξας διεψευσμένος περὶ τούτου.*
>
> If the same object cannot simultaneously contain opposed properties and convictions that have corresponding contradictory statements are opposed to each other—then, of course, one and the same man cannot simultaneously believe that one and same thing is and is not. Whoever would be in error here, would have opposed convictions at one and the same time [cf. Appendix II, 262, 6].[29]

[29] Ross (Aristotle 1992): "If it is impossible that contrary attributes should belong at the same time to the same subject, and if an opinion which contradicts another is contrary to it, obviously it is impossible for the same man at the same time to believe the same thing to be and not to be; for if a man were mistaken in this point he would have contrary opinions at the same time."

In this section, the interpretation of the following passage involves difficulties: *ἐναντία δ' ἐστὶ δόχα δόξη ἡ τῆς ἀντιφάσεως*. From formal logic, it is known that *ἐναντίωσις* "contrariety" (opposition *contraria*) and *ἀντίφασις* "contradiction" (*oppositio contradictoria*) are not only two *different* concepts, but mutually *exclusive* ones. How is contradiction to be brought into agreement with opposition in this passage? A key to the understanding of this problem is contained in the closing part of *De Interpretatione* where Aristotle poses the following question:[30]

> *De Int.* 14, 23a 27-39: *Πότερον δὲ ἐναντία ἐστὶν ἡ κατάφασις τῇ ἀποφάσει ἢ ἡ κατάφασις τῇ καταφάσει, ... οἷον ἔστι Καλλίας δίκαιος — οὐκ ἔστι Καλλίας δίκαιος — Καλλίας ἄδικός ἐστι' ποτέρα δὴ ἐναντία τούτων, εἰ γάρ τὰ μὲν ἐν τῇ φωνῇ ἀκολούθει τοῖς ἐν τῇ διανοίᾳ, ἐκεῖ δὲ ἐναντία δόξα ἡ τοῦ ἐναντίου, ... καὶ ἐπὶ τῶν ἐν τῇ φωνῇ καταφάσεων ἀνάγκη ὁμοίως ἔχειν. εἰ δὲ μὴ ἐκεῖ ἡ τοῦ ἐναντίου δόξα ἐναντία ἐστίν, οὐδὲ ἡ κατάφασις τῇ καταφάσει ἔσται ἐναντία ἀλλ' ἡ εἰρημένη ἀπόφασις. ὥστε σκεπτέον ποία δόξα ἀληθὴς ψευδεῖ δόξῃ ἐναντία, πότερον ἡ τῆς ἀποφάσεως ἢ ἡ τὸ ἐναντίον εἶναι δοξάζουσα.*
>
> Is the affirmative statement set opposite to the negative one or the affirmative to the affirmative one, for example, Callias is just—Callias is not just—Callias is unjust? Which of the (two latter) statements is set opposite (to the first)? If the statements expressed in words accompany the convictions in thought and an opposite conviction in thought is one that affirms the opposite properties, then the (corresponding) affirmative statements, expressed in words, must also remain in a similar relation to each other. But if in

[30] I am indebted to a work by H. Maier (1896, 1969) *Die Syllogistik des Aristoteles*, Vol.1, p.155, for this reference. In passim, this reference is also found in Aphrodisias: *ὅτι ἐναντίαι αἱ δόξαι τῆς ἀντιφάσεως, δέδεικται διὰ πλειόνων επὶ τέλει τοῦ περὶ 'Ερμηνείας.* Cf. *Scholiam in Aristotelem*, coll. Brandis, ed. Acad. Bor. Berolini (Brandis 1836), p.652.

> thought the conviction that affirms an opposed property is not in opposition, then the affirmative statement is not set against the affirming one, but the already mentioned negative one. Thus, one needs to find out which true conviction is set opposite to the false one:—the one that corresponds to the negative statement or the one that affirms the being of the contrary.[31]

The issue regarding the opposition of statements indicated in this fragment created a special difficulty for Aristotle: according to him, it is primarily *properties* that are set in opposition, and in particular those that take up the extreme opposed positions in a series of properties of the same kind; for example, black and white, good and evil. However, statements are not properties. Thus, it is difficult to speak of an opposition of statements. Aristotle, in order to circumvent this burden, transfers the entire problem to the *psychological* domain: the statements expressed in words correspond to convictions held in thought, and convictions can be conceived as *properties* of the mind in which they occur.[32] Thus, the convictions grounded as properties can be placed in opposition and it is possible to consider the statements that correspond to these convictions as opposed to each other. Supported by numerous arguments, Aristotle attempts to show that the convictions to which an affirmative and a negative statement correspond, each referring to the same object, are opposite to each other (for example, "Callias is unjust"—"Callias is not just"). With this, we read as conclusion:

> *De Int.* 14, 24b 1-3: *ὥστε εἴπερ ἐπὶ δόξης οὕτως ἔχει, εἰσὶ δὲ αἱ ἐν τῇ φωνῇ καταφάσεις καὶ*

[31] Ackrill (Aristotle 1992): "Is the affirmation contrary to the negation, or the affirmation to the affirmation, … take, for example, Callias is just, Callias is not just, Callias is unjust; which of these are contraries? Now if spoken sounds follow things in the mind, and there it is the belief of the contrary which is contrary … the same must hold also of spoken affirmations. But if it is not the case there that the belief of the contrary is contrary, neither will the affirmation be contrary to the affirmation, but rather the above-mentioned negation. So we must inquire what sort of true belief is contrary to a false belief, the belief of the negation or the belief that the contrary holds."

[32] Cf. H. Maier (1896), *Die Syllogistik des Aristoteles*, Vol.1, p.150.

> *ἀποφάσεις σύμβολα τῶν ἐν τῇ ψυχῇ, δῆλον ὅτι καὶ καταφάσει ἐναντία . . . ἀπόφασις*
>
> If accordingly acts of belief relate in this manner (that is, if affirmative acts of belief are in contrary opposition to the denying ones) and if the linguistic affirmations and denials are symbols of psychical processes, then apparently, the denial is also in contrary opposition to the (linguistic) affirmation [cf. Appendix II, 262 7].[33]

These investigations give the following results:

α) Here, *δόξα,* "opinion, conviction", signifies a psychical act, which is located in thought, *ἐν τῇ διανοίᾳ,* or in the soul, *ἐν τῇ ψυχῇ.* An affirmative, *κατάφασις,* or negative, *ἀπόφασις,* statement, presented as a sign, *σύμβολον,* in words, *ἐν τῇ φωνῇ*, corresponds to it. Here, *Δόξα*, means as much as *ὑπόληψις*, conviction, belief. Such an interpretation is confirmed by the following passage from *De Anima* (III 3, 428a 20-21):

> *οὐκ ἐνδέχεται . . . δόξάζοντα οἷς δοκεῖ μὴ πιστεύειν.*
>
> The one who believes cannot not believe in that which convinces him.[34]

β) *δόξα ἡ τοῦ ἐναντίου* means the same as *δόξα το ἐνατίον εἶναι δόξάζουσα*, that is, what is dealt with here is the conviction to which an opposed property corresponds in words as an affirmative statement. Similarly, *δόξα ἡ τῆς ἀπόφασεως,* signifies a conviction to which a contradictory statement corresponds in words. Accordingly, it is possible to render the expressions: *ἐναντία δ' ἐστὶ δόξα δόξῃ ἡ τῆς ἀντιφάσεως* as follows: "Convictions that have corresponding contradictory statements are opposite to each other."

[33] Ackrill (Aristotle 1992): "If then this is how it is with beliefs, and spoken affirmations and negations are symbols of things in the soul, clearly it is the universal negation about the same thing that is contrary to an affirmation."

[34] Smith (Aristotle 1992): "For without belief in what we opine we cannot have an opinion."

The difficulty mentioned above, how to square opposition and contradiction, has been removed in virtue of such an interpretation. Accordingly, contradictions are *statements*, and opposed *convictions*, which correspond to these statements. At the same time, it becomes increasingly clear that *Aristotle distinguishes between statement and conviction*. It is possible now to formulate the discussed proof of the *Metaphysics* as follows:

If no object can simultaneously contain contrary properties, and a man who simultaneously believes that something is and is not would simultaneously have two opposed convictions, and thus also two opposed *properties*—then it is impossible for any man to believe that something is and at the same time is not. In reverse: two convictions, to which contradictory statements correspond, cannot simultaneously exist in the same mind.

This should conclude the first part of the proof.

b) The second part establishes the justification of the assertion that no object can contain opposed properties. Aristotle derives this assertion from the logical principle of contradiction. We read:

> *Met. Γ* 6, 1011b 15-21: *ἐπεὶ δ' ἀδύνατον τὴν ἀντίφασιν ἀληθεύεσθαι ἅμα κατὰ τοῦ αὐτοῦ, φανερὸν ὅτι οὐδὲ τἀναντία ἅμα ὑπάρχειν ἐνδέχεται τῷ αὐτῷ. τῶν μὲν γὰρ ἐναντίων θάτερον στέρησίς ἐστιν οὐχ ἧττον, οὐσίας δὲ στέρησις. ἡ δὲ στέρησις ἀπόφασίς ἐστιν ἀπό τινος ὡρισμένου γένους. εἰ οὖν ἀδύνατον ἅμα καταφάναι καὶ ἀποφάναι ἀληθῶς, ἀδύνατον καὶ τἀναντία ὑπάρχειν ἅμα . . .*
>
> If it is impossible for contradictory statements stated about the same object to be simultaneously true, then of course the opposed properties also cannot be attributed to the same object. One no less than the other of these opposed properties is a lack and, specifically, a lack of substance. Lack, in turn, is a certain kind of negation. Thus, if it is impossible to simultaneously affirm and deny, in agreement with the truth, then the

> opposed properties also cannot exist simultaneously [cf. Appendix II, 263, 8].[35]

The phrase, "one no less than the other of the opposed properties is a lack", does not express clearly and precisely enough the thought that containing one of the opposed properties *connects* itself with not-containing the opposite one. If, for example, something is white, then it is not black, and conversely. A similar imprecision, by the way, is found in Spinoza's famous dictum: *omnis determinatio est negatio*. At a different location, Aristotle is more precise:

> Met. I, 1055b 18: *πᾶσα γὰρ ἐναντίωσις ἔχει στέρησιν θατέρου τῶν ἐναντίων.*
>
> Every object contains the absence of the contrary property.[36]

In this, it is shown that if the same object were to contain opposed properties, a contradiction would result. Two statements would be true, one of which attributes exactly the property to the object that the other *implicite* denies of it. This should conclude the second part of the proof. In its entirety, then, Aristotle's proof of the psychological principle of contradiction presents itself as follows:

If two convictions, to which contradictory statements correspond, were to be present in the same mind, then this mind simultaneously would have opposed properties. But it follows from the logical principle of contradiction that no object can contain opposed properties. Thus, two convictions, to which contradictory statements correspond, cannot simultaneously exist in the same mind.

Aristotle considered the psychological principle of contradiction as a consequence of the logical one. This logical principle constitutes, in the deliberations completed above, the *reason* for the

[35] Ross (Aristotle 1992): "Now since it is impossible that contradictories should be at the same time true of the same thing, obviously contraries also cannot belong at the same time to the same thing. For of the contraries, no less than of the contradictories, one is a privation—and a privation of substance; and privation is the denial of a predicate to a determinate genus. If, then, it is impossible to affirm and deny truly at the same time, it is also impossible that contraries should belong to a subject at the same time."

[36] Ross (Aristotle 1992): "Every contrariety involves, as one of its terms, a privation."

general rule that asserts the impossibility of the co-existence of any opposed properties. And, precisely because the logical principle is equivalent to the ontological one, the following statement would certainly agree with Aristotle's views: the psychological principle of contradiction presents a consequence of the ontological principle.

Chapter IV

Critique of the Aristotelian Proof of the Psychological Principle of Contradiction

One must admit that Aristotle proceeds very carefully in proving the psychological principle. It seems that he is fully aware that the simultaneous appearance—in the same mind—of two convictions, to which two contradictory statements correspond, would still not constitute an *obvious* contradiction. In fact, every conviction is a *positive* psychical act. Accordingly, there would never be an obvious contradiction if someone had the conviction that something is and simultaneously had another conviction that something is not, and an obvious contradiction would arise only if the same conviction *had* and had *not* been in the same mind at the same time.

Aristotle merely demonstrates that two convictions, to which contradictory statements correspond, contain an *opposition*, that is, a *hidden* contradiction, if they were to be in the same mind. Let us consider whether this proof procedure holds.

a) First, it rests on the assumption that convictions are properties of a mind in which they are located. Let us assume the same. If convictions are properties, then they can enter a contradictory relation. We accept this, too. We further assume that opposed properties exclude each other. But which convictions are the opposed ones? To find out which ones they are, one needs to order all convictions about any object into a series based on some principle and then determine the poles lying at the extremes of this series. These poles, precisely because of their extreme placement, will be opposed to each other. This corresponds to Aristotle's thought:

> *De Interpretatione* 14, 23b 22-23: *τὰ γάρ ἐναντία τῶν πλεῖστον διαφερόντων περὶ τὸ αὐτό.*

> Properties are opposed that are the most different from each other in the same respect.[37]

Aristotle arranges the convictions about some object in a series based on their truth and falsity. But because the series with respect to a property comes about only in case a hierarchical differentiation of this property does exist, the Stagirite must assume that some of the convictions are more true or, correspondingly, more false than the others. Indeed, we read:

> *De Interpretatione* 14, 23b 17: ... *μᾶλλον δὲ ἑκάστου ἀληθὴς ἡ χαθ' ἑαυτό* (scil. *δόξα*) ...
>
> Every conviction about something is truer if it asserts an essential property[38] (compared to a conviction that asserts an accidental property).
>
> *De Interpretatione* 23b 20-21: ... *μᾶλλον ἄν εἴη ψευδὴς τοῦ ἀγαθοῦ ἡ τῆς ἀποφάσεως ἢ ἡ τοῦ ἐναντίου δόξα.*
>
> The conviction that the good is not good (*δόξα ἡ τῆς ἀποφάσεως*) would be more false than the opposed one[39] (that is, that the good is bad).

These viewpoints lead to the conclusion that the relation of opposition arises between the truest and falsest convictions about a given matter—for example, "the good is good" and "the good is not good". But these are convictions to which an affirmative and a negative statement correspond.

One cannot agree with this consideration. One cannot assume that hierarchical differences occur in truth or in falsity. If one wants to speak about the *truth* of convictions at all, this can be done only if it is assumed that a true *statement* corresponds to a true conviction. But such an affirmative statement, which attrib-

[37] Ackrill (Aristotle 1992): "Contraries are among things which differ most with regard to the same thing."

[38] Ackrill (Aristotle 1992): "The more true belief about anything is the one about what it is in itself."

[39] Ackrill (Aristotle 1992): "The more false belief about the good would be that of the negation rather than that of the contrary."

utes a property to an object, is true if the object contains that property and this regardless of whether the property is essential or accidental, or whether the inherence of the property is essential or limited in time. We do not know of hierarchical differences in the relation of inherence to which a difference in truth would correspond. One would have to alter the definition of a true statement, if one wanted to accept the existence of statements that are more or less true.

Thus, if there are no hierarchical differences in truth and falsity, then there are also no opposed convictions, that is, convictions that are extremely polarized with respect to truth and falsity. Consequently, Aristotle's position that convictions, to which contradictory statements correspond, would be opposed is unjustified.

b) However, the deliberations from the fourteenth chapter of *De Interpretatione*, by which Aristotle demonstrates the opposition of convictions, is subject to an even more fundamental objection: *What is found here*—probably for the first time in the history of philosophy—*is the confusion of what is logical with what is psychological, which nowadays is so common.*

Though Aristotle does distinguish statement from conviction, the true nature of these facts remains unclear to him. Especially, the *psychical nature of convictions* escapes him, which should not be a cause for too much wonderment because these are extraordinarily subtle and even up to the present day not completely explained phenomena. Here, too, lies the source of his errors.

He investigates the problem of the opposition of *convictions,* a *psychological* matter at first, even though he wants to solve the problem of the opposition of *statements*, that is, a purely *logical* problem. Because of this, he tacitly begins with the false assumption that the same relations exist between convictions and between statements.[40]

However, this false assumption does not at all lead him into difficulties. Since he cannot provide a psychological analysis, *Aristotle considers convictions as statements* and constructs a logical investigation out of the intended psychological one.

α) *In this way, he imputes relations to convictions that only exist between statements*. In considering the following question—which

[40] Apparently, H. Maier does not see anything erroneous in this assumption when he says: "This method is allowed" (*Die Syllogistik des Aristoteles*, Vol.1, p.150).

of the false convictions: "the good is bad" and "the good is not good" is opposite to the true one "the good is good"—he notes among other points:

> *De Interpretatione* 14, 23b 25-27: *ἡ δὲ (scil. δόξα ἡ τῆς ἀποφάσως) τοῦ ὅτι κακὸν τὸ ἀγαθὸν συμπεπλεγμένη ἐστί καὶ γάρ ὅτι οὐκ ἀγαθὸν ἀνάγκη ἴσως ὑπολαμβάνειν τὸν αὐτόν.*
>
> The conviction (that the good is not good) is connected to the conviction that the good is bad; (whoever believes that the good is bad) must be convinced that it is also not good.[41]

This sentence is not right. Merely the fact is true that the statements "the good is bad" and "the good is not good" are connected because the first statement forms the reason for the second. But from this, however, it does not follow that the corresponding *convictions* (if anyone were to have such convictions of in the first place) also are connected. If is possible to be convinced that the good is bad and not think in the least that the good is not good. Aristotle illegitimately transposes the relation of dependence between statements into the sphere of psychical phenomena.[42]

β) Aristotle ascribes properties to convictions that in their proper sense belong only to statements, that is, truth and falsity.

Considered strictly, truth and falsity are not properties of objects or phenomena, but only of a certain *x*—initially we do not know, whether this is a statement or a conviction—that *means* that something is or is not, or in general, that some object contains or does not contains a property. Furthermore, what is dealt with here are relative properties, that is, properties such that they are attributed to *x* only because of *their relation of agreement* or *disagreement* with the facts about the containing or not containing of the property by an object. Is this *x* a statement or a conviction?

[41] Ackrill (Aristotle 1992): "The belief that the good is bad is complex; for the same person must perhaps suppose also that it is not good."

[42] It is an astonishing fact that the same mistake can be found in some more recent psychological textbooks of logic (cf, for example, Höfler—Meinong, *Logik*, Wien 1890, p.136); in this context, also cf. my treatise *Analiza i konstrukcja pojęcia przyczyny*, (Analysis and construction of the concept of causality) "Przegląd Filozoficzny" IX, 1906, p.138.

Statements *mean* that something is or is not, that some object contains a property or does not contain it; statements also are in the relation of *agreement* or *disagreement* with the facts of containing or not containing of a property by an object. They are a series of words or other signs that portrays such facts. Accordingly, statements may be true or false.

Convictions, on the other hand, do *not* mean that something is or is not; they are to be considered as certain feelings that are not to be determined but to be experienced. For example, in this way, I am sitting at the desk writing; my mother is in the next room. Even though I do not see her, I nevertheless sense that she is there. I am ready to tell her something through the door that is ajar or to simply get up and walk over to her, expecting that I find her sitting in a chair. This feeling is the conviction of the presence of my mother in the next room; however, it does not mean: "Mother is in the next room". It is not in a relation of agreement or disagreement with the "fact", but is connected to it through a so-called *intentional* relation. Every conviction is concerned with something, is something, has an intention. The first part of this intentional relation is formed by an act of conviction, the second by some actual or seeming matter of fact (Meinong's "*Objektiv*") that something is or is not, is so or not so—in a word, that some object contains some property or does not contain it. If we express the second part of an intentional relation in words, then a *statement* results, which is either true or false precisely because it portrays an actual or a seeming matter of fact. The conviction, on the other hand, the first part of the intentional relation, as a phenomenon, is *not* a rendering of some fact and, because of this, it is strictly speaking neither false nor true.

This constant confusion of statements with convictions has brought it about that in the psychology of cognition analyses are performed that primarily reduce logical to *a priori* assumptions and not to assumptions that refer to experience. Aristotle's consideration from the 14th chapter of *De Interpretatione* also belongs to such pseudo-psychological analyses. Thus, this consideration cannot justify the psychological thesis that convictions, to which contradictory statements correspond, are opposed. And if this thesis forms the premise of the Aristotelian proof of the psychological principle of contradiction, then it shows that *this proof is insufficient.*

Chapter V

Critique of the Psychological Principle of Contradiction

The incorrectness of the argument does not prove the incorrectness of the thesis. If Aristotle's proof is insufficient, then let us consider whether there are other arguments that justify the psychological principle of contradiction.

To reach this goal, it is not necessary, as Aristotle attempted, to show that convictions, to which contradictory statements correspond, are opposed; it would already be sufficient to demonstrate that they exclude each other. The concept of mutually exclusive properties has a greater scope than that of opposing ones. *We call two properties mutually exclusive of each other with respect to a class of objects, if they cannot simultaneously belong to the objects of this class*, and this without regard whether they take up the extreme opposite poles in some series (as "black" and "white") or whether they do not (as "white" and "grey" or "white" and "red").

We demonstrate the mutual exclusion of two properties either *a priori*, that is, based on assumptions and definitions that are determined in advance, or *empirically*, that is, based on experience. In this manner we prove, for example, that the properties "right-angled" and "equilateral" exclude each other with respect to the class of "triangles". From the assumptions and definitions of geometry, it does follow that no equilateral triangle is right-angled. On the other hand, we demonstrate empirically that the properties "metallic" and "emanating at the anode" are also mutually exclusive with respect to the class of chemical elements. We know based on experience, and *only* based on experience, that in the process of electrolysis all metallic elements always emanate on the side of the cathode, and not at the anode. In the present case, which of these methods of proof should be employed?

a) I claim that *the mutual exclusion of convictions, and thus the psychological principle of contradiction, too, cannot be proven a priori.* Let us assume that there are some assumptions and definitions with regards to convictions from which one could deductively derive the psychological principle of contradiction; despite this, such a proof would be neither *certain* nor *a priori*. Again and again, doubts would arise whether the concept determined by the assumed definition corresponds to actual conviction. The psychological principle of contradiction concerns *phenomena*, that is, *real* facts, and the concepts of such facts cannot be constructed in an arbitrary fashion but must contain properties that in fact belong to these facts. Thus, they have to be *real* concepts, that is, reconstructive concepts, which are created based on experience and not on the basis of ideal constructions of the mind. The correspondence of real concepts with reality, however, is always merely a more or less likely *hypothesis*, from which it follows that conclusions that rely on such concepts can also always merely be *probable* and ultimately belong to *experience*.

b) Accordingly, *the psychological principle of contradiction can be at the most an empirical law*. Such laws are never certain, but merely probable. We arrive at them through means of induction by searching for some cause, in the form of a universal statement, for phenomena of a certain class, for phenomena that behave constantly and without exception in the same fashion.

But is it possible to consider the above named principle as a *confirmed* empirical law? In this matter, Husserl[43] remarks the following: "It is impossible for contradictory acts of belief to persist in the same individual, or better still, in the same consciousness, for any time interval however small. But is this really a law? May we really assert it with unrestricted universality? Where are the psychological inductions that would justify such an assumption? Couldn't there have been, and still be, men that occasionally—confused, for example, by erroneous conclusions—considered opposites to be simultaneously true? Have scientific investigations been conducted whether such things do occur in the case of the mentally insane or perhaps even in cases of naked contradictions? What is the situation with regards to conditions of hypnosis, fever deliriums, and so forth? Does the law apply to animals as well?"

[43] Husserl (1900), *Logische Untersuchungen*, Vol.1, Halle 1900, Ch.V p.82; Chapter V contains an exquisite critique of the conceptions of some philosophers (i.e., Mill, Lange, Sigwart), who confuse the logical and the psychological principle of contradiction.

So far, we have not found any exhaustive answers to these questions. Psychologists probably do not concern themselves with them because they do not know how to distinguish the psychological principle of contradiction from the logical one—and they do not doubt the truth of the logical principle. But still, as long as all the investigations have not been completed with the greatest precision and strictness that any empirical investigation demands, and as long as it will not be shown on the basis of these investigations that no instances of such states of consciousness are known to us in which the same man believes that something is and simultaneously believes that the same is not—then nobody is permitted to pronounce the psychological principle of contradiction as a law of thought.

c) Thus, it is permissible to already doubt today whether these investigations *will demonstrate* this principle. To date, it is already possible to list facts that, in my opinion, cannot be squared with this principle, without having to draw on *additional auxiliary hypotheses*. Many philosophers taught that the same can simultaneously be and not be. In this context, Aristotle names Heraclitus—but in the fragments of his work no clear sentence about the principle of contradiction has been preserved.[44] Hegel, on the other hand, the modern supporter of Heraclitus, expresses himself clearly and unequivocally.

> Something moves, not in that it is here in this now, and there in another now, but only in that it is in one and the same now here and not here, in that it is and simultaneously is not in this here. One has to concede to the old dialecticians the contradictions that they demonstrate in movement, but from this it does not follow that movement consequently does not exist, but rather that movement is the *being-present* of contradiction itself [*der daseyende Widerspruch selbst*].[45]

To this, the defenders of the psychological principle of contradiction could say with Aristotle that "he who is speaking does not have to believe what he says." But then, however, they would have

[44] Cf. H. Diels (1901), *Heraklitos von Ephesos*.

[45] Hegel (1834), *Wissenschaft der Logik* in *Hegels Werke*, Vol.4, p.69.

to assume either that Hegel said and wrote something different from what he believed, or that he was confused about what he said and what he wrote. In both cases, they must adopt some *auxiliary hypothesis* that, by unnecessarily complicating the theory advocated by them, lowers its value and probability. Wouldn't it be much simpler to assume that Hegel *believed* what he wrote?

d) Finally, I want to present an argument from my own inner experience. On occasions, I have experienced certain sentiments in which I believed that something is and simultaneously believed that the same is not. Of course, this argument would not have any scientific value if it were not possible to produce similar states in other minds. I will nevertheless attempt to do so.

On many occasions, I have read the simple but great words of song by St. Athanasius in which he presents the symbol of the Holy Trinity. There, a *clear* contradiction is no more to be found than a latent one (in a corresponding theological interpretation). But whoever surrenders to the religious-aesthetic effect of this poetry, by leaving out theological problems, will experience for a moment that he believes two statements that appear contradictory. In the slow, serious, monotonous rhythm with its uniformly constructed sentences, the touching words resonate with majesty.[46]

Alia est enim persona Patris, alia Filii: alia Spiritus sancti.

Sed Patris, et Filii, et Spiritus sancti una est divinitas: aequalis Gloria, coaeterna majestas.

Qualis Pater, talis Filius: talis Spiritus sanctus.

Increatus Pater, increatus Filius: increatus Spiritus sanctus.

Immensus Pater, immensus Filius: immensus Spiritus sanctus.

Aeternus Pater, aeternus Filius: aeternus Spiritus sanctus.

Et tamen non tres aeterni: sed unus aeternus.

Sicut non tres increati, nec tres immensi: sed unus increatus et unus immensus.

Similiter omnipotens Pater, omnipotens Filius: omnipotens Spiritus sanctus.

Et tamen non tres omnipotentes: sed unus omnipotens.

Ita Deus Pater, Deus Filius: Deus Spiritus sanctus.

Et tamen non tres Dei: sed unus est Deus.

[46] I cite according to (Horae diurnae Breviarii romani 1886), Mechliniae, p.13-14.

Ita Dominus Pater, Dominus Filius: Dominus Spiritus sanctus.
Et tamen non tres Domini: sed unus est Dominus.[47]

A believing mind that simply receives these words and, reading them with inner concentration, does not strive for theological analysis, experiences the feeling of an impenetrable mystery. He believes that there were three different forms of God, wherein each of these three would be a true God—and simultaneously he believes, they were not three but only one uncreated, infinite, omnipotent and eternal God. In my opinion, it is precisely these acts of belief concerning these *apparently contradictory* statements that produce this feeling of mystery and horror. Surely it was under the influence of such states of mind that some theologians have searched for contradictions also in the concept of God; one might remember, for example, Cardinal Nicolas of Cusa, who saw in God a *coincidentia oppositorum*.

I have included this example so that the reader, immersing himself into the words of this symbol, may at least for a moment experience the feeling that I succumbed to in doing so. Whoever manages to reach this state of mind, will consider the argument as existent; whoever does not may skip over it.

If I am not mistaken, then the considerations above will at least be able to convince the reader that the psychological principle of contradiction is not as certain and indubitable as it is usually taken to be. And because an uncertain and doubtful principle may hardly

[47] Translator's note: Łukasiewicz cites an extended passage from the Athanasian Creed in the original Latin. The Athanasian Creed places great emphasis on the doctrine of the Trinity. In a popular 19th century English translation by Philip Schaff (1877), Łukasiewicz' selection of the Athanasian Creed is translated as follows:

"For there is one Person of the Father; another of the Son; and another of the Holy Ghost. But the Godhead of the Father, of the Son, and of the Holy Ghost, is all one; the Glory equal, the Majesty coeternal. Such as the Father is; such is the Son; and such is the Holy Ghost. The Father uncreated; the Son uncreated; and the Holy Ghost uncreated. The Father unlimited; the Son unlimited; and the Holy Ghost unlimited. The Father eternal; the Son eternal; and the Holy Ghost eternal. And yet they are not three eternals; but one eternal. As also there are not three uncreated; nor three infinites, but one uncreated; and one infinite. So likewise the Father is Almighty; the Son Almighty; and the Holy Ghost Almighty. And yet they are not three Almighties; but one Almighty. So the Father is God; the Son is God; and the Holy Ghost is God. And yet they are not three Gods; but one God" (Schaff 1877, II, 66-71).

constitute the foundation of logic, it is possible to omit it from subsequent considerations without any great loss. *The path to the foundations of logic does not run through psychology.*

Chapter VI

The Unprovability of the Ontological and Logical Principle of Contradiction

After the elimination of the psychological formulation of the principle of contradiction, the ontological and logical ones remain. We will now turn our attention to them.

As a reminder, the ontological principle of contradiction states: No object can simultaneously contain the same property and not contain it. The logical principle, on the other hand, says: Two statements, one of which attributes a property to an object that the other denies of it, cannot be simultaneously true. We already know that these sentences are equivalent, which means that one either accepts both or rejects both. In the following paragraphs, I primarily examine the ontological principle, which, as is well known, is the principle of contradiction *κατ' ἐξοχήν*.

Proofs that demonstrate the truth of some principle can prompt us to accept it. What are the proofs of the ontological or the logical principle of contradiction?

For Aristotle, this is apparently a rather delicate question, which clearly throws him off balance and puts words in his mouth that suggest a certain agitation. We read at *Met.* Γ 4, 1006 a 3-15:

> *ἡμεῖσ δὲ νῦν εἰλήφαμεν ὡς ἀδυνάτου ὄντος ἅμα εἶναι καὶ μὴ εἶναι, καὶ διὰ τούτου ἐδείξαμεν ὅτι βεβαιστάτη αὕτη τῶν ἀρχῶν πασῶν. ἀξιοῦσι δὴ καὶ τοῦτο ἀποδεικνύναι τινὲς δι' ἀπαιδευσίαν. ἀξιοῦσι δὴ καὶ τοῦτο ἀποδεικνύναι τινὲς δι' ἀπαιδευσίαν. ἔστι γὰρ ἀπαιδευσία τὸ μὴ γιγνώσκειν τίνων δεῖ ζητεῖν ἀπόδειξιν καὶ τίνων οὐ δεῖ. ὅλως μὲν γὰρ ἁπάντων ἀδύνατον ἀπόδειξιν εἶναι (εἰς ἄπειρον γὰρ ἂν βαδίζοι, ὥστε μηδ' οὕτως εἶναι ἀπόδειξιν)*[48] ... *ἔστι δ'*

[48] Translator's note: Parentheses by Ross (1924), not included in Łukasiewicz' citation

> *ἀποδεῖξαι ἐλεγκτικῶς καὶ περὶ τούτου ὅτι ἀδύνατον, ἂν μόνον τι λέγῃ ὁ ἀμφισβητῶν΄ ἄν δὲ μηθέν, γελοῖον τὸ ζητεῖν λόγον πρὸς τὸν μηθενὸς ἔχοντα λόγον … ὅμοιος γὰρ φυτῷ ὁ τοιοῦτος …*

I render these words in their figurative sense in order to emphasize more fittingly the mood that gained hold of me:

> Thus we have said that it is impossible that something simultaneously were to be and not to be, and showed *by this* (!) that this principle is the most secure of all. You want proofs? There are none! It is a lack of *education* not to know what requires proof and what does not. One cannot prove everything because we would become lost in infinity and in such a manner that then there would be no proof at all. But, by the way, if you really care that much about proofs, then they certainly can be found, but not simple ones, only 'elenctic' ones. Somebody should just try to oppose this even with a single word! But if he does not say anything, then it would be ridiculous to debate with him; it would be the same as talking to a wall [cf. Appendix II, 263, 9].[49]

Whoever expresses any opinion with such emphasis and self-assurance, whoever is irritated instead of arguing, has apparently no sufficiently strong arguments left and notices that things stand quite poorly with one's cause. Thus, he attempts to save face in this manner, apparently in order not to reveal his weaknesses.

[49] Ross (Aristotle 1992): "But we have now posited that it is impossible for anything at the same time to be and not to be, and by this means have shown that this is the most indisputable of all principles. Some indeed demand that even this shall be demonstrated, but this they do through want of education, for not to know of what things one may demand demonstration, and of what one may not, argues simply want of education. For it is impossible that there should be demonstration of absolutely everything; there would be an infinite regress, so that there would still be no demonstration. But if there are things of which one should not demand demonstration, these persons cannot say what principle they regard as more indemonstrable than the present one. We can, however, demonstrate negatively even that this view is impossible, if our opponent will only say something; and if he says nothing, it is absurd to attempt to reason with one who will not reason about anything, in so far as he refuses to reason. For such a man, as such, is seen already to be no better than a mere plant."

This is the impression that the cited passage from the *Metaphysics* made on me. But let us subject it to a logical analysis.

To begin with, I will pass over the (actual or apparent) contradiction, which consists in that Aristotle, determining that the principle of contradiction is unprovable, nevertheless introduces this possibility just a few lines later by saying: *ἔστι ἀποδεῖξαι ἐλενκτικως καὶ περὶ τούτου ὅτι ἀδύνατον*, and then tortures himself over several chapters with the proof. In this section, however, I am only concerned with the idea that the principle of contradiction is an *ultimate* and unprovable principle.

Aristotle asserts that it is impossible to prove everything; however, what he has in mind here are not particular statements about concrete facts, but principles, that is, *universal* statements. But if one wants to prove a principle, then one must show that another statement is true—and precisely that statement on which the principle to be proven rests. Then the truth of these reasons in turn needs to be proven based on some other reason and so forth. This chain of consequences and reasons must lead to an *ultimate* principle, which then would have no more consequences and reasons, but would be true by itself. If we were to assume that this chain of reasons was to be infinite, then we would get statements that are merely *hypothetical* truths, for example: statement S_1 is true if statement S_2 is true, statement S_2 is true if statement S_3 is true, and so on. One must determine *categorically* that in this chain some statement S_n is true *by itself*, without reference *to other statements*. Such a statement is an *ultimate* one, *πρώτη ἀρχή*, and an *unprovable*, *ἀναπόδεικτος*, principle. We read:

> *Post.An.* I, 3, 72 b 18-20: *ἡμεῖς δὲ φαμεν οὔτε πᾶσαν ἐπιστήμη ἀποδεικτικὴν εἶναι, ἀλλὰ τὴν τῶν ἀμέσων ἀναπόδεικτον*
>
> But we claim that not all knowledge can be proven, but the knowledge of statements in which the predicate directly belongs to the subject (this are precisely *τὰ ἄμεσα*), is unprovable.[50]

[50] Barnes (Aristotle 1992): "But *we* say that neither is all understanding demonstrative, but in the case of the immediates it is non-demonstrable."

Aristotle designates ultimate principles as *ἄμεσα*, because no term, *τὸ μέσον*, that mediates between subject and predicate exists. Let us assume that in some sentence, *A* is *B*, a mediating term *C* were to exist that would allow the following statements: "*A* is *C*" and "*C* is *B*". But then this principle could be proven based on the premises "*A* is *C*" and "*C* is *B*", which would mean that this sentence is anything else but ultimate.

One may agree with this conclusion though with a note whose meaning will only become clear later on: under principles, one should not understand only universal statements. Accordingly, it may be assumed that some *ultimate* principles do exist, that is, *those statements, which cannot be proven based on other statements, but which are true by themselves*. What is at hand now is to find these principles.

According to Aristotle, one of them, the most certain one, *βεβαιοστάτη*, the one that is most easily accessible to cognition, *γνωριμωτάτη*, and the one about which it is impossible to be in error at all, *περὶ ἣν διαψευσθῆναι ἀδύνατον*,[51] is precisely the principle of contradiction. But where is the proof for this? The Stagirite does not offer one but is content with the words:

> *Met. Γ* 4, 1006 a 10-11: *εἰ δέ τινων μὴ δεῖ ζητεῖν ἀπόδειξιν, τίνα ἀξιοῦσιν εἶναι μᾶλλον τοιαύτην ἀρχὴν οὐκ ἂν ἔχοιεν εἰπεῖν.*
>
> If one does not have to search for a proof for certain principles, then it would be difficult to give them (i.e., those who demand a proof for the principle of contradiction) an even more evident principle (that is, a principle in which the reason for its unprovability were to be have greater weight than in the case of the principle of contradiction).[52]

But what if such a principle does exist? What if one is able to not only assert it but also to *prove* that this principle, which is still unknown to us, is true in virtue of itself and unprovable, and thus that it is an ultimate principle even though it is not the principle of

[51] *Met.* Γ 3, 1005 b 12.

[52] Ross (Aristotle 1992): "But if there are things of which one should not demand demonstration, these persons cannot say what principle they regard as more indemonstrable than the present one."

contradiction? And finally, what if it becomes clear that the principle of contradiction, based on this *essential* principle, does *require* proof?

Aristotle does not think that the assertion that the principle of contradiction is an ultimate principle needs to be proven. Because of this, he accepts two ultimate and unprovable claims: the principle of contradiction and the claim that asserts that the principle of contradiction is an ultimate principle.

This is a weak position: We will soon be able to convince ourselves that it is unable to withstand the attacks of a logical critique.

Chapter VII

The Principle of Contradiction and the Principle of Identity

Among universal statements, there is a principle that could be considered as ultimate with better justifications than the principle of contradiction. This is the *principle of identity*.

However, Aristotle does not formulate it at any location in the form of a separate ontological or logical law.[53] It could be determined in a twofold manner according to a relation of inherence or non-inherence: *Every object contains the property that it contains; and no object contains the property that it does not contain.* These two formulas can also be expressed in conditional sentences: *If an object contains a property, then it contains it; if an object does not contain a property, then it does not contain it.* They are ontological formulations because they contain the concepts of object and property.

Logicians usually consider the principle of identity as a positive but nevertheless worthless and trivial formulation of the principle of contradiction.[54] This conception probably stems from the

[53] Cf. Maier (1896, 1969), *Die Syllogistik des Aristoteles*, I, 101—and also the already cited passage from the *Metaphysics* 7, 1011 b 20-27.

[54] For example, cf. Ueberweg (1882, 232): "As a tautological sentence, the formula A = A does not state anything and is by no means the necessary positive addendum to the principle of contradiction. It is a justified logical requirement that a thought that has been recognized as true is not canceled again by a contradicting one, but that it is to be identical to itself and always again true, that is a superfluous remark." Sigwart (1889, 186): "Thus, it is completely natural that Aristotle emphasizes the principle of contradiction alone as a principle and only occasionaly gives expression to its positive backside, just as for a long time the Aristotelian principle of contradiction was understood as the *Principium identitatis*." This last remark of Sigwart also applies to Trendelenburg, among others, who discusses the principle of contradiction in his *Logische Untersuchungen* [*Logical Investigations*] (Trendelenburg 1870) under the name principle of identity. Finally, I present an example from a more recent non-logical treatise to show how very common this

circumstance that the principle of contradiction is still frequently articulated in Leibniz' version, "*a* is not non-*a*".[55] And this version would correspond, as negation, to the positive formula assumed for the principle of identity: "*a* is *a*".

It is surprising how strongly certain opinions can persist within the sciences that are not only incorrectly formulated and without justification, but which are plainly *false*—most likely, as I believe, because what has been declared in the past is repeated uncritically again and again. The problem of the relation of the principle of contradiction to the principle of identity presents itself in the same manner.

a) The principle of identity is supposed to be a "positive" formulation of the principle of contradiction. This thesis, whose clarity and exactitude leaves a lot to be desired (cf. further the even murkier expression *positive backside* in the Sigwart citation in footnote [54] above), seems to mean as much as that these two principles express the same thought in different ways (one in an affirmative sentence, the other in a negative one), that is, that they have the same meaning. I already mentioned in Chapter II that no affirmative statement has the same meaning as a negative one; affirming is something different from denying. An affirmative statement can at most be equivalent to a negative one, whereby identity of sense and sameness of meaning are two *different* concepts. Accordingly, one may not assume that the formulas "*a* is *a*" and "*a* is not *non-a*" have the same meaning and, correspondingly, present the same statement.

b) However, the problem of the sameness of meaning of these formulas has no significance for our question because the sentence "*a* is not *non-a*" does not present the principle of contradiction at all. Scientific logic, which utilizes unequivocally determined symbols in its investigations and which avoids the unclear and shaky expressions of ordinary speech, considers this formula to be

mistake is. Dr. H. Kleinpeter, in his book *Die Erkenntistheorie der Naturforschung der Gegenwart* [*Epistemology in contemporary science of nature*] (Kleinpeter 1905, 103, 103): "if one states that the principle (of contradiction) consists in that the two judgments 'A is B' and 'A is not B' cannot be the case simultaneously … then what is stated is the same as the principle of identity".

[55] Cf., for example, Höfler and Meinong, *Logik* (Höfler 1890, 135, 135): "The principle of contradiction is often customarily expressed as: *A* is not non-*A*."

an imprecise formulation of the *principle of double negation*.[56] It can be shown that none of the three principles— contradiction, identity, and double negation—expresses the same thought, which is to say that the three principles do not have the same meaning.[57]

c) To justify this assertion properly, I list all these principles in the form of conditional sentence constructions because in this manner they adopt best to exact formulas of symbolic logic:

The principle of identity:
If x contains F, then x contains F.

The principle of double negation:
If x contains F, then x cannot not contain F.

The principle of contradiction:
If x is an object, then x cannot simultaneously contain F and not contain F.

Doubts may arise whether this third sentence construction is synonymous with the principle of contradiction expressed in categorical form ("No object can simultaneously contain and not contain the same property"). In my opinion, every universal statement, whether affirmative or negative, presents the connection between two statements: "All A are B" means that "if something is A, then it is also B", and "no A is B" means that "if something is A, then it is not B". The *equivalence* of these formulas cannot be doubted; their identical meaning, however, follows from the meaning of the words "all" and "no".

The words "all A" do not present one object but an indeterminate number of objects A_1, A_2, … A_n. Thus, the assertion "all A are B" expresses in abbreviated form the class of statements: "A_1 is B", "A_2 is B" … "A_n is B", whereby A_1, A_2, … A_n satisfy exhaustively the range of A. This means that whichever A_x we want to take, it is B; it means that "if something is A, then it is B". In the same way, the sentence "no A is B" presents in abbreviated form the class of statements: "A_1 is not B", "A_2 is not B", … "A_n is not B" whereby

[56] Cf. Schröder (1890–1905, , I, 350).

[57] Sigwart (1889, , I, 182, 23), too, agrees that the formula "a is not non-a" is not an expression of the principle of contradiction. In Chapter 10, I show that the the above named principles are not even equivalent.

$A_1, A_2, \dots A_n$ satisfy exhaustively the range of A. This in turn means that whichever A_x we want to take, it is not B. Accordingly, the concept of consequence contained in these sentence constructions is hidden in the words "all" and "no".

I am stating the principle of contradiction here in its conditional form because it is easier this way to detect the difference between this principle and the principles of identity and double negation. The same differences, however, are also decisive for the *categorical* form of the principle of contradiction, so that the following examination will remain correct even if the conditional form were to reveal itself as not identical in meaning with the categorical one. The properties in virtue of which we distinguish the principle of contradiction from the principle of identity and from the principle of double negation are the following:

α) The term "object" is found in the antecedent of the principle of contradiction, which is not found in the antecedents of the principle of identity and the principle of double negation. If we were to formulate these two principles with the aid of this term, we would merely get *singular* cases: "If x is an object, then x is an object" and "If x is an object, then x cannot not be an object". These singular cases are of course different from the *universal* principles of identity and double negation. It is possible to express the principle of contradiction in its converse form with the aid of an undetermined property F: "If x contains F, then x cannot simultaneously contain F and not contain F". However, I doubt whether this new formulation would be synonymous with the earlier one. It would mean: if one can assert anything whatever about any arbitrary object, then this object cannot simultaneously contain and not contain the same property. Accordingly, this formulation would be broader than the one that is usually assumed. However, I will pass over the problem whether the principle of contradiction in this new formulation expresses the same thought as the earlier one; the main difference between the three principles, after all, is not found in their antecedents but in their consequents.

β) The consequent of the sentence construction in which the principle of contradiction is expressed (as it is in its categorical form as well), contains terms without which this principle could not be formulated and which, on the other hand, are in fact completely dispensable for the determination of the principle of identity and the principle of double negation. They are the terms *and* and *simultaneously*, which present the concept of *logical multiplication*. In immediate connection with this difference is a *second*, no less relevant one: whenever logical multiplication comes about, there also must be at least *two* multiplicands, that is, *two* statements. The consequent of the principle of contradiction contains indeed two statements tied together with the terms "and" and "simultaneously". On the other hand, neither the consequent of the principle of identity nor in the consequent of the principle of double negation contain two statements that are connected by a relation of multiplication. Further, I see no possibility of deducing from the terms that appear in these principles—via some analysis—two statements that constitute a logical multiplication,

These differences bring about the result that the principle of contradiction expresses a new thought. A thought that is completely different from those that are expressed in the previous principles. *It is impossible to formulate the principle of contradiction if two statements, of which one is the negation of the other, and which jointly constitute a logical multiplication, are not available; it is possible, however, to formulate the principle of identity and the principle of double negation without two statements that form a logical multiplication. Furthermore, the principle of identity can be expressed without having to involve the concept of negation, which is completely out of the question with respect to the principle of contradiction.* As long as 'two' designates something different from 'one' and as long as negation and logical multiplication mean something different from the absence of negation and logical multiplication, so long will *the principle of identity be different from the principle of contradiction.*

From this it emerges that the conception articulated by many logicians, that the principle of identity is merely a positive formulation of the principle of contradiction, makes no sense at all. No wonder. None of them has bothered to present this assertion correctly and to further justify it in some form. Even with respect to the most fundamental logical problems, empty phrases are still strewn into the wind.[58]

[58] Perhaps Wundt alone does not place the principle of identity on the same level as the principle of contradiction, even though he, too, does not grasp precisely enough the connection between these two principles. Cf. *Logik*, Vol.1, (Wundt 1893, 564, 564): "… it [is] possible to utilize the principle of contradiction as a substitute for the law of identity (?), as it was done throughout by the older logic [following the

Aristotle is not free from similar charges. Full of confidence in the dialectical power of his method of proof, he exclaims: "Whoever does not want to accept the principle of contradiction without proof ought to name another principle that could be considered as ultimate with a better justification." There *is* such a principle that, distinct from the principle of contradiction, is simpler, more secure and easier to understand. Perhaps one ought to recognize *it* as the ultimate principle?

example of Aristotle—as Wundt added erroneously in the third edition], while it is not possible, on the other hand, to infer the principle of contradiction from the principle of identity. Because the first will also be valid if the function of negation were not exist."

Chapter VIII

The Ultimate Principle

The principle of identity is not the ultimate principle because it is possible to prove it based on another statement. What underlies the principle of identity is the *definition of a true statement.*

An affirmative statement is to be designated as true if it attributes a property to an object that the object contains. A negative statement is to be designated as true if it denies a property of an object that the object does not contain. These are definitions. It follows immediately from them: if an object contains a property, then it is true that it contains it, thus it contains it. And if it does not contain it, then it is true that it does not contain it, thus it does not contain it. These sentences are true precisely because I determine the truth in this manner. And, consequently, *the principle of identity is thus not an ultimate principle, but the definition of a true statement, on which this principle rests, is.*

We want to examine this assertion in detail.

a) The definition of a true statement is, as any other definition, a singular statement. Every definition contains, openly or hidden, the word that asserts the respective fact: I determine, I designate, I name, I understand. For example: "Under a true statement I understand such an affirmative statement that attributes a property to an object that the object does possess", or "the relation of inherence—*x* contains *F*—I designate with the letter *F*", or "a flat, closed, curved line on which every point is equidistant from the center, I call a circle". The words "understand", "designate", "name" may be omitted if the sentences, which are supposed to contain them, are clearly or implicitly determined as definitions. Then, instead of saying "Under a true statement, I understand ...", I simply say "an asserting statement that ... is true" and add "and this is a definition". If this sentence does not exist, or if it cannot be anticipated, a definition transforms itself into a universal statement, which in its appearance would be an ultimate principle. There is a passage in Aristotle, which initially looks like a formulation of the principle of identity, but which is only the definition of a true statement:

> *Met. Γ 7,* 1011 b 26-27: *τὸ ... γὰρ λέγειν ..., τὸ ὂν εἶναι καὶ μὴ ὂν μὴ εἶναι ἀληθές ...*
>
> To state that being is and that not-being is not, is true.[59]

Father Gabryl treats this sentence as an expression of the principle of identity.[60] And it would indeed be so if Aristotle had not brought it to our attention before that with these words he wants to give the *definition* of truth. Immediately before this sentence, he writes:

> *Met. Γ 7,* 1011 b 25: *δῆλον δὲ (scil. ὅτι οὐδὲ μεταξὺ ἀντιφάσεως ἐνδέχεται εἶναι οὐδέν) πρῶτον μὲν ὁρισαμένοις τί τὸ ἀληθὲς καὶ ψεῦδος.*
>
> That no (third) can exist between contradictory statements will become clear once we first determine what is true and what is false.[61]

Accordingly, one should distinguish the definition from the principle that follows from it. A definition is always a *singular statement*, which states that someone determines, designates and names an object in a certain way. A principle that rests on a definition is always a *universal* statement, which asserts a property about the defined object that the definition attributes to it.

b) Every definition forms a true statement because it asserts a property about its *author* that belongs to him. That is, whoever says or writes, "by circle, I understand a curved line", or "the relation of inherence '*x* contains *F*', I designate with *F*", *creates* with this the fact about which he speaks or writes. After all, he asserts, solely by uttering (or writing) those words, that by "circle" he understands a curved line and that he designates that relation by

[59] Ross (Aristotle 1992): "To say of what is that it is, and of what is not that it is not, is true."

[60] Gabryl, Franciszek (1903, 105). *Metafizyka ogólna, czyli nauka o bycie* (General metaphysics, or the science about being), p.105.

[61] Ross (Aristotle 1992): "There cannot be an intermediate between contradictories … This is clear, in the first place, if we define what the true and the false are."

the letter *F*. But here, doubts emerge: the author of a definition could be *lying* and, while defining a circle as a curved line, he could be convinced that a circle is something completely different. I admit that such cases do occur. But definitions do not exist, as some would have it, to express the acts of conviction or willed decisions that exist in some person, but rather they are supposed to determine the meaning of words and of other arbitrary sense-perceivable signs with the aim of mutual communication and the grasping of the facts of reality. Accordingly, what is at issue is not whether somebody, while formulating a definition, believes or does not believe what he says, or whether he really wants to define some sign in the way he indicates or merely pretends to do it this way; rather, what is at issue is what *words* he employs as he articulates the definition and how he *uses* the defined sign in assertions that are stated by himself. Thus, the expressions "understand", "designate", "determine", and so forth, one should always relate to *signs*, that is, to sentences in which they occur, and not to *psychical acts*. Thus, *every definition stands in relation to a fact, which comes about together with it and which is contained in it. It is because of this, that every definition is true.*

But not every definition is practical and useful. A definition is impractical if someone determines anew an expression that already has an established scientific meaning and does so in a manner that diverges from the generally recognized one. A definition is not useful if someone gives words and signs such a meaning, i.e., creates concepts, that neither correspond to reality nor allow of any direct application to reality in some form. The assertion that a concept created by a definition corresponds to reality is always merely a hypothesis that has to tested and confirmed based on experience.

c) The definition of a true statement is an ultimate principle, because it is true in virtue of itself and cannot be proven based on another statement. The definition of a true statement is true because every definition is true; and it is true in virtue of itself because its truth does not rest on the truth of another statement, but on its own truth. If somebody says: "By a true statement I understand a statement that attributes a property to an object that the object does possess", then he attributes to himself the property of "understanding-something-by-a-true-statement". He indeed does possess this property because he just asserted it in the utterance of this definition. Thus, this definition is true in virtue of the determination of truth contained in it. And this is the only case in which a statement can be true, in a literal and concise sense, by virtue of itself alone. If this property is asserted about other statements, then the expression "true in virtue of itself" is not used in a precisely determined manner. The definition of a true statement cannot be proven based on another statement. Let us assume some true statement would constitute its foundation. But then the truth of this foundation would have to rest, among other considerations, also on the truth of the definition of a true statement and, consequently, the proof would be a *petitio principii*.

d) There are no ultimate principles except the definition of a true statement. Ultimate principles are not:

α) Other definitions, because they rely on the truth of the definition of a true statement.

β) Statements about *facts* given directly in internal or external experience. Even though there are some statements, as "it thunders" or "I have a headache" that resemble the ultimate principle in their indemonstrability, but of course with the difference that they are not true in virtue of themselves. They do not state facts that are contained in them but concern phenomena that exist *outside of them*.

γ) Finally, *universal statements* also are not ultimate principles. From Chapter VII, we already know that every universal or affirmative statement as "all *A* are *B*" or, respectively, every negating one as "no *A* is *B*" present a connection of two statements. The sentence "all *A* are *B*" means that "if something is *A*, then it is *B*" and the sentence "no *A* is *B*" means that "if something is *A*, then it is not *B*". The truth of this connection is never found in the connection itself but always demands a proof, which in turn can rely only on either definition or experience.

The principle of contradiction is a universal statement that states: if something is an object, then it cannot simultaneously contain and not contain the same property. The truth of this relation is not located in (the principle) itself but unconditionally demands proof. But even the philosophers who consider the principle of contradiction as directly self-evident do not base its truth on (the principle) *itself*, but rather on a feeling of self-evidence (that is, on a *psychical fact*) that takes hold of them in front of this principle.

Accordingly, the principle of contradiction is therefore not an ultimate principle, and whoever accepts it or attempts to motivate others to accept it, must prove it first.

Chapter IX

Aristotle's Elenctic Proofs

No one, it seems, had a stronger desire to prove the principle of contradiction than Aristotle himself. He knew but could not get himself to agree with the conviction that the principle of contradiction, as ultimate principle, cannot be proven. This left him in a huge quandary: he entangled himself in contradictions while merely contemplating the principle of contradiction.

The way out of such a quandary, however, is well known to us: one picks out a verbal distinction that is meant to cover up the obvious contradiction. Quite rightfully, Goethe's Mephisto says somewhere in *Faust*: "When a concept is lacking, a *word* will turn up just in time."[62]

Aristotle, too, gets out of his quandary with one *word*, namely with the adverb *ἐλεγκτικῶς* (*elenktikos*). Even though the principle of contradiction cannot be proven, proofs for it do exist, even though they are not real but "elenctic" ones. How are they different from each other? Let us listen to Aristotle himself:

> Met. *Γ* 4, 1006 a 15-18: *τὸ δ' ἐλεγκτικῶς ἀποδεῖξαι λέγω διαφέρειν καὶ τὸ ἀποδεῖξαι, ὅτι ἀποδεικνύων μὲν ἂν δόξειεν αἰτεῖσθαι τὸ ἐν ἀρχῇ, ἄλλου δὲ τοῦ τοιούτου αἰτίου ὄντος ἔλεγκος ἂν εἴη καὶ οὐκ ἀπόδειξις.*
>
> However, I assert that the elenctic proof differs from the real one in that the proving speaker (who wants to prove the principle of contradiction the real way) appears to assume in advance that which is to be proven (i.e., he would commit a *petitio principii*); however, if someone else causes this (i.e., a *petitio principii*),

[62] Goethe (1990 [1828-29]) *Faust I*, verse 1995 f.

> then this would constitute an elenctic and not the real proof [cf. Appendix II, 263, 10].[63]

To me, the meaning of these words appears to be the following: Whoever proves the principle of contradiction the real way proceeds wrongly because he commits a *petitio principii*; on the other hand, whoever allows this error creates the possibility of a elenctic proof—and everything is in good order. To put it briefly: the elenctic method of proof differs from the real one in that the former is good in the discussed example, the latter one, however, is bad. Isn't this a precisely formulated difference?

To this day, Aristotle's authority is so great that even the most recent commentators take this sentence seriously to such an extent that they do not perceive any trickery in it. Schwegler writes: "The impossibility of the assumption that something was to be and not to be at the same time cannot be shown directly but only apagogically [sic!] (ἐλεγκτικῶς), namely by placing the burden of the proof of the opposite thesis on the one who doubts this impossibility, that is, on the one who doubts the principle of contradiction."[64] Maier, on the other hand, says: "As little as the same (*scil.* the principle of contradiction) can actually be given proof, a certain demonstration nevertheless can be conducted in the sense that the opposite account is refuted and the absurd consequences, which follow from it, are brought out."[65]

Not only will any given interpretation not be able to remove the contradiction that is found at the cited location of the Metaphysics, but it itself will not be free of it. To present this contradiction better let us first investigate what Aristotle means by "elenchus".

a) An *elenchus* (ἔλεγχος) is a syllogism that derives a contradictory result from a given thesis. It is brought about when

[63] Ross (Aristotle 1992): "Now negative demonstration I distinguish from demonstration proper, because in a demonstration one might be thought to be assuming what is at issue, but if another person is responsible for the assumption we shall have negative proof, not demonstration."

[64] Schwegler (1847, 1960-1968) *Die Metaphysik des Aristoteles*, Vol.3, p.162., At least this comment by Schwegler is significant in this pile of errors, namely, that it is possible to prove the principle of contradiction in some fashion.

[65] Maier (1896, 1969) *Die Syllogistik des Aristoteles*, Vol.1, p.47.

it is possible to get one's opponent to acknowledge his own mistakes, which together with the thesis defended by him, produce a contradictory conclusion. Thus, we read the following:[66]

> Pr.An. II 20, 66 b 6-13: *πάντων μὲν γὰρ συγχωρουμένων ... ἐγχωρεῖ γίγνεσθαι ἔλεγκον ... εἰ τὸ κείμενον εἴη ἐναντίον΄ τῷ συμπεράσματι, ἀνάγκη γίγνεσθαι ἔλεγκον ὁ γὰρ ἔλεγκος ἀντιφάσεος συλλογισμός. εἰ δὲ μηδὲν συγχωροῖτο, ἀδύνατον γίγνεσθαι' ἔλεγκον΄ οὐ γὰρ ἦν συλλογισμός πάντων τῶν ὅπων στερητικῶν ὄντων.*
>
> If the opponent agrees to everything, then the conditions for the emergence of an elenchus are given ... If the thesis is in contradiction to the conclusion, an elenchus must come about. An elenchus is the syllogism of contradictory statements. If the opponent does not agree with anything, an elenchus cannot arise: the syllogism does not exist if all terms are negating ones.[67]

For example, let us assume that our opponent does not recognize the principle of contradiction; if one can move him to accept those statements from which the principle follows syllogistically, then an elenctic syllogism, that is, an *elenchus*, comes about. This syllogism becomes elenctic exclusively *κατὰ συμβεβηκός,* that is, if someone were to be found arbitrarily who would have first contradicted the conclusion, but then would have accepted the premises. The elenctic syllogism constitutes at the same time the elenctic *proof* of the conclusion, for example, of the principle of contradiction, if this principle happened to be its conclusion. And because every correct syllogism (with true premises) is the real

[66] Cf. also *Sophistical Refutations*, 165 a 1-3, 170 b 1-2.

[67] Jenkinson (Aristotle 1992): "A refutation is possible whether everything is conceded, or the answers alternate (one, I mean, being affirmative, the other negative) ... if what is laid down is contrary to the conclusion, a refutation must take place; for a refutation is a deduction which establishes the contradictory. But if nothing is conceded, a refutation is impossible; for no deduction is possible (as we saw) when all the terms are negative."

proof of the conclusion, *the elenctic syllogism, too, proves its conclusion in the real way*. Because of this, Maier can say: "It (*scil.* the elenchus) is a syllogism that derives the opposite of a presented claim. . . . As a conclusion, it coincides with the demonstrative syllogism."[68]

If, correspondingly, the elenctic proof that builds a syllogism constitutes, according to Aristotle, a real proof, then does not Aristotle fall into a contradiction when he claims that the principle of contradiction cannot be proven but can be demonstrated elenctically? Not only does the Stagirite claim this, he also actually proves this apparently unprovable principle! And if it indeed were to be shown that his proofs are not convincing, this would not alter the fact that he did consider them to be so when he closes the elenctic argumentation with the words:

> Met. *Γ* 4, 1007 b 17-18: *εἰ δὲ τοῦτο, δέδεικται ὅτι ἀδύνατον ἅμα κατηγορεῖσθαι τὰς ἀντιφάσεις.*
>
> If this is the case, then *the proof has been produced* that one cannot simultaneously accept contradictory statements.[69]

b) Aristotle not only proves the principle of contradiction *elenctically*, but also *apagogically*. The apagogic proof, *ἡ εἰς τὸ ἀδύνατον ἀπαγωγή*, *reductio ad absurdum*, comes about if one assumes as starting point of the proof process a sentence that is contradictory to the given thesis and then shows that the syllogistic consequences of this sentence are nonsensical. From the falsity of the consequences one further deduces that the starting point of the proof process is false, too, and that the thesis contradictory to it, correspondingly, is true.

The difference between the elenctic and apagogic proof is of unusual importance especially regarding our problem. Let's make the difference more precise: The *elenctic* proof of a statement *B* consists in that one finds some premise *A* (respectively, two premises, as in a syllogism) which is the reason for the conclusion *B*. One furthermore claims that premise *A* is a true statement and forces the opponent to accept this statement. But whoever accepts

[68] Die Syllogistik des Aristoteles, Vol.2, p.359.

[69] Tredennick (Aristotle 1933-35): "And if this is so, we have proved [*dedeiktai*] that contradictory statements cannot be predicated at the same time."

the premise must also accept the conclusion. Thus, we get a schema:

> If statement *A* is true, then statement *B* is true.
> Statement *A* is true.
> ---
> Therefore, statement *B* is true

It is the inference form of *modus ponens*, known from formal logic.

The apagogic proof of statement *B* consist in that one assumes for the moment that statement *B* is false and then shows that in this case statement *A* must be false. Furthermore, one claims that statement *A* is true contrary to the conclusion, and forces the opponent to accept this statement, that is, to a contradicting of the drawn conclusion. But whoever contradicts the conclusion cannot accept its premises, which means, he has to assume that statement *B* in the given case is not false. Thus, we get a schema:

> If statement *B* is false, the statement *A* is false.
> Statement *A* is not false.
> ---
> Therefore, statement B is not false, i.e., it is true.

It is the inference form of *modus tollens*, known from formal logic.

Consequently, the elenctic and apagogic proofs are to be traced back to these two known forms of inference. Making an inference via *modus ponens*, however, *does not rely* on the principle of contradiction, except if someone were to use it to demonstrate the connection between premise *A* and conclusion *B*; on the other hand, an inference via *modus tollens* always *presupposes* the principle of contradiction. We will convince ourselves of this in Chapter XII. Thus, whoever wants to prove this principle apagogically, would commit a *petitio principii*, which is what Aristotle assumes, and of course could not convince the opponent.

This shows how much Schwegler is in error (see citation above) when he confuses the apagogic proof with the elenctic one; and his explanation, as if the *reductio ad absurdum* were to consist in that the opponent should prove the contradictory thesis, is practically nonsensical. The cited commentary by Schwegler together with the cited text by Aristotle brings a harmonic whole of incredible mistakes into unison.

How incredibly large the effect of a suggestion can be, if it is supported by an ingenious mind through determined words that spring from the depth of conviction! Aristotle categorically decided that the principle of contradiction is the ultimate law of thought and being; almost all believed in it—they still believe in it, up to the present day. Earlier, I have attempted to show that, at the least, it is a doubtful matter that this principle is a law of *thought*; after that I showed that it not only is not an *ultimately valid* law, but also that it demands proof; finally, I have claimed that Aristotle himself *attempts to prove* it. The entire fourth chapter of *Book Γ* of the *Metaphysics* is dedicated to these proofs. Clear, they are not. The train of thought is abstruse. Aristotle, as the first among philosophers, reaches for the deepest foundations of logic and ontology. The task of the next chapter is to decipher those proofs, to present them as clearly as possible, and to critically evaluate them.

Chapter X

The Principle of Contradiction and the Principle of Double Negation

In an elenctic proof, the opponent is compelled to accept statements that entail the conclusion that he refused to recognize. The statements whose acceptance Aristotle forces from the opponents of the principle of contradiction are *definitions*. Thus, we read:

> *Met. Γ* 4, 1006 a 18-25: *ἀρχὴ δὲ πρὸς ἅπαντα τὰ τοιαῦτα οὐ τὸ ἀξιοῦν ἢ εἶναί τι λέγειν ἢ μὴ εἶναι ..., ἀλλὰ τὸ σημαίνειν γέ τι καὶ αὑτῷ καὶ ἄλλῳ· τοῦτο γὰρ ἀνάγκη, εἴπερ λέγοι τι ... ἂν δέ τις τοῦτο διδῷ, ἔσται ἀπόδειξις· ἤδη γάρ τι ἔσται ὡρισμένον.*
>
> The starting point against all such accusations is not the demand that the opponent say that something is or that something is not, but that he at least should name a word that signifies something for himself and for others; that is precisely what he must do if he wants to say anything. If, however, someone indicates such a word, the proof will be completed; after all, there will already be something definite [cf. Appendix II, 263, 11].[70]

The fact that Aristotle's concern is not simply with the word as such, but with the *determination of its meaning*, that is, with a

[70] Ross (Aristotle 1992): "The starting-point for all such arguments is not the demand that our opponent shall say that something either is or is not ... but that he shall say something which is significant both for himself and for another; for this is necessary, if he really is to say anything. ... But if any one grants this, demonstration will be possible; for we shall already have something definite."

definition, shows itself in the subsequent course of the proof as well as in a parallel passage in *Metaphysics Γ* 7, where the principle of double negation is discussed:[71]

> *Met. Γ* 7, 1012 a 21-23: *ἀρχὴ δὲ πρὸς ἅπαντας τούτους ἐξ ὁρισμὸς δὲ γίγνεται ἐκ τοῦ σημαίνειν τι ἀναγκαῖον εἶναι αὐτούς ...*
>
> (To convince all those who do not recognize the principle of the excluded third or who do not accept it without proof) "one has to start from the definition. But the definition comes from the fact that they have to utter some word" [cf. Appendix II, 264, 12].[72]

Thus, one has to compel the opponent to provide a meaningful word, for example, "man", and bring him to utter the sentence: "By this word, I understand this and this", for example, "By the word 'man', I understand a living, two-footed being". Then the foundation of an elenctic proof is given.

In my appraisal, two proofs can be distinguished in the conclusion that follows from these introductory remarks (*Metaphysics Γ* 4, 1006 a 28 - 1007 b 18): with the first, complicated one, that is connected to the concepts of "essence" and "substance", I will deal with in the next chapter; the second, simpler one, slides into the investigations of the first series and is unconnected to the concept of substance. This second proof goes as follows:

> *Met. Γ* 4, 1006 b 28-34: *ἀνάγκη τοίνυν, εἴ τι ἔστιν ἀληθὲς εἰπεῖν, ὅτι ἄνθρωπος, ζῷον εἶναι δίπουν' τοῦτο γὰρ ἦν ὃ ἐσήμινε τὸ ἄνθρωπος. ει δ' ἀνάγκη τοῦτο, οὐκ ἐνδέχεται μὴ εἶναι τὸ αὐτὸ ζῷον δίπουν' τοῦτο γὰρ σημαίνει τὸ ἀνάγκη εἶναι, τὸ ἀδύνατον εἶναι μὴ εἶναι [ἄνθρωπον]. οὐκ ἄρα ἐνδέχεται ἅμα ἀληθὲς εἶναι εἰπεῖν τὸ αὐτὸ ἄνθρωπον εἶναι καὶ μὴ εἶναι ἄνθρωπον.*

[71] This detail was noted by Maier, *Die Syllogistik des Aristoteles*, Vol.1, p.48.

[72] Ross (Aristotle 1992): "And the starting-point in dealing with all such people is definition. Now the definition rests on the necessity of their meaning something; for the formula, of which the word is a sign, becomes its definition."

> Thus, if something can be signified as man, it must be a living and two-footed being; this is precisely what the word man [τὸ ἄνθρωπος] means. And if something must be a living, two-footed being, then it cannot not be this; 'something must be' means that it cannot not be. Thus, it is impossible that it might be simultaneously true that one and same is a man and is not a man (a living, two-footed being, respectively) [cf. Appendix II, 264, 13].[73]

This conclusion can be brought to general formula by employing letters for concepts: By *x*, I understand something that is *F*. Thus, *x* must be *F*. Accordingly, *x* cannot not be *F*, because of the determination of the word "must". Conclusion: *x* cannot simultaneously be *F* and not be *F*.

This deduction consists of two premises: the statement "*x* must be *F*", which is supported by the definition of the term *F*, and the principle "if *x* must be *F*, then it cannot not be *F*", which is supported by the definition of the words "must be". This second premise represents the *principle of double negation.* Thus, Aristotle tries to prove the principle of contradiction based on the principle of double negation. What is one to make of such a proof?

At first, it appears very convincing. The premises are true because they are supported by definitions; a *petitio prinicipii* does not occur because the premises are different from the principle of contradiction. The mistake consists only in that *these premises do not prove the conclusion that is at issue here.*

From the statements: "*x* must be *F*" and "If *x* must be *F*, then it cannot not be *F*" follows via *modus ponens* the conclusion: "*x* cannot not be *F*". Thus: "*x*, which must be *F*, cannot not be *F*". This is precisely the principle of double negation. We already know that the principle of contradiction and the principle of double negation do not mean the same (see Chapter VII); thus, Aristotle *has proven*, at most, the principle of double negation but *not the principle of contradiction* in the first elenctic proof.

[73] Ross (Aristotle 1992): "Therefore, if it is true to say of anything that it is a man, it must be a two-footed animal; for this was what 'man' meant; and if this is necessary, it is impossible that the same thing should not be a two-footed animal; for this is what 'being necessary' means—that it is impossible for the thing not to be. It is, then, impossible that it should be at the same time true to say the same thing is a man and is not a man."

But even though the above principles do not mean the same, they could nevertheless be *equivalent*—and even if they are not equivalent, a relation of *one-sided* deduction could connect them. So, let us continue Aristotle's investigation and consider whether the principle of contradiction does after all follow from the principle of double negation.

Logic teaches us that if statement B does follow from statement A, then no instances can exist in which statement A is true and statement B is false. If, however, at least one example could be found for the co-existence of the truth of statement A and falseness of statement B, then B cannot follow from A.

There are instances in which the principle of double negation is true and the principle of contradiction is not applicable or, put simply, where it is false. To find such peculiar instances, one needs to reach back to the domain of contradictory objects. Classic examples for *contradictory objects* are "wooden iron" (*σιδηρόξυλον*), "square circles" or "round squares". Some consider these strange combinations of words as empty, meaningless sounds. As far as I am concerned, I think that they are not merely empty sounds, like "abracadabra" or "mohatra", but that they still mean something. After all, one can assert about a round square that it is round, that it is a square, and that it is a contradictory object—whereas one cannot assert anything about "abracadabra" because this word does not mean anything. I do admit, however, that those artificially constructed examples of contradictory objects do not make much sense. Nevertheless, we do know other examples from the history of the sciences that are not at all nonsensical. Whoever has studied geometry will without doubt understand what this is: "A square, constructed with the aid of compass and ruler, whose surface area is identical to the surface area of a circle that has a radius of 1." How many men in all ages have tried in vain to construct such a square! Only in the 19th century did Hermite and Lindeman show that such a square is just as much a contradictory an object as a "round square". If it were indeed to be constructed with compass and ruler, then it must have sides that would be expressible by an algebraic number (rational or not rational, like $\sqrt{2}$); if, however, it should have an identical surface area to that of a circle with a radius of 1, then it must have sides that *cannot be expressed* by an algebraic number (its side = $\sqrt{\pi}$, and π is a transcendental number).

Such a square—let's designate it simply by *Q*—is a contradictory object though it does means something and whatever is something is an object.

Applied to square *Q*, the principle of double negation is undoubtedly true. *Q* must have *S*, that is, it must have sides that are expressible by an algebraic number. "Must have" means that it "cannot not have *S*". Thus, *Q* cannot not have *S*. Whoever accepts the principle of double negation, must recognize these two statements as true. But despite this, it is not true that *Q* cannot have *S* and not have *S* at the same time—on the contrary: *Q has S* and simultaneously *does not* have *S*. It is precisely because of this that *Q* is a contradictory object and the squaring of the circle a sentence that cannot be understood.

One could show in the same way that the principle of contradiction does not follow from the principle of identity. The principle of identity asserts that if *Q* has *S*, then it has *S*; and if in this context there is no *S*, then there is not *S*. But one cannot deduce from these statements that *Q* cannot simultaneously have *S* and not have *S*. Thus, the principle of contradiction does neither follow from the principle of double negation nor from the principle of identity. Accordingly, it emerges a fortiori that these two principles neither mean the same as nor are they equivalent to the principle of contradiction.

This entire conclusion is accurate only under this condition, that contradictory objects are *something*, that they are objects. If someone understands under "object" only objects that are not contradictory, the square *Q* would not be an object but *nothing*, and since it would not fall under the principle of contradiction, it would not constitute an exception. The principle of contradiction, after all, applies exclusively to objects, that is, to everything that is something and not nothing. Without doubt, the attentive reader will begin to see the result that these investigations are directed towards.

Chapter XI

The Principle of Contradiction and the "Essence" of Things

The second elenctic proof is connected to the concepts of "essence" and "substance".

Here too, definition forms the starting point. Aristotle requests that the opponent express any given word and determine its meaning. However, the word must signify some *one* thing, as we read:

> *Met. Γ* 4, 1006 b 7-9: *τὸ γὰρ μὴ ἕν τι σημαίνειν οὐδὲν σημαίνειν ἐστίν, μὴ σημαινόντων δὲ τῶν ὀνομάτων ἀνῄρηται τὸ διαλέγεσθαι πρὸς ἀλλήλους* ...
>
> Not to signify some one thing is to signify nothing, and if words mean nothing, then the possibility of communication ends.[74]

From the following passage, we learn what it is that Aristotle is thinking of when he says that the word ought to signify some one thing:

> *Met. Γ* 4, 1006 a 31-34: ... *εἰ τὸ ἄνθρωπος σημαίνει ἕν, ἔστω τοῦτο τὸ ζῷον δίπουν. λέγω δὲ τὸ ἓν σημαίνειν τοῦτο εἰ τοῦτ' ἔστιν ἄνθρωπος, τοῦτ' ἔσται τὸ ἀνθρώπῳ εἶναι.*
>
> If the word 'man' signifies one thing, then let that be a living, two-footed being. But the expression 'to signify one thing', I understand as follows: If this is a

[74] Ross (Aristotle 1992): "For not to have one meaning is to have no meaning, and if words have no meaning reasoning with other people, and indeed with oneself has been annihilated."

> man—if anything at all is a man—then humanness will be his essence [cf. Appendix II, 264, 14].[75]

Aristotle uses the words *τὸ ἀνθρώπῳ εἶναι* for the signification of the essence of man, which is one thing, immutable, different from matter, not perceptible by the senses and accessible to cognition only in its *concept.*[76] Thus, to signify any given entity (one thing) is to signify the *conceptual essence* of an object. A word has meaning only if it signifies something that is one thing according to its essence. A person who designates with 'man' something that, according to its essence, could just as well be a wall or a ship, does not use the word 'man' in a definite way and one cannot communicate with him. That is to say, t*he essence of every object is some one thing*. This principle, which Aristotle does not formulate clearly, is the foundation of the entire proof. The proof says:

> *Met. Γ 4, 1006 b 11-22: ἔστω δή ... σημαῖνόν τι τὸ ὄνομα καὶ σημαῖνον ἕν. οὐ δὴ ἐνδέχεται τὸ ἀνθρώπῳ εἶναι σημαίνειν ὅπερ μὴ εἶναι ἀνθρώπῳ, εἰ τὸ ἄνθρωπος σημαίνει ... ἕν ... καὶ οὐκ ἔσται εἶναι καὶ μὴ εἶναι τὸ αὐτὸ ἀλλ' ἢ καθ' ὁμωνυμίαν, ὥσπερ ἂν εἰ ὃν ἡμεῖς ἄνθρωπον καλοῦμεν, ἄλλοι μὴ ἄνθρωπον καλοῖεν τὸ δ' ἀπορούμενον οὐ τοῦτό ἐστιν, εἰ ἐνδέχεται τὸ αὐτὸ ἅμα εἶναι καὶ μὴ εἶναι ἄνθρωπον τὸ ὄνομα, ἀλλὰ τὸ πρᾶγμα.*
>
> Thus, a word is to be given that signifies something and signifies some one thing. Since, if the word man signifies one thing, then the word man cannot signify the same as the word not-man. Thus, one and the same thing cannot be man and not be man, unless it

[75] Ross (Aristotle 1992): "If 'man' has one meaning, let this be 'two-footed animal'; by having one meaning I understand this: if such and such is a man, then if anything is a man, that will be what being a man is."

[76] Cf. Trendelenburg, Aristotelis De anima libri tres, Jenae, 1833, p.471. Trendelenburg explains the expression τὸ τινὶ εἶναι with the following example: "τὸ μεγέθει εἶναι universam esse notionem, qua res constituitur, a materia avocatam, universa cogitatione conceptam, τὸ μέγεθος vero ad singula quaeque pertinere, quae sub sensus cadant."

> was through an equivalence of words such as when what we call man others were to call non-man. But it is of no concern whether one and same can be simultaneously man and not-man with regards to the name; it is, however, with regards to the thing [cf. Appendix II, 264, 15].[77]

This proof has not been formulated with enough clarity and precision. To begin with, I want to make it more precise and give it a general form, as in the case of the first proof, by using letters for concepts. The assumption is that the word x signifies something, that is, it signifies an object. This assumption is forced on the opponent, who does not accept the principle of contradiction, by compelling him to name some word that signifies something. The opponent has to do this, if he wants to enter into the discussion in the first place. As soon as this takes place, the conditions for an elenctic proof are met. This proof consists of the hypothetical syllogism and the *modus ponens* form of inference.

> *First premise:* If the word x signifies something, then it must signify something that is one thing according to its essence.
>
> *Second premise:* If the word x signifies something that is one thing according to its essence, then it cannot signify something that simultaneously is F and is not F according to its essence.
>
> *Conclusion:* If the word x signifies something then it cannot signify something that simultaneously is F and is not F according to its essence.
>
> *Assumption:* The word x does signify something.
>
> ---
>
> Thus: The word x cannot signify something that according to its essence simultaneously is F and is not F.

[77] Ross (Aristotle 1992): "Let it be assumed then ... that the name has a meaning and has one meaning; it is impossible, then, that being a man should mean precisely not being a man, if 'man' is not only predicable of one subject but also has one meaning ... And it will not be possible for the same thing to be and not to be, except in virtue of an ambiguity, just as one whom we call 'man,' others might call 'not-man'; but the point in question is not this, whether the same thing can at the same time be and not be a man in name, but whether it can in fact."

Proof of the first premise: If a word does not signify something that according to its essence is one thing, then it signifies nothing (τὸ γὰρ μὴ ἕν τι οὐδὲν σημαίνειν ἐστίν). At that point, the possibility of communication ends.

Proof of the second premise: If a word signifies something that according to its essence simultaneously is F and is not F, then it does not signify something that according to its essence is one thing. Being-man-according-to-essence signifies something different than being-not-man.[78]

I have tried to present Aristotle's investigation in the most precise form, a form in which it most of all concerns the words of a language. Of course, the conclusion in this form is not convincing, because:

a) Words may have meanings without signifying something that is one thing according to its essence. Let us assume, for example, that the word "hippocentaur" signifies a living being that is a man and simultaneously not a man, but a horse: even though this word signifies something that is non-existing, but it is not without meaning. After all, everybody understands what "hippocentaur" means, and must understand this if he wants to say that such a being is only a creation of phantasy and does not really exist. The assertion, which Aristotle appears to agree with or, respectively, which is often attributed to him in connection with this investigation, namely the assertion that meaningful words of a language cannot signify contradictory objects, because they must be *determined unequivocally*, is generally mistaken. "A square, constructed with ruler and compass, which has a surface area that is identical to the surface area of a circle with the radius of 1" is without doubt a phrase that is unequivocally determined and has a meaning, yet despite all this, it signifies an object with contradictory properties.

b) The proof presented above does not ground the ontological

[78] Cf. *Met. Γ* 4, 1007 a 27-29: *εἰ δ' ἔσται τι ἢ ὅπερ μὴ ἀνθρώπῳ εἶναι ἢ ὅπερ μὴ εἶναι ἀνθρώπῳ, ἄλλο τι ἔσται.* "If anything were to be not-man according to its essence, of if it were not *man*, then it would be *something else*." [Translator's note: Łukasiewicz' Greek text differs from Ross (1924).]

principle of contradiction. Even if every word of a language were to signify something that is one thing according to its essence, it would not follow from this that *reality does not* contain a contradiction. Human language could reproduce reality imprecisely. But Aristotle, too, understands his proof differently: he is not concerned with *words* but with *objects*. The words of a language must signify objects that contain an essence only because only such objects exist in fact. That is why the Stagirite says: "Thus, one and the same cannot be and not be man, except through a sameness of meaning of the words, if that what we call man others were to call not-man. But the concern is not whether one and the same thing can be man and not-man with reference to the *name*, but with reference to the *thing*"[79] (see also Chapter XII, 149 f).

From this it emerges that Aristotle's proof, even though he assumes as starting point the words of a language, is after all not concerned with words, but with the objects signified by them. Accordingly, one could formulate this proof more accurately in the following manner:

> The *assumption* is: Word x signifies something, which means, it signifies an object; thus, x is an object, which means, it is something. A hypothetical syllogism and a *modus ponens* conclusion follow:
>
> *First premise:* If x is an object, then it must be one thing according to its essence.
>
> *Second premise:* If x is one thing according to its essence, then it cannot be F and not be F according to its essence.
>
> *Conclusion:* If x is an object, then it cannot be F and not be F according to its essence.
>
> *Assumption:* x is an object.
>
> --
>
> Thus: According to its essence, x cannot simultaneously be F and not be F.

The first and second premises are proved in an analogous manner, as in the previous formulation.

[79] Translator's note : *Met. Γ* 4, 1006 b 19-22 as cited and translated on p.57.

This, then, is the second and perhaps more correct formulation of Aristotle's elenctic argument. But in this formulation, too, the argument is not convincing; it is subject to the following objections:

c) Even if it were correct, it would prove the principle of contradiction only for a narrow range of objects: it would concern merely the *essence* of things, but not accidental properties. Object *x*, if it were man, would have to be one thing according to its essence, thus it could not [*sic.*?] simultaneously be white and not be white, because the essence of object *x* is not whiteness, but humanness.

d) This argument is supported by the assumption that objects contain a certain conceptual essence that is different from accidental properties, a certain *universale in re. This assumption is the metaphysical foundation of the entire logic of Aristotle.* Already Socrates said that true knowledge is based on concepts; thus, something real must correspond to the concepts if actual knowledge about reality were to exist. Plato created from concepts the Idea existing in the beyond; Aristotle situated the Platonic Ideas in determined, concrete object. What are *universalia in re*? They are what Aristotle designated as the "essence of things", that is, *groups of properties* that always occur together, for example, some properties of the organic composition of human beings, like two-footedness. In order to explain the fact why these properties occur always together, we assume that some *one* thing underlies them at bottom, a some-thing that holds them together—some kind of *substantial being*, about which we actually do not know anything. Substance and properties that always occur together, that is the essence of an object. Aristotle, too, admits that his concern is with the concept of substance when he says:

> Met. *Γ* 4, 1007 a 20-21: *ὅλως δ' ἀναιροῦσιν οἱ τοῦτο λέγοντες οὐσίαν καὶ τὸ τί ἦν εἶναι.*
>
> Finally, those that talk this way (that is, those that do not acknowledge the acceptance of the presented proof), cancel substance and essence of things.[80]

[80] Ross (Aristotle 1992): "And in general those who use this argument do away with substance and essence."

Met. *Γ* 4, 1007 a 25-26: *ἓν γὰρ ἦν ὃ ἐσήμαινε, καὶ ἦν τοῦτό τινος οὐσία.*

The one was that which (the opponent) signified, and it was the substance of something.[81]

Met. Γ 4, 1007 b 16-18: *ἔσται ἄρα τι καὶ ὣς οὐσίαν σημαῖνον. εἰ δὲ τοῦτο, δέδεικται ὅτι ἀδύνατον ἅμα κατηγορεῖσθαι τὰς ἀντιφάσεις.*

Thus. it must be something that signifies substance. And if this is so, then proof has been brought that one cannot simultaneously accept contradictory statements [cf. Appendix II, 264, 16].[82]

Thus, in the end, the second proof of the principle of contradiction rests on the concept of *substance*. Perhaps it does not only spring from his metaphysical convictions, that Aristotle selected precisely such a proof, but most likely remains in connection to his polemic with the Megarians. The Megarians, after all, did not recognize the principle of contradiction by negating the distinction between substance and accident. They used to say Socrates is a man and simultaneously not a man because he is white, educated, and so forth, and being white, that is, the being-white, does not signify being-man.[83] Contrary to this, Aristotle wanted to show that the *accident*, to contain "white", means something different than to be white according to one's *essence*, that is, being-white. Every object may have many accidents and there is nothing contradictory about that; but the essence or substance of every object must be one thing and may not contain a contradiction. Aristotle attempts to prove the claim that substantial modes of being do exist with a series of arguments. I shall pass over these arguments; in my opinion, the history of the concept of substance showed in sufficient clarity that a statement, which [asserts] the existence of substantial modes of being, that is, the existence of an "essence" of

[81] Ross (Aristotle 1992): "There was some one thing which it meant, and this was the substance of something."

[82] Ross (Aristotle 1992): "There must, then, … be something which denotes substance. And it has been shown that, if this is so, contradictories cannot be predicated at the same time."

[83] Cf. Maier, *Die Syllogistic des Aristoteles*, Vol.2, Part 2, p.7, note 1.

things that is different from arbitrariness, can merely be probable, but never a certain *hypothesis*. Because of this, the conclusions that are supported by this hypothesis can also only be *probable*, so that the second elenctic proof, should it even be correct, would only demonstrate the *probability* of the principle of contradiction.

e) Nevertheless, let us assume that in every object there is indeed one essence and one substance, that is, we accept all factual assumptions of the proof. It will turn out that this proof contains a *petitio principii* because the justification of the premises of a hypothetical syllogism relies on the inference form of *modus tollens*, which in turn presupposes the principle of contradiction. The first premise: "if the word x means something, then it must signify something that is one thing according to its essence" (respectively, "If x is an object, then it must be one thing according to its essence"), Aristotle does not prove directly but only apagogically by asserting: if x were not to signify something—that is one thing according to its essence (respectively, if x were not one thing according to its essence), then it would mean nothing (respectively, it would be nothing). The proof of the second premise is also apagogical. I doubt that these premises can be proven directly; in any case, I do not find any indications regarding this in Aristotle.

Summarizing the last three objections: the first (c) shows that Aristotle's proof cannot justify the principle of contradiction as a *universal* law: the second (d) claims that this proof also does not justify the principle of contradiction as a logically *certain* law: finally, the third bears witness to a *formal mistake* in the method of proof. All these objections taken together testify that the second elenctic proof of Aristotle is also not convincing.

Chapter XII

Apagogic Proofs of the Principle of Contradiction

As we already know from Chapter IX, the apagogic proof rests on a *modus tollens* inference whose schema can be presented as follows:

If statement B is false, then statement A is false.

Statement A is not false.

Therefore, statement B is not false, i.e., it is true.

Every inference of this type presupposes the principle of contradiction. We assert that the denial of the falsity of statement B follows from the denial of the falsity of statement A only because in the reverse case a contradiction would arise. For, if the denial of the falsity of statement A were to coincide with the falsity of statement B, then it also would have to coincide with the falsity of statement A since the falsity of statement A follows from the falsity of statement B. Statement A then would be false and simultaneously not false, which contains a contradiction.

I shall explain the inference with an example. Let B designate a statement that a number n is divisible by 3; A is to designate that the number n is divisible by 6. If statement B is false, that is, if the number n is not divisible by 3, then statement A must be false, that is, the number n cannot be divisible by 6, which means but that statement A is false. If we were to assume that statement B is false, that is, that the number n is not divisible by 3, we also would have to accept the consequence of this statement, that is, accept that the number n is not divisible by 6. Then, however, n *would* be divisible by 6 and simultaneously *not* be divisible by 6, which contains a contradiction. To remove this contradiction, we assume that if statement A is not false, that is, if the number n is divisible by 6, the statement B cannot be false, that is, the number n must be divisible by 3.

The *modus tollens* inference, therefore, is based on the principle of contradiction. Thus, whoever does not recognize this principle, or wants to prove it first, can of course not make use of this inference. Accordingly, one can already claim in advance that the apagogic proofs have no force to convince.

Nevertheless, three such proofs that Aristotle advances deserve our attention; let us take a closer look at them.

a) The first proof, which repeats itself several times, asserts:

> *Met. Γ* 4, 1007 b 19-21: *εἰ ἀληθεῖς αἱ ἀντιφάσεις ἅμα κατὰ τοῦ αὐτοῦ πᾶσαι, δῆλον ὅτι ἅπαντα ἔσται ἕν. ἔσται γὰρ τὸ αὐτὸ καὶ τριήρης καὶ τεῖχος καὶ ἄνθρωπος.*
>
> If all contradictory statements about the same object are simultaneously true, then of course all is one. Then, the same will be ship and wall and man.[84]

Perplexing is the expression "all contradictory statements". Why *all*? Whoever doubts the principle of contradiction and, especially, whoever demands a proof for it does not have to assume that *all* contradictory statements are simultaneously true. The opponent of the principle of contradiction considers whether at least *one* case can be found in which even one *pair* of contradictory statements is true because this single case already would be sufficient to bring down this principle. In response, Aristotle shows him that anybody who was to assume that all contradictory statements were simultaneously true, would arrive at a nonsensical conclusion. That may be so, but conducting a proof in such a manner is similar to fighting windmills.

Aristotle's consideration in this passage is peculiar in its weakness. For example, we read there: If all were to be one, then in truth nothing exists.[85] Where does such a conclusion come from? If it is true that x is man and simultaneously is not man, the x is *in truth* man and it is in truth not man. This, after all, follows from the

[84] Ross (Aristotle 1992): "If all contradictories are true of the same subject at the same time, evidently all things will be one. For the same thing will be a trireme, a wall, and a man."

[85] *Met. Γ* 4, 1007 b 26: *ὥστε μεθὲν ἀληθῶς ὑπάρχειν.* Ross (Aristotle 1992): "We thus get the doctrine of Anaxagoras, that all things are mixed together; so that nothing really exists."

definition of a true statement. Also, we furthermore read the following strange sentences:

> Met. *Γ* 4, 1007 b 32-35, 1008 a 1-2: ... *εἰ ἀληθὲς εἰπεῖν τὸν ἄνθπωπον ὅτι οὐκ ἄνθπωπος. δῆλον ὅτι καὶ οὐ τριήρης ... εἰ δ' αὕτη (scil. ἡ ἀπόφασις τῆς τριήρους ὑπάρχεὶ), καὶ ἡ κατάφασις.*
>
> If it is true that man is not man, then of course he is not a ship. And if the negation is true (that he is not a ship), then the affirmation is true also (that he is a ship).[86]

I do not understand how one can draw such conclusions from the non-recognition of the principle of contradiction. Does Aristotle mean that if someone does not recognize the principle, he is permitted to disregard all rules of inference?

b) The second apagogic proof is only a sketch. According to Aristotle, this conclusion follows from not accepting the principle of contradiction:

> Met. *Γ* 4, 1008 a 28-30: *πρὸς δὲ τούτῳ (scil. δῆλον) ὅτι πάντες ἂν ἀληθεύοιεν καὶ πάντες ἂν ψεύδοιντο, καὶ αὐτὸς αὐτὸν ὁμολογεῖ ψεύδεσθαι.*
>
> Furthermore, all would speak truth and untruth, and everyone would admit by himself that he is speaking untruth.[87]

This conclusion stays in connection with the definition of false statements, which is assumed by Aristotle:

> Met. *Γ* 7, 1011 b 26-27: *τὸ μὲν γὰρ λὲγειν τὸ ὂν μὴ εἶναι ἢ τὸ μὴ ὂν εἶναι, ψεῦδος.*

[86] Ross (Aristotle 1992): "If it is true to say of a man that he is not a man, evidently it is also true to say that he is either a trireme or not a trireme."

[87] Ross (Aristotle 1992): "Further, it follows that all would then be right and all would be in error, and our opponent himself confesses himself to be in error."

> To say that that, which is, is not, and that that, which is not, is, that is false.[88]

From this follows: If x is F, then the statement that x is not F is false; and if x is not F, then the statement that x is F is false. Thus, whoever would assert that x is F and simultaneously not F would consider both these statements as true and not true, and he himself would have to admit this if he merely accepts the above definition of false statements.

This conclusion will not persuade anyone that one may not fail to recognize the principle of contradiction because it itself (the conclusion) is an expression of its non-acceptance. In this context, one needs to note that in *Aristotle's formulation*, this conclusion does not at all follow from the non-acceptance of this sentence. Whoever does not accept the principle of contradiction is not immediately forced to attribute contradictory properties to *all* objects and to consider *every* statement as simultaneously true and false, which is what Aristotle appears to assume. Here, he repeats the mistake that we already pointed out in the first apagogic proof.

c) The third apagogic proof is connected to the practical behavior of man. Aristotle says:

> Met. *Γ* 4, 1008 b 12-19: *ὅθεν καὶ μάλιστα φανερόν ἐστιν ὅτι οὐδεὶς οὕτω διάκειται οὔτε τῶν ἄλλων οὔτε τῶν λεγόντων τὸν λόγον τοῦτον. διὰ τί γὰρ βαδίζει Μέγαραδε ἀλλ' οὐχ ἡσυχάζει οἰόμενος βαδίζειν; οὐδ' εὐθέως ἕωθεν πορεύεται εἰς φρέαρ ἢ εἰς φράγγα, ἐὰν τύχῃ, ἀλλὰ φαίνεται εὐλαβούμενος, ὡς οὐκ ὁμοίως οἰόμενος μὴ ἀγαθὸν εἶναι τὸ ἐμπεσεῖν καὶ ἀγαθόν; δῆλον ἄρα ὅτι τὸ μὲν βὲλτιον ὑπολαμβάνει τὸ δ' οὐ βέλτιον.*

> From this it shows itself most clearly that no one thinks in this manner, neither those who talk this way nor anyone else. After all, why does one, who talks this way, go to Megara instead of staying at home convinced that he is going? Why doesn't he throw

[88] Ross (Aristotle 1992): "To say of what is that it is not, or of what is not that it is, is false."

> himself directly down a well or abyss on some beautiful morning, if it were to happen that way, but instead apparently does take care so that falling in is not in the same way good and not good? Clearly, he considers one to be better and the other to be worse.[89]

This proof, which undoubtedly would find the highest recognition among the adherents of pragmatism, which is currently so fashionable, is no stronger than the previous ones. In the first place, Aristotle seems to assume that whoever does not accept the principle of contradiction is unable to act. But people do act, even those who deny the principle, who accordingly prefer one mode of behavior to another but in doing so do not hold that one and the same mode of behavior is good and not good.

In my opinion, there is no connection at all between acting and recognizing, or not recognizing, the principle of contradiction. Actions quite often come about mechanically, under the influence of some external circumstances which cause movement as reaction. But *conscious* action, too, which is based on a willed decision, can arise in the case of a non-acceptance of the principle of contradiction. I can believe that motion contains a contradiction and that I, by walking to Megara, simultaneously do not walk: furthermore, I can believe that falling into a well is simultaneously something good and not good. Despite all that, I decide to engage in that contradictory action of motion, and walking I follow a path around the well so as not to fall into it because the *not-falling-into-the-well* is also something that is simultaneously good and not good. After all, everything is supposed to contain a contradiction, according to the assumption: thus I am allowed to prefer the second instead of the first possibility. A suicidal person would prefer the first one. Secondly, Aristotle appears to assume that whoever does not accept the principle of contradiction has to consider affirming and denying as *one and the same*. In this way someone might hold that, as

[89] Ross (Aristotle 1992): "Thus, then, it is in the highest degree evident that neither any one of those who maintain this view nor any one else is really in this position. For why does a man walk to Megara and not stay at home thinking he ought to walk? Why does he not walk early some morning into a well or over a precipice, if one happens to be in his way? Why do we observe him guarding against this, evidently not thinking that falling in is alike good and not good? Evidently he judges one thing to be better and another worse."

often as he walks, he does not walk—but from this it does not follow that walking would be the same as not walking, that it would not make any difference to go to Megara or to stay at home.

However, the main mistake of this proof, as of the two previous ones, is a *μετάβασις ἄλλο γένος*,[90] that is, an *ignoratio elenchi.* Aristotle attempts to show that someone who would accept a contradiction everywhere would have to arrive at conclusions that would make speaking and acting impossible. But that is not the point at all! One cannot force the assertion that *everything* is contradictory on anyone who doubts the principle of contradiction or demands a proof of it. In doing so, one merely postpones the disputed problem and the arguments lose their force to convince.

Accordingly, if one leaves out the formal mistake that is found in each of the apagogic proofs of the principle of contradiction, none of the presented three arguments prevails against a critique. And because Aristotle did not offer any other proof of the principle of contradiction besides the elenctic and apagogic arguments, it follows that *he was unable, despite the attempts, to prove this principle.*

[90] Translator's note: *μετάβασις ἄλλο γένος*—transition to another genus

Chapter XIII

Ignoratio Elenchi in Aristotle's Proofs

The fallacy of postponing solutions to problems in the Aristotelian proofs of the principle of contradiction (such a mistake is called *ignoratio elenchi*) is so odd, it deserves a special explanation. The original intention of Aristotle was to prove this sentence, that *no* object can simultaneously contain and not contain one and the same property. At the beginning of the fourth part of book *Γ* of the *Metaphysics*, where he presents his proofs, the Stagirite clearly says:

> *Met. Γ* 1006 a 3-4: *ἡμεῖς δὲ νῦν εἰλήφαμεν ὡς ἀδυνάτου ὄντος ἅμα εἶναι καὶ μὴ εἶναι ...*
>
> With this, we have accepted that it is impossible that something simultaneously is and is not.[91]

Further, he adds:

> *Met. Γ* 1006 a 11-13: *ἔστι δ' ἀποδεῖξαι ἐλεγκτικῶς καὶ περὶ τούτου ὅτι ἀδύνατον, ἐὰν μόνον τι λέγῃ ὁ ἀμφισβητῶν.*
>
> One can show elenctically that it is impossible not to accept this principle, too, as soon as the opponent only says something at all.[92]

In fact, the first two elenctic proofs, even though insufficient, display a tendency to prove the principle in its entire breadth. To wit, the reasoning ends with the words:

[91] Ross (Aristotle 1992): "But we have now posited that it is impossible for anything at the same time to be and not to be."

[92] Ross (Aristotle 1992): "We can, however, demonstrate negatively even that this view is impossible, if our opponent will only say something."

> Met. Γ 4, 1007 b 17-18: *εἰ δὲ τοῦτο, δέδεκται ὅτι ἀδύνατον ἅμα κατηγορεῖσθαι τὰς ἀντιφάσεις*
>
> If the matter is so, then proof has been produced that contradictory statements cannot be simultaneously accepted.[93]

However, the deeper we immerse ourselves in considerations of the mentioned passage, the more this initial goal of the investigation is pushed back and, in the end, the Aristotelian proofs strive towards the justification of the thesis that *not all objects contain a contradiction*. This is a thesis that is not only completely different from the principle of contradiction but that in fact stands in contradiction to it if one considers that it contains the acknowledgment of the existence of contradictory objects. Before showing in which way Aristotle could come to such a strange and unexpected thought, let us first examine the traces of the emergence of this thought.

Already at the onset of the elenctic method of proof we encounter a short, inserted sentence to which Aristotle does not appear to pay any greater attention:

> Met. Γ 4, 1006 a 29-31: *πρῶτον μὲν οὖν δῆλον ὡς τοῦτό γ' αὐτὸ ἀληθές, ὅτι σημαίνει τὸ ὄνομα τὸ εἶναι ἢ μὴ εἶναι τοδί' ὥστ' οὐκ ἂν πᾶν οὕτως καὶ οὐχ οὕτως ἔχοι. ἔτι εἰ τὸ ἄνθρωπος σημαίνει ἕν κτλ.*
>
> To begin with, at least this is obviously true, that the words 'to be' and 'not to be' have a definite signification; thus, not everything would be so and not so. Further, if the word 'man' signifies some one thing ...[94]

For a moment, thus, the conclusion already shows itself here, namely, that not everything is so and not so, that is, not all objects

[93] Ross (Aristotle 1992): "And it has been shown that, if this is so, contradictories cannot be predicated at the same time."

[94] Ross (Aristotle 1992): "First then this at least is obviously true, that the word 'be' or 'not be' has a definite meaning, so that not everything will be so and not so. Again, if 'man' has one meaning ..."

contain a contradiction. Apparently this conclusion satisfies Aristotle and it does not engage him any further because he immediately moves on to the second argument, which is confirmed by the sentence following the passage. However, one must admit that this thought is not yet in disagreement with the principle of contradiction; rather, it could count as a first step towards a justification of the principle. After all, if one shows for individual cases that *at least* some objects are not contradictory, then the path is cleared for a universal statement that *no* object contains a contradiction.

This thought, innocent so far, takes on quite a different shape in the passages dedicated to the apagogic proofs. There we read:

> Met. *Γ* 4, 1008 a 8-12: *ἔτι ἤτοι περὶ ἅπαντα οὕτως ἔχει, καὶ λευκὸν καὶ οὐ λευκὸν καὶ ὂν καὶ οὐκ ὄν. καὶ περὶ τὰς ἄλλας φάσεις καὶ ἀποφάσεις ὁμοιοτρόπως, ἢ οὔ. ἀλλὰ περὶ μέν τινας, περὶ τινας δ' οὔ. καὶ εἰ μὲν μὴ περὶ πάσας, αὗται ἂν εἶεν ὁμολογούμεναι. εἰ δὲ περὶ πάσας κτλ.*
>
> Further, either it is the case that all objects behave this way, that is, they are contradictory and (everything) is white and not white, and being and not being, and the same applies to every other affirmation and denial, or they do not, and some behave this way but the others do not. If, however, not all are (contradictory), then these exceptions should be accepted. But if all are, then …[95] (and so forth).[96]

I have again presented the passage of the next sentence to show that Aristotle has already closed the preceding thought. This thought, then, is not that easy to bring into agreement with the principle of contradiction. I understand it the following way: "Either everything is contradictory or not everything is. Whoever asserts

[95] Ross (Aristotle 1992): "Again, either the theory is true in all cases, and a thing is both white and not-white, and being and not-being, and all other contradictories are similarly compatible, or the theory is true of some statements and not of others. And if not of all, the exceptions will be agreed upon; but if of all …"

[96] I translate the expressions *περὶ τινας* and *περὶ πάσας,* which refer to *φάσεις,* as if they sound like *περὶ τινα* and *περὶ παντα* (that is, 'object' and not 'sentences'). The parallel expression *περὶ ἅπαντα* at the beginning of the citation justifies me to do so. Aristotle's thought, which has not always been expressed clearly, comes out more distinctly in such an interpretation.

that not everything is contradictory must assume the existence of non-contradictory objects besides the existence of contradictory objects." And that would be all. Would this assessment of the facts, i.e., that *not all* but some objects do not contain a contradiction, be sufficient for Aristotle? That he does think this way and not differently seems to follow from the conclusion of this citation:

> Met. *Γ* 4, 1008 a 12-16: *εἰ δὲ περὶ πάσας, πάλιν ἤτοι καθ' ὅσων τὸ φῆσαι καὶ ἀποφῆσαι καὶ καθ' ὅσων ἀποφῆσαι καὶ φῆσαι, ἢ κατὰ μὲν ὧν φῆσαι καὶ ἀποφῆσαι, καθ' ὅσων δὲ ἀποφῆσαι οὐ πάντων φῆσαι. καὶ εἰ μὲν οὕτως, εἴη ἄν τι παγίως οὐκ ὄν, καὶ αὕτη βεβαία δόξα.*
>
> If, however, all (objects behave this way), then one can in turn deny of them what one affirms, and affirm what one denies, or one can nevertheless deny of everything what one affirms, but one cannot affirm of everything what one denies. And if so, then it would be true that there is not-being and this conviction would be certain [Appendix II, 264, 17].[97]

I understand this sentence the following way: If objects exist about which one cannot assert what one denies, then an object would be possible that would contain only negations. This would most certainly be a non-existing object, but it would not contain a contradiction. Contradictions only arise if *affirmation* and *denial* were to take place simultaneously. And once again, it seems as if this *one*, non-existing but contradiction free object would be sufficient for Aristotle, whereas all other objects may contain contradictions.

Here the fallacy of postponing solutions to problems comes into clear view. The sentence that at least some objects are not contradictory agrees with the principle of contradiction; but the assertion that though non-contradictory object do exist, there are *only* a

[97] Ross (Aristotle 1992): "But if of all, again either the negation will be true wherever the assertion is, and the assertion true wherever the negation is, or the negation will be true where the assertion is, but the assertion not always true where the negation is. And in the latter case there will be something which fixedly *is not,* and this will be an indisputable belief."

few of them (while others may even be contradictory) is the expression of a thesis that in fact stands in contradiction to the principle of contradiction.

This almost improbable thought of Aristotle shows itself most clearly at the closing of the proof of the principle of contradiction. We read:

> Met. *Γ* 4, 1008 b 31 – 1009 a 5: *ἐτι εἰ ὅτι μάλιστα πάντα οὕτως ἔχει καὶ οὐχ οὕτως, ἀλλὰ τό γε μᾶλλον καὶ ἧττον ἔνεστιν ἐν τῇ φύσει τῶν ὄντων' οὐ γὰρ ἂν ὁμοίς φήσαιμεν εἶναι τὰ δύο ἄρτια καὶ τὰ τρία, οὐδ' ὁμοίως διέψευσται ὁ τὰ τέτταρα πέντε οἰόμενος καὶ ὁ χίλια. εἰ οὖν μὴ ὁμοίως, δῆλον ὅτι ἅτερος ἧττον, ὥστε μᾶλλον ἀληθεύει εἰ οὖν τὸ μᾶλλον ἐγγύτερον, εἴη γ' ἄν τι ἀληθὲς οὗ ἐγγύτερον τὸ μᾶλλον ἀληθές. κἂν εἰ μὴ ἔστιν, ἀλλ' ἤδη γέ τι ἐστὶ βεβαιότερον καὶ ἀληθινώτερον. καὶ τοῦ λόγου ἀπηλλαγμένοι ἂν εἴημεν τοῦ ἀκράτου καὶ κωλύοντός τι τῇ διανοίᾳ ὁρίσαι.*
>
> And further, let us even assume that everything would behave so and not so, then at least a "more" and a "less" is contained in the nature of things. Because we would not call the numbers two and three even in the same way, and someone who takes four to be five and someone who takes four to be a thousand do not err to the same extent. But if they do not err to the same extent, then one of course errs less and thus says something that is truer. But if that, which is truer, approaches the truth more closely, then there would be a (not-relative) truth, which is approached more closely precisely by that which is truer. And even if indeed there were no such truth, then there would be at least something (relatively) certain and true, and we would at last be rid of this crazy thought that does

> not allow us to rationally determine anything [cf. Appendix II, 264, 18].[98]

In reading these words, one gains the impression that Aristotle, in a desperate effort of thought, is searching for Archimedes' *δός μοι ποῦ στῶ!*[99] If only one could find truth, even *a single one*, secure, unspoiled by any mistakes, and free of contradiction! Or, at least, if one could win the certainty that there are some probable statements, statements that are approaching the truth! This single certainty would have restored his faith in the capacity of rational thinking and liberated him from these waves of contradictions that appear to engulf him!

The deepest logical problems sometimes give rise to unusual moods. The light of the most evident, highest and untouchable truth shines for a moment. We fly towards this light to view its full sheen. Too late! The closer, the darker; we lose direction, go astray on complicated ways of thought and slowly doubt arises: Was there no light? Is all just appearance? This bothersome thought returns again and again and tortures us without end. Fear overwhelms us in this mysterious, dark isolation. We would like to have at least a *spark* from the flame that rose just a short while ago to brighten up this darkness and to get rid of the nightmare, which mixed up our thoughts and took away our understanding.

I find traces of such a mood in Aristotle. He almost runs out of breath when he exclaims at the end: 1009 a 3-5 *καὶ τοῦ λόγου ἀπηλλαγμένοι ἂν εἴημεν τοῦ ἀκράτου καὶ κωλύοντός τι τῇ διανοίᾳ ὁρίσαι!* ("And finally we are rid of this crazy thought that did not allow us to rationally determine anything"). How different the end is from the beginning! Proud self-assuredness and scornful disdain for the opponent in one place; hopeless exertion to save at

[98] Ross (Aristotle 1992): "Again, however much all things may be so and not so, still there is a more and a less in the nature of things; for we should not say that two and three are equally even, nor is he who thinks four things are five equally wrong with him who thinks they are a thousand. If then they are not equally wrong, obviously one is less wrong and therefore more right. If then that which has more of any quality is nearer to it, there must be some truth to which the more true is nearer. And even if there is not, still there is already something more certain and true, and we shall have got rid of the unqualified doctrine which would prevent us from determining anything in our thought."

[99] Pappus of Alexandria reports Archimedes to have said: *δός μοι ποῦ στῶ καὶ τὰν γᾶν κινάσω*— give me a place to stand and I will move the earth."

least some remnants in the other. It seemed as if the Stagirite, filled with trust in his own strength and certain of victory, entered head-on into a fight. Like arrows from a quiver, he takes out one proof after the other; but he does not notice that the arrows have no effect. He has exhausted the arguments and none of them has demonstrated the principle that was so dear to him. So, he defends with what is left of his strength and faith the last position: that of only *one* contradictory free being and only *one* contradiction free truth.

Or perhaps it has been different? Perhaps his pride and self-assuredness were just pretended? Sometimes one wants to assume that Aristotle, sensing the practical and ethical importance of the principle of contradiction with his acute and deep understanding, *deliberately* formulated it as an untouchable dogma to replace the lack of factual arguments with his *sic volo sic iubeo.*[100] But in the depth of his soul, he himself was not sure about this matter. He hid himself behind this thought; the debate, however, made him grow passionate. And in this way, he let slip a moan of despair against his will.

It is difficult today to conduct the analysis of a psychic event that took place centuries ago. One thing, at any rate, appears to be certain: it would be erroneous to claim that Aristotle, by delaying the critical point in the proofs of the principle of contradiction, only wanted to make as wide-ranging concessions as possible to the opponent of the principle. It will be shown soon that he had in fact enough reasons to doubt the universal significance of the principle of contradiction, but apparently did not have enough courage to admit this outright.

[100] Translator's note. Łukasiewicz' reference is to a (slight) misquotation of the Roman poet Juvenal by Martin Luther (1483-1546), who wrote in response to the charge that he made an error in his translation of Paul's letter to the Romans: *Sic volo, sic jubeo. Sit pro ratione voluntas*—I want this, I order this. Let my will stand for a reason.

Chapter XIV

Characteristics of Aristotle's Proofs

In the discussion of the Aristotelian proofs of the principle of contradiction, it needs to be kept in mind that they have a primarily *polemical* character. The second elenctic proof, which is based on the concept of substance, is directed, as Maier correctly suspects,[101] against the Megarians who did not accept the difference between substance and accident. Also the third apagogic proof is apparently directed against the Eristics from Megara, which seems to be indicated only by the choice of the example "to go to Megara".[102] But Aristotle undoubtedly also fights for the principle of contradiction against the school of Antisthenes, which is indicated by the word *ἀπαιδευσία* that both Plato and Aristotle always use in connection with Antisthenes.[103] Aristotle treats all of these Eristics with anger and disdain, he calls their account crazy (*ἄκρατος λόγος*) and says about the authors of this account that they propagate it only for the sake of argument, *λόγου χάριν λέγουσιν*.

Aristotle sees more formidable opponents of the principle of contradiction in the followers of the sensualist epistemology of Protagoras and related currents which he deals with in Chapters V and VI of *Book Γ* of the *Metaphysics*. According to this theory, all of our knowledge rests on sense perception. But numerous contradictions are contained in perception itself and in the perceived phenomena. What one person takes to be sweet appears bitter to another, and even one and the same phenomenon presents itself differently to one and the same person, depending on the circumstances in which the perception takes place. Because of this, different and even contradictory statements about one and the same

[101] Cf. *Die Syllogistik des Aristoteles*, ibid Vol.2, Part 2, p.7, n.1.

[102] Ibid, p.8, n.1.

[103] Ibid, p.11, n.3; and p.15, n.2

thing may exist and all of these statements are true, because they are based on sense perception. Further, the phenomena perceived by the senses do change continuously; as Heraclitus put it, they flow—thus, in reality they do not exist but in each moment they arise and dissolve at the same time. But if on the basis of one and the same phenomenon contradictory phenomena arise, then some kind of opposite, and therefore also contradictory, germs must be in them. In this way, the entire sensible world is full of contradictions.

Aristotle takes a peculiar position with respect to this theory. He rejects as mistaken the core assumption that human knowledge is exclusively based on sense experience but nevertheless appears to accept those consequences of the theory, which are most dangerous for the principle of contradiction. I put together the following passages:

> *Met. Γ* 5, 1009 a 22-36: *ἐλήλυθε δὲ τοῖς διαποροῦσιν αὕτη ἡ δόξα ἐκ τῶν αἰσθητῶν, ἡ μὲν τοῦ ἅμα τὰς ἀντιφάσεις καὶ τἀναντία ὑπάρχειν ὁρῶσιν ἐκ ταὐτοῦ γιγνόμενα τἀναντία. εἰ οὖν μὴ ἐνδέχεται γίγνεσθαι τὸ μὴ ὄν, προϋπῆρχεν ὁμοίως τὸ πρᾶγμα ἄμφω ὄν, ὥσπερ καὶ Ἀναξαγόρας μεμῖχθαι πᾶν ἐν παντί φησι καὶ Δημόκριτος· καὶ γὰρ οὗτος τὸ κενὸν καὶ τὸ πλῆρες ὁμοίως καθ᾽ ὁτιοῦν ὑπάρχειν μέρος, καίτοι τὸ μὲν ὄν τούτων εἶναι τὸ δὲ μὴ ὄν. πρὸς μὲν οὖν τοὺς ἐκ τούτων ὑπολαμβάνοντας ἐροῦμεν ὅτι τρόπον μέν τινα ὀρθῶς λέγουσι τρόπον δέ τινα ἀγνοοῦσιν· τὸ γὰρ ὂν λέγεται διχῶς, ὥστ᾽ ἔστιν ὃν τρόπον ἐνδέχεται γίγνεσθαί τι ἐκ τοῦ μὴ ὄντος, ἔστι δ᾽ ὃν οὔ, καὶ ἅμα τὸ αὐτὸ εἶναι καὶ ὂν καὶ μὴ ὄν, ἀλλ᾽ οὐ κατὰ ταὐτὸ ὄν· δυνάμει μὲν γὰρ ἐνδέχεται ἅμα ταὐτὸ εἶναι τὰ ἐναντία, ἐντελεχείᾳ δ᾽ οὔ.*
>
> Those who perceive true difficulties [and who do not negate the principle of contradiction merely for the purpose of debate] have reached this position, i.e., the position that contradictory and opposite properties can exist simultaneously; they did see that contradic-

> tions arise based on one and the same thing. If, however, that, which does not exist, cannot come to be, then the given thing [based on which the contradictions were to arise] would before have to be one as well as the other. And in this way Anaxagoras says that all is mixed with all, and Democritus, who assumes that in every part what is empty is included as well as what is full, even though the one is being and the other is not-being, expresses himself in a similar manner. We will answer those who have reached this position in this fashion that they are right in some ways, but that in other ways, they show ignorance of the matter. The word "being" has two senses so that in the first sense something can come to be out of not-being, but precisely not so in the second sense, and one and the same can be and simultaneously not be, but not regarding the same kind of being. Potentially (*in potentia*), one and the same can simultaneously have opposite properties, but not in actuality (*in actu*) [cf. Appendix II, 265, 19].[104]

The last sentence of this passage is of utmost importance to our problem: it contains in the clearest possible words the limitation of the principle of contradiction. According to Aristotle, *potential being, τὰ δυνάμει ὄντα*, does not fall under this principle because it may contain simultaneously opposite and, therefore, also contradictory properties. *The principle of contradiction applies only to actual being, τὰ ἐντελεχείᾳ ὄντα.* But what constitutes the potential being that does not fall under the principle of contradiction? The answer to this question we find at the following passage:

[104] Ross (Aristotle 1992): "Those who really feel the difficulties have been led to this opinion by observation of the sensible world. They think that contradictions or contraries are true at the same time, because they see contraries coming into existence out of the same thing. If, then, that which is not cannot come to be, the thing must have existed before as both contraries alike, as Anaxagoras says all is mixed in all, and Democritus too; for *he* says the void and the full exist alike in every part, and yet one of these is being, and the other non-being. To those, then, whose belief rests on these grounds, we shall say that in a sense they speak rightly and in a sense they err. For 'that which is' has two meanings, so that in some sense a thing can come to be out of that which is not, while in some sense it cannot, and the same thing can at the same time be and not be—but not in the same respect. For the same thing can be potentially at the same time two contraries, but it cannot actually."

> *Met. Γ* 5, 1010 a 1-5: *αἴτιον δὲ τῆς δόξης τούτοις ὅτι περὶ τῶν ὄντων μὲν τὴν ἀλήθειαν ἐσκόπουν,τὰ δ' ὄντα ὑπέλαβον εἶναι τὰ αἰσθητὰ μόνον· ἐν δὲ τούτοις πολλὴ ἡ τοῦ ἀορίστου φύσις ἐνυπάρχει καὶ ἡ τοῦ ὄντος οὕτως ὥσπερ εἴπομεν· διὸ εἰκότως μὲν λέγουσιν, οὐκ ἀληθῆ δὲ λέγουσιν.*
>
> The cause for such a position [i.e., the non-acceptance of the principle of contradiction] lies in that they have been searching for the truth of being but considered being as merely that which can be perceived by the senses. The objects of perception, however, are predominantly of an indeterminate nature and belong to that being about which we talked earlier. Because of this, they speak convincingly, but they do not speak the [whole] truth [cf. Appendix II, 265, 20].[105]

From this it would follow, that precisely *the objects of perception, which means, appearances, would be potential being*. And even though Aristotle did not muster the courage to express this clearly and decisively, and was satisfied with the diplomatic reference to the preceding passage, the word *ἀόριστον*, "indeterminate", does not leave any room for doubt as to what mode of being these objects should be attributed to. Already before this, the Stagirite had noted:

> Met. *Γ* 5, 1007 b 28-29: *τὸ γὰρ δυνάμει ὂν καὶ μὴ ἐντελεχείᾳ τὸ ἀόριστόν ἐστιν.*
>
> Because that which is potentially, and not actually, is indeterminate being.[106]

Thus, we arrive at the following conclusion: *The objects of perception, because they are potential being, can simultaneously contain opposite properties and, therefore, also contradictory ones.* The sensible world, continuously changing and bearing the

[105] Ross (Aristotle 1992): "But the reason for this opinion is that while these thinkers were inquiring into the truth of that which is, they thought that which is was identical with the sensible world; in this, however, there is largely present the nature of the indeterminate of that which exists in the peculiar sense which we have explained; and, therefore, while they speak plausibly, they do not say what is true."

[106] Ross (Aristotle 1992): "For that which exists potentially and not actually is the indeterminate."

germs of contradictory phenomena within itself, would not be subject to the principle of contradiction. Whoever assumes, as for example the sensualists do, that only that exists which is perceptible with the senses, may rightfully not accept this principle, and he does not need to accept contradiction free being.

Now it is easy to understand why Aristotle delays the original point of view in his proofs and attempts with the entire effort of his thought to prove the thesis that there must also be an absolute and contradiction-free truth apart from contradictory things. In the domain of the sensuous world, he might lose the fight; but in truth this world does not exist, and the only true, eternal, unchanging and contradiction-free being is the *essence* of things and the *substance* that *rests* on the foundation of every concrete object. Substance, however, we do not perceive with the senses, but we cognize it with the understanding. Thus, the manner of demonstration of the sensualists is convincing insofar as it concerns the sensuous world; but it does not constitute the *entire* truth because, aside from phenomena and matter, there further are contradiction-free substance and form, which are accessible exclusively by concept.

Aristotle expresses this thought a number of times while confronting the sensualists. So, for example, he ends the first of the cited passages with the words:

> Met. *Γ* 5, 1009 a 36-38: *ἔτι δ' ἀξιώσομεν αὐτοὺς ὑπολαμβάνειν καὶ ἄλλην τινὰ οὐσίαν εἶναι τῶν ὄντων ᾗ οὔτε κίνησις ὑπάρχει οὔτε φθορὰ οὔτε γένεσις τὸ παράπαν.*
>
> And beyond this, we ask that they also recognize the existence of another substance that does not underlie any change and that as a whole neither perishes nor comes about.[107]

About the second of the cited passages, Aristotle says instead:

> Met. *Γ* 5, 1010 a 32-35: *ἔτι δὲ δῆλον ὅτι καὶ πρὸς τούτους ταὐτὰ τοῖς πάλαι λεχθεῖσιν ἐροῦμεν· ὅτι*

[107] Ross (Aristotle 1992): "And again we shall ask them to believe that among existing things there is another kind of substance to which neither movement nor destruction nor generation at all belongs."

> *γὰρ ἔστιν ἀκίνητός τις φύσις δεικτέον αὐτοῖς καὶ πειστέον αὐτούς.*
>
> And furthermore, we shall of course tell those the same that we have said before, namely, that there is an unchanging nature; one ought to show them this, and they should believe this.[108]

It is only in this light, that the second elenctic argument, which I take to be the most important one, gains its actual significance. In vain does Aristotle remark with emphasis in the presentation of this argument that one needs to assume something *definite*, *τὶ ὡρισμένον*, something that would be one according to its essence, if the possibility of understanding and thinking is to be given. Sense objects, "which are most of the time of an indeterminate nature", *ἐν οἷς πολλὴ ἡ τοῦ ἀορίστου φύσις ἐνυπάρχει*, could not be the *ὡρισμένον* but rather the substantial being that constitutes the essence of things. The original paradigm of this being is pure form, which is completely free of contradictory matter, and this form is a divine being.[109] This being, i.e., the substantial forms, we grasp with *concepts*, whereby the signs of these concepts are the *words* of a *language* that have been unequivocally determined with the aid of *definitions. This unequivocal meaning of words, which is based on the existence of homogenous substantial being, is the ultimate foundation of the principle of contradiction, which consequently ought to be recognized as the highest law of true conceptual thought and true essential being.*

Everything appears to be in favor of the view that *Aristotle limited the significance of the principle of contradiction to substantial being*. Who knows whether the Stagirite was not thinking exactly about this delimitation when, after the famous formulation of the principle: *τὸ γὰρ αὐτὸ ἅμα ὑπάρχειν τε καὶ μὴ ὑπάρχειν ἀδύνατον τῷ αὐτῷ καὶ κατὰ τὸ αὐτό* (one and the same cannot at the same time and in the same respect belong to and not belong

[108] Ross (Aristotle 1992): "And again, obviously we shall make to them also the same reply that we made before; we must show them and persuade them that there is something whose nature is changeless."

[109] Because of this, Pater Gratry could expound the view that the existence of God refutes the—in his opinion—pantheist and atheist doctrine that negates the principle of contradiction. (*Logique*, Vol.1, p.317).

to one and the same thing)—he immediately added the following words:

> Met. *Γ* 4, 1005 b 20-22: *καὶ ὅσα ἄλλα προσδιορισαίμεθ' ἄν, ἔστω προσδιωρισμένα πρὸς τὰς λογικὰς δυσχερείας.*
>
> And whatever additional considerations we were to add, they should be added in order to avoid logical difficulties.[110]

What could these other considerations be, if this principle is not already formulated with the greatest of care, namely with the qualifications *ἅμα, κατὰ τὸ αὐτό,* etc., which unequivocally determine that what is dealt with is *one and the same property*, which *cannot simultaneously* and in *the same way* belong and not belong to *one and the same* object?

It needs to be noted that *the principle of contradiction is not only an ontological principle in the writings of Aristotle, but has an additional metaphysical significance.* Most likely, it is based on the metaphysical presupposition that contains the existence of substances, and it is as closely as possible connected to this presupposition. But it is precisely this presupposition that weakens its currency; metaphysical presuppositions never have the certainty of logical laws. Aristotle certainly was aware of this weak point in his account. Perhaps he grew doubtful whether some enduring substantial being does in fact exist behind the changeable, sensuous world? If not, could the Sensualists be right? But then the Eristics from Megara would not be that far from the truth and this entire, artful construction would plunge into an abyss. But that cannot be possible! Because then man could neither think nor speak nor act! And consequently, as final resort, Aristotle holds on, tense and tight, to his absolute truth, that is, to substantial being.

The investigations above show that Aristotle did not at all solve the problem of the principle of contradiction. We need a new and a better justification of this principle. This need becomes the more urgent as Aristotle used his principle of contradiction most of all in its application to substantial being and derived the validation of the truth of this principle in a way from the domain of the

[110] Ross (Aristotle 1992): "we must presuppose, in face of dialectical objections, any further qualifications which might be added."

supernatural world. After all, today we apply it without exception to all objects, and thus, also to the sensible world, and even to illusions. However, based on the almighty rule of empiricism, which today permeates all aspects of human knowledge, we are more inclined to dedicate more attention to the objects of *experience* rather than non-experiential being—like substances—because we consider substances, rightfully or not, merely as products of the human mind. Because of this, a renewed examination of the principle of contradiction as it has been received from Aristotle will be necessary for this reason as well.

Chapter XV

The Principle of Contradiction and the Syllogism

Not only are logical and ontological principles more secure, they also are more general than metaphysical principles; this is so because they concern the metaphysical modes of being, which make up the nature of the world, as well as the objects of experience and the constructions of the human mind, which in reality do not exist, as well as anything that is something and is not nothing. If the Aristotelian principle of contradiction were merely a metaphysical law, then the position that its logical and ontological significance is small, would *primae facie* not be improbable.

However, the Stagirite asserts that the principle of contradiction is the highest and most secure of all [principles]. It is a *final* principle not only because it does not need any proof, but also in this sense, in that it serves as the logical foundation for all other principles. We read:

> *Met. Γ* 3, 1005b 32-34: *διὸ πάντες οἱ ἀποδεικνύντες εἰς ταύτην ἀνάγουσιν ἐσχάτην δόξαν, φύσει γὰρ ἀρχὴ καὶ τῶν ἄλλων ἀξιωμάτων αὕτη πάντων.*
>
> Because of this, everybody who wants to prove something will lead his proof back to this final principle: because of the nature of the matter, this is the foundation of all other axioms.[111]

This sentence has not been formulated exactly, because we do not know whether Aristotle took the principle of contradiction for a *sufficient* or a *necessary* foundation of all other axioms.

[111] Ross (Aristotle 1992): "It is for this reason that all who are carrying out a demonstration refer it to this as an ultimate belief; for this is naturally the starting-point even for all the other axioms."

The difference between a sufficient and a necessary foundation, as it is commonly known, is the following: *If two statements A and B stand in a relation to each other where B follows from A, that is, where A is the antecedent of B, then the truth of statement A is a sufficient condition for the truth of statement B, and the truth of statement B is a necessary condition for the truth of statement A.* If the antecedent is true, so must be the consequent: thus, the truth of the antecedent is a *sufficient* condition for the truth of the consequent, but not a necessary one because the consequent may very well be true even if the antecedent is false. Secondly, if the consequent is false, the antecedent must be false as well: thus, the truth of the consequent is a *necessary* but not a sufficient condition for the truth of the antecedent, since the antecedent may be false despite the truth of the consequent.

I do not want to deepen the problem whether the principle of contradiction is a sufficient condition for all other principles, even though it is not hard to prove that an affirmative answer in regard to this problem would be decisively in error. All I want to demonstrate here is *that this principle—even according to Aristotle himself—is not a necessary condition for one of the most significant rules of inference, syllogistic reasoning.* In other words: syllogistic reasoning and syllogistic inferences would remain correct, even if the principle of contradiction as such were to contain errors.

We have learned recently that Aristotle did in fact assert this. Under the influence of the conviction that the principle of contradiction was the highest and final foundation of thought, this section in the *Analytics,* which the English author Isaac Husik[112] first brought to greater attention,[113] has not been understood sufficiently. This passage, which Waitz,[114] for example, did not understand at all, Maier had already explained in full accuracy prior to

[112] Translator's note: Isaac Husik (1876—1939), a Russian born, American historian of philosophy.

[113] Isaac Husik (1906), *Aristotle on the Law of Contradiction and the Basis of the syllogism*, Mind, Vol.15. In Husik we find, despite the appropriate leading idea, numerous inaccuracies; for example, the first two sentences of the section from the *An. Post.* cited above are translated with errors.

[114] Translator's note: Theodor Waitz (1821—1864), German philosopher, psychologist and anthropologist. Waitz advocated psychologism in philosophy and was a severe critic of Fichte, Schelling, and Hegel.

Husik. However, Maier was unable to appreciate the fundamental importance, which it has within the entire Aristotelian logic, so that his remarks in this regard, since they are made without corresponding emphasis, are lost among the many other details of his extensive work.[115]

> *An. Post.* I 11, 77a 10-22: *τὸ δὲ μὴ ἐνδέχεται ἅμα φάναι καὶ ἀποφάναι οὐδεμία λαμβάνει ἀπόδειξις, ἀλλ᾽ ἢ ἐὰν δέῃ δεῖξαι καὶ τὸ συμπὲρασμαι οὕτως. δείκνυται δὲ λαβοῦσι τὸ πρῶτον κατὰ τοῦ μέσον, ὅτι ἀληθές, ἀποφάναι δ᾽ οὐκ ἀληθὲς. τὸ δὲ μέσον οὐδεν διαφέρει εἶναι καὶ μὴ εἶναι λαβεῖν, ὡς δ᾽ αὕτως καὶ τὸ τρίτον. εἰ γὰρ ἐδόθη, καθ᾽ οὗ ἄνθρωπον ἀληθὲς εἴπειν, εἰ καὶ μὴ ἄνθρωπον ξῷον εἶναι, μὴ ξῷον δὲ μή· ἔσται γὰρ ἀληθὲς εἰπεῖν Καλλίαν, εἰ καὶ μὴ Καλλίαν, ὅμως ξῷον, μὴ ξῷον δ᾽ οὔ. αἴτιον δ᾽ ὅτι τὸ πρῶτον οὐ μόνον κατὰ τοῦ μέσον λέγεται ἀλλὰ καὶ κατ᾽ ἄλλου διὰ τὸ εἶναι ἐπὶ πλειόνων, ὥστ᾽ οὐδ᾽ εἰ τὸ μέσον καὶ αὐτό ἐστι καὶ μὴ αὐτό, πρὸς τὸ συμπὲρασμα οὐδὲν διαφέρει.*
>
> No proof (syllogism) presupposes that one cannot simultaneously affirm and deny, except that the conclusion would also have to affirm such a principle. However, this is demonstrated by assuming that the affirmation of the upper term is true with respect to the middle term, but the denial is false. But insofar as the middle term is concerned, and the lower term as well, the assumption that this term is or is not does not affect the conclusion. Let us assume that there is an object, which corresponding to the truth can be called man; if it is true that he is also not-man—should it only be true that man is a living being and not a not-living being—then this also will be true, namely that Callias, even if he were to be not-Callias, is nevertheless a living being but not a not-living being. The reason for this is that one can assert the upper

[115] *Die Syllogistik des Aristoteles*, Vol.2, ibid., p. 238 and 239, note 3.

> term not only with respect to the middle term, but also with respect to other objects because its scope is larger than that of the middle term so that even in the case in which the middle term is and is not, it does not influence the conclusion [Appendix II, 265, 21].[116]

I have attempted to translate this quite difficult passage both as faithfully to the text and as clearly as possible. Its interpretation is as follows: We designate the upper term, *τὸ πρῶτον*, with the letter *A* (living being), the middle term *τὸ μέσον*, with *B* (man), the lower term *τὸ τίιτον*, with *C* (Callias). Then we obtain the following syllogism:

B is *A* Man is a living being
C is *B* Callias is a man

C is *A* Callias is a living being

The principle of contradiction presupposes the syllogism only in the case in which the conclusion has to confirm clearly that *C* is *A* and not simultaneously non-*A*. With that, the premise listed above must assert that *B* is *A* and not simultaneously non-*A*. That is the meaning of the first two sentences of the passage cited.

The next two sentences confirm that a syllogism is possible even in the case in which *C* were to be simultaneously *B* or not-*B* or simultaneously *C* and not-*C*. In the case of this assumption, not only the conclusion '*C* is *A*' remains true, but furthermore the addition '*C* is not simultaneously *non-A*' can also be true, if only this addition is found in the upper premise. And, consequently, the following forms of syllogisms are correct:

[116] Barnes (Aristotle 1992): "That it is not possible to affirm and deny at the same time is assumed by no demonstration—unless the conclusion too is to be proved in this form. It is proved by assuming that the first term is true of the middle and that it is not true to deny it. It makes no difference if one assumes that the middle term is and is not; and the same holds of the third term too. For if it is granted that that of which it is true to say man, even if not-man is also true of it—but provided only that it is true to say that a man is an animal and not not an animal—for it will be true to say that Callias, even if not Callias, is nevertheless an animal and not not an animal. The explanation is that the first term is said not only of the middle but also of something else, because it holds of several cases; so that even if the middle both is it and is not it, that makes no difference with regard to the conclusion."

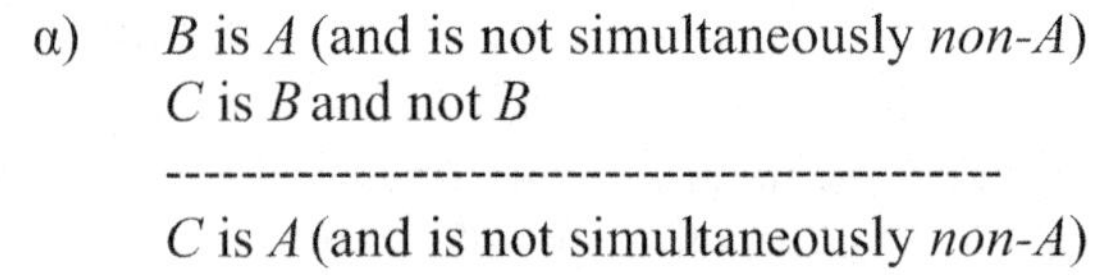

α) *B* is *A* (and is not simultaneously *non-A*)
C is *B* and not *B*

C is *A* (and is not simultaneously *non-A*)

β) *B* is *A* (and is not simultaneously *non-A*)
C, which is not *C*, is *B*

C is *A* (and is not simultaneously *non-A*)

Syllogism (α) is correct because *C* is *B*. In this case, *C* is not *B* not only does not harm the conclusion '*C* is *A*' but also does not affect the addition '*C* is not simultaneously *non-A*'. Term *A* has a greater scope than term *B* and correspondingly includes also those objects which are not *B*. Let us assume that, in the example given by Aristotle, Callias is simultaneously man as well as horse, but that means, not man. Since a horse is also a living being, in this special case term *A* also belongs to term *non-B*. Thus, the conclusion can be formulated that Callias is a living being but not a not-living being.

Syllogism (β) is correct because here, too, *C* is *B*. That in this case *C* is simultaneously not *C* does not harm the conclusion and it also does not need to affect the mentioned addition, because *B* has a greater scope than *C*. With this, Callias, who is not Callias but, for example, Socrates, does not stop being a man and he is accordingly a living being and not a not-living being.

This is the meaning of the passage cited from the *Analytic*. It is regrettable that Aristotle unnecessarily obscured his interesting deliberation with the "addition" to the conclusion and offered an explanation that, strictly considered, misses its mark. In general, it is true that the upper term *A* has a greater scope than the middle term *B*; thus, as a rule, *A* also includes some, but not all, *non-B*. And, because of this, it can happen that some not-*B*, which belongs to the term *C*, is not contained within the scope of *A*. If, in the imagined example, Callias were to be a man *B* and also a rock, thus, not-man, that is, *non-B*, then the term *A* "living being" does in this special case not include term *non-B,* and one cannot say in the conclusion that Callias is *living*, but not a *not-living* being. Because of this, I used in the interpretation the form of expression that the contradiction of the term *C* does no harm to the conclusion and does not *have to have* an effect on the addition; with that I want to note that it *can* have an effect on it.

This problem, of course, is of no consequence for the relation between the principle of contradiction and syllogistic reasoning. Important in this is Aristotle's admission that the conclusion "*C* is *A*", *despite the contradiction* that the lower premise contains, is dependent only on the correctness of the premises "*B* is *A*" and "*C* is *B*". The relation of *subsumption*, expressed in the premises by the word "is", belongs to *transitive* relations, i.e., it means that if between the classes of objects a relation *A* and *B* and *B* and *C* exists, then it also must exist between *A* and *C*. The meaning of the syllogism principle relies precisely on this: *quidquid de omnibus valet, valet etiam de quibusdam et de singulis*.[117] Thus, insofar as the premises of the syllogism are true, insofar the conclusion must be true as well. Then let us assume that any one of the premises of the syllogism contains a premise, for example "*C* is *B* and simultaneously not *B*". For a contradiction to arise, both statements must be true at the same time. And if the statement "*C* is *B*" and the other premise "*B* is *A*" are true, then the conclusion "*C* is *A*" must be true as well. The syllogism principle maintains its validity even though the principle of contradiction has ceased to be true. Thus, it has been shown that the principle of contradiction *is not a necessary foundation of syllogistic reasoning*.

This result is confirmed in its entire breadth by contemporary symbolic logic. Further, even based on only a superficial acquaintance of this logic, it is possible to convince oneself that there are numerous other rules and principles of demonstration, which do not depend on the principle of contradiction.[118] One could also demonstrate the same, though with lesser precision, without logical symbolism by using examples of conclusions from daily life. However, to give visibility to the great independence of thought from the principle of contradiction and to simultaneously take up the fight against this deeply rooted conception of the almighty significance of this principle more effectively, I permit myself to construct a few cases of inference, under the preliminary assumption that the principle of contradiction has become irrelevant.

[117] Translator's note: Whatever applies to all also applies to some and to each individual.

[118] Cf. Appendix, The principle of contradiction and Symbolic Logic, § 9.

Chapter XVI

Non-Aristotelian Logic

As far as I know, no one has yet created fictions in logic, even though they are a means of scientific research, which can clarify the *significance* of the laws, causes or peculiarities of the objects investigated. For example, by bracketing certain laws, which apply to a given domain of phenomena, and by trying to investigate what happens without them, we recognize most clearly to what extent the bracketed laws influence the course of events. So, let us for a time use a fiction in these logical investigations.

Imagine a society that lives in the same world as we do, but whose intellectual organization is different. Namely, let it be assumed, that the members of this society are taking every negated statement as true. Then, it would always and everywhere be true for them that the sun does not shine, that man is not mortal, that two times two is not four, and so forth, even if sunshine, mortality and concepts like two, four, multiplication and equality would mean the same for them as they do for us. It certainly is not easy to place oneself into this way of thinking; I nevertheless do think that despite all of this the following consideration facilitates a fair understanding of the intellectual disposition of these fictitious beings.

If the sun is shining, then it shines only insofar as it emits rays that reach our eyes; however, insofar as it rotates around its own axis or moves together with the entire planetary system towards some celestial constellation, it does *not* shine. Thus, the sun not only does not shine at night, but it also does not shine during the day, that is, it even does not shine when it does shine. After all, it is always true that the sun, apart from the property of shining, has a great number of *other* properties, and shining is not among them. The same inference can be performed in every other case. That man is not mortal is true also when he dies, because man dies only insofar as necrotic processes take place in his tissue, but he does not die insofar as he lies in bed or exerts pressure on the bed sheet with his body weight, and so forth. Thus, every negating statement is true. I explicitly reserve to myself not to list this inference as an argument against the principle of contradiction; I am not at all concerned whether this consideration is accurate or mistaken. Rather, I only want to facilitate in this way the relation of fiction.

The beings, for which the negating statements are always true, certainly would not care about the negation. They would consider each negating statement as something obvious that does not warrant any deliberation. Their language would probably have only *one* expression that would signify simultaneously all possible negations.

These beings would not recognize the principle of contradiction; this principle would be just as inconceivable to them as its rejection appears to be inconceivable to us. Everything that exists would be contradictory for them, insofar as negating would always be true. Only certain non-existent and unlikely objects, about which nothing positive could be asserted, would contain no contradictions.

But let us consider whether this society, which is composed of such beings, could rationally think, act and produce sciences. Let us take concrete examples into consideration:

a) A physician attending to a patient suffering from severe throat pain, diagnoses high fever, grayish-white plaque on the mucous membranes of the tonsils, a deep reddening of the neighboring mucous membranes, a swelling of the thyroid and all other symptoms of emerging diphtheria. At the same time, he knows that there is no fever, that the throat is not reddened, that the glands are not swollen and so forth; however, he does not pay any attention to these negations, which are always true. He only ascertains that which is and not that which is not. *These, as well as all other facts, he asserts based on sense experience: the principle of contradiction is completely useless for him.*

b) The physician treats the patient with a certain serum; he could convince himself in all previous cases that this medication, taken at the right time, removes the illness. These again were facts, which the physician ascertained based on experience and *condensed into one formula*: in all cases, so far, the serum treatment eliminated the illness. He nevertheless knows at the same time that the serum treatment does not eliminate the illness since the patients did not only regain health, but they lay in bed while doing so, enjoyed domestic care, remained in family relations with other persons; and insofar as someone lies in bed and is a brother or a son, he will not regain his health. The physician did not consider these facts; they were obvious. He merely ascertained that in the previous cases a continuous improvement of the patients took place under the effect of the serum. *However, it is not necessary to know the principle of contradiction in order to condense a series of individual facts, for example, A_1 is B, A_2 is B, ... , A_{10} is B, into one formula: all ten A's are B.* This is an abbreviated manner of expression that does not at all presuppose any factual logical rule.

c) The one-sidedness of the cases so far needs an explanation. The physician infers that a certain serum *always* cures diphtheria because it neutralizes the toxic substances that are the causes of the disease. That is, he assumed a universal statement: Every *A*, not just those previous ten, is *B*. By assuming such a universal rule, he could explain the regularity of the phenomena; they all were consequences of the same reason. Nevertheless, the physician knew that the serum does not help all the time and that it in fact never heals diphtheria; each medication only heals insofar as it takes effect in immediate contact with the organism, but it does not heal insofar as it is expensive or affordable, was bought in this pharmacy or that and so forth. However, the physician does not pay attention to these *negative* details; he only wanted to explain the positive phenomena. Because of this, he infers *inductively* by searching for a universal reason for the given statements from which they then would follow. He could infer this way even though he did not know the principle of contradiction. Inductive inferences consist of a search for the point of origin of the conclusion for the given certain statements, a search for another statement from which the given statements would follow. Because the statements "A_1 is *B*", "A_2 is *B*", ..., "A_{10} is *B*" and so forth, follow without doubt from the universal statement "Every *A* is *B*". *However, one does not need the principle of contradiction to find such a universal statement and to confirm that an entailment relation exists between it and the statements, and thus, to make an inductive inference.* This, by the way, shows itself already in that this entire inference does not contain a negating statement; but where there are no negating statements, the principle of contradiction cannot find application.

d) While keeping an eye on the general rule, which he had posited already earlier, the physician infers that in the present case as well the patient being treated with the serum will recover. Namely, if all the patients who are treated with the serum regain their health. Of course, at the same time this patient will not recover because everyone is healthy only insofar as he happens to possess this immeasurable treasure of health; on the other hand, he is not healthy insofar as he has just recently been born and will die soon. But this *negative* fact is self-explanatory; the physician wants to predict and justify the *positive* fact of the recovery. Because of this, he infers *deductively* by constructing a syllogism. But he can reason this way because syllogistic reasoning does not presuppose the principle of contradiction. All deductive inferences consist in that from those statements, that form the starting point of the inference, other statements are derived, which in this way follow from the given statements. *But to assert that, for example, the statement "A is C" follows from the statements "A is B" and "B is C", thus, to infer deductively, one does not need to know the principle of contradiction.* Here, too, we have exclusively positive statements and, thus, the principle of contradiction has no application here. The physician, supported by the conclusion indicated above, bravely applies the tried medication, and his hope for a good result will not be disappointed.

This example shows that beings that do not recognize the principle of contradiction, that ascertain matters of experiential fact, can reason inductively and deductively and can act effectively based on such conclusions. If, however, these thought processes are possible in *one* case, then they must be possible in *all* cases. If, by the way, the intellectual organization of our fictitious beings would not be different from the human one, then they would be able to develop the same sciences as the ones developed by man. From that society, a second Galileo would emerge who would calculate the paths of balls rolling along tilted chutes and who would postulate the laws of free falling objects based on the foundation of those facts; there would further be a second Newton, who would synthesize the discoveries of Galileo, Kepler and Huyghen into one unified account by determining the highest principles of mechanics. There would be a second Lavoisier, who would found the science of chemistry, a second Harvey, who would discover blood circulation. Gradually, sciences would emerge that range from the comparatively simplest mathematics to the most complicated sociology. These sciences ascertain certain experiential facts and then form their syntheses by making use of inductive or deductive inferences. In turn, these are methods of scientific investigation that would be known to the fictitious beings. But if this society were also to develop logic, and if a second Aristotle were to appear, then he would accept all the basic rules of thought that the author of the *Analytics* already has formulated, except for the principle of contradiction and those logical rules that depend on this principle. If one may call a system of logical laws, in which the principle of contradiction is not valid, non-Aristotelian logic, then this society would commit to *non-Aristotelian* logic.

* * *

The fiction of a non-Aristotelian logic appears to me as the final boundary that an opponent of the principle of contradiction can approach without leaving the path of strict logical reasoning and without resorting to the phrases that Hegel was so fond of using in his struggles. All the deliberations so far were an incessant struggle against the principle of contradiction. By following the footsteps of Aristotle, I have attempted to show those mistakes and shortcomings, which abound in his presentation of the matter. The tip of the charges that have been leveled against the Stagirite did at least reach the principle itself. Let us recall those charges: a) It has been shown that it is at the very least a *doubtful* matter whether the principle of contradiction is a *psychological* principle of thought. b) The principle of contradiction is not a *final* law but it demands proof. c) Aristotle has not provided proof because his arguments were insufficient. Thus, if no one else delivers a proof, the principle of contradiction remains an *unjustified* principle in which we have blind faith. d) This principle is not *universal* since apparently Aristotle himself restricted it to substantial modes of being. e) This principle is not a *necessary* law of thought because even Aristotle himself admits that it is possible to make inferences without having to apply this principle. f) There are cases in which this principle is certainly *false*, namely with respect to contradictory objects. Put briefly, it would follow from these charges that the principle of contradiction is *uncertain* in its psychological formulation, *unjustified* in its logical and ontological formulation, *superfluous* in many and *false* in some cases.

It is possible that not all of these charges are accurate and it even could be that all of them contain mistakes though I have so far been unable to detect any mistakes in them. But even if this were the case, I still believe that these deliberations will not lack in utility. It seems to me that whoever will work scientifically on the principle of contradiction in the future will not be able to simply assert verbally that this principle is true in itself, that only an insane person cannot believe in it and that it is useless to discuss it with someone who denies it—in accordance with the old scholastic maxim: *contra principia negantem non est disputandum*. In the future, one will have to engage with numerous arguments that do not permit such an facile, I would say *irresponsible*, treatment of such a serious scientific matter; one will have to go further and deeper. For any problem, however, an increase in critical depth can only be an advantage to science and the desire for truth.

Chapter XVII

Proof of the Principle of Contradiction

I have completed the primarily critical part of the investigations. The more the results turned out negative, the stronger the need grew to add a positive part. Despite all this, nobody seriously doubts the principle of contradiction; in addition, both in everyday life and in the sciences, this principle provides us with indisputable services. Because of this, one must demonstrate where this certainty stems from, wherein its primary significance lies, why we do believe in it so unconditionally, and most of all—one must *prove* this principle.

a) I want to point out in advance, that I consider it insufficient to refer to the factual or supposedly *immediate evidentness* of the principle as proof of the principle of contradiction. In the first place, because this principle is not evident to me; secondly, because I do not consider evidentness as a criterion of truth. If the word "evident" is supposed to mean anything other than "true", then it probably signifies a *psychic condition*, a *feeling* that is not further determined except that we have it when we believe in some statements. After all, the fact that some statement appears evident to somebody does not entail its truth.

We do know examples of false statements that were considered as evident. Descartes, who is to blame for having introduced the concept of evidentness to modern logic, considered his mistaken proof of God's existence as evident. He argued that if I find in myself the idea of an infinite being, i.e., the idea of God, and I, as a finite being, could not produce this idea by myself, then it is not I that is the cause of this idea but this really existing infinite being. This proof appeared to Descartes as evident, even though it is false. If evidentness can deceive us in *one* case, then it can deceive us just as well in others. It shows itself that there is no necessary connection between evidentness and truth.

The use of the concept of evidentness as a criterion of truth is a remnant of "Psychologism", which led philosophical logic astray. Psychologism is closely connected with subjectivism and skepticism. If evidentness is a criterion of truth, then every statement is true that appears evident to someone. And because it may happen that the same statement appears evident to one person, but not to another, the same statement will be true for one person, but for another person it does not need to be true and may even be false. Every truth then becomes something subjective and relative, and absolute and objective truth ceases to exist. If, however, someone says that a statement that is evident for one person must also be evident for all, then he asserts a conviction that does not correspond to the facts. Not to pursue these examples any further, I want to note again that the principle of non-contradiction, which appears evident to so many, is not evident to *me*. This is a definite fact at which brings discussion to an end. It is not my fault, if someone does not believe me. We see right away to what senseless consequences the criterion of evidentness may lead in every case: the truth or falsity of any given statement could depend on someone's *word of honor* or *oath*. Fortunately, evidentness is a criterion of truth *on paper* only, that is, in the psychological textbooks of logic and epistemology. In *actual* scientific research, no one will be satisfied with evidentness, but everyone demands and searches for *proof*.

b) Furthermore, it is not possible to prove the principle of contradiction by appealing to some *psychological necessity*, which is supposedly located within our intellectual organization and which forces us to acknowledge this principle. This necessity, if it were to exist, would reveal itself most of all in the form of the *psychological principle of non-contradiction*. It has already been seen above (V), that it is at the very least a rather doubtful matter, whether the principle of contradiction is a psychological law of thought; thus, the existence of a psychic *necessity*, which would push such a principle on us, correspondingly doubtful. And, it may be permissible for me to again appeal to a definite fact: in myself, I do not sense such a necessity.

But even if this necessity were to exist, the principle of contradiction does not have to be true. Where is the guarantee that the real external world follows the requirements of the inner organization of man? Kant skillfully circumvented this difficulty in that he made the world of appearances in a certain sense into a product of the human mind; accordingly, he could hold the position that our forms of intuition and categories of understanding are also effective in the external world. But Kant's Copernican thought is merely a hypothesis. If we were to assume, what Kant did not claim, that the principle of contradiction is a synthetic statement *a priori*, which results from our intellectual organization, then this principle in its application to the sensible world would be merely an assumption, because it would depend on a hypothesis which considers the world of appearances as a product of the human understanding.

In general, it should be noted that basing the truth of statements on a feeling of *evidentness* and *intellectual organization*, are two closely related ways of arguing. The difference consists mainly in that in the first case the purported basis of truth is provided by some psychic *act*, which consequently is constituted by a phenomenon that endures merely for a *preliminary* moment, in the second case, however, some psychic *disposition*, which we consider as a *permanent* property of the understanding. In my opinion, both ways of argumentation lead to subjectivism and skepticism.

c) If one wants to prove the principle of contradiction, then one needs to search for *objective* arguments, thus one needs to search out a proof such that the truth of the matter would follow from it by *itself*, and not—at best—the truth of a statement that we have to accept this principle. One can prove a statement either *a posteriori* by basing it on *experience*—such a proof never provides certainty—or *a priori*, by basing it on *definitions*. The principle of contradiction is generally considered an *a priori* statement, thus one must base it on a definition.

The appearance may arise that just as the definition of *true* statements forms the basis of the principle of identity (PI), the definition of *false* statements may form the basis of the principle of contradiction—if not by itself, then at least in connection with the definition of true statements. The definitions under consideration are the following:

(α) An affirmative statement is false if it attributes a property to an object that it does not contain; a negative statement is false, if it denies a property of an object that it contains.

Similarly, the reverse is valid:

(β) No object contains a property that a false statement ascribes to it; and every object contains the property that a false statement denies of it.

From the connection of the definition of true statements with the definition of false statements results that if any *affirmative* statement is true or false, then a corresponding negative statement also must be true or false, and, reversed, if any negative statement is true or false, then a corresponding affirmative statement has to be true or false. One might believe that two contradictory statements cannot be simultaneously true and that the principle of contradiction, which rests on generally recognized definitions, is just as certain as the principle of identity.

At the onset, Aristotle was of this opinion, when he expressed himself as follows while proving the principle of contradiction:

> *Met. Γ* 4, 1008 a 34—b 1: *ἔτι εἰ ὅταν ἡ φάσις ἀληθὴς ᾖ, ἡ ἀποφασις ψευδής, κἂν αὕτη ἀληθὴς ᾖ, ἡ κατάφασις ψευδής, οὐκ ἂν εἴη τὸ αὐτὸ ἅμα φάναι καὶ ἀποφάναι ἀληθῶς.*
>
> And further, if the negation is false, the affirmation is true, and if the affirmation is false, the negation is true, then one cannot, in agreement with the truth, affirm and deny one and the same at the same time [Appendix II, 266, 22].[119]

However, in the next line he adds:

> 1008 b 1-2: *ἀλλ' ἴσως φαῖεν ἂν τοῦτ' εἶναι τὸ ἐξ ἀρχῆς κείμενον.*
>
> This, however, one might consider a *petitio principia* [Appendix II, 266, 23].[120]

It is strange: in this instance, Aristotle refutes his own false argument with a false counterargument. The conclusion above does not fall under the accusation of *petitio principii*. Neither the definition of true statements nor that of false statements contains the principle of contradiction; if one could derive the principle from these definitions, then it would be fully founded.

But nevertheless, this conclusion is false, because the principle of contradiction does not follow from the specified definitions. On their foundation, one can only say that if a statement *a* is true, then a statement *a*' that is contradictory to it is false; however, despite

[119] Ross (Aristotle 1992): "Again, if when the assertion is true, the negation is false, and when this is true, the affirmation is false, it will not be possible to assert and deny the same thing truly at the same time."

[120] Ross (Aristotle 1992): "But perhaps they might say we had assumed the very thing at issue."

its falsity, statement *a*' can also be true, for example, if it pertains to a contradictory object. In this way, the definitions of truth and falsity can be satisfied, even though the principle of contradiction is rendered invalid. It furthermore should be noted that the principle of contradiction contains the concept of *logical multiplication*, which cannot be derived from the definitions of truth and falsity.

Still, it should be admitted that the above listed definition of false statements gives a hand to the principle of contradiction. Whoever would not recognize this principle could construct a different definition.

We use statements to reproduce reality with sense-perceptible signs. One may assume, therefore, that *a statement is false only if it does not agree with reality, that is, if it does not reproduce reality*. If the principle of contradiction is invalid, we receive the following three cases:

1) x contains F	It is true that x contains F. It is false that x does not contain F.
2) x does not contain F	It is true that x does not contain F. It is false that x contains F.
3) x contains F and x does not contain F	It is true that x contains F. It is true that x does not contain F.

It follows from this schema that if the negative statement is false, then the object contains this property that the statement denies of it; but if the affirmative statement is false, then the object does not contain the property that the statement attributes to it. However, the reverse does not follow, that is, in case the object contains the property, that the negative statement is false, which denies the property of it, and in case the object does not contain the property, that the affirmative statement is false, which attributes the property to it; after all, the object x may contain a contradiction. *Thus, only if the object x does not contain a contradiction and contains a property or does not contain it, then the statement is false which denies it of it or attributes it to it.*

If one compares these sentences with the earlier definition of false statements, then it is not hard to notice that only assertions (β) remains standing, assertions (α) on the other hand do not agree with the new conception. However, I do not know why the new definition should be worse than the earlier one, on the contrary, it appears to me that it is better. After all, it gives—as did the previous one—expression to the general conviction that falsity rests on the *disagreement of statements with reality*, and it is more cautious because in the case of the non-existence of the principle of contradiction, it does not force us to call one and the same statement simultaneously true and false.

Whatever the facts in this matter may be, it is nevertheless clear that the principle of contradiction cannot be derived from the concept of false statements. With this, Sigwart's conception also falls; Sigwart sees the basis of this principle in the concept of *negation*, but traces negation back to false statement. He assumes that the negative statement "*x* does not contain *F*" is the negation of the affirmative statement "*x* contains *F*" and means: "It is not true that *x* contains *F*."[121] The definition, which could support the principle of contradiction, has to be found elsewhere.

d) The considerations above indicate a certain characteristic moment in the principle of contradiction, which I would call without hesitation a *synthetic* moment. There is a lot more in this principle than in the definitions of truth and falsity: affirmation and denial, truth and falsity cannot exist *next to each other;* they *cancel* and *exclude* each other. One and the same statement cannot be simultaneously true and false, one and the same object cannot have and not have one and the same property at the same time. This mutual *cancellation* of truth and falsehood and of affirmation and denial contains the actual meaning of the principle of contradiction.

We nevertheless encountered during these considerations examples of such objects in which affirmation and denial do not cancel each other. These are *contradictory* objects. A square constructed with the aid of ruler and compass, which equals in its area to that of a circle with a radius of 1, has sides that are expressible with an algebraic number, and at the same time it does not. Both the affirmative statement, which attributes this property to the square, as well as the negative statement, which denies it this property, must be true. Since, if one of these statements were not true, that square would not contain a contradiction, and the squaring of the circle would be a problem that can be solved. Thus, if there are

[121] Sigwart, *Logik*, Bd.1, p.182

cases in which affirmation does not cancel denial, *then the principle of contradiction is not a universal law that governs all objects.*[122] Every proof of the principle of contradiction must take this fact into account; there is only *one* way to circumnavigate this difficulty: it must be assumed that contradictory objects are no objects at all, that they are not something but *nothing*. Anything, then, that is an object and which therefore is something and not nothing, does not contain contradictory properties.

And here we have the proof of the principle of contradiction, *the only strict and formal proof* that, in my opinion, does exist. We presuppose, from the start, that *what is to be understood as an object cannot simultaneously contain and not contain one and the same property.* From this assumption, which can be considered as the *definition* of "object", it immediately follows based on the principle of identity, that no object can simultaneously contain and not contain the one and the same property.

I doubt that this proof will deceive anyone. It appears to be so simple, cheap and superficial. And in fact, these complaints would not lack a certain justification, if the matter where to end here. But this is not the case; this proof can only be a *starting point* for further investigations.

According to the first definition, we will call "object" everything that is something and not nothing: i.e., things, persons, phenomena, events, relations, the entire external world and everything that takes place within ourselves. Also all scientific concepts and theories are objects. According to the second definition, we will call everything an "object" which does not contain a contradiction. The question arises: *are objects in first sense also objects in the second sense?* And, if it is consequently true, that things, persons, phenomena, events, relations, thoughts, feelings, concepts, theories, etc., do not contain contradictions? This is the real problem and we have been looking for its solution from the beginning.

The proof presented in this section, then, is only formal, but not material. Nevertheless, its significance is not minor: it allows

[122] As far as I know, Meinong was the first to express this opinion; in the discussion of some of Russell's objections in his work On the Position of the Theory of Objects in the System of the Sciences, Leipzig 1907, p.16, he writes: "what B. Russell places real emphasis upon is that by the recognition of such (scil. Impossible) items, the principle of contradiction would loose its unlimited validity. Naturally, I cannot avoid this consequence in any way [...] nobody has ever brought the principle of contradiction into relation to anything other than what is real or what is possible."

us to formulate the problem of contradiction in a suitable manner and shows us the way that leads to a factual solution. The way does not go into the wasteland of dry formalism and *a priori* speculation, but directs our steps to the rich and full forms of being. The real material of facts, which experience as well as scientific theory provides, will give the final statement on the principle of contradiction. And it is to this material of facts that we will turn in the following.

Chapter XVIII

The Principle of Contradiction and Constructions of the Mind

To solve the problem whether objects—in the first sense of the word—contain no contradiction, it is not necessary to examine each object by itself, but it is sufficient to divide them up into some larger groups and within these groups to consider especially those objects of which one may suspect in advance that their examination will present a certain value for the principle of contradiction.

a) The problem of the *division of objects* and the related question of the *classification of the sciences*, which is connected to it, belongs to the most difficult logical tasks. I cannot treat these problems at length here and offer only a division of objects that corresponds best to the goal of this investigation.

The principle of this division forms a *relation* that connects objects with properties. Two kinds of objects can be distinguished. Objects belong to the first kind, if the assertion of any determinate property of them results in a statement that is either true or false; following Meinong, I call such objects *complete objects*. Objects belong to the second kind if the just mentioned property does not apply to them—I call them *incomplete objects*.[123] A few examples will clarify this division.

When I consider a concrete object, for example, the Mickiewicz-Column in Lemberg, then I always obtain a statement that is either true or false, no matter what properties I may assert about the column. When I say that this column stands on Mariacki Square, that it consists of granite, that it is higher than the Mickiewicz monument in Cracow, etc., then I enunciate true statements. If, however, I were to say that this column stands on the Unia-Lubelska Hill, that it is made of plaster, that it is taller than the

[123] Meinong presented this division in his winter semester 1908/09 lectures in Graz.

Napoleon Column on the Place Vendôme in Paris, that it is reasonable, modest and so forth, then I would be making a series of false statements. I will not find a predicate that with "the Mickiewicz Column in Lvov" as subject will not generate a true or false statement. In other words: any property that one can conceive of can be attributed to this object or denied of it. The Mickiewicz Column in Lvov is *determined* in all its minutest details—it is a complete object.

In contrast, let us consider the object "column as such", without any closer determination. About this object, too, a series of true or false statements can be made. Accordingly, one can say that this column fills a space, that it is a material thing, that it is not a sphere, and so forth. But should the following statement "columns are made of bronze" be considered true or false? Some columns are made of bronze, but others are *not*. The "column as such" is undetermined in this respect. Because of this, one can neither attribute nor deny this property, and the statement "A column (as such) is made of bronze" is neither true nor false.[124] First, one would need to *mark* which column is concerned, for example, the one on the Place Vendôme in Paris, or the Mickiewicz Column in Lemberg, that is, one would need to first *complete* the object, and then the above statement would become either true or false. "Column as such" is an *incomplete* object.

It is not difficult to realize that concrete objects are complete, and abstract ones are incomplete. Not a surprise. Abstract objects usually come about in this manner: we compare a series of objects and take out their *shared* properties, but omit the *differing* ones. In that way, we build an incomplete object that, thanks to this incompleteness, is universal and which, as genus, can grasp numerous concrete objects.

Incomplete, that is, abstract objects do not exist in reality; rather, they are merely products of the human mind. Some of them

[124] Here, I adopt Meinong's conception for the moment. However, the question arises whether one should not consider judgments like "A column is made of bronze", "A column is not made of bronze", "A triangle is equilateral", "A triangle is not equilateral", nevertheless as false. This question stays connected with the *principle of the excluded third* which, as is known, forms a *pendant* to the principle of Non-Contradiction. If one were to consider the mentioned judgments as false, then the *non-applicability* of the principle of the excluded third to incomplete objects would be a characteristic mark of these objects.

have come about because they grasp concrete objects, and they then acquire this property, that one can obtain these concrete objects from them through certain completions. These are the objects of *empirical* concepts, like man, plant, crystal, ray, and so forth. I call such objects (following Bieganski[125]) *reconstruction objects*.

Other incomplete objects do not have the goal of grasping concrete objects: by completing them we either do not obtain any concrete objects at all or, at the least, we are not concerned with that. They are the objects of *a priori* concepts, which are primarily the concern of mathematics and logic. These objects I call *construction objects*. Reconstruction objects, that is, *reconstructions*, are based on experience; in comparison, construction objects, that is, *constructions*, are independent of experience.

The division sketched here is sufficient for our purposes. In the following section, I shall deal with construction objects.

b) Construction objects, which include among other items *numbers* and *geometric* figures, are without doubt objects in the first sense of the word, that is, they are something and not nothing. To begin with, this is witnessed by the big part that they play in science as well as in praxis. These objects do not exist and are independent of experience. About them, one can say together with Dedekind, that they are *free creations of the human mind.*[126] Consequently, it could be the case that we have unlimited freedom in their construction, that it depends only on *us* whether these objects turn out contradictory or not contradictory: but because we do believe in the principle of non-contradiction, we construct them in such a way that they *would* not be contradictory. Accordingly, we may assert at least about construction objects with certainty that none of them can simultaneously contain and not contain the same property.

But even in the domain of such objects contradictions nevertheless do occur. It is enough to mention the "greatest prime number" or the "square constructed with ruler and compass that has the same area as a circle with the radius of 1". To this one can reply that those contradictory objects, which obviously are *not* objects, have found their place among other constructions only erroneously

[125] Translator's note: Wladyslaw Bieganski (1857-1917), a pioneering Polish writer in the history of philosophy of medicine.

[126] Dedekind (1888). *Was sind und was sollen die Zahlen?*

and *by accident*, and this because our imperfect intellect is unable to grasp the entire manifold of properties and relations in a single moment and cannot in all cases detect a contradiction right away. But we have immediately removed such objects from science as soon as it became apparent that the objects mentioned are contradictory, and nowadays we already know that the squaring of the circle is impossible and that the greatest prime number does not exist.

But the doubt remains: If we are unable to recognize contradictions right away, then how do we know that constructions, which are held to be not contradictory, do not contain a contradiction? Perhaps we simply have not discovered it until now? This doubt can be expressed in the form of a *charge on principle*: *Where is the guarantee that non-contradictory construction objects exist at all?* Constructions are only *seemingly* free products of mind. Of course, one can assume that the definition of any construction object is whatever is desired: but we create *many* such objects and attribute to each of them *many* different properties. Together with arbitrary objects, certain *relations*, which are no longer dependent on our will, also arise. In fact, every mathematician and every logician senses that he encounters a *resistance* of the investigated material while examining these "free products" of the intellect. This resistance proves that the properties of numbers, figures, functions, etc., in turn do not entirely depend on us. And if this is the case, could one not suspect that as often as we create even only *two* constructions certain *contradictory relations* also co-arise immediately between them. Could not this contradiction be an *essential* and *indispensable* characteristic of all construction objects? And where is the proof that it is not so?

And once again, someone might object at this point that if every construction were to contain a contradiction, we then would, more frequently than up to now, encounter contradictory objects. In the meantime, one should consider the examples just mentioned merely as *exceptions*. They are simply leftovers in the workshop of science, impurities on the surface of gray, molten iron. However, that this nevertheless is not the case, and that the purity of the metal itself is strongly under suspicion, that is testified by the newest investigations of the foundations of mathematics.

Today, researchers consider the so-called *series of natural numbers*: 1, 2, 3, 4, 5, 6, ... *ad inf.*, as the foundation of the mathematical sciences. From these numbers, thanks to the operations of arithmetic, new numbers arise, positive and negative ones, whole fractions, rational and irrational ones, and so forth, and these new numbers are only certain relations of the previous ones. Various areas of mathematics, as for example, lower and higher analysis, function theory, number theory, etc., deal with the connections between numbers. Even in geometry, numerical laws can be applied up to a certain degree in that one defines connections of one-to-one, reciprocal orderings, that is, *depictions* of spatial elements and numbers. In this manner, scientists attempt to trace practically all of mathematics back to *laws of arithmetic* and then speak of an "arithmetisation" of mathematics.

However, within these fundamental mathematical objects, which the natural numbers are, apparently strange contradictions are hidden. There are many of such numbers; and one may very well ask, *how many*? The answer: there are as many as, for example, there are even numbers. After all, one can determine a one-to-one mapping between the series of natural numbers and the series of even numbers, that is, a relation such that to every number in the first series there corresponds only *one* number in the second series, and in reverse also:

1, 2, 3, 4, 5, 6, ... ad inf.
2, 4, 6, 8, 10, 12, ... ad inf.

The basis of the ordering is constituted by the relation: "the number twice as large" or, respectively, "the number smaller by half". The second series of course should contain as many numbers as there are in the first series. However, on the other hand, we see that the numbers of the second series make up only a part of the numbers of the first series. Accordingly, we get as conclusion: *the part is equal to the whole.*

Already Leibniz noticed this contradiction and Bolzano discussed it. Its solution, in my opinion, is as follows:

One cannot claim *ex definitione* that the part is smaller than the whole; rather, one needs to assume the following determination of a part: Set *A* is part of set *B* if each element of *A* is an element of *B*, but not the reverse, not every element of set *B* is an element of set *A*. An example: Catholics and Christians.

Further, one cannot claim *ex definitione* that that which is smaller forms a part, rather one needs to assume the following determination of smallness: Set *A* is smaller than set *B* if a relation exists that coordinates each element of set A one-to-one to the elements of set B; however, in reverse, there is no relation that would coordinate each element of set B one-to-one to the elements of set A. An example: Calvinists and Catholics. Defined in this manner, it does not follow from the concepts of part and smallness that the part must be smaller than the whole. The contradiction mentioned ceases to exist. But at what price! At the cost of the assumption that the part can be equal to the whole! However, based on what do we know that we have finally removed the contradiction, and that it will not re-appear again in consequences of this determination that are still not known to us?

The fate of the theory of transfinite numbers is testimony that such a doubt is not without reason. Georg Cantor could create this theory only because he omitted the contradiction mentioned. *After all, the transfinite number is such that it possesses a part that is equal to the whole.* The quantity of numbers in the series of natural numbers, which is not only equal to the number of even numbers, but also to the number of real fractions and indeed equal to the number of all algebraic numbers—is the *smallest* transfinite number. Cantor designated it with the Hebrew letter "aleph null". The number of elements in a continuum is larger than it (aleph null), for example, the number of points in a segment of a line. Cantor designates this number with "aleph one" and claims, even though at the present no exact proof for this exists, that this number follows *immediately* after "aleph null". After "aleph one" follows "aleph two" and so forth, and in this manner, the series of transfinite numbers is brought about, like the series of finite numbers. And mathematicians have found new contradictions, so-called "antinomies" which they are unable to solve now, precisely in this series.[127] It thus appears as if Cantor merely repositioned the contradiction from one corner to another, but that the contradiction itself cannot be thought away from the foundations of mathematics.

However, I shall skip over this problem, since it cannot be presented in an elementary fashion. But I cannot omit the other contradiction, which Bertrand Russell discovered, and which is positioned within the *logical* foundations of mathematics and

[127] Here, I am thinking about the Burali-Forti-Antinomy and related ones.

which thus concerns the shared trunk from which all *a priori* construction sciences grow. This contradiction is one of the strangest and the most interesting logical discoveries that have ever been made.[128]

The concept of number remains in a close connection to the concept of a class. And already I must once again disregard the question what this connection is and will concern myself only with the concept of a class. *We call a class a set of elements, that is, of individuals, that have some shared properties and which for this reason can be traced back to one concept.* If, for example, we designate as "human being" a living creature endowed with a capacity for reason and with such and such a physical constitution that is more precisely determined by zoology, then this set of individuals, which have these properties and which accordingly can be traced back to the concept of human being, are a *class* of human beings. We say about the objects that belong to a class that they are *subordinated* to this class.

Most of the time it happens that a class is not subordinated to *itself* because, as a set of elements, it usually displays other properties than each element by itself. The set of human beings is not human, the set of triangles is not a triangle, and so forth. But this is different in some cases. For example, let's consider the concept of a "fulfilled class", that is, a class to which some individuals do belong. Not all classes are fulfilled, some are empty; for example, the classes "pure gold mountain", "*perpetuum mobile*", "square circle" are empty because there are no individuals that belong to them. Thus, one can distinguish them from those classes to which some individuals *belong* and which in this way bring about the concept of a "fulfilled class". Entire *classes*, as individuals, fall under this concept, for example, the class of human beings, of triangles, of even prime numbers (this class contains only one element, the number 2), and so forth. The set of all these classes forms a new class, namely, "the class of fulfilled classes". Since this class of fulfilled classes is also a fulfilled class, it is therefore subordinated to itself.

Thus, if some classes are subordinated to themselves while others are not, then the following concept can be introduced: "The class that is not subordinated to itself". As individuals, the classes

[128] Cf. Russell, *The Principles of Mathematics*, Vol.1, Cambridge 1903, Ch. X: *The contradiction.* Also Frege, *Gurndgesetze der Arithmetik*, Vol. 2, Jena 1903, p.253.

of human beings, of triangles, or even prime numbers, and so forth, fall under this concept. The set of all these classes forms a "*class of all classes that are not subordinated to themselves*". Let's call this class simply class *K*.

The question arises: Is class *K* subordinated to itself or not? If we assume that it is, then we conclude that class *K is not* subordinated to itself, because every class that is subordinated to class *K* is not subordinated to itself. In this way, a contradiction arises, because from class *K's* being subordinated to itself it follows that it is not subordinated to itself.

If we want to avoid this contradiction, we need to assume that class *K* is not subordinated *to itself*. But if it is not subordinated to itself, then it belongs to class *K* and thus is subordinated to itself. Because of this, here too a contradiction arises, because from class *K's* not being subordinate to itself it follows that it is subordinated to itself. Whichever way we turn, we run into this contradiction. What to do?

I have deliberately presented this situation more extensively to show that the contradiction here emerges from an apparently innocent concept that has been created quite correctly with the aid of a most strictly deductive process. Thus, this is no sophism or dialectical artifice. This contradiction furthermore deserves our attention because it cannot be solved as easily as other cases of mathematical contradictions that we have come to know so far. In this sense, let us compare the case above with the contradiction that is contained in "the greatest prime number".

If we assume that a prime number *N* is the greatest one, then we arrive at the conclusion that it is not the greatest one. This is so because the number *P*, which is the result of the multiplication of all prime numbers up to *N* (inclusive) plus 1, i.e., $P = 2\ 3\ 5\ 7\ 11 \ldots N + 1$, is either a prime number *itself* and, naturally, larger than *N*, or it must be *divisible* by a prime number that is larger than *N*. If, however, we assume that the prime number *N is not* the greatest, then no contradiction does follow from this. Thus, let us assume that no prime number is greatest prime number—and everything will remain in the best of order.

Russell's contradiction cannot be resolved in this manner: the first assumption that the class *K is* subordinated to itself and the second assumption that it *is not*, both lead to the contradiction. Thus, if one wanted to avoid the contradiction in *this case*, then one should assume that the class *K is* neither subordinated to itself nor that it is not, that is, one would have to violate the *principle of the excluded third*. Thus, we may choose: either not to follow the principle of contradiction or to discard the principle of the excluded third.

This is indeed a difficult dilemma. For several years now, Russell attempts to solve it by developing ever more artful theories. After all, this contradiction is not merely a logical *toy*, but it is deeply connected with the foundations of mathematics and logic. Frege admits that the result of many years of work, his two volumes on the foundations of mathematics,[129] has been cast into doubt by this contradiction.

I shall not attempt to resolve this difficulty even though I do suspect that a *salvis principiis exclusi tertii et contradictionis*-solution[130] can be found. I want to return to the problem to which this chapter is dedicated. We did ask whether construction objects, that is, the *a priori* concepts of mathematics and logic, are objects in the second sense of the word, which is to say, whether they contain contradictory properties or not. The presented examples were to show that we cannot answer the question unequivocally. *In fact, we do encounter strange contradictions in these objects and never can we know with certainty whether seemingly contradiction-free objects really are such.*

We cannot penetrate the unlimited number of *relative properties*, which belong to the constructions of the mind in virtue of the innumerable *relations* that exist independently of us. At most, we can say that as often as a contradiction appears somewhere, a possibility to remove it *occasionally*, at least for a moment, will always be found. *But whether it will be possible to remove it once and for all, that is a problem whose solution does not lie within the limits of human knowledge.*

There are extensive disciplines of *a priori* sciences, which are clear and distinct to our eyes. But this clear and glorified lump appears to be surrounded by darkness. We are engaged in a fierce battle with this hostile force and are gaining more and more room for light. However, the defeated darkness does not *disappear*, it merely *retreats* from us; and we have no assurance that at some

[129] Cf. *Grundgesetze der Arithmetik*, ibid p.253, Nachwort

[130] Translator's note: a solution that saves or perserves the principles of the excluded third and non-contradiction.

point all the darkness will completely disappear or whether it is perhaps an *essential* condition for the existence of light.

Chapter XIX

The Principle of Contradiction and Reality

It is not only constructions, that is, abstract objects that are incomplete objects, but *also re-constructions*. It is possible to obtain concrete, that is, real objects from re-constructions through corresponding completions. After all, we create re-construction objects with the intention that they should grasp reality. The re-construction objects of man, plant, crystal, ray are directed towards actual men, plants, crystals, and rays; in other words: re-constructions are not products of mind, but they depend on experience and rest on it.

From these determinations, it follows that: If correctly created re-construction objects contain a contradiction, then this contradiction, as an expression or reproduction of actually existing contradictory properties, would be merely a *derived* one. Then, instead of examining the re-constructions of the mind, it is better to direct oneself immediately towards reality and to ask whether concrete objects, such as things, conditions, phenomena, events, do contain contradictory *properties* or not—that is, whether they are objects in the second sense of the word or not. Nobody doubts that they are objects in the first sense of the word, that is, that they are *something* and not *nothing*. In this, I must assume that under "reality" I certainly do not understand a thing-in-itself, but that I adopt the expression in its ordinary meaning by signifying all those objects as real that I see around me and that I altogether perceive with my senses, or that I intuit as feelings, convictions, willed acts, etc.

There does not seem to be anything easier than the answer to the question above. If there is anything that cannot be doubted, then it is *this* fact: real existing phenomena, things and their qualities, do not contain contradictory properties. If I am now sitting at my desk and write, then it cannot be true at the same time that I am not sitting and not writing, but that instead I am on a stroll through town and talking with my colleague. If sunlight enters my room through the open window and, reflected by the smooth window-pane, a flickering ray of light appears on the opposite wall, then this phenomenon exists, and it cannot simultaneously not exist or exist differently. To claim that the sunshine simultaneously does and does not enter my room, that it is reflected by the windowpane and nevertheless not reflected by it, that it is and is not thrown onto the wall, that would mean to contradict the obvious facts.

In fact, such and similar considerations taken from daily life are the strongest arguments for the principle of contradiction. Neither the apparent obviousness of the principle nor the abstract demonstrations of the logicians have as much power of persuasion as those small facts of experience that we encounter all the time. Under no circumstance are they to be analyzed in detail, but simply taken (as they come), and no doubt about the principle of contradiction will arise.

Things are completely different, if someone is not satisfied with the merely superficial consideration of the appearances and engages in a subtler analysis. Whoever does this, moves away from "healthy common sense" and has only to blame himself if he gets caught in contradictions. Zeno of Elea will remain a deterring example of this for eternity. For years, he wandered across Greece and tortured "reasonable" persons with strange mind-bending puzzles. And because of this, he bit off his own tongue in his old age and ended his life rather miserably!

All objections against the principle of contradiction that have been produced over the centuries, and which—by the way—were not very numerous had their source not in the analysis of the principle itself or in the deconstruction of some abstract objects, but precisely in the analysis of the facts of experience. Zeno did not take position against the principle that Aristotle had not yet formulated, but he attempted to demonstrate, by showing actual or apparent contradictions in the sensible world, that this world is an illusion and in truth does not exist. However, for the sensualists of the school of Protagoras, who did not accept any other being than the sensible world, Zeno's subtle arguments were merely demonstrations against the principle of contradiction. We already have seen previously that even Aristotle did not dispute that this conception had a certain import, and Hegel already says very clearly that one

> "has to concede to the old dialecticians the contradictions that they demonstrate in motion, but from this it does not follow that motion does not exist, but rather that motion is the *being-present* of

> contradiction itself [*der* daseyende *Widerspruch selbst*]."[131]

Thus, it appears that if it is possible to cast doubt on the principle of contradiction at all, then it is in the area of concrete objects, that is, in the area of facts of experience.

Let us consider to what extend these doubts are justified. The weakest point of the principle of contradiction, its Achilles' heel, is the simple word *ἅμα*, "simultaneously". If abstract objects are concerned, then this expression signifies the concept of *logical multiplication*. We already know, thanks to this word, that the principle of contradiction can be derived neither from the principle of identity, nor from the principle of double negation, nor from the definition of a false statement. In the application to concrete objects, the little word "simultaneously" gains the characteristic of a *temporal* determination. Concrete objects may contain contradictory properties, but not "simultaneously", that is, not at one and the same time. I may sit or not sit, the windowpane may reflect the sunshine or it may not reflect it, but not "simultaneously", not at one and the same instant. One even might say that time exists only so that objects and phenomena can have contradictory properties—without detriment to the principle of contradiction. But they must have these properties because if they did not, the world would be dead. After all, the entire movement and every change, which do not merely appear to be a *measure* of time but also its *condition*, take place in this manner: the object that is changing loses properties that it did have, and takes on new ones that it did not have. A contradiction would result in the first and in the second case if different time determinations did not exist.

If change is *continuous*, for example, the motion of an arrow shot from a bow, the rotation of the earth around the sun, the constant reduction of the intensity of light or the uninterrupted decrease in temperature, then, in each smallest of time intervals, the changing object loses a series of properties and acquires others. The moving arrow is at any *two* time-moments in separate locations. Even if one assumes that the distance between these time-moments is smaller than any arbitrarily small magnitude, the arrow is located at *different* positions, as long as this distance is limited

[131] Cf. Chapter V

but not equal to zero (these days, even mathematicians do not believe anymore in the existence of infinitely small magnitudes). However, what does happen if the distance is reduced to zero, if we consider only *one* instant as a non-continuous point on the time line?

We all have heard the fairy tale of the princess who pricks her little finger with a needle and immediately falls into a 100-year slumber and everybody around her falls asleep with her. In this fashion, the court of Popiel was instantly turned into stone because Rzepicha cast a spell on him in the songs of *Król Duch*.[132] Let us assume that what was merely poetic fiction has become reality. Let us imagine a transverse section cut across the entire world of phenomena, performed at some arbitrary point in time. In this transverse section, on its immobilized surface, there would be no change and no time. The arrow would have to freeze motionless at some location. But how do we know that it would have to be at only *one* location? For if it was moving, it continuously changed its location in space and, consequently, it was present at many locations even within each smallest of time-moments. Why, then, could it not also be at least at *two* different places in the not extended time-point of the transverse section, why could it not *be* at one place and also *not be* at that same place at the same time? How do we know that it is not the case that each and every object that undergoes some kind of change contains a similar contradiction? If, however, all is changing continuously and flows, then couldn't it be that the entire sensible world is full of contradictions, which would show themselves in a dissecting cut?

There are no answers to these questions. One cannot gain anything here with *a priori* considerations because one would have to already rely on the principle of contradiction, which is what we are trying to ground. Experience, too, is silent in this matter, since a not extended time-moment is not an object of experience. All appearances that we do perceive have a shorter or longer *duration*—and they *must* persist for a minimum time period so that we can perceive them at all. We do not know what takes place in a not extended time-moment. And still, it is exactly this moment that concerns the principle of contradiction, because if we say that the arrow cannot *simultaneously* be and not be at the same location,

[132] Translator's note: The reference is to characters in a work by Jóliusz Słowacki which was written in the period of Polish Romanticism.

then the little word 'simultaneously' refers to the *same*, that is, only *one* not extended moment.

Thus, the investigations of this chapter lead us to the same result as the ones of the previous chapter: Just as we cannot say with certainty whether there are construction objects that are free of contradiction, we also have no guarantee that there are concrete objects that are free of contradictions. This result could have been seen in advance. After all, if our understanding cannot grasp the unlimited number of properties and relations in the domain of those objects which are the free products of mind, and thus only apparently dependent of us, then the infinitely complicated objects of experience that exist independently of us are even less accessible to our comprehension. All that logic has taught us for some time about the laws of reality agrees with this result as well. There are no *a priori* and thus necessary and certain laws of experience. Even if we could penetrate to the bottom of all perceived phenomena and were to find no contradictions in them, then the doubt still would remain whether such a state of affairs did always exist in the world and whether it will stay that way forever. *A priori* laws are based on definitions: because of this they are certain; because of this they are dogmas. But that our definitions agree with reality, that is not a dogma of science but merely a hypothesis that will never be confirmed with complete certainty.

But despite all this, the case of the principle of contradiction is stronger in the domain of real objects than in the sphere of mental constructions. There we encountered *factual* contradictions, whose solution is not at all easy, and here, on the other hand, the existence of contradiction is merely *possible*. Further, should we actually encounter at some point a contradictory object in experience, then this contradiction could be easily *removed* by a matching interpretation. Let us assume that a material, continuously moving point is actually located at two different locations at *one* instant and that we can catch it in experience. Initially, one might say that it is not *one* point but two; and two points not only can but must be at two different locations. Later, once this interpretation did show itself to be erroneous due to other circumstances, one could still claim that it does not contain a contradiction if the point *would* not simultaneously *be and not be*. However, we do assume that if an object is located at one place, it cannot simultaneously be at another place, and because of this we are inclined to suspect a *latent* contradiction, if the point is located simultaneously at different locations. This suspicion, however, is based on experience. Thus, if we were to cognize opposed facts in experience, then that suspicion would have to be dropped and we would have to assume that the same object *can* in that way simultaneously be at many places without contradiction, just as it can simultaneously have many different properties, because it can be round as well as white, and at the same time it can also be hard. In experience, *pure negation* never arises but it always relates to position. If a button is not black, then it must have a different color, for example, it must be white and if in being this it also was to be black at the same spot, then we would say that there is no contradiction here but instead that one and the same object *can* be simultaneously white and black at the same spot. We would have rejected the position with the negation (not-white). It seems to me that if we are to proceed in this manner in every instance of an apparent or factual contradiction, we will never encounter any such actual objects that one should consider irrevocably as contradictory.

If this opinion is correct, then the principle of contradiction would remain in a similar relation to experience as the *principle of causation*. We claim that every phenomenon has a cause. It is impossible to prove this law, but there is no reason for the concern that a case could be found that would refute it. After all, if it there was no cause in some case, we could always say that a cause does exist, but we just cannot find out what it is. The situation looks exactly the same for the principle of contradiction. The principle cannot be proven based on experience, but there is also no reason for concern that experience might be able to refute it. Even if we were to encounter a factual contradiction in a concrete instance, of course without knowing anything about it, there would always be a remedy to remove it. Because of this, the principle of contradiction can be applied without concerns to the facts of experience.

The result of the last two chapters has in principle been negative: *It is impossible to show in an indubitable manner that contradictory objects exist.* Long centuries of scientific work separate us from that moment during the origins of philosophy when Aristotle sought to prove the existence of at least *one* contradiction-free being. Today we are older—and, thus, more modest.

Chapter XX

The Significance of the Principle of Contradiction

Whoever expected to encounter a complete and final proof of the principle of contradiction in this concluding, positive part of this work—has been disappointed. It turned out that *only a formal, a priori proof is possible; a factual one on the other hand cannot be executed.* It is good that at least the difficulties that question the existence of this principle can be removed!

The principle of contradiction had validity throughout the centuries as the highest and most complete *ontological* law. That it *is* such a law cannot be demonstrated. It merely *could* be that. One should learn modesty. Man did not create Being and he cannot force his a priori laws on it. He is barely able to grasp the products of his own mind! We are only permitted to *guess* at the *divine* laws that are effective in the universe and their cognition *a posteriori,* whereby we are only permitted to consider a priori knowledge as merely a *tool* of this cognition.

This position is far removed from philosophical dogmatism. On the contrary, even a skeptical note resonates within it. But this skepticism should not have any influence on the methods of scientific investigation nor on practical behavior. Even though the proof of the principle of contradiction is not complete, it should not be underestimated. After all, we do not have any better proofs for other principles either. The laws of geometrical figures are based just as much on definitions as the principle of contradiction, and we are permitted to doubt their truth in their application to real figures just as much as we doubt the application of the principle of contradiction to the real world. We do not know either, whether the definition of Euclidean space corresponds to real space, nor do we have a guarantee that the definition of an object corresponds to the real object. However, since we do not encounter any resistance at all in the application of these laws to reality, we use them without scruples and will continue to do so if it is successful.

But the impression cannot be suppressed that if all these critical considerations should be accurate, then they would significantly diminish the value of the principle of contradiction. Until very recently, we believed that this principle is absolutely true; today we can no longer make this claim; and who knows whether clarity on this matter will ever be won. If this is true, then we mistakenly *valued* this principle and *believed* in it without reason; unless, that is, there is a value other than that of a *logical* category, a value that one would have to attribute to our principle because it is of equal magnitude and importance. We should answer two more questions: Why is it that we believe in a principle whose truth cannot be demonstrated, and why do we attribute a value to it that exceeds even the value attributed to statements that are true with certainty?

a) That we believe so universally in the principle of contradiction is due significantly to the authority of Aristotle. Let us consider how rarely the knowledge of an individual person is based on an independent, critical examination of a matter, and how often we have to rely on the respect of others, even in the sciences! Any claim that does not obviously disagree with the known or accepted facts easily gains scientific credit. Most scientists do not concern themselves with logic and accept uncritically the investigations of specialists. Logicians, on the other hand, belong to the most diehard conservatives for the longest time and held on to the traditional views without change all the way to the most recent past. High up on the list of these views the principle of contradiction is found. For centuries, no one criticized it. Aristotle announced it with passionate conviction. Who would be surprised that everyone believed in it? Even into the 17th century Aristotle was believed word by word, that heavier bodies fall faster than lighter ones, and that heavy bodies only fall down because below there is a place for them, the lighter ones go up because they belong up there. Galileo finally refuted these opinions. The natural sciences and especially mechanics developed quicker and sooner than logic. The development of logic only took place in the second half of the 19th century. Thus, it is only now that one can critically check the older logical conceptions and subject them to a revision. Further, the *absence* of any facts that did *not agree* with the principle of contradiction has also exerted a significant influence on the general belief in this principle. In experience, analyzed superficially, these facts did not exist at all. Recently they were discovered in intellectual constructions, but only a few people know about this. Examples from daily life seemed to confirm this principle at every step. The difficulties raised by Zeno were considered to be sophisms. Finally, how often has the principle of contradiction been *confused* with other principles, for example, the principle of identity or the principle of double negation! For a long time, the principle of contradiction was known in Latin as *principium ... identitatis.*[133] This is the best proof of how *carelessly* the principle has been treated.

It is of course a mark of the genius of the Aristotelian spirit, that it could convince all of humanity of two things: First, that the principle of contradiction is true *even though there is no proof for it*; and further, that the principle of contradiction *does not require proof at all.* Has there ever been anything comparable in the history of any other science?

But nevertheless, there exists an almost logical instinct in man that *shows itself* on occasions and which does not permit him to accept as true that for which there is no proof. When Hegel raised objections against the principle of contradiction, he immediately found supporters. Even our compatriot Trentowski,[134] following the master, repeated that this law of the old logic is not worth much. Still, Hegel did not take this principle *critically* apart. And, thus, it appears that our belief in the principle of contradiction is, despite it all, not so strong that it could not be shaken. Something or other is not quite in order with this principle. After all, why has no one ever seriously negated the truth of the claim that two times two is four? It is possible to indulge in a mean-spirited joke and claim that for some "two times two is five plus lamp" and one may use this claim as the title of a *comedy*, but no one will *seriously* claim that two times two is five. Hegel, however, *seriously* claims that the principle of contradiction is false.

These brief remarks sufficiently explain why we do believe in the principle of contradiction even though it cannot be proven. A simple matter: *a logical reason is only one reason among many and by far not the strongest of belief-motivations.*

b) The answer to the second question will be different: How does it happen that we attribute a value to the principle of contradiction

[133] See above the citation in the note to Chapter VII.

[134] Translator's note: A nineteenth century Polish Hegelian.

that is even greater than the value of statements that are true with certainty?

Truth is a *logical* value. We treasure truth, even if it were to be of no utility to us, just as we treasure beauty and virtue. Logical statements are logically *valuable*; they are the logical *good*. False statements are the logical *evil*, just as a violation is a *moral* evil. Those statements about which we do not know whether they are true or false do not contain any logical value as long as their truth cannot be determined. They are logically *valueless* statements. The principle of contradiction belongs to these statements insofar as we apply it to being in general, and actual being in particular. Thus, if this principle is to have a value, then this value must belong to *another* category, and not to the category of logic.

There are logically valueless statements that are nevertheless treasured in practice. To these statements belong virtually all empirical laws and the theories and hypotheses of the natural sciences. The law of the preservation of energy, the theory of evolution, the aether and electron hypotheses—cannot be proven. Even though all the facts known to us apparently correspond to these laws and theories; however, whether this agreement will end at some point—that we do not know. Nevertheless, even though these statements are not true to the same degree as, for example, the sentences of mathematics, and even though one cannot suspect that they are false without a reason, they nevertheless have a tremendous practical value because they join a great many different phenomena into a whole, by establishing an order among them, and because they permit the prediction of future phenomena. Even if Newton's *leges motus* should be shattered at some point and it would turn out that these highest laws of mechanics are not a precise expression of reality, they would even then, despite their falsity, continue to have practical value in that they give order to the complicated chaos of phenomena and mechanical formulae, and join them all into one systematic whole. Does such a practical value also belong to the principle of contradiction?

This question, too, has to be answered negatively. The principle of contradiction does not join diverse phenomena and laws into a whole nor does it order any facts at all. And we have never used it with the aim of predicting future events based on it. If this principle has a practical significance, it must be found elsewhere.

And this is the place to present the final and probably most important idea of this treatise. It seems to me that so far nobody has brought this thought into clear awareness, even though Aristotle was perhaps closest to it: *the value of the principle of contradiction is not of a logical but of a practical-ethical nature: this practical-ethical value, however, is so great that the lack of logical value does not count in comparison.* To explicate and justify this idea appropriately, I will allow myself to first present a few examples. Not all statements, which we use in life or in the sciences, can be *proven* or, in whatever manner, be *justified.* This concerns especially statements about past events and phenomena. Most often, such statements are based on *memory*, and we know from experience, how often memory deceives us. But neither in life nor in the sciences can we do without such statements. Whole passages of history would have to be forfeited, empirical psychology, whose introspective method relies not so much on the direct observation of phenomena, but rather on holding them in memory, would then become nearly impossible, and even in the natural sciences this or that fact would have to be excluded. And even less could we manage practical life without these statements. Thus, in all these cases, we must rely either on our *own* memory, or on somebody else's memory and *truthfulness*.

Knowing this, let us assume that we live in a society that does not accept the principle of contradiction and that does not even know it. Now, a Mr. X comes up to me and tells me that he saw me yesterday evening on a street outside. I, on the other hand, do remember quite well that I did not leave the house yesterday. I have numerous witnesses who spent the evening with me and who confirm my word. Apparently, Mr. X is mistaken, or perhaps he is lying. I cannot ask him to prove his claim because it is impossible to prove such statements; only memory and the truthfulness of the speaker serve us as guarantees for them. At most, I might attempt to verify my *own* assertion with corresponding witness testimonies, that is, that I was at home and thus I could not have been outside my house. But if the principle of contradiction does not exist, then my attempts do not make any sense: my opponent will calmly agree with me, but he will nevertheless not give up on his own opinion. *Both* statements may be true at the same time, that I *was* at home and that I *was not there*. But accordingly, how am I to refute the claim of my opponent? Let us consider an even more drastic example!

Somebody has been wrongfully accused of having murdered his friend. There are false witnesses who testify under oath that they have seen the accused on the day of the crime in the house of the victim, that they observed a fight from a distance, that at last they had to watch the sad final scene and that they were unable to come to the aid of the attacked person in time. The accused ceremoniously declares his innocence, appeals to his untroubled life, his quiet and peaceful character, the friendship of many years that connected him to the deceased, and finally he introduces several credible witnesses who establish his *alibi* in a clear and undisputable manner. But how is all this to benefit the accused? At best, he can justify the claim that he *did not murder* his friend. However, the truth of this statement does not preclude the truth of the statement contradictory to it, that is, that he nevertheless *did murder* him, if the principle of contradiction should not exist. The false testimony of the dishonest witnesses cannot be refuted by any means—the judge must assume that even though the accused *did not murder* his friend he nevertheless *did murder* him—and a mistrial is declared.

These examples show what the practical and ethical significance of the principle of contradiction consists in. *This principle is the only weapon against mistakes and lies.* If contradictory statements were to be *reconcilable* with each other, if affirmation were *not to nullify* denial, but if the one were to be able to meaningfully co-exist next to the other, then we would have no means at our disposal to discredit falsity and unmask lies. It is because of this that in every inference in which we apply this principle, for example in an apagogic proof, the concern is to demonstrate the falsity of some statement. And it is also because of this, that the accusation that somebody is caught in contradictions—be it in a scientific treatise or on the witness stand—is such a sensitive matter. Without mercy, it reveals mistakes or lies. Thus, it is the principle of contradiction that makes it possible to victoriously fight a variety of untruths, and on this relies its entire significance.

When I remarked earlier that I wanted to add a positive part following the negative one, a positive part that would ground again Aristotle's shaky principle, what I had in mind was primarily this: its *a-logical* value. Not only does the practical and ethical need to recognize this principle fail to prove its truth, but it can even further diminish what is left of its remaining logical value. It becomes apparent how very *relative* the acceptance of this principle is! If we only could be satisfied with such statements that follow with inexorable necessity from definitions and which have been proven with precision, like the simplest sentences of mathematics, then the principle of contradiction would be without any use to us. Of course, in that case we would be unable to indicate either error or lie, but because we would recognize only statements that have been *proven*, the falsities, which cannot be proven, would be of no concern to us. Because of this, I do not see any danger for the sciences if some contradiction in the *a priori* sciences, for example Russell's contradiction, cannot be resolved. After all, in the sciences we accept only exactly demonstrated statements. And if there should be a contradiction that can be proven, then we can acknowledge this fact with reassurance and even consider it a valuable scientific achievement. However, a careless good-bye to the principle of contradiction in the empirical sciences or in life in general would not bring any certainty. It then would be not easy to determine the boundaries in which this principle is valid and in which ones it is not. We would gradually stop applying it and as result there would arise perhaps not *skepticism* but rather some unjustified *faith* in certain statements.

Even if the human understanding were to be *infallible* and the human character completely *pure*, even then one would not have to accept the principle. Then there would be neither errors nor lies. If then we were to encounter a contradiction, its acceptance would not bring any harm with it. But man is a weak and limited creature: *Aristotle's principle is precisely an expression of man's impotence!* Thus, we must accept it, and only the highest being could do without it.

Aristotle already sensed the practical value of the principle of contradiction when he said that we, while contradicting this principle, could neither think reasonably nor communicate with each other nor even act. The Stagirite, asserting this, did not have any justification for his claim, but he was not at all that far from the truth. He simply was unable to make it clear to himself on what the practical signification of this principle is based upon, and he did not grasp the difference between that and its logical value. He was, however, on the right track, but in the end, no one followed him on this path.

And no one followed him because, for centuries, there was no need to defend this principle. Such a need existed only in the time of Aristotle. And Aristotle did not merely fight for the preservation of the principle of contradiction as one might fight for a possibly correct, but emotionally neutral *theoretical* opinion, he fought for it as one fights for *life's essential goods*. Let us remember, if only briefly, those distant moments! It was the era of the largest social expansion of Ancient Greece, an era of national division and political corruption, which was exploited to a considerable extent by Philip of Macedonia. As the family's doctor and educator of Alexander, Aristotle certainly belonged to Philip's faction. But possibly he also was on the Macedonian side because he was a supporter of the social order and saw the only rescue for his decaying homeland in a strong and powerful monarchy. But he also must have felt heart break over the battle of Chaeronea.[135] In this politically most difficult moment, which made practical life so distasteful to Aristotle and encouraged him to treasure theoretical life above all, the sophists introduced the elements of intellectual and moral laxness. This constituted a hundred times greater a defeat than the might of Macedonia. It not only destroyed the foundations of social being but also the foundations of the individual; it destroyed the principles of the understanding. Aristotle saw the future of his homeland in the cultural work that was to remain the only free area of activity for the Greeks for centuries to come. And he himself took on an inexhaustible part in this labor by establishing the considerable foundations of *scientific* culture and, by combining his own research and that of others, created a series of new and systematic branches of knowledge. The sophists have proven themselves as the enemies of such a goal-oriented, creative, and systematic labor—not the older wandering teachers who deserve serious consideration, like Protagoras or Prodicus, who Aristotle mentions not without considerable respect, but the younger Eristics from Megara, cynics from the school of Antistheses, and skeptics such as Cratylus. The sophistries and paradoxes of these clever speakers were known in all of Greece. Perhaps there wasn't anyone who took these strangely distorted thoughts too seriously, but they nevertheless ridiculed science in the public eye and instigated chaos in the minds of men. These sophists denied the principle of contradiction. Even though their charges were vacuous, the positive proof of this principle was nevertheless not possible and we were able to convince ourselves in this treatise that Aristotle himself was

[135] Translator's note: Battle of Chaeronea, 338 AD. Philip defeated the Theban and Athenian armies. According to Paul K. Davis, "Philip's victory ended Greek independence for decades and laid the groundwork for Alexander the Great's championship of Hellenism in his conquests" (Davis 1999, 27).

aware of the weakness of his arguments. Entering the argument itself was not without danger because in doing so Aristotle took on the fight in the territory of the opponent. Counter-arguments existed for the arguments, and the sophists were professional dialecticians. Thus, there was nothing else left than to declare the principle of contradiction a *dogma*, and to set authoritarian limits to any destructive works. Only in this way was the Stagirite able to forge armors against sophistries and errors and to clear the path for positive work.

Generations have gone by and the Hellas of Antiquity no longer exists. The times and social conditions have changed and public opinion has taken on a different mood. Still, one encounters even today skeptics and annihilators of scientific work, but their harmful activities do not find support. Science, whose foundations were created by Aristotle, has grown into a giant edifice that encompasses all of aspects of man's life. Its incredible *practical achievements*, which everybody brings up against the skeptics, are a clear proof of its enduring significance. Thus, if we did subject the principle of contradiction to such a sharp critique and want to strike it from the set of scientific dogmas, then this deed and intention will no longer shake the foundations of science, but will instead allow us to view the strange construction of this principle in complete and truthful illumination.

Chapter XXI

Summary of Results

Because the problems that have been considered in this treatise are so diverse and numerous, it seems to me that a clear summary of the most important results, including the shorter proofs, will be advantageous for the orientation of the reader. The summary of results will also make the task of critical review easier. My main concern is not so much that my theses should prove themselves to be correct and generally acceptable, but rather to reach the truth in this important logical problem.

I divide the results of this treatise into two categories: in the first one, I place *historical* theses, including Aristotle's opinions as well as critical commentaries; in the second one, I posit *factual* theses, that is, my own opinions about the principle of contradiction.

I. Historical Theses

1) Aristotle formulates the principle of contradiction in its ontological, logical, and psychological meaning, even though he does not clearly distinguish between these meanings.

> a) The ontological formulation: "The same cannot simultaneously belong and not belong to and the same thing."[136]
>
> b) The logical formulation: "Contradictory statements are not simultaneous-ly true."[137]
>
> c) The psychological formulation: "Nobody can believe that one and the same thing is and is not."[138]

[136] *Met.* Γ 3, 1005 b 19-20.

[137] *Met.*.Γ 6, 1011 b 13-14.

[138] *Met.* Γ 3, 1005 b 23-24.

2) Aristotle silently assumes that the ontological and the logical principle of contradiction are equivalent.

This claim can be derived from Aristotle's view of the relation between true statements and being: statements, as signs, must correspond to being.[139]

3) Aristotle attempts to prove the psychological principle of contradiction based on the logical one. The proof consists of two parts:

> a) "If the same object may not have opposed properties at the same time, and convictions, to which contradictory statements correspond, are opposite to each other—then, of course, one and the same man cannot simultaneously believe that one and the same is and is not. Thus, whoever would be mistaken here would have opposite convictions."[140]
>
> b) "If contradictory statements that are asserted about the same object cannot be simultaneously true, then, of course, the opposed properties also cannot belong to the same object at the same time."[141]

4) The Aristotelian proof of the psychological principle of contradiction is insufficient.

> a) Aristotle did not prove that the convictions to which contradictory statements correspond are opposite to each other, that is, that they form the extreme poles of the chain of properties that exclude each other.
>
> b) But he did not prove this for this reason, namely, because he only performed a logical analysis instead of a psychological one. (The first traces of Psychologism in logic, that is, of "Logicism" in psychology).[142]

5) Aristotle considers both the ontological and the logical principle of contradiction to be ultimately valid; thus, this means that he

[139] *De Int.* 9, 18 a 39—b 2; *Met.* Θ 10, 1051 b 3-4.

[140] *Met.* Γ 3, 1005 b 26-32.

[141] *Met.* Γ 6, 1011 b 15-18.

[142] De Int. 14

claims that this principle cannot be proven on the basis of other statements, but that it is instead true by itself.

Aristotle does not prove this claim, but makes the appeal that some final principles must exist and that there is no other principle that could be ultimately valid with a better justification than the principle of contradiction.[143]

6) This opinion is false insofar as there are principles that one could take as ultimately valid with a better justification than the principle of contradiction. Such principles, for example, are the *principle of identity* or the *definition of a true statement.*

7) Even though Aristotle considers the principle of contradiction as unprovable, he nevertheless admits that it can be proven elenctically—and he does prove it both elenctically as well as apagogically.[144]

8) Aristotle falls into a contradiction by considering the principle of contradiction as unprovable but then proves it nevertheless elenctically and apagogically. This contradiction cannot be removed by any interpretation, because:

> a) The elenctic proof is a syllogism which comes about if the opponent initially does not accept a given thesis and further must accept premises from which it follows. Thus, as a syllogism, the elenctic proof is a proper proof.[145]
>
> b) Aristotle finishes his elenctic argumentation with the words: "Thus, if the matter is this way, then proof has been produced that contradictory statements may not be simultaneously accepted."[146]

9) Two elenctic proofs and three apagogic ones can be distinguished among the Aristotelian proofs of the principle of contradiction.

The assumption of the elenctic proofs, which the opponent has to accept, insofar as he wants to debate the matter, is this: there is

[143] *Met.* Γ 4, 1006 a 3-11.

[144] *Met* Γ 4, 1006 a 11-12 and the entire chapter 4 of book Γ.

[145] *Prior Analytics* II, 20, 66 b 4-15.

[146] *Met.* Γ 4, 1007 a 17-18.

a word that signifies something that is one according to its essence, for example, there is a word "man" that signifies a two-footed living being.[147]

> a) The first elenctic proof arises in connection with the principle of double negation: "Thus, if it is possible to signify something as man, it must be a two-footed living being; this is, after all, what the word 'man' indicates. And if something must be a two-footed living being, then it cannot not be that; 'something must be' means that it cannot not be. Thus, it is impossible that it would simultaneously be true that one and the same is a two-footed living being and is not a two-footed living being."[148]

> b) The second elenctic proof remains connected to the concept "essence" and "substance": "Thus, a word should be given that signifies something and that signifies some one thing. The word humanness (the essence of humanity) cannot signify the same as the word not-humanness, if the word man signifies one thing. Thus, one and the same cannot be man and not be man."[149]

Another formulation of this proof: Every object must be one in its essence (a substantial being); thus, in its essence, it cannot simultaneously be the same and not be the same, because then it would not be one.

> c) The first apagogic proof: "If all contradictory statements about the same object are simultaneously true, then of course everything is one. One and the same will be ship, wall, and man."[150]

> d) The second apagogic proof: "Furthermore, everyone would be speaking truly and falsely, and everyone would admit by himself that he is speaking falsely."[151]

[147] *Met.* Γ 4, 1006 a 18-25; b 11-13.

[148] *Met.* Γ 4, 1006 b 28-34.

[149] *Met.* Γ 4, 1006 b 11-15, 18.

[150] *Met.* Γ 4, 1007 b 19-21.

[151] *Met.* Γ 4, 1008 a 28-30.

e) The third apagogic proof: If the principle of contradiction were not to exist, action would be impossible. However, men do act, and so do even those who contradict this principle, thus: they do not believe that the same action is simultaneously good and not good.[152]

10) The critique of these proofs:

a) The first elenctic proof justifies only the principle of double negation, from which the principle of contradiction does not follow. Because:

α) The principle of contradiction contains the concept of logical multiplication, which cannot be derived from the principle of double negation.

β) In the case of contradictory objects, the principle of double negation remains true even though the principle of contradiction becomes false.

b) The second elenctic proof, which relies on substantial being and the concept of the "essence" of things, is primarily subject to three objections:

α) This proof does not justify the principle of contradiction as a universal law because it concerns only essence and substance, but not contingent properties.

β) It does not justify this principle as a logically certain law, because the existence of substantial being is merely a hypothesis.

γ) It contains a formal error because it uses the *modus tollens* form of inference, which presupposes the principle of contradiction.

c) All apagogic proofs (9c, 9d, 9e) are subject to the following two objections:

α) They contain the error of *petitionis principii* because they rely on the *modus tollens* form of inference, which presupposes the principle of

[152] *Met.* Γ 4, 1008 b 12-19.

contradiction.

β) They contain the error of *ignorationis elenchi*, because they attack the universal statement that all objects are contradictory instead of demonstrating the falsity of the particular statement that some objects are contradictory.[153]

11) Aristotle probably delayed the controversial point in his proofs because he apparently shared the opinions of the sensualists, who saw contradiction in the sensible world and, consequently, he himself did not believe in the universality of the principle of contradiction. The proofs:

a) Aristotle admits that potential modes of being may contain contradictions.[154]

b) He says about the objects of perception, that is, about the phenomena of the sensible world, that they belong primarily to potential being. They are indeterminate, continuously changing, emerge and disappear, from the same phenomena oppositions arise, etc.[155]

12) Accordingly, the second elenctic proof is Aristotle's main argument. This proof, in addition to the existence of the sensible world, also assumes the existence of substantial, immutable and eternal being.[156] For Aristotle, thus, the principle of contradiction rests on a fundamental metaphysical presupposition.

13) While in the *Metaphysics* Aristotle considers the principle of contradiction to be the foundation of all axioms,[157] he nevertheless admits in the *Analytics* that this principle is not an indispensable foundation of syllogisms. The minor premise may contain a contradiction, but despite this, it will not touch the validity of the syllogistic inference.[158]

[153] Regarding the fallacy of postponing the solution of problems in the Aristotelian proofs, see *Met.* Γ 4, 1006 a 28-31; 1008 a 8-16; 1008 b 31—1009 a 5.

[154] *Met.* Γ 5, 1009 a 22-36.

[155] *Met.* Γ 5, 1010 a 1-5; Γ 4, 1007 b 28-29.

[156] Cf. *Met.* Γ 5, 1009 a 30-38; 1010 a 32-35.

[157] *Met.* Γ 3, 1005 b 32-34.

[158] *Posterior Analytics* I 11, 77 a 10-22.

14) Chapter 4 of the *Metaphysics*, where Aristotle proves the principle of contradiction, contains expressions that indicate a certain excitement of the author. (Aristotle accuses his opponents of ignorance, compares them to plants, and calls their teachings irrational: *Metaphysics* Γ 4, 1006 a 5-7, 13-15, 1008 b 10, 11, 1009 a 3-5). This excitement could be explained as follows:

> a) In these passages, Aristotle engages in polemics against the Eristicians from Megara, Anthisthenes, the Sophists, all of which are hostile towards him.
>
> b) Aristotle sensed the practical significance of the principle of contradiction and he fought, by defending himself, for valuable social and cultural goods.
>
> c) Most likely, Aristotle also sensed the inadequacy of his arguments, which in connection with the conviction of the indispensability of this principle, could momentarily throw him off balance.

II. Factual Theses

1) There are three formulations of the principle of contradiction:

> a) Ontological: no object can contain and simultaneously not contain one and the same property.
>
> b) Logical: Two statements, one of which attributes to an object exactly that property, which the other statement denies of it, cannot be simultaneously true.
>
> c) Psychological: Two convictions, to which two contradictory statements correspond, cannot exist simultaneously in one and the same mind.

2) These formulations do not mean the same because they contain different concepts (object and property, statement and truth, conviction and temporal co-existence). At most, they can be equivalent.

3) The ontological and logical formulations are equivalent: true statements, affirmative or negative, do agree with the objective facts, that is, with the containing or not containing of a property by

an object.

4) The psychological principle of contradiction cannot be a certain *a priori* statement, but only a probable empirical law, because it concerns existing phenomena.

5) The psychological principle of contradiction is not a justified law, but instead an empirically rather dubious one, because:

> a) No extensive psychological investigations in this direction have so far been done (Husserl's argument).
>
> b) There are known cases of intellectual conditions which either directly contradict this principle, or which cannot be made tolerable without the aid of additional hypotheses (the negation of the principle of contradiction by Hegel, mystical moods, etc.).

6) The principle of contradiction, in its logical or ontological formulation, is not an ultimate principle. The proof:

> a) An ultimate principle is a statement that cannot be proven based on other statements, but that is true by itself.
>
> b) The principle of contradiction is not true by itself: The only statement that is true by itself is the definition of true statement.

Thus, the principle of contradiction requires proof.

7) The principle of contradiction is not a highest logical law, which means, it is also not an indispensable foundation (and also not a sufficient one) for other logical laws. This is witnessed by the fact that one can make deductive inferences by moving in a circle of affirmative statements to which the principle of contradiction cannot be applied; after all, this principle always simultaneously concerns affirmation and denial.[159]

8) The principle of contradiction is distinct from the principle of identity and cannot be derived from it. The proof:

> a) One cannot formulate the principle of contradiction if one does not have two statements of which one is the negation of the other and which together form a logical product. The principle of identity, however, can be

[159] See Appendix I § 9 δ

formulated without the aid of logical product and without the aid of negation.

b) Applied to contradictory objects, the principle of contradiction is false even though the principle of identity remains true.

9) The principle of contradiction is distinct from the principle of double negation and cannot be derived from it. The proof:

a) The principle of contradiction cannot be formulated without the aid of logical product, but the principle of double negation can be formulated that way.

b) Applied to contradictory objects, the principle of contradiction is false even though the principle of double negation remains true.

10) One cannot prove the principle of contradiction by appealing to its immediate self-evidence, because:

a) Self-evidence is not a criterion of truth if false statements can also be considered as self-evident.

b) The principle of contradiction is not self-evident to everybody.

11) One cannot prove the principle of contradiction by appealing to a psychological necessity which supposedly is situated within our mental organization and which forces us to recognize this principle; because:

a) False statements, too, can be psychologically necessary.

b) Not all perceive the necessity to recognize this principle.

12) The principle of contradiction follows neither from the definition of false statements nor from the concept of negation.

a) The concept of logical product, which is contained in this principle, cannot be derived from the definition of false statements. Thus, one may merely claim that if statement *a* is true, *a*', the statement contradictory to it, is false, but not that statement *a* can simultaneously be true and false.

b) One can construct a more cautious definition of false

statements, which would not force the simultaneous designation of the same statement as true and false.

13) The only formal proof of the principle of contradiction (in its ontological formulation) relies on the definition of object: It is only because one is to understand by object that which may not contain any contradictory properties, that no object can simultaneously contain and not contain one and the same property.

14) To prove the principle of contradiction not only formally but also factually, one would have to show that anything that is an object in the first sense, thus, everything that is something and not nothing, is also an object in the second sense, which is to say, that it does not contain a contradiction. Such a proof cannot be performed because:

a) We encounter numerous contradictions in the domain of a priori constructions of the mind (transfinite numbers, Russell's contradiction); thus, there is no guarantee that apparently contradiction-free constructions do not also contain contradictory properties.

b) In the domain of reality, contradiction has been perceived for the longest time in the phenomenon of continuous change, which underlies the entire actual world. Experience does not confirm this contradiction, but it also does not deny it; thus, there is no guarantee here as well that the apparently contradictory things and phenomena do not contain contradictory properties.

15) Because the principle of contradiction cannot be factually proven, even though it needs proof, it has no logical value. However, it does have a considerable practical and ethical value in that it is the only weapon against error and lies. That is the reason why we should recognize it.

Appendix I

The Principle of Contradiction and Symbolic Logic

Note: Since symbolic logic, except for a small circle of experts, is almost unknown, I would like to present its principles in greater detail so that anyone who wants to work through this appendix can acquire the fundamentals of this science. Furthermore, the principles of symbolic logic are so intertwined with each other that one needs to familiarize oneself with all of them in order to be able to determine the position that the principle of contradiction takes up amongst them.

In this basic sketch, I rely most of all on the excellent textbook by Couturat (1905, 1914), *L'Algèbre de la logique,*[160] but I diverge from it in many details. Sections §2, §8 and §9, as well as all notes to the other sections are written independently from other works of this orientation. I have taken over the symbolism of Couturat, which is the simplest one and does not require any new printing types.

A detailed bibliography on the subject can be found in J.Venn's book, *Symbolic Logic* (1894), as well as in the work by E.Schröder, *Vorlesungen über die Algebra der Logik* (1890–1905).

[160] Paris 1905, publisher "Scientia", for math-physics classes, Nr.24.

§ 1 Explanation of Symbols

E.1 *a*, *b*, *c*, ... signify affirmative statements: *X* contains *a*, *X* contains *b*, *X* contains *c* ...

E.2 a', b', c', ... signify negative statements: *X* contains no *a*, *X* contains no *b*, *X* contains no *c*...—a' is the negation of *a*.

E.3 1 (logical one) signifies the statement: *X* is an object, i.e., it is something.

E.4 0 (logical zero) signifies the statement: *X* is not an object, i.e., it is nothing. 0 is the negation of 1.

E.5 *ab* means that *X* contains *a* and simultaneously *b*. *ab* is called *logical product.*

E.6 $a+b$ means that *X* contains *a* or *b* whereby the case that *X* simultaneously contains *a* and *b* is not excluded. In any case, *X* has to contain at least one of these properties. $a+b$ is called *logical sum.*

E.7 $a<b$ means that *b* follows from *a*, i.e.: if *X* contains *a*, then it contains *b*, too. The $<$ sign is the symbol of *one-sided* entailment.

E.8 $a=b$ means that from *a* follows *b* and from *b* follows *a*. The = sign is the symbol of *mutual* implication, i.e., of *equivalence.*

E.9 As in mathematics, round () and square [] brackets serve to perform separations within a unified formula.

Note: To simplify, I assume that all statements *a*, *b*, *c*, ... , and respectively, a', b', c', ... , which are contained in a given formula, have the shared subject *X*. I also consider those relations of entailment ($a<b$) as statements that can be given the following meaning: "*X* has the property that if it contains *a*, then it also contains *b*".

§ 2 Axioms that are based on Properties of the Inference Relation

The inference relation is a fundamental logical relation. From statement *a* follows statement *b*, if *b* has always to be given in case *a* is given. In words, we express this relation with the aid of a relative composite sentence: "If *a* is, *b* also is." If, for example, a number is divisible by 6, it is also divisible by 3. The first statement *a* is also called the *reason*, the second the *consequence*. Using signs, we write: $a<b$ (E.7). This relation has the following properties:

α) The inference relation is *reflexive*, that is, every statement is related to itself in this relation. The expression of this relation is the *principle of identity*:

A1 $a<a$

Put into words: From *a* follows *a*, or if *X* contains *a*, then *X* contains *a*. Based on explanation 8 (E.8), this axiom can also be presented in the form of equivalence:

A1a $a=a$

β) The inference relation is *transitive*, that is, it must hold between *a* and *c*, if it holds between *a* and *b* and between *b* and *c*. The expression of this relation is the axiom of syllogism:

A2 $(a<b)(b<c) < (a<c)$

Put into words: If *b* follows from *a* und *c* follows from *b*, then *c* follows from *a*. The axiom of syllogism is of course important for the equivalence relation:

A2a $(a=b)(b=c) < (a=c)$

γ) The inference relation is *asymmetrical*, that is, it may, but does not need to hold in the direction from *b* to *a*, if it holds in the direction from *a* to *b*. This property is the basis for the differentiation between *deductive* and *reductive* reasoning (rozumowanie). The deductive inference proceeds accordingly *in agreement* with the direction of the entailment relation, the reductive inference proceeds in the opposite direction. Thus, I infer deductively, if I derive from statement *a* a statement *b*, which follows from statement *a*. I infer reductively, if for a given statement *b* I find a statement *a* from which *b* follows.

Inference and testing are types of deductive reasoning. An inference takes place if a *certain* statement forms the starting point of the reasoning process and I infer some consequences from it. For example, if the number 1908 is divisible by 6, then it is also divisible by 3. A test is performed if an *uncertain* statement is the starting point of the reasoning process, which I want to make more probable by finding *true* consequences. For example: A friend of mine, who I missed at his place, should have gone to the theatre. If this is true, then other facts agree with this, that he left the house around 7:00 pm, that he took binoculars with him, that he walked along a certain street, etc.

Proof and *explanation* are types of reductive reasoning. Proof takes place if an *uncertain* statement forms the starting point for the reasoning process and I search for a true logical antecedent for it. For example, I do not know that 157 is a prime number. I prove this statement by discovering the true reasons: 157 is not divisible by 2, nor by 3, 5, 7, 11. An explanation takes place if one or more *certain* statements form the starting point of the reasoning process and I search for some logical antecedent from which these statements would follow. For example, a free-falling body traverses 5 meters in 1 second, 20 meters in 2 seconds, about 45 meters in 3 seconds, about 80 meters in 4 seconds. I find the reason for these certain statements in a general law: a body in free-fall traverses in t seconds approximately 5 t^2 meters. Every *inductive* reason is an explanation.

Symbolic logic, as all formal logic, is neither a deductive nor an inductive logic because it investigates only the *connections* between statements without any concern whether these statements are certain or uncertain. Searching for these connections, symbolic logic states the laws for inferences of any kind. Deduction and induction—this is not a *theory* of logic but the solution to certain logical *tasks* based on a theory of reasoning.

§ 3 The Axioms of Logical Multiplication and Addition

The axioms stated below (except for A7) follow from symbol explanations E.5 and E.6, that is, they rely on the meaning of the words "and" as well as "or", just as the principle of identity and the principle of syllogism rely—at least in part—on the meaning of the words "if—then". The axioms and theorems of logical multiplication and addition correspond to each other in pairs due to the so-called law of *duality*. This law states that from a certain axiom of multiplication a certain axiom of addition comes about if we transform a product into a sum or a sum into a product and change the inference sign.

The law of duality, first discovered empirically, relies on the axiom of contraposition and De Morgan's formulas (see below S27, S28). It has significance in the sense that it orders the axioms of multiplication and addition, but it only concerns those expressions that contain a sign of entailment or equivalence. 1 and 0 correspond to each other dually.

A3	$ab<a$	A4	$a<a+b$
	$ab<b$		$b<a+b$

Put into words: *a* follows from *a* and *b*, just as *b* follows from *a* and *b*.—*a* or *b* follows from *a*, just as *a* or *b* follows from *b*. A3 is self-explanatory. If there is *a* and simultaneously *b*, then there is without a doubt *a*. The existence of *b* does not cancel [aufheben] the existence of *a*. A4 becomes clear once we consider that "*a* or *b*" means the existence of *at least* one of the terms of the sum (E.6). But if there is *a*, then there is, based on the principle of identity, at least *a*. Correspondingly, if there is *a*, then there is *a* or *b*. A3 and A4 are called the axioms of *simplification*.

A5 $(c<a)(c<b) < (c<ab)$

A6 $(a<c)(b<c) < [(a+b)<c]$

Put into words: if *a* follows from *c* and *b* follows from *c*, then likewise *a* and *b* follows from *c*. If *c* follows from *a* and *c* follows from *b*, then *c* follows from *a* or from *b*. Here, too, A5 is self-explanatory. A6 becomes clear once we consider that the existence of at least one of the terms of the sum "a or b" is sufficient for c due to the assumption $(a<c)$ and $(b<c)$. A5 and A6 are called the axioms of *composition*.

A7 $(a+b)c < ac+bc$

Put into words: If there is a or b and simultaneously c, then there also is a and c or b and c. This is the so-called simple axiom of distribution. The reciprocal (odwrotna) axiom of distribution: $ac+bc < (a+b)c$, as well as the formula $(a+c)(b+c) < ab+c$, which corresponds dually to A7, can be demonstrated on the basis of the previous axioms; thus, in the relevant sense of the word, they are no longer axioms but theorems (see A14 and A15 below) The simple axiom of distribution, however, is independent of the previous axioms. In it, a new logical thought is expressed that does not follow from the concepts of multiplication and addition. Up to now, no one has extensively investigated this thought.[161]

§ 4 Sentences that follow from the First Seven Axioms

Based on axioms A1-A7, which all *agree* with each other and are *independent* of each other, several derived logical claims can be proven. I list the most important ones and order them, in the sense of the law of duality, into pairs, and give a proof for each theorem.

Note on the proofs: All proofs consist of a series of formulas each of which either presents an inference relation (stosunek wynikania) or an equivalence relation. The *left* part of these formulas must consist of true statements, that is, of already proven axioms or theorems. Of not proven statements, this part can only contain the assumption of the thesis.

α) If there are *no* assumptions but only true statements in the left part, then it may altogether be omitted and the right part can be considered as a proven claim. An example from S4:

Thesis: $ab = ba$

[161] The independence of the simple axioms of distribution from other axioms was discovered and proven by Schröder (see *Vorlesungen über die Algebra der Logik*, Vol.1, p.282).

The first line of the proof

$$(ab<b)(ab<a) \qquad < \qquad (ab<ba)$$

The left part of this formula consist of axioms, thus, of true statements

The right part has been proven based on the left part

Thus, one may omit the left part and apply the right part, as an already proven claim, in the subsequent steps of the proof:

$$(ab<ba)(ba<ab) \qquad < \qquad (ab=ba)$$

The thesis: $ab = ba$ is proven, because the left part of the formula contains exclusively true statements.

β) If the left part of the formula contains the *assumption* of the thesis, then the assumption must be kept and brought into connection with the conclusion after the true statements have been left out. An example from S2:

Thesis: $(c<ab) < (c<a)$. — $(c<ab)$

is the assumption of the thesis.

Proof: $(c<ab)(ab<a) \qquad < \quad (c<a)$

The left part of the formula contains the assumption of the thesis: $(c<ab)$ and the axiom $(ab<a)$.

The right part is proven under the condition that we accept the assumption $(c<ab)$

Thus, after leaving out the axiom, we obtain in the conclusion:

$$(c<ab) \qquad < \quad (c<a)$$

With this, the thesis has been proven.

The numbers and letters in square brackets next to each formula (starting at Proof S2 below) indicate the axioms and theses from which that formula follows. The numbers are important since they indicate what axioms each sentence is based upon.

S1 $(a=b) \quad = (a<b)(b<a)$

S1a $(a<b)(b<a) < (a=b)$

S1b $(a=b) \quad < (a<b)(b<a)$

These sentences express explanation 8 (E.8) in symbols. They do not belong among the *axioms* because they do not present *factual* logical laws but are merely rules of *notation* (*prava znakowania*).

S2 $(c<ab) \quad < (c<a)$
$(c<ab) \quad < (c<b)$

S3 $(a+b<c) < (a<c)$
$(a+b<c) < (b<c)$

Proof S2:

$(c<ab)(ab<a) \quad < \quad (c<a)$ [A3, A2]
$(c<ab) \quad < \quad (c<a)$ *q.e.d.*

Proof S3:

$(a<a+b)(a+b<c) < (a<c)$ [A4, A2]
$(a+b<c) < (a<c)$ *q.e.d.*

Because $(c<a)$ as well as $(c<b)$ follow from $(c<ab)$, and also $(a<c)$ as well as $(b<c)$ follow from $(a+b<c)$, it is possible to say based on A5:

S2a $(c<ab) \quad < (c<a)(c<b)$
S3a $(a+b<c) < (a<c)(b<c)$

S2a and S3a present the inversion (*odwrócenie*) of axioms 5 and 6. Thus, based on S1, these axioms can be formulated as equivalences:

S2b $(c<a)(c<b) = (c<ab)$
S3b $(a<c)(b<c) = (a+b<c)$

S4 $ab = ab$ S5 $a+b = b+a$

Proof S4:

$$(ab<b)(ab<a) < (ab<ba) \quad [A3, A5]$$
$$(ba<a)(ba<b) < (ba<ab) \quad [A3, A5]$$
$$(ab<ba)(ba<ab) < (ab=ba) \quad [S1a]$$
$$ab = ba \quad q.e.d.$$

Proof S5:

$$(a<b+a)(b<b+a) < (a+b<b+a) \quad [A4, A6]$$
$$(b<a+b)(a<a+b) < (b+a<a+b) \quad [A4, A6]$$
$$(a+b<b+a)(b+a<a+b) < (a+b=b+a) \quad [S1a]$$
$$a+b = b+a \quad q.e.d.$$

S4 and S5 present the law of commutation.[162]

S6 $a=aa$ S7 $a=a+a$

Proof S6:

$$(a<a)(a<a) < (a<aa) \quad [A1, A5]$$
$$(a<aa)(aa<a) < (a=aa) \quad [A3, S1a]$$
$$a = aa \quad q.e.d.$$

Proof S7:

$$(a<a)(a<a) < (a+a<a) \quad [A1, A6]$$
$$(a<a+a)(a+a<a) < (a=a+a) \quad [A4, S1a]$$
$$a = a+a \quad q.e.d.$$

[162] Couturat does not provide proofs for these laws.

S6 and S7 are called the laws of *tautology*. To say twice that "X contains a" and "X contains a" means the same as to say once "X contains a".

S8 $\quad a+ab=a$ $\qquad$ S9 $\quad a(a+b)=a$

Proof S8:

$$\begin{aligned} (a<a)(ab<a) &< (a+ab<a) && \text{[A1, A3, A6]} \\ (a+ab<a)(a<a+ab) &< (a+ab=a) && \text{[A4, S1a]} \\ a+ab &= a && \textit{q.e.d.} \end{aligned}$$

Proof S9:

$$\begin{aligned} (a<a)(a<a+b) &< [a<a(a+b)] && \text{[A1, A4, A5]} \\ [a(a+b)<a][a<a(a+b)] &< [a(a+b)=a] && \text{[A3, S1a]} \\ a(a+b) &= a && \textit{q.e.d.} \end{aligned}$$

S8 and S9 are called the laws of *absorption*. In S8, a absorbs all the parts of the sum in which it appears as a factor, as it were; in S9, a absorbs all factors in which it appears as a part of the sum.

S10 $\quad (a<b)<(ac<bc)$ $\qquad$ S11 $\quad (a<b)<(a+c<b+c)$

Proof S10:

$$\begin{aligned} (ac<a)(a<b) &< (ac<b) && \text{[A3, A2]} \\ \alpha)\quad (a<b) &< (ac<b) && \\ (ac<b)(ac<c) &< (ac<bc) && \text{[A3, A5]} \\ \beta)\quad (ac<b) &< (ac<bc) && \\ \alpha\,\beta\ [(a<b) &< (ac<bc)] && \text{[A2]} \\ (a<b) &< (ac<bc) && \textit{q.e.d.} \end{aligned}$$

Proof S11:

$$\begin{aligned} (a<b)(b<b+c) &< (a<b+c) && \text{[A4, A2]} \\ \alpha)\quad (a<b) &< (a<b+c) && \\ (a<b+c)(c<b+c) &< (a+c<b+c) && \text{[A4, A6]} \end{aligned}$$

$\beta)$ $(a<b+c) < (a+c<b+c)$
$\alpha\,\beta$ $[(a<b) < (a+c<b+c)$ [A2]
$(a<b) < (a+c<b+c)$ *q.e.d.*

It is easy to prove that S10 and S11 are also valid as equivalences:

S10a $(a=b) < (ac=bc)$
S11a $(a=b) < (a+c=b+c)$

It is not possible to infer inversely (odwrótnie), as in simple algebra, from the equivalences $(ac=bc)$ or $(a+c=b+c)$, which are given *separately*, that $(a=b)$. However, from the two equivalences $(ac=bc)$ and $(a+c=b+c)$, if they are given *jointly*, $(a=b)$ does follow.[163]

S12 $(a<b)(c<d) < (ac<bd)$
S13 $(a<b)(c<d) < (a+c<b+d)$

Proof S12:

$\alpha)$ $(a<b)(c<d) < (a<b)$ [A3]
$(ac<a)(a<b) < (ac<b)$ [A3, A2]
$\beta)$ $(a<b) < (ac<b)$
$\alpha\,\beta < [(a<b)(c<d) < (ac<b)]$ [A2]
I) $(a<b)(c<d) < (ac<b)$
$\gamma)$ $(a<b)(c<d) < (c<d)$ [A3]
$(ac<c)(c<d) < (ac<d)$ [A3, A2]
$\delta)$ $(c<d) < (ac<d)$
$\gamma\,\delta < [(a<b)(c<d) < (ac<d)]$ [A2]
II) $(a<b)(c<d) < (ac<d)$
I II $< [(a<b)(c<d) < (ac<b)(ac<d)]$ [A5]
A) $(a<b)(c<d) < (ac<b)(ac<d)$
B) $(ac<b)(ac<d) < (ac<bd)$ [A5]
A B $< [(a<b)(c<d) < (ac<bd)$ [A2]
$(a<b)(c<d) < (ac<bd)$ *q.e.d.*

[163] See S16.

Proof S13:

$$\begin{array}{llcll}
 & \alpha) \quad (a<b)(c<d) & < & (a<b) & [A3] \\
 & (a<b)(b<b+d) & < & (a<b+d) & [A4, A2] \\
 & \beta) \quad (a<b) & < & (a<b+d) & \\
 & \alpha\,\beta < \; [(a<b)(c<d) & < & (a<b+d)] & [A2] \\
\text{I)} & (a<b)(c<d) & < & (a<b+d) & \\
 & \gamma) \quad (a<b)(c<d) & < & (c<d) & [A3] \\
 & (c<d)(d<b+d) & < & (c<b+d) & [A4, A2] \\
 & \delta) \quad (c<d) & < & (c<b+d) & \\
 & \gamma\,\delta < \; [(a<b)(c<d) & < & (c<b+d)] & \\
\text{II)} & (a<b)(c<d) & < & (c<b+d) & \\
 & \text{I II} < \; [(a<b)(c<d) & < & (a<b+d)(c<b+d)] & [A5] \\
\text{A)} & (a<b)(c<d) & < & (a<b+d)(c<b+d) & \\
\text{B)} & (a<b+d)(c<b+d) & < & (a+c<b+d) & [A6] \\
 & \text{A B} < \; [(a<b)(c<d) & < & (a+c<b+d) & [A2] \\
 & (a<b)(c<d) & < & (a+c<b+d) & q.e.d.
\end{array}$$

Shorter proof S13:

$$\begin{array}{llcll}
 & (a<b)(b<b+d) & < & (a<b+d) & [A4, A2] \\
 & \alpha) \quad (a<b) & < & (a<b+d) & \\
 & (c<d)(d<b+d) & < & (c<b+d) & [A4, A2] \\
 & \beta) \quad (c<d) & < & (c<b+d) & \\
 & \alpha\,\beta < [(a<b)(c<d) & < & (a<b+d)(c<b+d)] & [S12] \\
\text{A)} & (a<b)(c<d) & < & (a<b+d)(c<b+d) & \\
\text{B)} & (a<b+d)(c<b+d) & < & (a+c<b+d) & [A6] \\
 & \text{A B} < [(a<b)(c<d) & < & (a+c<b+d) & [A2] \\
 & (a<b)(c<d) & < & (a+c<b+d) & q.e.d.
\end{array}$$

Note on proofs S12 and S13: -- Couturat gives the proofs in a considerably shortened form.[164] Proof S12, for example, runs like this:

$$\begin{array}{lcl}
(ac<a)(a<b) & < & (ac<b) \\
(ac<c)(c<d) & < & (ac<d) \\
(ac<b)(ac<d) & < & (ac<bd)
\end{array}$$

In a more expanded form, this proof would have to be presented in the following way:

[164] *L'Algèbre de la Logique*, cit. edition, p.14.

$$
\begin{array}{lrcl}
 & (ac<a)(a<b) & < & (ac<b) \\
\alpha) & (a<b) & < & (ac<b) \\
 & (ac<c)(c<d) & < & (ac<d) \\
\beta) & (c<d) & < & (ac<d) \\
 & \alpha\,\beta < [(a<b)(c<d) & < & (ac<b)(ac<d)] \\
\mathrm{A}) & (a<b)(c<d) & < & (ac<b)(ac<d) \\
\mathrm{B}) & (ac<b)\,(ac<d) & < & (ac<bd) \\
 & \mathrm{A}\,\mathrm{B} < \quad [(a<b)(c<d) & < & (ac<bd)] \\
 & (ac<b)\,(ac<d) & < & (ac<bd) \qquad q.e.d.
\end{array}
$$

However, in this form, which corresponds entirely to the shorter proof of S13 listed above, the proof contains a *petitio principii*. The inference relations, as $(a<b)$ or $(c<d)$, should be treated as statements;[165] thus, one may apply to them the axioms that are used in respect to simple expressions a, b, c, d. If we designate: $(a<b)=A$, $(c<d)=C$, $(ac<b)=B$, $(ac<d)=D$, then Couturat's proof contains the following inference:

$$
\begin{array}{lccc}
\alpha) & A & < & B \\
\beta) & C & < & D
\end{array}
$$

$$
\begin{array}{rcl}
\alpha\,\beta & < & (AC<BD) \qquad \text{thus} \\
(A<B)(C<D) & < & (AC<BD)
\end{array}
$$

This inference is precisely an application of the claim that was to be demonstrated. This shows how careful one has to be in the demonstration of claims of symbolic logic. The shorter proof of S13 does not contain a *petitio principii* because the already demonstrated S12 can be applied.

It is easy to prove that S12 and S13 are also valid as equivalences:

$$
\begin{array}{lrcl}
\text{S12a} & (a=b)(c=d) & < & (ac=bd) \\
\text{S13a} & (a=b)(c=d) & < & (a+c=b+d) \\
\text{S14} & ac+bd & < & (a+b)c \\
\text{S15} & ab+c & < & (a+c)(b+c)
\end{array}
$$

[165] See note at the end of § 1.

Proof S14:

$$
\begin{array}{llcll}
 & (a<a+b) & < & [ac<(a+b)c] & [A4, S10] \\
\alpha) & ac & < & (a+b)c & \\
 & (b<a+b) & < & [bc<(a+b)c] & [A4, S10] \\
\beta) & bc & < & (a+b)c & \\
\alpha\,\beta < & [ac+bc & < & (a+b)c] & [A6] \\
 & ac+bc & < & (a+b)c & q.e.d.
\end{array}
$$

Proof S15:

$$
\begin{array}{llcll}
 & (ab<a) & < & (ab+c<a+c) & [A3, S11] \\
\alpha) & ab+c & < & a+c & \\
 & (ab<b) & < & (ab+c<b+c) & [A3, S11] \\
\beta) & ab+c & < & b+c & \\
\alpha\,\beta < & [ab+c & < & (a+c)(b+c)] & [A5] \\
 & ab+c & < & (a+c)(b+c) & q.e.d.
\end{array}
$$

S14 presents the *inverse* (*odwrotne*) law of distribution. It is remarkable that the inverse law of distribution can be proven whereas the simple one—as Schröder demonstrated—belongs to the ultimate axioms of logic. S14 together with A7 gives the following equivalence:

S14a $\quad (a+b)c \;=\; ac+bc$

S14a is called in short the principle of *distribution*.

Note: S15 presents the dual law of distribution, which is distinct from the actual one in that in it addition instead of multiplication takes place, and conversely. This law is unknown in ordinary algebra. It states that if one adds an expression to a product in such a way that one adds it to both factors and multiplies the resulting sums.

The inverted sentence:

S15a $\quad (a+c)(b+c) \;<\; ab+c$

is proven as follows:

$$
\begin{array}{llcll}
\alpha) & (a+c)(b+c) & < & a(b+c)+c(b+c) & [A7] \\
 & a(b+c) & < & ab+ac & [A7, S4] \\
 & c(b+c) & < & c & [A3]
\end{array}
$$

$$
\begin{array}{llll}
\beta) & a(b+c)+c(b+c) & < ab+ac+c & [S13] \\
& \alpha\,\beta < [(a+c)(b+c) & < ab+ac+c] & [A2] \\
\text{I}) & (a+c)(b+c) & < ab+ac+c & \\
& ac+c & < c & [S8, A3, A2] \\
\text{II}) & ab+ac+c & < ab+c & [S11] \\
& \text{I II} < [(a+c)(b+c) & < ab+c] & [A2] \\
& (a+c)(b+c) & < ab+c & q.e.d.
\end{array}
$$

Together, S15 and S15a result in the equivalence:

S15b $\quad (a+c)(b+c) = ab+c$

S16 $\quad (ac=bc)(a+c=b+c) < (a=b)$

Proof S16:

$$
\begin{array}{ll}
(a+c=b+c) < [a(a+c)=a(b+c)] & [S10a] \\
[a=a(a+c)][a(a+c)=a(b+c)] < [a=a(b+c)] & [S9, A2a] \\
[a=a(b+c)][a(b+c)=ab+ac] < (a=ab+ac) & [S14a, A2a] \\
(a=ab+ac)(ab+ac=ab+bc) < (a=ab+bc) & [S11a, A2a]
\end{array}
$$

Based on S11a, $(ab+ac=ab+bc)$ follows from the *assumption* $(ac=bc)$.

$$
\begin{array}{ll}
(a=ab+bc)[ab+bc=b(a+c) < [a=b(a+c)] & [S14a, A2a] \\
[a=b(a+c)][b(a+c)=b(b+c)] < [a=b(b+c)] & [S10a, A2a]
\end{array}
$$

Based on S10a, $b(a+c)=b(b+c)$ follows from the *assumption* $(a+c=b+c)$.

$$
[a=b(b+c)][b(b+c)=b] \quad < \quad (a=b) \qquad [S9, A2a]
$$

It is permitted to omit all mediating parts and keep only the assumption:

$$
(ac=bc)(a+c=b+c) < (a=b) \qquad q.e.d.
$$

S17 $\quad (a<b) = (a=ab)$
S18 $\quad (a<b) = (a+b=b)$

Proof S17:

$$
\begin{array}{llll}
& (a<a)(a<b) & < (a<ab) & [A1, A5] \\
\alpha) & (a<b) & < (a<ab) &
\end{array}
$$

	$(a<ab)(ab<a)$	$<$	$(a=ab)$	[A3, S1a]
$\beta)$	$(a<ab)$	$<$	$(a=ab)$	
$\alpha\,\beta <$	$[(a<b)$	$<$	$(a=ab)$	[A2]
I)	$(a<b)$	$<$	$(a<ab)$	
$\gamma)$	$(a=ab)$	$<$	$(a<a)$	[S1b, A3, A2]
$\delta)$	$(a<ab)$	$<$	$(a<ba)$	[S2]
$\gamma\,\delta <$	$[(a=ab)$	$<$	$(a<b)]$	[A2]
II)	$(a=ab)$	$<$	$(a<b)$	
I II $<$	$[(a<b)$	$=$	$(a=ab)]$	[S1a]
	$(a<b)$	$=$	$(a=ab)$	*q.e.d.*

Proof S18:

	$(a<b)(b<b)$	$<$	$(a+b<b)$	[A1, A6]
$\alpha)$	$(a<b)$	$<$	$(a+b<b)$	
	$(a+b<b)(b<a+b)$	$<$	$(a+b=b)$	[A4, S1a]
$\beta)$	$(a+b<b)$	$<$	$(a+b=b)$	
$\alpha\,\beta <$	$[(a<b)$	$<$	$(a+b=b)$	[A2]
I)	$(a<b)$	$<$	$(a+b=b)$	
$\gamma)$	$(a+b=b)$	$<$	$(a+b<b)$	[S1b, A3, A2]
$\delta)$	$(a+b<b)$	$<$	$(a<b)$	[S3]
$\gamma\,\delta <$	$[(a+b=b)$	$<$	$(a<b)]$	[A2]
II)	$(a+b=b)$	$<$	$(a<b)$	
I II $<$	$[(a<b)$	$=$	$(a+b=b)]$	[S1a]
	$(a<b)$	$=$	$(a+b=b)$	*q.e.d.*

S17 and S18 permit the transformation of any inference relation into an equivalence relation.

§ 5 The Principles regarding 0 and 1

We do know, based on the explanations E.3 and E.4, that 0 signifies a statement "*X* is not an object", and 1—"*X* is an object". These symbols concern the following axioms:

A8 $0<a$ A9 $a<1$

Put into words: If *X* is not an object, then it contains some property *a*, thus everything follows from 0. If *X* contains some property, then *X* is an object, thus 1 follows from everything.

A10 $aa'<0$ A11 $1<a+a'$

In words: If *X* contains *a* and simultaneously does not contain *a*, then *X* is not an object. If *X* is an object, the *X* contains *a* or it does not contain *a*.

Axioms A8 and A10 as well as A9 and A11 can be brought together in these equivalence formulas:

A10a $aa'=0$ A11a $a+a'=1$

Symbolists call A10 the principle of contradiction, A11a the principle of the *excluded third.* The axioms A8-A11 require some additional explanation.

A9 does not pose any difficulty. If *X* is an object, then it is valid: whatever property *X* may contain, it always is an object. A8, however, may appear unusual. Here we cut into a problem that is already in close connection to the principle of contradiction.

First and foremost, one needs to realize that the statement, which is symbolized by the logical zero, contains a contradiction. *X*, after all, is an object; and by saying that "X is not an object" we give the object *X* contradictory properties. However, this does not explain why *X* is supposed to have *any* property at all. One can try to justify this principle in numerous ways:

α) One could appeal to the law of *contraposition*[166] by which it is *permitted* to reverse any entailment relation by simultaneously negating its parts. Via contraposition we receive from A9: ($a<1$) the formula ($0<a'$); but because *a*' as well as *a* signify an *arbitrary* property of 0 and 1, one may replace *a*' with *a* and get A8 in this manner. The law of contraposition, however, already presupposes the four principles above, thus it is based on axiom A8.[167]

β) Further, one could try to demonstrate this axiom with the aid of the concept of *entailment.* Quite often, an entailment relation is determined with the aid of the concept of a "contradictory object". In the sense of this definition, "From *a* follows *b*", that is, "if there is *a*, then there is *b*", would mean that *a* contains a contradiction if there is no *b*. But 0 always contains a contradiction; thus, it must be true that b follows from 0 because it is true that if there is no b,

[166] Translator's note: contraposition (*p*->*q*) iff (not-*q* -> not-*p*)

[167] See S26

0 contains a contradiction. However, 0 also contains a contradiction if there is b; 0, after all, is a contradictory object. And because of this, everything follows from a contradictory object. This claim was already known to the Scholastics; they said, *ad impossibile sequitur quodlibet* (that is, $0<a$, because 0 is *impossibile*), and also *necessarium sequitur ad quodlibet* (that is, $a<1$, because 1 is *necessarium*). Duns Scotus puts it clearly: "... *est prima conclusio, quod ad quamlibet statementem implicantem contradictionem de forma, sequitur quaelibet alia statement in consequential formali*".[168] However, the concept of entailment mentioned above already presupposes - as does the law of contraposition - the four axioms listed; thus, it also relies on axiom A8.[169]

γ) Furthermore, one might try to support axiom A8 based on the consideration that one may attribute arbitrary properties to contradictory objects since such objects are of no concern to us in the first place. Whether they contain a few pairs of contradictory properties or more does not matter, and is even more convenient in the formal logical treatment. The claim, however, that it is permissible to attribute arbitrary properties to contradictory objects, appears to be ad hoc. It would have to be justified first.

δ) Finally, one might suspect that axioms A8 and A10 taken together express the *definition* of logical zero and consequently, that their truth is based on a definition. Such a solution would be the one that is most correct, and beyond this, it would explain axiom A10. But first one would have to examine what logical *need* could move us to postulate such a definition.

From the above considerations, it is apparent that the problem of the justification of the axiom A8, just as that of A7, is neither clear nor easy to solve. It would be of the utmost significance to discover the logical ideas that are hidden at the foundation of these axioms.

The situation is no different with respect to axioms 10 and 11. These axioms, too, contain some *new factors* that can neither be

[168] *Librum Priorum Analyticorum Aristotelis Questiones.* Questio X (Ed. Wadding, Vol.1, p.288, § 14). In Scholastic logic, which is unfamiliar but nevertheless considered with disregard, valuable truths are hidden which should be retrieved from the past.

[169] See S24

derived from the fundamental explanations nor from the other logical axioms. Axiom 10 states that if the object X contains a and simultaneously does not contain a, then X is not an object, that is, it is nothing. One could base this axiom on the definition of "*object*" by assuming that an object is that which does not contain a contradiction; and, whatever does contain a contradiction, is not an object. But now again the question arises, what utility such a definition might have for us, and why we accept it. I have tried to answer this question in Chapter XX of this treatise. In my opinion, both the principle of contradiction and the definition of "object" as something free of contradiction are based on the *practical* need to have a weapon at hand against errors and lies. Who knows whether similar practical needs or, respectively, unconscious generalizations of the simplest of facts of experience are also hidden in other principles? A11 presents the principle of the excluded third in Aristotle's formulation: "If X is an object, then it must either contain a or not contain a." *Tertium non datur*. In this principle, too, a new idea is present, the development of which should be dedicated to a separate treatise. One ought to suppose, however, that A10, even in connection to A8, that is, in the form of A10a, is not the principle of contradiction in Aristotle's sense, even though it has the same name. Soon we will be able to convince ourselves that *the principle of contradiction in Aristotle's formulation is not at all a principle of symbolic logic, but merely a derived claim.*

The sole purpose of the remarks above was *to refer to* certain problems; their solution belongs to the most difficult tasks of logic.

§ 6 Assertions that follow from Axioms 8-11

S19 $a\text{x}0=0$[170] S20 $a+1=1$

S21 $a+0=a$ S22 $a\text{x}1=a$

Proof S19 and S21:

[170] Translator's note: Łukasiewicz introduces 'x' without explanation. The notation corresponds to Couturat's formulas introduced in his "Definitions of 0 and 1", pp.17-20 (Couturat 1914). In particular, Łukasiewicz's formulations S19—S22 are identical to Coutarat's "formulas comprising the rules for the calculus of 0 and 1" on p.19 (ibid).

$(0<a)=(a\text{x}0=0)=(a+0=a)$ [A8, S17, S18]

Proof S20 and S22

$(a<1)=(a+1=1)=(a\text{x}1=\text{a})$ [A9, S17, S18]

The assertions above (except S20) justify the selection of symbols. The logical symbols 0 and 1 behave in logical multiplication and logical addition the same way as the arithmetic symbols 0 and 1 behave in arithmetic multiplication and arithmetic addition.

S23 $a''=a$

Proof S23:

$$
\begin{array}{lrcll}
 & (aa'=0)(0=a'a'') & < & (aa'=a'a'') & [\text{A10a, A2a}] \\
\alpha) & aa' & = & a'a'' & \\
 & (a+a=1)(1=a'+a'') & < & (a+a'=a'+a'') & [\text{A11a, A2a}] \\
\beta) & a+a' & = & a'+a'' & \\
 & \alpha\,\beta & < & (a''=a) & [\text{S16}] \\
 & a'' & = & a & q.e.d.
\end{array}
$$

S23 presents the principle of *double negation.*

S24 $(a<b)=(ab'=0)$ S25 $(a<b)=(a'+b=1)$

Proof S24:

$$
\begin{array}{lrcll}
\alpha) & (a<b) & < & (ab'<bb') & [\text{S10}] \\
 & (ab'<bb')(bb'<0) & < & (ab'<0) & [\text{A10, A2}] \\
 & (ab'<0)(0<ab') & < & (ab'=0) & [\text{A8, S1a}] \\
 & (a<b) & < & (ab'=0) & [\text{A2}]
\end{array}
$$

β) In order to show that $(ab'=0) < (a<b)$, a supplemental assertion needs to be demonstrated first:

$$a < ab+ab'$$

$a = a\mathrm{x}1$	$=$	$a(b+b') = ab+ab'$	[S10a, S14a, S22, A11a]
a	$=$	$ab+ab'$	[A2a]
$(a=ab+ab')(ab'=0)$	$<$	$(a=ab+0)$	[S11a, A2a]
$(a=ab+0)$	$<$	$(a=ab)$	[S21, A2a]
$(a=ab)$	$<$	$(a<b)$	[S17]
$(ab'=0)$	$<$	$(a<b)$	[A2]
$\alpha\,\beta < [(a<b)$	$=$	$(ab'=0)]$	[S1a]
$(a<b)$	$=$	$(ab'=0)$	*q.e.d.*

Proof S25:

α) $(a<b)$	$<$	$(a'+a<a'+b)$	[S11]
$(1<a'+a)(a'+a<a'+b)$	$<$	$(1<a'+b)$	[A11, A2]
$(1<a'+b)(a'+b<1)$	$<$	$(a'+b=1)$	[A9, S1a]
$(a<b)$	$<$	$(a'+b=1)$	[A2]

β) In order to show that $(a'+b=a) < (a<b)$, a supplemental assertion needs to be demonstrated first:

$$b < (a+b)(a'+b)$$

$$\begin{aligned} b &= b+b = b+b\mathrm{x}1 \\ &= b+b(a+a') \\ &= b+ba+ba' \\ &= 0+ab+ba'+bb \\ &= aa'+ab+ba'+bb \\ &= (a+b)(a'+b) \end{aligned}$$

[A10, A11a, S4, S5, S7, S11a, S14a, S21, S22]

b	$<$	$(a+b)(a'+b)$	[A2a]
$[b=(a+b)(a'+b)](a'+b=1)$	$<$	$[b=(a+b)\mathrm{x}1]$	[S10a, A2a]
$[b=(a+b)\mathrm{x}1]$	$<$	$(b=a+b)$	[S22, A2a]
$(b=a+b)$	$<$	$(a<b)$	[S18]
$(a'+b=1)$	$<$	$(a<b)$	[A2]
$\alpha\,\beta <$ $[(a<b)$	$=$	$(a'+b=1)]$	[S1a]
$(a<b)$	$=$	$(a'+b=1)$	*q.e.d.*

S24 and S25 allow us to transform relations of implication into relations of equivalence—in a different manner than S17 and S18. These two assertions rely on all for axioms A8-A11. Based on S24, the relation of implication could be defined with the aid of the symbol 0.[171]

S26 $(a<b) = (b'<a')$

Proof:

$(a<b) = (ab'=0)$		[S24]
$(b'<a') = (b'a'=0)=(b'a=0)(ab'=0)$		[S24, S23 S4, S2a]
$(a<b) = (b'<a')$		*q.e.d.*

S26 presents the law of *contraposition*. This important law states: if *b* follows from *a*, then the negation of *a* follows from the negation of *b* and conversely. This is the foundation of the *modus tollens* inference and of the apagogic proofs. By relying on S24, this law relies on all four axioms A8-A11.[172]

S26a $(a<b') = (b<a')$

Proof:

$(a<b') = (ab''=0)$
$= (ab=0)=(ba=0)=(b<a')$ [A2a, S4, S23, S24]

S27 $(a+b)' = a'b'$ S28 $(ab)' = a'+b'$

Proof S27:

α) Supplemental assertion: $a+b = ab+ab'+a'b$

$a+b=a\text{x}1+b\text{x}1=a(b+b')+b(a+a')$	[S22, S10a, S11a,
$=ab+ab'+ba+ba'=ab+ab'+a'b$	S14, S4, S7, A11a]
$a+b = ab+ab'+a'b$	[A2a]*q.e.d.*
$(a+b)+a'b' = ab+ab'+a'b+a'b'$	[S11a, S14a,
$=a(b+b')+a'(b+b')=a+a'=1$	A11a]
$[(a+b)+a'b'=1] = [(a+b)'<a'b']$	[A2a, S25]
$(a+b)'< a'b'$	

[171] See above § 5 β.

[172] See above § 5 α.

β) $(a+ba'b'=aa'b'+ba'b'=$
$0\text{x}b'+bb'a'=0\text{x}b'+0\text{x}a'=0+0=0$ [S14a, A10a, S19, S4, S7]
$[(a+b)a'b'=0] = [a'b'<(a+b)']$ [A2a, S24]
$a'b' < (a+b)'$
$\alpha\,\beta < [(a+b)' = a'b']$ [S1a]
$(a+b)' = a'b'$ *q.e.d.*

Proof S28:

α) It is possible to prove the supplemental assertion $a'+b' = a'b'+a'b+ab'$ based on the formula from the previous proof $a+b = ab+ab'+a'b$ by substituting a and b with a' and b' and a' and b' with a and b.

$a'+b' = a'b'+a'b+ab'$
$(a'+b')+ab=a'b'+a'b+ab'+ab$ [S11a, S14a, A11a]
$=a'(b'+b)+a(b'+b)=a'+a=1$
$[(a'+b')+ab=1] = [(ab)'<a'+b']$ [A2a, S25]

$(ab)' < a'+b'$

β) $(a'+b')ab =a'ab+b'ab$ [S14a, A10a,
$=0\text{x}b+b'ba=0\text{x}b+0\text{x}a=0+0=0$ S19, S4, S7]
$[(a'+b')+ab=0] = [a'+b'<(ab)']$ [A2a, S24]
$a'+b' < (ab)'$
$\alpha\,\beta < [(ab)' = a'+b']$ [S1a]
$(ab)' = a'+b'$ *q.e.d.*

S27 and S28 teach us how to negate a product or a sum. The negation of a sum is equivalent to the product of the negated parts of the sum. These assertions bear the name *De Morgan's Laws* after De Morgan, who first discovered them.[173]

S29 $(ab<c)=(c'a<b')=(bc'<a')=(c'<a'+b')=(b<c+a')=(a<b'+c)$

Proof:

All the expressions are equivalent with the following formulas:

[173] De Morgan, an English logician and mathematician; he lived 1806-1871.

$$(abc'=0) = (a'+b'+c=1) \quad [S23\text{-}S28]$$

One might call S29 the *expanded* law of contraposition. Similar assertions are easily proven for any number of statements.

In this way, I have given the proofs for the 29 most important assertions of symbolic logic. Together with the 11 axioms, they form the fundamental laws of inference. Thus, we have met a total of 40 logical laws. I am listing them below to make it easier to keep an overview of them.

§ 7 Summary of the Axioms and Assertions of Symbolic Logic

A1	$a<a$	principle of identity
A2	$(a<b)(b<c)<(a<c)$	principle of syllogism
A3	$ab<b$	principles of simplification
A4	$a<a+b$	
A5, S2	$(c<a)(c<b)=(c<ab)$	principles of composition
A6, S3	$(a<c)(b<c)=(a+b<c)$	
A7, S14	$(a+b)c=ac+bc$	principle of distribution
A8, S10	$aa'=0$	principle of contradiction
A9, S11	$a+a'=1$	principle of excluded third
S1	$(a=b)=(a<b)(b<a)$	definition of equivalence
S4	$ab=ba$	laws of commutation
S5	$a+b=b+a$	
S6	$a=aa$	laws of tautology
S7	$a=a+a$	
S8	$a+ab=a$	laws of absorption
S9	$a(a+b)=a$	
S10	$(a<b)<(ac<bc)$	
S10a	$(a=b)<(ac=bc)$	
S11	$(a<b)<(a+c<b+c)$	
S11a	$(a=b)<(a+c=b+c)$	
S12	$(a<b)(c<d)<(ac<bd)$	
S12a	$(a=b)(c=d)<(ac=bd)$	
S13	$(a<b)(c<d)<(a+c<b+d)$	
S13a	$(a=b)(c=d)<(a+c=b+d)$	
S16	$(ac=bc)(a+c=b+c)<(a=b)$	
S15b	$(a+c)(b+c)=ab+c$	dual law of distribution
S17	$(a<b)=(a=ab)$	

S18 $(a<b)=(a+b=b)$
S19 $a\times 0=0$
S20 $a+1=1$
S21 $a+0=a$
S22 $a\times 1=a$
S23 $a''=a$ law of double negation
S24 $(a<b)=(ab'=0)$
S25 $(a<b)=(a'+b=1)$
S26 $(a<b)=(b'<a')$ law of contraposition
S27 $(a+b)'=a'b'$ De Morgan's laws
S28 $(ab)'=a'+b'$
S29 $(ab<c)=(c'a<b')=(bc'<a')=$
$(c'<a'+b')=(b<c+a')=(a<b'+c)$

§ 8 The significance of symbolic logic

In conclusion to the above outline of symbolic logic, I would like to add a few words about its significance. There are frequent objections, especially from philosophers, that formal logic in general and symbolic logic, in particular, is a mere *intellectual toy* without any greater significance. Quite often it is the case that the ones who advance such objections do not know the teachings that they are fighting. Thus, there is no merit in answering them but instead one has to ask them to first acquaint themselves in greater detail with the matter that they are judging. But whoever has worked through the few paragraphs above and has gained familiarity with the foundations of symbolic logic will without doubt admit that its value is based on the following points:

α) This logic forms a *system of truths*, which are appropriately justified and framed in an exact symbolism, like a system of any mathematical truths. Thus, whoever acknowledges that, for example, the theory of algebraic functions or number theory does have value as such even though they do not have a "practical" application will also have to admit that symbolic logic has at least the same value as those mathematical sciences. Every truth is valuable because it gives anyone who can grasp and perceive it the gift of bright moments of pure and untarnished enjoyment.

β) Should symbolic logic not offer any further significance, then the fact alone that *themes, which are not mathematical, can be grasped by symbols with mathematical precision*, gives it enduring theoretical value. After all, the conviction that only mathematics and physics are "exact" sciences proves itself to be wrong. Logic is just as exact a science as mathematics. The symbolic treatment of logic reveals a deep relationship between logic and mathematics, which leads to the viewpoint that all a priori sciences grow from the same root. This viewpoint is a valuable scientific gain for both the philosophy of mathematics and the theory of knowledge.

γ) Beyond this, symbolic logic has the value that it forms an *incomparably more exact and extensive theory of logical facts* than traditional formal logic. Here, for the first time, the attempt of an exact determination and grasp of fundamental logical principles emerges; for the first time, the possibility presents itself of investigating what relation these principles stand to each other, which ones of them are independent of the others, and which ones can be demonstrated based on the others. Here, a larger number of new logical themes emerge, which—by arousing our curiosity—give new life to the skeleton of traditional logic, which had been withering away for centuries, and demand new research. Who could predict to what scientific discoveries this direction of research will lead us?

δ) But for the practice of scientific thinking, too, symbolic logic shows just as much value. I would like to recall a fact, which is often forgotten or not known at all, about the great part that was played by formal logic during the beginning of the development of the natural sciences. Whoever has read the treatises by Galileo or the works on physics by Pascal will without doubt have noticed the precision and delicacy with which the thought of these great minds had been endowed. Good observation of just a few facts had been enough for them to develop excellent theories with great universality, and in these theories, the element of deductive and formal thought dominates. The capacity for such thinking, however, they acquired because they came out of a good school of scholastic logic and grew up in an atmosphere that favored logic. How tremendously useful a similar knowledge of logic and a similar precision of thought would be for contemporary scientists and, even more so, for philosophers, philologists, historians and sociologists! If the imperfect traditional logic had such a great significance for the precision of thought, then the more complete symbolic logic should gain an even greater significance in this respect. However, the objections of the opponents aim precisely at this point. Symbolic logic has no practical value because its theories are *a priori*; they do not take account of the *facts* of thinking. I put aside that such an objection reveals a lack of knowledge on the side of the opponents regarding the difference that exists between *logic* and the *psychology of cognition*: I put this counter-argument aside because the awareness of this difference is steadily growing in modern philosophy and because "psychologism" in logic fortunately no longer continues to be fashionable. I want to bring attention to another matter: symbolic logic is with certainty just as dispensable for every day thought as algebra is dispensable for the accounting of personal finances; to account for ordinary expenses it is sufficient to master, at most, also multiplication apart from addition and subtraction. But does it follow from this that algebra is superfluous? Engineers, surveyors, astronomers, physicists and even artillery officers—all of them cannot function without knowledge of algebra. In the same way, symbolic logic will show itself to be indispensable wherever complicated logical tasks arise that can no longer be solved with the aid of ordinary everyday methods of thinking. The reason that so far only a few of such tasks exist is perhaps due to the inability of scientists, unfamiliar with more delicate logical methods, to generate sufficient intellectual effort to develop more complicated tasks in the first place! In the course of the perfection of the logical instrument and the spread of its findings, more difficult logical tasks will certainly present themselves.

ε) As a last point one should note that a new science has already grown from symbolic logic that should gain an even greater significance for the praxis of thought than its origin: it is the general *theory of relations*. This science, which is also *a priori* and employs symbols, will some day, as an enrichment and generalization of symbolic logic, become the foundation of methodology. All scientific syntheses could be produced precisely because some *relations* exist by which we connect a multitude of facts into a unity. Depending on the kind of the connecting relation, the character of the synthesis and the method of investigation change. To provide an explanation and to offer an example, I am mentioning the earlier method of *generalization* and the newer *genetic* method. Previously, human beings had been considered in terms of a *symmetric* relation of similarity, which connects them to other human beings, and the species human being was created by a search for universal laws that apply all human beings. Today, based on the genetic method, human beings are treated also with respect to *asymmetric* relations of descendence, which connect a human being with his parents and in this way not universal laws are created but chains of development. This difference in synthesis springs from the difference in the connecting relations. Symmetric relations are the foundation of the universal laws of series.[174] Should symbolic logic have only this merit, namely, that it made possible the emergence of the theory of relations, then it should be studied and appreciated for this reason alone.

Despite all this, symbolic logic will not gain popularity with a certain type of philosopher. The creation of snappy syntheses with beautifully sounding words is after all a nice and conceivable matter. Symbolic logic, however, has to be *learned* first and learned the same way in which one learns mathematics, pencil in hand, not omitting a single letter, not passing over a single proof. One must want to work *scientifically* and one has to be able to do so. But this is a much too dry and boring a labor for those spirits that yearn for the absolute.

§ 9 The Principle of Contradiction in the Light of Symbolic Logic

As I have mentioned above, the principle of contradiction in Aristotle's formulation does not present an axiom of symbolic logic. This formulation states: "One and the same cannot at the same time belong and not belong to the same under the same conditions", which means "no object can simultaneously contain and not contain the same property". I assume that this formulation is equivalent to the following conditional sentence: "If X is an object, then X cannot simultaneously contain a and not contain a". This conditional sentence can be presented symbolically in the following way:

S30 $1 < (aa')'$

[174] See my note on the theory of relations in "Przegląd Filozoficzny" XI, 1908, pp. 344-347.

Thus, S30 would present the principle of contradiction in Aristotle's formulation.

α) Let us consider in which way this assertion could be demonstrated. We have only two ways of conducting a proof: because S30 contains the negation of a product and if one wants to trace it back to already known axioms or, respectively, already proven laws, then one must use either the law of contraposition or De Morgan's laws.

1) Applying the law of contraposition, we get:

$$[1<(aa')'] \quad = \quad (aa'<0) \qquad [S26, S23]$$

From this, based on S1b, it follows:

$$(aa'<0) \quad < \quad [1<(aa')']$$

Thus, S30 can be derived from A10 with the aid of the law of contraposition.

2) Applying De Morgan's laws, we get:

$$[1<(aa')'] = (1<a+a')$$

From this, based on S1b, it follows:

$$(1<a+a') < [1<(aa')']$$

Thus, S30 can also be derived from A11 with the aid of De Morgan's laws. Either way, the principle of contradiction in Aristotle's formulation can be *proven* with the aid of axioms of symbolic logic; thus, it is a *derived assertion.*

β) Now let us consider which of the 11 axioms of symbolic logic constitutes the basis of the principle of contradiction.

1) The proof via contraposition relies on S26. This assertion follows from S24, and S24 relies immediately on axioms A2, A8, A9, A10 and A11, but indirectly on the axioms that, among others, are contained in S14a and S17. S14a contains A7 and S14, which in turn relies on axioms A4 and A6; S17 relies on axioms A1, A3, and A5. Thus, from this follows that in proof 1) the principle of contradiction relies on all eleven axioms, and the law of contraposition and S24 also rely on them.

2) The proof via De Morgan's laws relies on S28, which, among others, presupposes S24. It already turned out earlier that this assertion relies on all eleven axioms; thus, in proof 2) as well, the principle of contradiction presupposes all axioms. But because there are no other simple proofs of the principle of contradiction, it follows from this that *all axioms of symbolic logic taken together form the sufficient reason of this principle.*

It appears from the considerations α) and β) that the principle of contradiction is not a highest law if there are logical systems that have been formulated just as precisely, if not more precisely than Aristotle's system, in which this principle is merely a derived assertion (α) and, even further, a very complicated assertion (β). Each of the eleven axioms of symbolic logic, on which the principle of contradiction relies, presents without doubt a *simpler* thought than this principle and has a significance that is far more *important.*

γ) However, someone might object that the fight here is merely about words because, even if axiom A11, which is an expression of the principle of the excluded third, does not present the principle of contradiction, then at least axiom A10 does present it, though in a different formulation. We already knew beforehand not only that due to the law of contraposition S30 follows from A10, but also in reverse that A10 follows from S30. Thus, these two formulas are *equivalent.* If we take into consideration that in any case A10 in connection with A8 bears the name of principle of contradiction in symbolic logic, then the hunch that S30 and A10 are not only equivalent but that they also *mean the same* is not improbable In order to solve this problem and to cast away even the shadow of a doubt, one needs to work on this problem as extensively as possible.

If we compare these two formulas, no matter whether they are expressed in signs:

$1<(aa')'$ and $aa'<0$

or in words (I select here the formulations which correspond to each other the most):

"That which is an object cannot simultaneously contain and not contain the same property."

"That which simultaneously contains and not contains the same property cannot be an object",

We find that the subjects as well as the predicates in them (respectively, antecedent and consequent) are *different* and mean *something else*. Insofar as we want to hold on to the definition of sameness of meaning stated in Chapter II, we have to state that *these formulas, or statements, cannot be the same in meaning in any way*.

But let us go further and let us assume that that definition of sameness of meaning is too narrow and that cases are possible in which two statements with differing and *not sense-identical* subjects and predicates nevertheless have the same meaning. If such cases do exist, one should look for them most of all in the range of statements that contain the same concepts, only ordered differently. It would be the following statements: "No *A* is *B*" and "No *B* is *A*". If we present the classes of objects A and B with the aid of circles, as it is usually done,

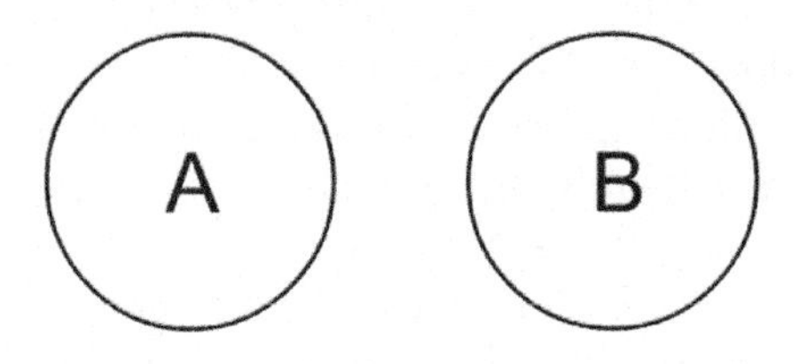

then the sameness in meaning of these statements could be proven in the following manner: -- The statement "No *A* is *B*" means that the class of objects *A* excludes the class of objects *B*. Accordingly, all of *A* lies outside the circumference of *B*, that is, *A* and *B* have no shared elements. The statement "No *B* is *A*" means that the class of objects *B* excludes the class of objects *A*. Accordingly, all of *B* lies outside the circumference of *A*, that is, *B* and *A* have no shared elements. Whether I say that *A* and *B*—or *B* and *A*—contain no shared elements amounts to the same thing based on the law of commutation. And because the first statement "No *A* is *B*" as well as the second statement "No *B* is *A*" mean the same as what a third statement means: "*A* and *B* (or *B* and *A*, respectively) contain no shared element", it shows that these statements are not only equivalent but also the same in meaning. In fact, that which corresponds to these statements, the relation between the two circles above, is the same in all cases.

S30 and A10 are also statements of the kind "No *A* is *B*" and "No *B* is *A*". The formulas do not look like this because the signs, which follow the symbol of implication, not only express the affirmation but also the negation of the copula (łącznika). But if we write:

A10: "That which is simultaneously *a* and *a*', is not 1 [that is, it is 0]."

S30: "That which is 1, is not simultaneously *a* and *a*' [that is, it is (*aa*')']", then the identity of the conceptual components in these two formulas becomes visible. Thus, one might claim that S30 and A10 have the same meaning; but in this case the principle of contradiction in Aristotle's formulation would be not merely a *derived assertion*, but also an *axiom*.

Are these deliberations acceptable? It seems to me that this is not the case—and for the following reasons:

1) Even though the statements "No *A* is *B*" and "No *B* is *A*" contain the same concepts in reverse order, the third statement, to which both these statements must be traced back to demonstrate their sameness in meaning, already contains a *new* concept. That "*A* and *B* do not have any shared elements" or that "*A* and *B* exclude each other" or that "No *A* exists that would simultaneously be *B*, or respectively, no *B* that would be simultaneously *A*"—all these statements contain the concept of *logical multiplication*, indicated by the word "and" as well as "simultaneously". Thus, the third statement has not the same meaning as the first or the second one. And is there anyone who can justify the sameness of meaning of the first two statements in a different manner and without the assumption of a third statement?

2) If two statements have the same meaning, then their difference relies only on the *signs,* and the factual state of affairs that the signs designate must be *the same* in both cases. The equivalence of statements with the same meaning is thus always *unconditional*, that is, it does not presuppose any *factual* conditions and is not dependent on the truth of any assumption, with the sole exception of the statement that determines the sameness of meaning of the signs In our case, the matter looks different; the equivalence of the statements "No *A* is *B*" and "No *B* is *A*" is not unconditional, but rather relies on the law of contraposition and on all the axioms of

symbolic logic. If somebody does not accept just one of these axioms, cases might occur in which these two statements would not be equivalent. This can be shown by an example. Let us assume that somebody does not accept axiom A8, thus he does not accept that everything follows from a contradictory object. Let us further assume, that *A* designates "a number that belongs to the series of natural numbers", and *B* designates "the last number of the series of natural numbers". *B* is a contradictory object and any *B* is simultaneously not *B*. Because it is true that "No *A* is *B*", that is, no number, which is the last in our series, belongs to this series. On the contrary, the last number of the series of natural numbers belongs to this series, and it does so according to the law of simplification A3. Schematically:

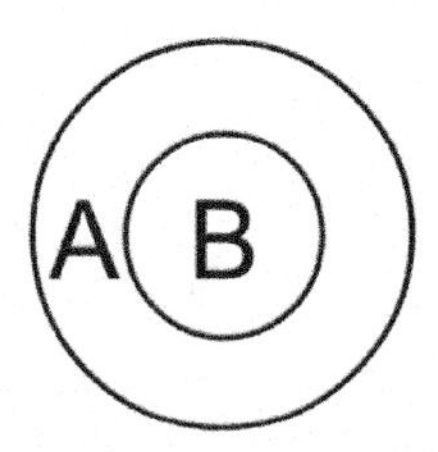

It is only then simultaneously true that "No *B* is *A*", if we assume A8. After all, *B* is a contradictory object, thus if something is *B* in the sense of A8, then it contains some property and does not contain that property.

In this it shows itself that the equivalence of the statements "No *A* is *B*" and "No *B* is *A*" is not unconditional, and conditionally equivalent statements cannot be the same in meaning. Conditional equivalence is a sure indicator that a *factual* difference exists in the statements and not just an external difference of the *signs*.

Thus, S30 and A10 are not unconditionally equivalent statements. Their equivalence depends on the law of contraposition, which presupposes indirectly all axioms of symbolic logic, amongst them A10. *Accordingly, it appears to be clear that S30 and A10 are not synonymous statements.* The result of the considerations α) and β), which prove that the Aristotelian principle of contradiction is a *complicated derived assertion*, remains entirely in force.

δ) I consider this result to be very important because it reveals that the principle of contradiction, despite Aristotle's proofs and the generally accepted opinion, is neither a *final* nor an *unprovable* law. Symbolic logic, in fact, proves something further; many logical laws have no connection at all to the principle of contradiction; consequently, this principle is not only not *final*, but it also does not form an *indispensable* foundation of logical thinking.

Let us assume the case that is most advantageous for our opponents, namely that the principle of contradiction stands in a very close connection with the axioms A8-A11 (without doubt, some connection does exist); in this case, at most merely sentences S19-S29 would presuppose this principle. Axioms A1-A7 and sentences S1-S18, on the other hand, are completely independent of the principle of contradiction. From this it also follows that the principle of identity and of the syllogism, the principle of simplification and composition, the principle of distribution, the laws of commutation, of tautology, absorption and many other laws for which we do not have individual names, would be true even if the principle of contradiction would cease to be a valid principle. And these laws are sufficient to be able to make deductive and inductive inferences and build up a science. It would be high time that we stop repeating uncritically with Aristotle that the principle of contradiction is the highest law and ultimate foundation of our entire knowledge.

In this context, one must note that there are also doubts whether all sentences S19-S29 presuppose the principle of contradiction. A9, as well as S20 and S22, which follow from it, certainly do not depend on this principle. It further appears that the principle of the excluded third, that is A11, is independent of the principle of contradiction. But to reach some certainty in this matter, many lengthy and detailed investigations would have to be carried out, which would have taken up too much room in this appendix. But whatever the result might be, it could only confirm the opinion about the significance of the principle of contradiction that was expressed above, but never refute it.

ε) I have frequently mentioned that contradictory objects do not fall under the principle of contradiction. Symbolic logic, however, does employ a contradictory object in its formulas, namely, the logical zero. Thus, it appears that even in symbolic logic the principle of contradiction is not a universal law but a law that has exceptions.

In fact, we do know that, based on A8, everything follows from logical zero. Thus, it is also true, that a as well as a' follows from logical zero, that is:

S31 $0 < aa'$

Put into words: If X is not an object, then it contains property a and simultaneously it does not contain it S31, thus, stands in contradiction to the principle of contradiction and this principle has no universal significance.

Confronted with this consequence, one cannot hide behind the argument that S31 has 0 and not 1, as S30, in the antecedent clause. It is possible to show, based on the following considerations, that this, which is not an object, is nevertheless also an object:

$(0<a)(a<1) < (0<1)$ [A8, A9, A2]

From this, we get:

S32 $0 < 1$

Based on S17, this formula can be transformed into the following equivalent: $0=1.0$.

Thus, in S31 one may write 1.0 instead of 0 and through this receive the following sentence:

S33 $1.0 < aa'$

Put into words, If X is an object and simultaneously is not an object, then X contains a and simultaneously does not contain a. In the end, there are certain objects that do not fall under the principle of contradiction.

Nevertheless, despite S33, the principle of contradiction has universal significance in symbolic logic, not only because S31 and S33 are true, but also because this sentence is true as well:

$0 < (aa')'$

It is possible to confirm this based on the following consideration:

$$(0<1)[1<(aa')'] < [0<(aa')']$$

Thus, even though the logical zero does not fall under the principle of contradiction, the principle does not have an exception in spite of this because it is simultaneously true that the logical zero does fall under this principle. There is nothing strange about this; the logical zero contains a contradiction, thus one may judge everything from nothing. Thus, thanks to the seemingly unusual axiom A8, symbolic logic does not divide into two logical systems—into an Aristotelian one in which this principle would be invalid, instead all symbols and all objects are subject to Aristotle's principle.

ε) In connection to S32, there is a principle of symbolic logic, which I have not mentioned so far only because it does not form the basis for *any* derived sentence, thus, it does not have any influence at all on the quantity and quality of the logical sentences.

According to S32, the logical 1 follows from the logical zero. If, conversely, the logical zero were to follow from the logical 1, that is:

$$1 < 0$$

then the logical 1 would—based on S1a—be equivalent to the logical zero, that is:

$$1 = 0$$

From this, it would furthermore follow that every statement would be equivalent with 1 as well as 0, because for any a we would get:

$$(0<a) = (1<a) \text{ and } (a<1) = (a<0)$$

that is,

$$a = 0 \text{ and } a = 1$$

One could assert everything about everything.

To circumvent this consequence, symbolic logic assumes that 0 does not follow from 1, that is, that 1 and 0 are not equivalent. With the signs:

A12 $1 \neq 0$

whereby the crossed-out sign of equivalence (synonymity) signifies the opposite of this relation, that is, *non-equivalence*. Couturat calls axiom A12 the *existence postulate*.[175]

Let us consider in which relation axiom A12 stands to the principle of contradiction. Would the principle of contradiction be false if axiom A12 were not to exist? Of course, it would not. The principle of contradiction would continue to remain true, but simultaneously an exactly opposite sentence would be true. If we assume that 0=1, then we get based on S31:

$1 < aa'$

Put into words: If *X* is an object, the *X* contains the property *a* and simultaneously does not contain it. This sentence would be a universal truth because every object would simultaneously not be an object.

The significance of axiom A12 consists in that it postulates the *existence of contradiction-free objects*. The principle of contradiction by itself does not guarantee the existence of such objects. It is, like any other law of symbolic logic, merely a *hypothetical* sentence, which states: If X is an object, then it cannot simultaneously contain a and not contain a. But from this it does not follow that X *is* an object, that is, that it is simply an object in that it is simultaneously not a non-object. This requires a special assumption, or better, a postulate. Whether this postulate is satisfied, about this—as the deliberations in chapters XVIII and XIX testify—we cannot know anything; but even if it were to be not satisfied, the rules of logical thinking will not be changed by this and remain true forever.

η) The above remarks do not claim to present the topic of the principle of contradiction in the light of symbolic logic in an exhaustive manner. Such a presentation is today, at least in this

[175] Postulat d'existence (Op. cit., p.28)

respect, impossible because symbolic logic is continuously developing and has not yet reached the peak of its development. Thus, it could happen that in the future we shall become acquainted with simpler logical laws and simpler logical systems. Every moment new works in this direction appear.[176] However, it seems to me that the negative results that are contained in the explications presented here (especially in α and β) will stand up to the test of scientific critique and open a path to a correct view of the significance of the principle of contradiction.

[176] See, for example, Huntington: *Sets of Independent Postulates for the Algebra of Logic* ("Transactions of the American Mathematical Society", Vol. V, 1905), as well as B. Russell: *The Theory of Implication* ("American Journal of Mathematics", Vol. XXVIII, 1906) and *Mathematical Logic as Based on the Theory of Types* (in the same journal, Vol. XXX, 1908).

Appendix II[177]

[1] ... the sentence "contradictory statements cannot be simultaneously true" is the most certain of all ... (*Met. Γ* 6, 1011 b 13-14; see Chapter I, 84 above).

[2] to each affirmation a negation and each negation is set opposed to it. And this, opposed affirmation and negation, is supposed to be contradiction. But I understand by opposite, that the same is affirmed and denied of the same, ... (*De Int.* 6, 17 a 32-35; see Chapter I, 85).

[3] There is a science that investigates being as being and what is attributed by itself to the same (*Met.* 1003 a 22; see Chapter I, 87).

[4] Because, if it is true to say that something is white or that it is not white, then it must be white or not white ... (*De Int.* 9, 18 a 39 – b 1; see Chapter II, 91).

[5] ... and if it is white or not white, then it was true to assert or to deny this (*De Int.* 9, 18 b 1-2; see Chapter II, 92).

[6] But now, if it is not possible that one and the same be attributed with the opposite, ... but in a contradiction one opinion is set opposite to the other, then it is apparently impossible that one and same man were to assume that one and the same thing is and is not; because whoever is in error about this would after all have opposite opinions at the same time (*Met. Γ* 3, 1005 b 26-32; see Chapter III, 95).

[7] If the matter is such regarding the opinion and if the affirmations or denials that are expressed by the voice are symbols or signs of what is in the soul, then apparently is the denial contrary to the affirmation with respect to the same ... (*De Int.* 14, 24 b 1-3; see Chapter III, 97).

[177] Appendix II contains supplementary translations by Łukasiewicz of certain key phrases from Aristotle's text.

[8] But since it is impossible to assert in truth simultaneously a contradiction about the same object, it is apparent that it is also impossible for contraries to belong simultaneously to the same object. Because one part of a contrary opposition is no less a privation than the other, a privation of essence. Privation, however, is the negation asserted about a certain kind. Now, if it is impossible to truly assert and deny simultaneously, then it is just as impossible that contraries were to belong simultaneously to the same object ... (*Met. Γ* 6, 1011 b 15-21; see Chapter III, 99).

[9] On the other hand, we have accepted that it is impossible that something simultaneously is and is not, and have demonstrated from this, that this is the most certain of all principles. Now, from a lack of education, some demand proof of this as well; because it is a lack in education if one does not know of what to ask proof and of what not to ask for proof. Because it is impossible for there to be proof for everything, since otherwise an infinite regress would set in and no proof at all would be obtained. Even though no proof should be sought for some things, they are unable to state what they would take to be such a principle with greater justification. But a refuting proof for the impossibility of the assertion can be produced as long as the one opposed to it does speak; but if he does not, it would be ridiculous to attempt to debate with someone who does not answer anything, especially insofar as he does not answer; as such, he is the same as a vegetable (*Met. Γ* 4, 1006 a 3-15; see Chapter VI, 113).

[10] The refuting proof, I distinguish from the proper direct proof; if one wanted to conduct that one, it would appear as if one presupposed what is to be demonstrated; but if the other, debating one is to blame, then a refutation comes about, but not a proper proof (Met. *Γ* 4, 1006 a 15-18; see Chapter IX, 129).

[11] The starting point in discussions of this sort is not that one demands of the opponent that he should declare that something is or is not (because this would already be seen as an assumption of what is to be proven), but that he signifies something in speech for himself and for someone else; because this is necessary insofar as he wants to say something at all. If not, such a person would have nothing to say, neither to himself nor to someone else. Once this is admitted, then the truth of the axiom can be shown to him; because something is already firmly determined (*Met. Γ* 4, 1006 a 18-25; see Chapter X, 135).

[12] Against all these, the beginning (of the refutation) results from the determination of the concept. This comes about because they necessarily need to signify something (*Met. Γ* 7, 1012 a 21-23; see Chapter X, 136).

[13] Thus, it is necessary, if one can say about something in truth that it is man, that it is two-footed living being; because it was this that the word man signified. And if this is necessary, then it is not possible, that the same were also not to be two-footed living being; because "to necessarily be man" signifies precisely the impossibility of not to be man. Thus, it is not possible that it would simultaneously be true to assert that the same was man and was not man (*Met. Γ* 4, 1006 b 28-34; see Chapter X, 136).

[14] Further, if the word man signifies something definite, this, for example, might be "two-footed living being". That it signifies one thing, I mean by this; if "man" means this, then, in case something is a man, his nature to be man, will lie in that (*Met. Γ* 4, 1006 a 31-34; Chapter XI, 140).

[15] Thus, it may stay with the sentence spoken at the beginning, that the word signifies something and that it signifies one thing. Then it is not possible that being-man signifies the same as not-being-man, insofar as the word man signifies one thing … (*Met. Γ 4, 1006 b 11-22;* see Chapter XI, 141).

[16] Thus, there must be something that signifies essence, and if that, then it is proven that it is impossible that contradictions can simultaneously be predicated (*Met. Γ* 4, 1007 b 16-18; Chapter XI, 146).

[17] If this, however, were to be the case with all, then in turn either denial will also take place for all those for which affirmation takes place, or affirmation will also take place for all those for which denial takes place, or negation will also take place in the cases where affirmation takes place, but not the reverse, that is, not in all cases, where denial takes place, affirmation will also take place. If the latter where the case, then there would be something that is persistent and firmly not-being, and this assertion would be certain (*Met. Γ* 4, 1008 a 12-16; Chapter XIII, 157).

[18] Further, even if indeed everything behaves so and also not so, there at least is found the more and less in the nature of what has being; because we would not call the two odd the same way as the

three, and who takes four to be five does not find himself in the same error as one who takes it to be a thousand. So, if these do not err in the same way, then one errs less and thus has more truth. Now, if the more is closer, then there also must be what is true and that which is truer comes closer to it. And even if not this, there nevertheless must already be something secure and true, and with that we are liberated from the teaching that does not admit any difference and which does not permit a firm delimiting in thought (*Met. Γ* 4, 1008 b 31 – 1009 a 5; see Chapter XIII, 158).

[19] The original reason of this position, for those who arrived at it by true doubt, lay in what is sensuous. (1.) First of all, it was believed that contradictions and oppositions exist at the same time because one saw opposites growing out of one and the same. Now, if it is not possible that something was but is not [now], then the thing already was both beforehand; as Anaxagoras says, all is found mixed into all, and so also Democritus, who lets void and plenum exist equally in each part, even while designating the one as being and the other as not-being. We shall reply to those, who have gotten from here to that position, that in a certain sense they are right, and in a certain sense they do not recognize the truth. Being is used in two significations, so that in one sense something can come out of not-being, but in the other sense it is not, and it is possible that one and same could simultaneously be and not be, but not in the same signification. In its capacity, one and same can simultaneously be opposites, but not but not according to reality (completion) (*Met. Γ* 5, 1009 a 22-36; see Chapter XIV, 162).

[20] For them, the cause of this position lay in that in the investigation into the truth of being; they only considered what is sensuous as being; this, however, contains the nature of the indeterminate and that, which according to the signified mode, is dominant. Because of this, their teaching has the appearance of truth, but not truth itself (*Met. Γ* 5, 1010 a 1-5; see Chapter XIV, 164).

[21] That it is not possible to affirm and to deny something at the same time, that itself is not assumed by any proof except in the case where the conclusion is demonstrated in this manner. In this proof, one assumes that it is true to affirm the first (greater) term of the middle one, but false to deny it. It does not make any difference with respect to the middle term to acknowledge being or not-being, or with respect to the third (= smaller) term.

Presupposed that that (particular) about which one asserts man truthfully is a living being, but not a not-living being—be it that it also may be true to assert not-man, as long as it is true to assert man—then it will be true to call Callias—even if it is so for not-Callias as well—a living being, but not a not-living being. The cause of this is that the first (term) is not only asserted of the middle one, but also of others, since it includes more (and the contradictory opposite). Therefore, if then the middle term is and is not itself (that is, it can also be asserted of what is opposite), this does not make any difference to the conclusion (*An. Post.* I 11, 77 a 10-22; see Chapter XV, 171).

[22] Further, in the case where, if the affirmation is true, the negation is false, and where it is true, the affirmation is false, it would not be possible to assert and deny the same in truth (*Met. Γ* 4, 1008 a 34—b 1; see Chapter XVII, 184).

[23] This, however, one would want to explain as an assumption of what is to be proven (*Met. Γ* 4, 1008 b 1-2; see Chapter XVII, 184).

Works Cited

Brandis, Christian August. 1836. Scholia in Aristotelem. Berolini: Reimer.

Couturat, Louis. 1905. L'Algebre de la logique, Scientia, Phys. Math. 24. Paris: Gauthiers-Villars.

Dedekind, Richard. 1888. Was sind und was sollen die Zahlen? Braunschweig: Vieweg.

Diels, Hermann ed. 1901. Fragmente : Griechisch und deutsch / Herakleites von Ephesos. Berlin: Weidmann.

Gabryl, Franciszek. 1903. Metafizyka ogólna czyli Nauka o bycie. Kraków: Ksi?garnia Spó?ki Wydawniczej Polskiej.

Gratry, titled "*La Logique du Panthéisme*". (Cf. his *Logique*, 5th ed., Paris 1868, Vol.I,

Goethe, Johann Wolfgang von. 1828-29. Faust : eine Tragödie. Erster Teil.

Hegel, Georg Wilhelm Friedrich. 1834. Wissenschaft der Logik. Edited by L. v. Henning. Vol. 4, Georg Wilhelm Friedrich Hegel's Werke / Vollständige Ausgabe durch einen Verein von Freunden des Verewigten: Ph. Marheineke, J. Schulze, Ed. Gans, Lp. v. Henning, H. Hotho, K. Michelet, F. Förster. Berlin Duncker und Humblot.

Höfler, Alois, Alexius Meinong. 1890. Logik, Philosophische Propaedeutik. Prag: Tempsky.

Horae diurnae Breviarii romani. 1886. Mechliniae.

Husik, Isaac. 1906. Aristotle on the Law of Contradiction and the Basis of the Syllogism. Mind 15 (58):215-222.

Husserl, Edmund. 1900. Logische Untersuchungen : Theil 1, Prolegomena zur reinen Logik. Halle a.S.: Niemeyer.

Kleinpeter, Hans 1905. Die Erkenntnistheorie der Naturforschung der Gegenwart. Leipzig: Barth.

Maier, Heinrich. 1896. Die Syllogistik des Aristoteles. (3 Theile) 2 vols. Tübingen: Laupp.

Meinong, Alexius. 1907. Über die Stellung der Gegenstandstheorie im System der Wissenschaften. 1st ed. Leibzig: R. Voigtländer Verlag.

Russell, B. *The Principles of Mathematics*, Vol.1, Cambridge 1903, Ch.1.

Schröder, Ernst. 1890–1905. Vorlesungen über die Algebra der

Logik. 3 vols. Leipzig: B.G. Teubner.

Schwegler, Albert 1847. Die Metaphysik des Aristoteles : Grundtext, Übersetzung und Kommentar nebst Anmerkungen. 3 vols. Tübingen: Fues.

Sigwart, Christoph. 1889. Die Lehre vom Urteil, vom Begriff und vom Schluss. 2 vols. Vol. 1, Logik. Tübingen: Mohr.

Trendelenburg, Friedrich Adolf. 1870. Logische Untersuchungen. 3rd ed. 2 vols. Leipzig: Hirzel.

Ueberweg, Friedrich. 1882. System der Logik und Geschichte der logischen Lehren. Edited by J. B. Meyer. 5th ed. Bonn: Marcus.

Venn, John. 1894. Symbolic logic 2nd, revised and rewritten ed. London: Macmillan.

Waitz, Theodor. 1844-46. Aristotelis Organon Graece. 2 vols. Leibniz: Hahn.

Wundt, Wilhelm. 1893. Erkenntnislehre. 2nd, revised ed. 2 vols. Vol. 1, Logik. Eine Untersuchung der Principien der Erkenntnis und der Methoden wissenschaftlicher Forschung Stuttgart: Enke.

Commentary

Commentary – Introduction

The Greek epigraph at the beginning of Łukasiewicz' introduction states: "we seek proof for which there is proof" (*λόγον ζητοῦμεν ὧν ἔστι λόγος*). It is both an allusion and a rebuttal to Aristotle's polemic response (at *Met.* Γ6) to those who dared to ask for a proof of the principle of contradiction (PC). Aristotle swiftly dismisses the demand for a proof of the PC and claims that those who seek proof for the principle "search for a proof for something that has none (*λόγον ζητοῦσιν ὧν οὐκ ἔστι λόγος*)" (1011a 12, Łukasiewicz' translation; Introduction, 77).

But Łukasiewicz' epigraph does not merely refer back to Aristotle and his seminal account of the PC, it also reiterates and endorses a programmatic demand made by one of Łukasiewicz' contemporaries, the German mathematician Richard Dedekind (1831-1916) in his influential 1888 monograph, *Was sind und sollen die Zahlen?* (*What are numbers and what is their purpose?*) In the very first sentence of that work, Dedekind proclaims that in the domain of science, "whatever is provable ought not to be believed without proof" (Dedekind 1888, vii; 1995).[34] Łukasiewicz adopts Dedekind's stance with respect to the principle of contradiction and demands—contra Aristotle—that the principle requires proof before it can be accepted in a scientific setting. Thus, Łukasiewicz connects his critique of the traditional Aristotelian account of the PC and its acceptance as the most secure of all logical and metaphysical principles with the modern scientific demand that proof is the non-negotiable condition for the acceptance of any claim, no matter how obvious the claim may appear.

The indication of a close connection between Aristotle's treatment of fundamental logical and metaphysical principles in the *Metaphysics* and the demands of late nineteenth century mathematics and logic, as suggested by his epigraph, presents an apt characterization of Łukasiewicz' overall approach and methodology. This becomes even more apparent in light of a second major theme—also introduced by Dedekind only a few lines later in the same work—which provides an additional important guiding thread to Łukasiewicz' investigation into the foundations and purpose of logic. "Numbers are the free creation of the human mind," Dedekind writes, "they serve as a means to comprehend the diversity of things with greater ease and precision" (Dedekind 1888, vii-viii).[35] For Łukasiewicz, the same can be said about logical objects and their construction. Łukasiewicz describes logic as an instrument that aids and facilitates the scientific acquisition of knowledge about the world. His critical examination of the fundamental principles of logic aims to "put logic on a more secure foundation" and to "refine its entire structure and . . . form a flexible and strong armor for a victorious battle for the cognition of the world" (Introduction, 8).

The importance of Dedekind's program to Łukasiewicz' own effort becomes even clearer in a later chapter where Lukasiewicz cites Dedekind's statement about the nature of numbers as free creations of the human mind in a crucial discussion of the logical consistency of abstract conceptual constructions (XVIII, 97). For Łukasiewicz, logical concepts—akin to Dedekind's numbers—are also free creations of the human mind and, thus, include a degree of creativity and variability. However, as soon as such concepts are articulated and defined, they are part of a manifold of relations that are not immediately transparent in their range and consequences. Thus, the relations and consequences that arise from the positing of logical concepts are far from obvious or "self-evident" but require careful analysis and investigation.[36]

Furthermore, a third thread connecting Łukasiewicz and Dedekind's investigations into the foundations of logic and mathematics is Dedekind's demand that an immediate or direct intuition of the truth of certain basic statements is not sufficient for the acceptance of these statements. Instead, Dedekind pursues an exploration of "the possibility to reduce such truths to other and more simple ones, even if the series of inferences are long and seemingly artificial" (Dedekind 1888, ix).[37] Dedekind's goal is to show that "a convincing proof is never given immediately through inner intuition, but always and only through the more or less complete repetition of individual inferences" (Dedekind 1888, ix).[38] Some ten years earlier, Frege advocated the same approach in his efforts to "prevent anything intuitive [*Anschauliches*]" from occurring within the proofs of basic statements of arithmetic and, thus, "to keep the chain of inferences free of gaps" (Frege 1879, Preface, 5).

Łukasiewicz' analysis of the principle of contradiction and other fundamental logical principles proceeds along similar lines of thought as advocated by Frege and Dedekind. As Frege and Dedekind before him, Łukasiewicz does not accept immediate or direct intuition of the truth or self-evidentness of fundamental logical principles as sufficient warrants for their acceptance. Instead, he follows the approach pursued by Frege and Dedekind and attempts to determine the content of fundamental logical principles and the relations between these principles and their dependence on other and simpler ones through carefully constructed chains inferences that do not contain any appeals to intuition or self-evidence.

Łukasiewicz lists several key questions regarding the nature of fundamental logical principles and their relations to each other, which his investigation aims to answer or illuminate:

What is the significance of these principles, how are they to be formulated, how can assurance for their certainty be given, what consequences result from each one of them, is it possible to give up some of them and replace them by others, are they useful for the investigation of facts, and so forth (Introduction, 79).

He coins the term "meta-logical" as a suitable descriptive term for his investigation into the foundation of logic and repeatedly emphasizes the work of contemporary mathematicians and logicians as models for his own work. He mentions Russell, Couturat, Frege, Hilbert, and Peano as the authors of important mathematical contributions to the understanding of logic and its foundations and, among logicians, he mentions Boole, De Morgan, Jevons, Peirce, and Schröder in addition to Russell, Peano, and Leibniz. Thus, Łukasiewicz clearly aligns himself and his work with the exponents of early analytic and mathematical philosophy. However, the problem that he aims to address and solve, the nature of fundamental logical principles and their relations to each other, stems from Aristotle and Hegel. It is by applying the newly developed methods and techniques of contemporary formal logic to this problem, that Łukasiewicz hopes to usher in a third and decisive moment in the history of the principle of contradiction.

Commentary – Chapter I
Formulations of the Principle of Contradiction

- Ontological Formulation
- Logical Formulation
- Psychological or Doxastic Formulation
- Formulation of the Target Principle
- Conviction, Statement, and Meinong's *Objektiv*

Łukasiewicz distinguishes three formulations of the principle of contradiction (PC) in Aristotle's discussion of the principle in the *Metaphysics*. These three formulations articulate the principle in ontological, psychological, and logical terms. Łukasiewicz restates Aristotle's formulations in the form of declarative statements that assert (or deny) a relation that does (or does not) obtain between an object and a property. This method of analytic reconstruction allows Łukasiewicz to reformulate the different versions of the PC in a form that is more suitable for a logical analysis than Aristotle's original formulations. Finally, he discusses the differences between his conception of a statement and Meinong's account of objektives (*Objektive*).

Ontological Formulation

The first formulation of the PC that Łukasiewicz identifies is the ontological formulation, which Aristotle states in Book IV of the *Metaphysics* at 1005b 19-20: "the same attribute cannot at the same time belong and not belong to the same subject in the same respect" (Ross translation). Immediately after presenting this formulation, Łukasiewicz cites a second formulation, which Aristotle offers much earlier in the text, at the beginning of Book III B, where Aristotle aims to determine the scope and subject matter of his envisioned new science that is to investigate being *qua* being. Aristotle discusses the "starting points of demonstration" on which all proofs are based and mentions two principles specifically. The first is a version of the principle of excluded third, which is expressed by the claim that "everything must be either affirmed or denied." The second principle, stated immediately after the first, is that "a thing cannot at the same time be and not be" (996b 30, Ross translation). Łukasiewicz considers the latter formulation to be a briefer (and less complete) version of the same ontological principle of contradiction that Aristotle subsequently introduces in Book IV.

Two questions arise about Łukasiewicz' analysis of these two formulations:

1) Why does Łukasiewicz consider the two formulations to be expressions of the same (ontological) principle, given that the two formulations are markedly different?

2) Why does he cite the short version of the principle given at 996b instead of the almost identical formulation that Aristotle presents at 1006a 2 (near the ontological formulation at 1005 b 19)?

The answer to both questions is closely connected to Łukasiewicz' method of analysis, which—as Jan Woleński (2000, 7-8) points out—relies on an analytic reconstruction of Aristotle's text. The method proceeds by reformulating Aristotle's statements into a more precise form that is suitable for logical analysis. The sentence form favored by Łukasiewicz is that of a declarative statement with a singular subject/predicate structure. Thus, the preferred form of his analytic reconstructions is a statement, which asserts that an object does (or does not) have a property. Aristotle's original formulations do not exactly exhibit this structure and tend to include numerous indexical expressions, which complicate the parsing of their content.

The shorter formulation of the ontological PC offered at 1006a 2 (*ἀδύνατον εἶναι καὶ μὴ εἶναι*), which Łukasiewicz chooses not to cite, contains its noun-phrase in the term *ἀδύνατον* … (translated as "it is impossible …"), which governs the infinitives (*εἶναι καὶ μὴ εἶναι*—to be and not to be) that follow and which do not contain a separate noun-phrase. However, the formulation at 996b 30 (*ἀδύνατον (scil. τί) ἅμα εἶναι καὶ μὴ εἶναι*), which Łukasiewicz does cite, does include an explicit, albeit indexical, noun-phrase (*ἅμα*—the same). Thus, this formulation corresponds more closely to a singular subject/predicate sentence, which Łukasiewicz prefers for his method of reconstructive analysis. The expression at 1006a 2, on the other hand, lacks an explicit noun-phrase that could be interpreted as the subject of the statement. Therefore, it is less suitable for Łukasiewicz' method of analysis.

However, while this suggests a reason for Łukasiewicz' choice of citation for the shorter formulation, the two ontological formulations of the principle that Łukasiewicz does cite are themselves markedly different. The version at 1005b 19-20 ("the same attribute cannot at the same time belong and not belong to the same subject in the same respect") articulates the principle in terms of objects and their properties, whereas the shorter version (996b 30) asserts that it is impossible for "a thing" to be and not be at the same time. Finally, the even shorter version at 1006a 2 asserts a necessary incompatibility between being and not-being as such, without reference to an object. Later writers drew a sharp distinction between the formulations and considered the two shorter versions (996b 30 and 1006a 2) as expressions of the proper ontological principle and the longer formulation in terms of a subject and its attributes (1005b 19-20) as an object-theoretical formulation of the principle.[39]

For Łukasiewicz, however, both the short formulation at 996b 30, which declares that "a thing cannot at the same time be and not be," and the object-theoretical formulation at 1005b 19-20, which states that "the same attribute cannot at the same time belong and not belong to the same subject in the same respect," are both formulations of the ontological PC. Thus, they both articulate the PC with respect to being *qua* being, the subject of Aristotle's investigation in the *Metaphysics*. The latter formulation, which articulates the principle in object-theoretical terms, presents the most concise articulation of Aristotle's ontological PC. It is an ontological formulation, Łukasiewicz argues, because it expresses the PC in relation to being (τὸ ὄν) and employs the ontological categories of object and property to articulate the principle. Because of this, it permits the reformulation of Aristotle's original formulation as a universal statement about the relation between objects and their properties, which Łukasiewicz expresses as follows: "*No object can contain and simultaneously not contain the same property*" (I, 84).

Łukasiewicz argues that this formulation is equivalent to Aristotle's because it "does not alter Aristotle's thought, it merely posits the nouns 'object' and 'property' instead of the stylistically awkward 'the same' and 'something'" (I, 84). The crucial concepts in Łukasiewicz' reformulations of Aristotle's statements of the PC are those of object and property. The relation between an object and its property is the foundation and touchstone of Łukasiewicz' logical analysis. It is this relation that is affirmed or denied in a statement.

According to Łukasiewicz, an object is "any something whatever that is 'something' and not 'nothing'" (I, 84). This conception of an object is based on the intentional approach developed by two of his most influential mentors and teachers, Alexius Meinong and Kazimierz Twardowski. Both had been students of Franz Brentano, who developed a highly influential concept of the nature of an object based on his analysis of intentionality. Broadly put, intentionality consists in the directedness of the mind towards an object. Intentionality is often considered to be *the* characteristic trait of consciousness and distinguishes it from purely physical, inanimate phenomena, which lack intentionality.

In Brentano's original account, an object is anything whatsoever that consciousness can direct itself towards. As such, Brentano's objects are intrinsically part of and generated as mental phenomena. They are "inexistent" but possess an immanent objectivity. Their status as objects is the result of an intentional activity and thus inseparable from consciousness. Brentano characterizes the directedness towards an object or "immanent objectivity" as the defining feature of intentionality.

> Every mental phenomenon is characterized by what the Scholastics of the Middle Ages called the intentional (or mental) inexistence of an object, and what we might call, though not wholly unambiguously, reference to a content, direction towards an object (which is not to be understood here as meaning a thing), or immanent objectivity. Every mental phenomenon includes something as object within itself, although they do not all do so in the same way. In presentation something is presented, in judgment something is affirmed or denied, in love loved, in hate hated, in desire desired and so on. This intentional in-existence is characteristic exclusively of mental phenomena. No physical phenomenon exhibits anything like it. We could, therefore, define mental phenomena by

> saying that they are those phenomena which contain an object intentionally within themselves (Brentano 1995 [1874], 88-89).

Łukasiewicz deliberately frames the concept of an object as an intentional object in the broadest terms possible, i.e., as any item that is "any something whatever", no matter how vague or indeterminate, as long as it is "'something' and not 'nothing'" (I, 84). An object is anything that stands before (or opposite to) the mind, as the German word "*Gegenstand*" or the Latin "*objectivum*" suggest. As long as there is something that is present in a mode that the mind can seize upon, as long as it is something before the mind, it is an object.

Thus, for something to constitute an object, it must have a positive aspect, a presence in a mode that can be attended to by the mind. However, *prima facie*, this presence of an intentional object as a mental phenomenon is independent of the extra-mental existence of an actual or ideal object. The point is emphasized by Twardowski in his 1894 monograph *On the Content and Object of Presentations,* where he notes that "every presentation presents an object, whether the object exists or not. Even presentations whose objects *cannot* exist are no exception to this law" (Twardowski 1977 [1894], 24). Most importantly, among the intentional objects that cannot exist apart from their presentations before a mind are impossible and contradictory objects, which—in Twardowski's account—nevertheless do exist as presented objects. "The object of a presentation in whose content contradictory characteristics are presented does not exist; yet one asserts that it is presented; hence it exists after all, namely as a presented object" (Twardowski 1977 [1894], 22).

The intentional conception of an object, which Łukasiewicz adopts for his analysis of the PC admits contradictory objects as bona fide, presentable objects. They are "not nothing" since they have positive constitutive features that can be brought before the mind. In Łukasiewicz' account, the positive constitutive features of an object arise in contrast to the consideration of a negative aspect, from the notion of absence, of 'nothing' in the sense of a complete lack of any presence whatsoever.

The objection might be raised that, in this sense, 'nothing' too is a proper object—even though it can be an object only as a negative presentation, as a presentation of absence. Still, in this way, nothingness *is something* that the mind can seize upon and present to itself, albeit only in the form of a negative determination. However, it lacks what one might call a positive "object-hood" since it does not offer any aspects in virtue of which it could be made manifest in a positive mode of presentation. The conception of object, then, is closely connected to the fundamental distinction between 'being' and 'not-being', a distinction that lies at the core of the PC. In its positive aspect, whatever is present to a mind is an object as long as it *is* something and, in its negative determination, it is an object as long as it *is not* nothing.

In Łukasiewicz' conception, the fundamental structure of an object is that of the relation between properties and an (unifying and underlying) entity that—akin to Aristotle's *hypokeimenon* of the *Categories*—is the bearer of properties. Objects have properties and an item that does not have at least one property is a 'nothing'—it is not an object. Łukasiewicz presents his understanding of property in the broadest possible terms. A property is "everything that can be asserted about any object" (I, 84).

Properties, in this sense, are dependent on objects. However, an object also depends on its properties. As mentioned, in Łukasiewicz' account an object is anything that is something and not nothing, but to be "something" means precisely that some property, however vague, is present to the mind. Łukasiewicz does not address the question of ontological dependence between object and property at this point. An object is an object *iff* it is something that has some property. If there *is* a property, then there also *is* an object to which this property belongs. For Łukasiewicz, the object-property relation constitutes the fundamental ontological relation. Aristotle's account of the PC attempts to provide an account of the logical structure of this relation.

Logical Formulation

In this section, Łukasiewcz proceeds to reformulate Aristotle's statement of the logical PC in terms of object and property. Aristotle's formulation occurs towards the end of his discussion of the PC, in the concluding remarks that follow a battery of arguments and reasons offered in support of the validity of the PC, at 1011b 13-14. In the original Greek, the logical formulation reads as follows: *βεβαιστάτη δόχα πασῶν τὸ μὴ εἶναι ἀληθεῖς ἅμα τὰς ἀντικειμένας φάσεις* (Ross 1924).

The crucial phrase in the interpretation of Aristotle's formulation is *ἀντικειμένας φάσεις*, which Łukasiewicz—together with Ross and others—translates as "contradictory statements" and, consequently, the entire passage as: "The most certain of all principles is that *contradictory* statements are not simultaneously true" (I, 84; *italics* added for emphasis). However, Kirwan translates the expression as "opposite assertions", which is closer to the meaning of *ἀντικειμένας* (opposite to each other) and which, most importantly, does not limit Aristotle's logical formulation to statements that are contradictories in the strict sense, i.e., the affirmation and denial of the same statement, as it is the case in the translations by Ross and Łukasiewicz. Instead, Kirwan's translation preserves the scope of Aristotle's formulation in that it addresses and includes all pairs of statements that stand in a relation of opposition to each other. Thus, in Kirwan's translation, Aristotle's logical formulation of the PC reads: "The opinion that *opposite* assertions are not simultaneously true is the firmest of all" (Kirwan 1993, 23, italics added for emphasis).

With respect to Aristotle's account of the PC as the first and fundamental metaphysical principle of being *qua* being, the two most important groups of opposed statements are contradictory pairs, consisting of an affirmation and a denial of one statement, and contrary pairs, consisting of two distinct statements that ascribe incompatible properties to one and the same object. The analysis and distinction between these two modes of opposition plays a crucial role throughout Aristotle's metaphysical and logical considerations. Contrary pairs of statements, however, are included only in Kirwan's rendering of Aristotle's formulation, and excluded in the translations by Łukasiewicz and Ross. Clearly, the inclusion or exclusion of contraries in the logical formulation of the PC has far-reaching and philosophically substantial consequences to an interpretation of Aristotle's account of the PC.

Łukasiewicz perceives the tension between contradictory and opposed pairs of statements[40] and tries to support his interpretation of Aristotle's logical formulation of the PC by drawing on a passage from *De Interpretatione* 6. The cited passage appears to strengthen Łukasiewicz' claim that the pair of statements, which form the subject term in Aristotle's formulation, consists of an affirmation and a negation of a *single* statement (as contrasted to a contradiction between statements that results from inferences drawn from either one or both as, for example, in the case of contraries). However, in the passage cited by Łukasiewicz, Aristotle merely offers an account of what he means by a contradiction, and the most explicit and clearest form of a contradiction is the pairing of an affirmative statement and its denial. Aristotle does not discuss the difference between contrary and contradictory opposition at the location cited, even though this discussion is taken up at numerous locations in *De Interpretatione* and the *Categories*, where it forms one of the key points of interest.

The question whether Aristotle's logical formulation of the principle includes contrary pairs of statements or whether Aristotle limits it to contradictory pairs of statements, is also of great importance in the reading that Whitaker defends in his monograph on the *De Interpretatione* (1996). Whitaker challenges the traditional positioning of *de Interpretatione* as the work following the *Categories* and preceding the *Prior Analytics*. In this account, *De Interpretatione* is part of a series of books that introduces and develops Aristotle's logic.

According to Whitaker, a comprehensive and careful reading of *De Interpretatione* suggest that the treatise "does not take as its subject propositions, seen as the components of the syllogism, but rather contradictory pairs, which are central to the working of dialectic" (Whitaker, 2). However, while Whitaker emphasizes the importance of the analysis and treatment of contradictory pairs for the practice of dialectic debate and reasoning, it is important to note that this discussion of contradictory pairs takes place within the context of the development of an account of the nature and distinctions between forms of opposition, a task that is introduced in the *Categories* and elaborated and refined in the *De Interpretatione*.

In Whitaker's analysis, the true purpose and topic of the discussion in the text is further obscured by the work's commonly used title, *De Interpretatione*, which "is not supported in other works of Aristotle, and should be rejected as spurious" (Whitaker, 7). In his monograph, Łukasiewicz opts to refer to the Greek name of the treatise and refers to it as the *Hermeneutics* instead of its latinized name. The most apt name for the treatise, according to Whitaker, would be "'On the Contradictory Pair' (*περὶ ἀντιφάσεως*)" (Whitaker, 7). Following the thrust of Whitaker's analysis, "On Opposing Assertions" may be even more appropriate since this title would not restrict the treatise topic to contradictory pairs but to logically opposed statements and their distinctions.

Finally, Whitaker argues that one of the central tasks of the *De Interpretatione* is to enable the practitioner of dialectic debates to distinguish contradictory pairs "for which it is not the case that one member is true and the other false" (Whitaker, 3). This may appear to be the case where contradictories omit certain qualifications and thus appear to be equally true, but only erroneously so. However, another important class of such contradictory pairs are contrary statements, which may appear contradictory, but which nevertheless may be both false in certain cases. In such a situation, the demand that a respondent in a dialectic debate must accept the truth of one of a pair of contradictory statements fails. As Whitaker points out, "the dialectical question based on the contradictory pair cannot be answered" and—most importantly—a "refutation will be impossible" (Whitaker, 3).

Even in a most charitable reading, Łukasiewicz' reference to *De Interpretatione* by itself does not establish that Aristotle's formulation of the logical PC is meant to take only contradictory pairs of statements as its subject term. However, it is the interpretation that Łukasiewicz adopts and implements into his analysis.

For Łukasiewicz, the opposed statements that are addressed in Aristotle's formulation are of the form "p and not-p", with p representing a (object/property) statement and not-p its negation. The corresponding predicate form is "$F(x)$ and not-$F(x)$", with x standing for an object and F for a property. Łukasiewicz, in agreement with Aristotle, assumes that all statements are of subject/predicate form. Łukasiewicz, even though he should have known better, reformulates Aristotle's formulation based on this assumption in terms of a single statement about one object and one of the object's properties and the negation of that statement: "*Two statement, of which one attributes precisely that property to an object that the other denies of it, cannot be simultaneously true*" (I, 85).

The formulation presents the logical PC because it presents the PC in terms of statements and their truth-values. As Łukasiewicz puts it, the formulation addresses "logical facts" (I, 85). However, it is important to note that Łukasiewicz' formulation of the logical PC does not accommodate pairs of contrary statements, since each of two contrary statements attributes a different property to the same object and the incompatibility of the two properties is not a logical fact *per se*, but only if additional stipulations or conditions are introduced. The distinction between contrary and contradictory opposition will gain additional importance and significance in subsequent discussions.

Psychological or Doxastic Formulation

Łukasiewicz turns to the psychological formulation of the principle, again with the aim of reformulating it in terms of object and property. He analyzes Aristotle's statement, "no one can believe that one and the same (simultaneously) is and is not" (1005b 23), which occurs shortly after the object-theoretical version at 1005b 19-20, in terms of beliefs or convictions and their objects. Convictions are transitive, that is, they require an object. The object of a conviction is expressed by a statement or, more precisely, the object of conviction corresponds to the content of a statement. A statement, for Łukasiewicz, is "*a series of words or other signs, which say that some object contains a property or does not contain it*" (I, 87).

Beliefs or convictions are psychological states, psychical phenomena (I, 87), that manifest themselves in the form of dispositions or attitudes, which are subjectively ascertained and directed towards a statement. The relevant psychological attitudes with respect to the PC are the acceptance or rejection of the assertion that is articulated by a statement. A judgment, then, expresses the relation between a *psychological fact*, i.e., an attitude or disposition of acceptance or rejection of what is asserted by a statement, and a *logical fact*, i.e., the truth or falsity of the statement as such.

Applying the distinction between convictions and statement to Aristotle's formulation of the psychological PC, Łukasiewicz reformulates the principle as follows: "*Two convictions, for which there are corresponding contradictory statements, cannot exist simultaneously in one and the same intellect*" (I, 87). Thus, the psychological PC asserts a constraint on a certain class of psychical phenomena, beliefs or convictions that belong to one intellect. The beliefs or convictions are distinguished with respect to the logical properties of the statement, which in turn constitute the objects of the beliefs or convictions.

The Target Principle

The difficulties of determining a formulation that captures the core or target principle has already been touched upon in the introductory discussion (32). With regards to Aristotle's three formulations, Łukasiewicz notes that Aristotle pays "the greatest attention to the *ontological* formulation, which aims to grasp the entire principle in its most complete form" (I, 87). The Aristotelian PC is first and foremost an ontological principle; for Aristotle, it is the first principle of the science that investigates the nature of being *qua* being. It is because of its relation to being, as Łukasiewicz points out (I, 87), that Aristotle discusses and defends the principle at length in the *Metaphysics* and not in the logical and semantic treatises of the *Analytics* or *De Interpretatione* and not as a primarily psychological principle in the context of his discussion of the soul or psyche in *De Anima*

If Łukasiewicz is right, then Aristotle considers the ontological formulation to be the formulation that articulates most closely the core or target principle, but Aristotle's selection itself may be contentious. Aristotle's ontological formulation is one of three distinct formulations presented by Aristotle, but Aristotle's formulations present only a first set of distinctions that generate a surprisingly large number of formulations of the principle. According to Patrick Grim (2004), more than 240 different formulations of the principle of contradiction are generated, if standard contemporary conceptual and logical distinctions are taken into account. According to Grim, this large number of formulations of the PC is the result of:

> four basic forms of approach—semantic, syntactic, pragmatic, and ontological—multiplied by (1) a distinction between implicit and explicit contradictions, multiplied by (2) contradictions as pairs or single statements, multiplied by (3) the number of distinctions between token sentences, types, statements, propositions, assertions, and claims, with that in turn multiplied by (4) the number of senses of negation (Grim 2004, 54-55).

Thus, the selection and determination of a formulation of the principle that is held to expresses the core content of the principle requires a sophisticated argument in its support. Even further, the existence of such a formulation may be doubted. The range of formulations, at any rate, suggest the possibility of a plurality of formulations of the principle with each formulation expressing a shared core content with respect to different core parameters, be they ontological, psychological, metaphysical, ethical, or logical in nature.

In this context, it is interesting to note that the British-German philosopher and Buddhist scholar, Edward Conze (1904–1976), encountered a similar multiplication of formulations in his 1932 work *Der Satz vom Widerspruch* (*The Principle of Contradiction*).[41] Conze, who at one point had been a student of Heinrich Scholz (the same Scholz who later became Łukasiewicz' close friend and associate at the University of Münster during the nineteen-thirties and forties, cf. 28 f. above),[42] adopts Łukasiewicz' distinction between ontological, logical, and psychological formulations of the principle in his own analysis. However, Conze expands Łukasiewicz' account and introduces two additional distinctions: first, he distinguishes Aristotle's broad ontological formulation at 1006a 2 (it is impossible to be and not to be) from the object-theoretical formulation favored by Łukasiewicz and, secondly, he introduces an additional formulation of the principle that is not found directly in Aristotle's writings, a formulation that articulates the principle of contradiction in its socio-linguistic dimension(Conze 1932, Sec.2-3). Through the introduction of further criteria to his initial five formulations, i.e., differences in the type of objects, statements, and concepts to which the principle is applied, Conze develops an extended range of distinct formulations of the principle, which prompts him to also raise the question which of the formulations expresses the core content of the principle of contradiction (Conze 1932, Sec.4 ff.).

Like Łukasiewicz before him, Conze argues that Aristotle's ontological formulation expresses what Aristotle took to be the core principle. However, Conze disagrees with Łukasiewicz about which of Aristotle's formulations expresses the proper ontological principle. For Conze, it is the formulation at 1006a 2, which articulates a fundamental incompatibility of being and not-being as such (*qua* being), without any reference to particular objects. In Conze's view, the Aristotelian PC constitutes a principle with respect to objects, statements, and beliefs, only in a secondary and derived form. In its essence and core intent, it is "an assertion about the relation of being and not-being" (Conze 1932, Sec.95). According to Conze, the PC addresses the essential nature of being *qua* being. For Łukasiewicz, on the other hand, the ontological focus of the PC is contained and most clearly articulated in its object-theoretical formulation, where it directly addresses the relation between object and property. Furthermore—and crucial for Łukasiewicz' method of reconstructive analysis—this relation is articulated by Aristotle himself in the form of a *statement* about object and property at 1005b 19-20.

Conviction, Statement, and Meinong's *Objektiv*

In a note at the end of the chapter, Łukasiewicz emphasizes the importance of a clear distinction between convictions and statements. Convictions, judgments, and beliefs are psychological phenomena whereas (logical) statements are presentations of (logical) facts. Łukasiewicz credits Meinong with the development of a precise theoretical distinction between statement and belief through the introduction of Meinong's concept of an *Objektiv*, which—roughly—corresponds to a fact or state of affairs (*Tatsache*). However, Łukasiewicz emphasizes that he uses the term "statement" in a way that "is not identical in sense" to Meinong's use of *Objektiv* (I, 88). The two terms are not synonymous. He qualifies his use of the term "statement" by giving the following definition: "A statement is an *Objektiv* that is *expressed in words or by other signs*" (I, 88).

Meinong introduces the technical term *Objektiv* in his mongraph *Über Annahmen* (*On Assumptions*) in order to articulate and develop the distinction between the psychological *act* of judging (or assuming or believing) from the *object* that is judged (or assumed or believed) (Meinong 1902). The object that is judged in a judgment (or assumed in an assumption or believed in a belief) is an *Objektiv*. According to Meinong, a great deal of unnecessary labor can be avoided, if a decision is made "to use the word 'judgment' [*Urteil*] only in the sense of experience [*Erlebnis*] and to explicitly posit opposite to it the object, which is grasped in the judgment, by the term *Objektiv*" (Meinong 1907, 125).[43]

Łukasiewicz endorses Meinong's distinction between the psychological act of judging or believing and the *Objektiv* that the psychological act is directed towards. However, as Łukasiewicz points out (I, 88), in Meinong's account, the *Objektiv* itself constitutes the *fact* or *Tatsache* that is grasped in an act of cognition. According to Meinong,

> that which is, the 'fact', without which no cognition could be considered as cognition, is the *Objektiv*, which is grasped through a respective act of cognition, and which has a precise constitution [*Bestand*], may it be positive or negative, may it be being or being-so (Meinong 1904, 25).[44]

The difference between Meinong and the young Łukasiewicz lies in their different understanding of what constitutes a fact and the ontological commitments involved in Meinong's identification of fact and *Objektiv*. Meinong aims to develop a theory that allows the cognition of an *Objektiv* independently of the existence of the items that are constitutive parts of an *Objektiv*; a theory that includes facts about non-existent and impossible items.

In Meinong's account, any fact or *Objektiv* has a specific mode or ontological domain in which it is or is not the case (*bestehen*). Meinong distinguishes between two primary ontological domains: being and being-so (*Sein* and *Sosein*). An *Objektiv* that presents of the actual, concrete being or existence of an object—the *Sein* of an object—is called a *Seinsobjektiv*. An *Objektiv* that presents the properties of an object that does not have concrete existence or being, for example, an abstract or ideal object like a number or geometrical figure, is a *Soseinsobjektiv*.

One of the crucial cornerstones of Meinong' theory of objects is the Independence Principle, which asserts that the being-so of an object is independent of the being of that object. While every proper object has a specific being-so in virtue of its properties, not every proper object has being in the sence of concrete existence. Thus, an object that has no being may be a constitutive part of a *Soseinsobjektiv*. According to Meinong,

> the being-so [*Sosein*] of an object is, in a manner of speaking, not affected by its not-being [*Nichtsein*]. This fact is important enough to formulate it explicitly as the principle of independence of being-so from being, and the domain of validity of this principle is best illuminated with respect to the circumstance that not only those objects are subject to this principle which do not in fact exist, but also those that cannot exist, because they are impossible. Not only is the much called upon golden mountain made of gold, but the round rectangle is as surely round as it is rectangular" (Meinong 1904, 8).[45]

Meinong's division of ontological domains allows him to include impossible and contradictory objects, which do not exist but nevertheless have a definite being-so, into the scope of his theory. But, once included as a proper object, a contradictory object like a square circle does present contradictory facts or *Objektive,* facts that do obtain (*bestehen*)—a situation that was intolerable to otherwise sympathetic critics like Russell (1905).

In light of this, Łukasiewicz' caution about Meinong's concept of *Objektiv* becomes understandable. Łukasiewicz' definition of a statement avoids Meinong's commitments to multiple and distinct ontologicalical domains (including the admission of contradictory objects) while preserving Meinong's distinction between beliefs and facts. Łukasiewicz limits the ontological commitments of his account to objects and properties. Statements are truth-bearers and distinct from the facts or state of affairs that a statement describes or articulates. In this sense, Łukasiewicz' position is closer to Aristotle where a state of affairs is distinct from its linguistic or symbolic presentation and constituted by the being of the object that is addressed in a statement. Łukasiewicz' conception of a statement matches Aristotle's better than Meinong's *Objektiv* because "according to Aristotle, a *statement is a sequence of words, which state that something is or is not*" (I, 89). In its clearest and most concise form, Łukasiewicz' statement is a declarative sentence about a property and its object. Thus, Łukasiewicz' conception of a simple logical sentence or a statement coincides in its characteristic features with Russell's "atomic sentence" or Wittgenstein's "elementary statement".[46]

Commentary – Chapter II
The Relation of the Ontological Principle of Contradiction to the Logical Principle

- Equivalence between Statements
- Proof of Equivalence between the Ontological and Logical
Formulations

Prompted by the question whether the three formulations of the PC (ontological, logical, and psychological) articulate three distinct principles or whether they are different formulations of one and the same principle, Łukasiewicz first investigates "in what cases two statements, composed of different words, express the same thought" (II, 90). He distinguishes between statements that have the same meaning and statements that are logically equivalent. Then, based on his account of propositional equivalence, he offers a proof of the equivalence of the ontological and logical formulations of the PC that relies on a realist conception of truth.

Equivalence between Statements

Łukasiewicz' analysis focuses on logical sentences or statements that have the form "object x contains property F" or the negation of a sentence of this form. He then distinguishes two cases: a) statements that have the same meaning and express the same thought and b) statements that are logically equivalent, that is, statements that logically imply each other.

Two statements are equivalent iff two statements mutually entail each other, that is, if the (material) conditionals, $p \rightarrow q$ and $q \rightarrow p$, are logical truths. Thus, Łukasiewicz' definition of equivalence between statements corresponds to the logical truth of the biconditional of classical logic.

If two statements are equivalent, then they have the same meaning. Two statements are identical in meaning if each refers to the same object and attributes the same predicate/property to that object. Consequently, if one of a pair of such statements is true, so is the other. However, Łukasiewicz recognizes that two logically equivalent statements, statements that have the same meaning, may nevertheless have different senses. Two statements with differents senses are equivalent if they mutually entail each other, but they are not identical in meaning, as Łukasiewicz' example 'Plato was a teacher of Aristotle' and 'Aristotle was a student of Plato' illustrates. Thus, two sentences that differ in senses may nevertheless be logically equivalent to each other.

It is important to note from the start that, in this discussion, Łukasiewicz does not explicitly distinguish between the sense and meaning of individual words or expressions in a way that would correspond to Frege's distinction between *Sinn* and *Bedeutung* (Frege 1966 [1892]). However, he does use both "thought" and "sense" to describe what is expressed by a sentence as a whole as distinct from the items that a sentence refers to. Further, Łukasiewicz distinguishes between a word or expression, which is a symbol or sign, and the meaning of a word or expression, which is its referent, that is, an object that is denoted by the word or expression.

Furthermore, Łukasiewicz does not assert or suggest that the referent of a logical sentence or statement is its truth-value as, of course, Frege famously does. At one point, though, Łukasiewicz appears to come very close to Frege's account. With respect to the example of a pair of sentences in which all the component parts of two sentences have exactly the same referents, i.e., where *x* and *x'* both refer to the same object and *F* and *F'* refer to the same property, Łukasiewicz writes: "The two sentences "*x* contains *F*" and "*x'* contains *F'*" *express the same object* in different words" (II, 90)—my Italics.

Prima facie, it is not obvious what Łukasiewicz means by "express the same object" in this passage; the phrase might be interpreted as a reference to Frege's truth-values. Given that the component parts of the two statements have the same meanings, i.e., that they refer to the same object and property, it generally is the case that the two statements also have or "express" the same truth-value.[47] However, Łukasiewicz makes no mention of truth-values as objects that are the referents of statements, nor does he mention Frege in this discussion.

An alternative interpretation would be to say that Łukasiewicz intended the term "object" to refer to a Meinongian *Objektiv*, which is to say, the two sentences express the same (Meinongian) fact. However, given Łukasiewicz' distinction between his use of the term statement or logical sentence and Meinong's use of *Objektiv* (as discussed in Commentary to Chapter I, 286 above), this interpretation seems unlikely to be an adequate rendering of what Łukasiewicz is saying. Plus, if this interpretation were correct, then why didn't Łukasiewicz simply use *Objektiv* instead of object?

A third possibility is to interpret the somewhat awkward wording of the phrase "express the same object" as equivalent to "express the same meaning". In this case, "the same object" indicates as a reference to a shared but not further specified *meaning* of the two sentences. However, this interpretation again comes very close to Meinong's account in which meanings are objects. In light of Łukasiewicz' expressed reservations regarding Meinong's account, this interpretation too seems unlikely to catch Łukasiewicz' intended meaning.

The most plausible interpretation is that "the same object" refers to the statement or, more specifically, to the content that is expressed by the two sentences.[48] After all, the component parts of the two sentences in the example refer to the same object and property, and the two sentences both assert that the same relation holds between the object and property. Thus, the two sentences express the same statement with different words. In this interpretation, what Łukasiewicz calls the *thought* that is expressed by a logical sentence is the same as the propositional content that is expressed by the sentence. This interpretation furthermore fits in seamlessly with the example that Łukasiewicz offers immediately following the passage. In that example, the noun-phrases of the two sentences are different but have the same meaning, i.e., "Aristotle" and "the Stagirite", which are two names or signs that both refer to the same person. The two sentences in turn attribute the same property to the object designated by the name that occurs in it as grammatical subject and, therefore, attribute the same property to the same object. Thus, Łukasiewicz concludes, the two sentences "express *the same thought* with partially different words" (II, 90, my *italics*).

In his discussion, then, Łukasiewicz derives the following condition under which two sentences have the same meaning: Two distinct sentences, i.e., sentences that are contain different words, have the same meaning iff they express the same thought (II, 90).

Before moving on to a discussion of logical equivalence, Łukasiewicz inserts the claim that an affirmative statement and its negation can never have the same meaning since the *sense* of "affirming" is different from the *sense* of "denying" (II, 90). Here, Łukasiewicz appears to use "sense" and "meaning" as equivalent terms. At least, he does not offer an explicit distinction between the two terms, nor does he address at this location the distinction between the psychological acts of affirmation or denial (as acceptance and rejection) and the logical fact of a statement asserting or denying a relation between an object and a property. According to Łukasiewicz, the reason for the necessary difference in meaning and/or sense of a propositional affirmation and its denial is that it is impossible to reduce either statement to the other.

Next, Łukasiewicz introduces the concept of propositional equivalence, which relies on the concepts of semantic truth and logical entailment. In his account, two statement p_1 and p_2 are equivalent iff p_1 follows from p_2 and p_2 follows from p_1; thus, two statement p_1 and p_2 are (logically) equivalent precisely in case p_1 iff p_2 holds logically. Thus, two equivalent statements have the same truth-value and they entail each other.

Łukasiewicz notes that on this account of equivalence, it follows that if two statements are not equivalent, then they do not have the same meaning. However, two statements that differ in *sense* may nevertheless be logically equivalent and this, of course, presents a philosophically and logically interesting case. Łukasiewicz considers the following sentences as an example in which two sentences are logically equivalent but have different senses: "Aristotle was a student of Plato" and "Plato was a teacher of Aristotle". He claims that the difference in sense is a result of the differences in the meanings, considered as referents, of the expressions employed in the two sentences. The sentence with Aristotle as grammatical subject is a sentence about a different person/object than the sentence that has Plato as its subject. Further, the property ascribed to the object is also different in each sentence.

Still, the first sentence follows from the second and vice versa and the two sentences thus are equivalent. However, while this is the case, the entailment relation does require a further premise that establishes the logical equivalence of the two relations and that is precisely the conclusion Łukasiewicz asserts, i.e., a premise that states "x is a teacher of y iff y is a student of x", or formalized as two-place predicates: T_{xy} iff S_{yx}. In standard logic, T_{xy} does not follow from S_{yx}, nor does S_{yx} follow from T_{xy} without this premise.

In a note, Łukasiewicz comments that he considers the task of an analytic distinction between statement with identical senses from statement with different senses to be not only one of the most difficult tasks of logic but also one of the most important ones. For Łukasiewicz, the problem is to find a criterion by which a determination can be made that shows whether or not a difference in signs corresponds to a difference in the actual being of the object(s) denoted by a sign or whether the difference is merely one of appearance (only a difference between signs), but not real (II, 91, n.23). Łukasiewcz takes up the problem again and specifically in relation to the PC in the Appendix at §9 γ.

The three formulations of the principle of contradiction developed in Chapter I are three different sentences that express distinct thoughts. They each address different items: objects, beliefs, and statement. The question is: are they logically equivalent?

Proof of Equivalence between the Ontological and Logical Formulations

Łukasiewicz claims that the ontological and logical formulation of the PC are equivalent and offers arguments to show that this is indeed the case. He presents two arguments, the first aiming to show that the ontological formulation of the principle of contradiction (PC_{ont}) entails the logical formulation (PC_{log}) and a second argument to show that the logical formulation (PC_{log}) entails the ontological one (PC_{ont}).

II.a) $(PC_{ont}) \rightarrow (PC_{log})$

Łukasiewicz' argument has the following form (with '*T*' standing for 'is true'):

$$(1) \quad T{<}F_x{>} \rightarrow F_x$$
$$(2) \quad T{<}{\sim}F_x{>} \rightarrow {\sim}F_x$$

Premise (1) and (2) correspond to Łukasiewicz' analysis of the passage cited from *De Int.* (18a 39 –b1), which he interprets as asserting the following two premises: (1) "If a statement, which attributes a property to an object, is true, then this object contains that property." (2) "If a statement, which denies a property of an object, is true, then it does not contain it" (II, 92).

Next, Łukasiewicz introduces a premise that includes a contradiction, i.e., (3) "if two contradictory statement were to be true, then the same object would contain and simultaneously not contain a property" (II, 92).

(3) $T<(F_x \mathbin{\&} {\sim}F_x)> \rightarrow \quad F_x$ and ${\sim}F_x$

This, however, Łukasiewicz points out, "is not possible in virtue of the *ontological* principle of contradiction" (II, 92), which reads in its *T*-schema:

$(\mathrm{PC}_{ont})\ T<{\sim}(F_x \mathbin{\&} {\sim}F_x)> \leftrightarrow {\sim}(F_x \mathbin{\&} {\sim}F_x)$

"Thus," Łukasiewicz concludes, "two contradictory statements cannot simultaneously be true" (II, 92).

II.b) $(PC_{\mathrm{log}}) \rightarrow (PC_{\mathrm{ont}})$

Łukasiewicz again relies on an Aristotelian theory of truth to derive the ontological principle from the logical one, i.e., $(\mathrm{PC}_{log}) \rightarrow (\mathrm{PC}_{ont})$.

> If an object contains a property, that is, if it has been put together with it, then that statement is true that ascribes the property to the object. If it does not contain it, that is, if the object remains separate from the property, then that statement is true which denies the property of the object (II, 92).

(1) $\quad F_x \quad \rightarrow T<F_x>$
(2) $\quad {\sim}F_x \quad \rightarrow \quad T<{\sim}F_x>$

As in the previous proof, Łukasiewicz now introduces a premise that includes a contradiction, i.e., (3) "should the same object contain and not contain a property, the two contradictory statement would be simultaneously true" (II, 92).

(3) F_x and ${\sim}F_x \quad \rightarrow \qquad T<(F_x \mathbin{\&} {\sim}F_x)>$

The logical principle, however, establishes that it is impossible for two contradictory statements to be true (5):

$$(PC_{log})\ T <\sim(F_x \ \& \sim F_x)> \ \leftrightarrow \ \sim(F_x \text{ and } \sim F_x)$$

Thus, Łukasiewicz concludes, "no object can simultaneously contain and not contain the same property" (II, 92). The ontological formulation of the PC follows from the logical formulation.

Łukasiewicz considers his arguments sufficient to establish the equivalence between (PC_{ont}) and (PC_{log}). However, there is the issue of the correct translation and interpretation of the logical principle. Łukasiewicz' proofs operate with the restricted version of the logical principle, i.e., the version that asserts that it is impossible for two *contradictory* statements to both be true. However, the equivalence between the ontological and logical formulations is far less certain if the broader version of the logical formulation is taken into consideration which includes pairs of contrary statements in its formulation.

Thus, based on an Aristotelian correspondence theory of truth, and a classical, bivalent logic, and the logical formulation that takes contradictory statements as its subject, the two formulations do entail each other. However, the appeal to a realist conception of truth, which underlies Łukasiewicz' arguments, raises its own set of questions. The adoption of an Aristotelian, realist conception of truth by itself does not entail the validity of the PC. Łukasiewicz' introduction and application of a proto *T*-schema as a crucial part of his proofs by itself is not sufficient to establish the validity of the PC. However, joined with *modus ponens* as a rule of inference, Łukasiewicz' proto *T*-schema is sufficient to demonstrate the equivalence between the two formulations.

Commentary – Chapter III
The Relation of the Ontological and Logical Principle of Contradiction to the Psychological Principle

- Aristotle's Argument
- Łukasiewicz' Analysis
- Scope and Objective of Aristotle's Argument

Łukasiewicz turns his attention to the psychological formulation of the principle, which he discusses over the span of three chapters (Chapters III – V). Chapter III presents an analysis and elucidation of Aristotle's account of the psychological version of the principle. Łukasiewicz argues that Aristotle considers the psychological PC as a consequence of the logical and ontological principles and that Aristotle presents an argument which aims to show that this is so. In Chapter IV, Łukasiewicz raises critical objections to Aristotle's argument and charges Aristotle with a failure to maintain an exclusive and exhaustive distinction between truth and falsity in his argument by admitting that beliefs may be more or less true (or, correspondingly, more or less false). Further, Łukasiewicz claims that Aristotle's argumentation trades on a confusion of psychological and logical principles. Finally, in Chapter V, Łukasiewicz presents a critique of the psychological PC that denies its status as an *a priori* principle.

Łukasiewicz begins his analysis of Aristotle's account of the psychological version of the principle of contradiction by pointing out that Aristotle, even though he does not explicitly state this, nevertheless considered the ontological and logical formulations of the principle to be equivalent. Neither of the two formulations can be proven directly since the principle they express is a first principle or *arche*. The situation is different with respect to the psychological formulation of the PC. Here, Aristotle does present an argument that, in Łukasiewicz' analysis, aims to derive the psychological version of the principle from the ontological and logical formulations.

Aristotle's Argument for the Psychological Principle

"It is impossible for anyone to believe the same thing to be and not to be" (1005b 32). Aristotle's psychological formulation of the principle of contradiction presents a startling and provocative claim. If Aristotle is right, then even the most thoughtful opponents of the principle do not (and cannot) believe the positions they articulate. Anyone who believes that an object or situation contains an actual contradiction, i.e., anyone who believes that something is the case and at the same time believes that it is also simultaneously not the case, would not just be mistaken about that object or situation—they would be mistaken about their own beliefs!

Aristotle appears to be aware that this claim lacks in persuasive force, not only for opponents who deny the truth of the principle of contradiction, but also for philosophers who would agree with Aristotle that the principle is true and universally applicable. Aristotle is pushing things too far when he claims that opponents of the PC cannot and, thus, *do not actually believe* what they assert as their considered beliefs, namely that there are contradictory objects and states of affairs.

In asserting that it is impossible to hold such beliefs, Aristotle is not merely trying to provoke or antagonize his opponents. Rather, in Aristotle's view, the principle of contradiction is a universally valid principle that not only governs the properties that any object may or may not have at the same time, it also governs the beliefs that an individual can simultaneously hold. In support his claim, Aristotle presents the following argument:

> If it is impossible that contrary attributes should belong at the same time to the same subject (the usual qualifications must be presupposed in this statement too), and if an opinion which contradicts another is contrary to it, obviously it is impossible for the same man at the same time to believe the same thing to be and not to be (1005b 26-32, Ross translation).

Łukasiewicz' Analysis

Łukasiewicz distinguishes two main parts in Aristotle's proof that correspond to the two main premises of the argument. Stated in the order in which Łukasiewicz discusses them, the premises are:

(P1) An opinion, which contradicts another, is contrary to it.[49]

(P2) It is impossible that contrary attributes should belong at the same time to the same subject.

In addition, the argument relies on an important but unstated premise:

(P3) Beliefs (opinions, convictions) are attributes (properties) of an individual mind or psyche (conceived as an object)

a) Beliefs in Contradictory Statements are Contrary to Each Other

Łukasiewicz begins his analysis with premise (P1). According to Łukasiewicz, the main problem in Aristotle's attempt to derive the psychological PC from the logical and ontological formulations lies establishing a connection between contrary beliefs and contradictory statements. The two concepts, in Łukasiewicz' account, "are not only two *different* concepts, but mutually *exclusive* ones" (III, 96). Furthermore, Łukasiewicz argues, Aristotle considers contrariety primarily as an opposition between properties. Statements, however, are not properties and, Łukasiewicz concludes, "it is difficult to speak of an opposition of statements" (III, 97).

According to Łukasiewicz, Aristotle bridges the gap between the concepts of contrariety and contradiction, and between statement and properties, by transposing the problem from logic to psychology (III, 97). In Aristotle's account, beliefs are properties of an individual mind and, further, beliefs in contradictory statements constitute contrary properties. But contrary properties cannot coexist simultaneously in one mind. Thus, according to Łukasiewicz, Aristotle derives the psychological PC from the incompatibility of contraries which, in Aristotle's account, is a consequence of the ontological and logical formulations of the principle of contradiction (III, 99).

The crucial claim that Aristotle's argument requires is that beliefs contradictory claims are (psychologically) incompatible in the sense that only one of the two beliefs can be held by a person at a given point in time. Beliefs in contradictions are contrary and, thus, exclusive to each other. If a person holds the belief that *p* is false, then that person does not (and cannot) also hold the belief that p is true (or vice versa).[50] Representing the intentional state of 'believing that p' by 'Φp', Aristotle holds (but does not demonstrate) that

$$\Phi{\sim}p \rightarrow {\sim}\Phi p$$

It is this interpretation of the behavior of beliefs that lies at the heart of Aristotle's claim that beliefs in contradictory statements are contrary to each other. If the claim is accepted, then the psychological act of holding two contrary beliefs at the same time, if it were to occur, would entail a (logical and ontological) contradiction. If a person were to believe that p is true and at the same time somehow also believed that p is not true and, if believing that p is false entails that it is impossible to believe that p is true, then it would follow that that person would believe and not believe that p is true—a clear and unmistakable contradiction (if beliefs are properties). Presented formally:

$$(\Phi p \ \& \ \Phi{\sim}p) \rightarrow (\Phi p \ \& \ {\sim}\Phi p)$$

Thus, if Aristotle's assumption is admitted, then the consequence of holding a pair of contrary beliefs is that each of the two beliefs is held and not held at the same time. This, however, presents a state of affairs that contradicts both the logical and ontological formulations of the PC—a belief is and is not held at the same time.

Finally, if Aristotle's assumption about the (psychological) behavior of contrary beliefs is admitted, the principle of contradiction in its logical or ontological formulation applied to beliefs entails the psychological formulation of the principle:

$${\sim}(\Phi p \ \& \ {\sim}\Phi p) \rightarrow {\sim}(\Phi p \ \& \ \Phi{\sim}p)$$

No contrary beliefs in contradictory statements exist simultaneously.

The question is whether Aristotle's theory about contrary beliefs is correct. Is it impossible to believe that p is true and at the same time to believe that p is not true? A dialetheist will say it is not only possible but, furthermore, that he or she is fully justified in holding both beliefs with respect to certain dialethias, certain existing contradictions. If Aristotle's claim is rejected, simultaneous beliefs in contradictory statements do not engender a contradiction with respect to the beliefs that are held or not held by a person—without Aristotle's assumption, beliefs simply no longer enter contrary relations to each other and beliefs in contradictory statements co-exist simultaneously.

b) The Principle of Contrariety

In the second part of his analysis (III, 99 ff.), Łukasiewicz examines the second premise (P2) of Aristotle's argument, which formulates the principle of contrariety, i.e., the claim that a given object cannot have contrary properties at the same time. According to Łukasiewicz, Aristotle considers this premise a consequence the logical formulation of the principle of contradiction. In a passage that occurs much later (at 1011b 15-21) in the text than the argument in support of the psychological principle (1005b 26-32, cited above), Aristotle presents an argument that aims to show that the principle of contrariety is a direct consequence of the logical formulation of the principle, which Aristotle had just introduced and stated in the preceeding lines at 1011b 13-14. The argument Aristotle presents is the following:

> Since it is impossible that contradictories should be at the same time true of the same thing, obviously contraries also cannot belong at the same time to the same thing. For of the contraries, no less than of the contradictories, one is a privation—and a privation of substance; and privation is the denial of a predicate to a determinate genus. If, then, it is impossible to affirm and deny truly at the same time, it is also impossible that contraries should belong to a subject at the same time (*Met.* 1011b 15-21; Ross translation).

Łukasiewicz points out that this argument provides "the justification of the assertion that no object can contain opposed properties", i.e., the second premise of Aristotle's argument for the psychological principle and concludes that "Aristotle derives this assertion from the logical principle of contradiction" (III, 99). In Łukasiewicz' analysis, the argument shows that "if the same object were to contain opposed properties, a contradiction would result"

(III, 100). This is so, because the presence of a property in an object *implicitly* denies the presence of any other property that is contrary to it. Thus, Łukasiewicz concludes, the logical PC constitutes "the *reason* for the general rule that asserts the impossibility of the co-existence of any opposed properties" in Aristotle's account (III, 100). Finally, since Aristotle considered the logical and ontological formulations are equivalent, Łukasiewicz concludes that his analysis of Aristotle's account demonstrates that Aristotle thought that the psychological formulation of the PC "presents a consequence of the ontological principle" (III, 100).

Scope and Objective of Aristotle's Argument

Łukasiewicz interprets the argument as an attempt to derive the psychological PC from the ontological and logical PC (and, of course, the additional premises contained in the argument). A similar position is taken by Ross (1949) who holds that Aristotle's PC, as an objectively stated "law of being," entails the subjective, psychological principle (Ross 1949, 159).

Conze (1932), on the other hand, distinguishes between the connection of the psychological formulation to the logical one and its connection to the object-theoretical (ontological) formulation. He argues that even though Aristotle considered the psychological PC a direct consequence of the object-theoretical one, the connection of the psychological PC to the logical one is the stronger and more important connection (Conze 1932, Sec.5, Sec.76-77).

Kirwan (1993) considers the argument primarily as an attempt to show that the (ontological) PC does meet the criteria required of a first principle, i.e., that it is indeed the firmest and most certain of principles, by showing that it is impossible to be in error about it (Kirwan 1993, 89). Lear (1980) also takes this position but argues that even though Aristotle's argument does require that the PC is true, it does not directly depend on the PC as a premise (Lear, 100-101). Rather, as Lear puts it, in Aristotle's view, "there is no conceptual space" in which contrary beliefs could be rationally articulated (Lear, 114).

Opinions diverge even further among writers who treat the psychological formulation as a *law of thought* and challenge the priority of the ontological and logical formulations. For example, Barnes (1969) argues that "the Law of Contradiction is a Law of Thought" (Barnes 1969, 309). Upton (1983) emphasizes the close connections between the "explicitly psychological and metaphysical grounds and dimensions of the PC" against strictly logical or dialectical interpretations of the relations between the different formulations of the principle (Upton 1983, 592). Finally, Halper (1984), who also considers the psychological PC a law of thought, argues that Aristotle is primarily concerned to show the universal scope of the principle and holds that Aristotle "is not expressing a psychological principle" in his argument about contrary beliefs because the PC "is at once a claim about the nature of things and about our capacity to know them" (Halper 1984, 371).

A further alternative is that Aristotle's argument does not derive the psychological formulation from the ontological or logical versions of the principle, but instead that the argument derives the psychological formulation directly from Aristotle's premise about the nature of contrary attributes. An example of such an interpretation is articulated by Dancy (1975), who argues that Aristotle's argument "relies on a corollary of the principle of non-contradiction, to the effect that contraries cannot belong to the same thing at the same time" (Dancy 1975, 3).

This interpretation holds that the ontological PC (in its object-theoretical formulation) is insufficient to establish the psychological formulation of the principle because the psychological PC relies on a *contrary* opposition among beliefs, and not on the *contradictory* opposition of statement and their negations. Contrary opposition, in Aristotle's account of relations of opposition, is distinct from contradictory opposition. The psychological formulation of the PC is grounded in the contrary opposition between certain beliefs, whereas the ontological, object-theoretical formulation of the PC is grounded in the contradictory opposition between a statement and its negation.

If Łukasiewicz' reconstruction of Aristotle's argument is accurate, and if Aristotle's argument succeeds in demonstrating the psychological PC, then the psychological PC is just as much an *a priori* first principle as the logical and ontological ones—a view that very plausibly corresponds to Aristotle's account. However, as it turns out, Łukasiewicz holds that the psychological principle is neither *a priori* nor a first principle in Aristotle's sense and, consequently, that Aristotle's argument fails. In the next two chapters, Łukasiewicz presents his critical objections to Aristotle's argument.

Commentary – Chapter IV
Aristotle's Proof of the Psychological PC

- Degrees of Truth in Statement and Belief
- Logicism in Psychology

Łukasiewicz presents two critical objections to Aristotle's account. The first charges that Aristotle sorts the strength of opposition between beliefs by appealing to different degrees of truth contained in the beliefs. However, in Łukasiewicz' view, the distinction between truth and falsity is applicable only to statements and, further, the distinction is exclusive and exhaustive. Every statement has exactly one of two truth-values; either a statement is true or it is false, and nothing else. Beliefs, on the other hand, are not the type of object that can be sorted in terms of truth or falsity and even less so in terms of degrees of truth or falsity. Thus, Łukasiewicz points out, if there is no range or hierarchy of degrees of truth in beliefs, then there are no corresponding degrees of opposition between beliefs. Without a range in degrees of opposition, Aristotle's argument collapses.

Łukasiewicz' second objection holds that Aristotle fails to sufficiently distinguish the psychological nature of beliefs from the logical nature of statements. A consequence of this error is that Aristotle mistakenly ascribes relations and properties to beliefs which do not belong to beliefs but only to statements. Thus, in Łukasiewicz' analysis, Aristotle's account illegitimately attempts to answer a psychological question, i.e., is the psychological PC an instance of the ontological and logical formulations, by treating it as if it were a logical one.

In his 1910 article "On the Principle of Contradiction in Aristotle," Łukasiewicz presents a shortened version of these two critical points. He argues that "Aristotle's proof of the psychological principle is incomplete because Aristotle did not demonstrate that acts of believing which correspond to contradictory statement are incompatible" (Łukasiewicz 1971 [1910], 491). According to Łukasiewicz, the proof is incomplete for two reasons: (1) Aristotle ascribes degrees of truth and falsity to beliefs, which is erroneous because truth and falsity do not admit of degrees and, further, because beliefs are not strictly true or false. (2) Aristotle confuses psychological connections with logical relations and "commits the very common fallacy of 'logicism in psychology,' which can pass for the counterpart of 'psychologism in logic' (Łukasiewicz 1971 [1910], 491).

Degrees of Truth in Statement and Belief

Łukasiewicz begins his discussion by pointing out that holding two beliefs in corresponding contradictory statement does not constitute an obvious (formal) contradiction, but a hidden one. The contradiction contained in such a pair of beliefs must be brought out first in order to be recognized as such. Thus, Łukasiewicz' view agrees with Upton's (1983) in holding that Aristotle's account allows for the possibility that hidden contradictions may be contained in beliefs that are simultaneously held by an individual. Beliefs are *positive* psychical acts, Łukasiewicz notes, and "an obvious contradiction would arise only if the same conviction *had* and had *not* been in the same mind at the same time" (IV, 102).

Examining Aristotle's proof, Łukasiewicz accepts the first three of Aristotle's premises:

> (1) Convictions are properties of a mind in which they are located.
>
> (2) Since convictions are properties, they can enter contradictory relations.
>
> (3) Opposed properties exclude each other.

However, as Łukasiewicz points out, the crucial question remains unanswered: exactly which beliefs constitute opposed properties? Aristotle arranges opposed beliefs in a series of increasing difference in truth (or falsity), where the most distant points in the series are the most opposed properties. And, consequently, Aristotle holds that convictions may be more or less true and, correspondingly, more or less opposed to each other.

Furthermore, Aristotle distinguishes beliefs in true statements about accidental properties from beliefs in true statements about essential properties, claiming that true beliefs about essential properties contain a qualitatively different truth than those about accidental properties. This, of course, reflects Aristotle's metaphysical view that knowledge or cognition of the essence of a thing is more comprehensive (and more desirable) than knowledge of some accidental feature. To know that something is a man constitutes a more penetrating cognition of *what* something is, the cognition of its unchanging substantial being. In comparison, knowing that something is white, presents a cognition of *how* something is, i.e., that it has some accidental property, which may change over time.

Łukasiewicz strongly rejects Aristotle's distinction of the cognitive value or scope that statements contain in addition to their truth-value. There is only one way in which a statement acquires a truth-value: a statement is true (or false) iff it asserts that something has or does not have a property and that object either has or does not have that property. Truth, for Łukasiewicz, is strictly a relation between a statement and the state of affairs presented by the statement. Metaphysical distinctions between essential and accidental predicates do not alter or affect the truth-value of the statement in which they occur.

Furthermore, Łukasiewicz rejects the idea that beliefs, in addition to statement, are proper bearers of truth and claims. "To speak about the *truth* of convictions at all," Łukasiewicz argues, requires that "a true *statement* corresponds to a true conviction" (IV, 103). Beliefs, to the extent to which a (logical) truth-value can be attributed to them at all, then take the truth value of the statement that is the object of the belief. Since there is no hierarchy or degree to which a statement is true or false, beliefs are also either true or false, and nothing in-between. Thus, Łukasiewicz concludes,

> if there are no hierarchical differences in truth and falsity, then there are also no opposed convictions, that is, convictions that are extremely polarized with respect to truth and falsity (IV, 104).

Aristotle, however, not only distinguishes between the quality of truth expressed by essential and accidental predications, he also allows for degrees of truth (or falsity) in statements. The notion of truth that Łukasiewicz insists on is a privileged point of a scale in Aristotle's account. This point is characterized by the opposition between being and not-being, the opposition between contradictories; it marks a change in the quality of truth and a corresponding change in its opposition to falsity. Here, statements are completely governed by strict bivalence, that is, any statement is exclusively and exhaustively either true or false. This is the case equally for all statements as truth bearers in the form of declarative sentences, including substantial, accidental or any other kind of predication.[51]

In adopting this position, Łukasiewicz agrees (in 1910) with Twardowski, who held and defended the view that truth is an absolute property that does not admit degrees. In 1900, Twardowski published an influential article "On so-called relative truths" (Twardowski 1999 [1900]) in which he rejects the notion of relative truth. His thesis is that "there are no truths which are true only in certain circumstances, under certain conditions, and which would cease to be true, thus becoming false, with a change in these circumstances and conditions" (Twardowski 1999 [1900], 148). According to Simons (2009),

> the effect of Twardowski's adopting this position was to cement the idea of the absoluteness of truth as the default position in Polish philosophy and logic (Simons, 7).[52]

However, Aristotle's account allows the possibility that statements may be graded in terms of degrees of truth (or falsity). The distinction between false statements is characterized by the opposition of contraries. Since any two of such statements may both be false, they are outside the scope of contradictory opposition in terms of being and not-being (the falsity of one does not—and cannot—imply the truth of the opposing, contrary one since it is just as false as the other).

Aristotle argues that the claim that some statements are more true or false than others requires that there is a determinate point at which a statement is simply true and not false. Thus, iff there is truth *simpliciter*, then it is possible to determine (at least to some extent) the magnitude of error or distance to truth that is contained in a false statement. Aristotle, responding to the theories of Protagoras and Anaximander, puts the point as follows:

> there is a more and a less in the nature of things; for we should not say that two and three are equally even, nor is he who thinks four things are five equally wrong with him who thinks they are a thousand. If then they are not equally wrong, obviously one is less wrong and therefore more right. If then that which has more of any quality is nearer to it, there must be some truth to which the

> more true is nearer (*Met.* 1008b 31 – 1009a 5, Ross translation).

In Aristotle's account, the degree to which a belief is more or less true corresponds to the extent to which the statement that is the object of the belief approximates truth. Łukasiewicz, on the other hand, rejects the idea of degrees of falsity (in statements or beliefs) by insisting on Aristotle's theory of truth as the exclusive method of evaluating the truth-values of statements. In his critique of Aristotle's account, Łukasiewicz does not mention Aristotle's argument (cited above) which relies on the idea that "there is a more and a less in the nature of things" and that the concept of truth provides the foundation for a distinction of degrees of falsity. Apart from this, the main thrust of Łukasiewicz' critique is that Aristotle's account requires a hierarchical ordering of beliefs in terms of truth to generate the opposition between contrary beliefs, which makes it impossible for an individual to simultaneously hold beliefs in contradictory statements. However, Aristotle mentions only beliefs in statements that contradict each other in his argument. Contradictory statements are such that one is true and the other false. Accordingly, a pair of contradictory statements would generate a pair of contradictorily opposed beliefs, which, in Aristotle's conclusion, cannot be held simultaneously. Thus, Aristotle's argument does not rely on degrees of truth, but on the opposition between strictly true and false statements.

Logicism in Psychology

According to Łukasiewicz, Aristotle's way of arguing for degrees of truth and falsity of convictions and, especially, Aristotle's account in *De Int.* 14, presents one of the first instances of "*the confusion of what is logical with what is psychological, which nowadays is so common*" (IV, 104).

Łukasiewicz is referring to key issues at the center of the psychologism debate, which evolved into a major dispute during the second half of the nineteenth century. In the German-speaking discourse, the debate about the proper domain of logic took place under the heading of *Psychologismus-Streit* and reached its peak in the years between 1890 and 1914 (Kusch 2007). The central issue of this dispute was the question of the relationship between logic and psychology in general and, more specifically, whether logic and epistemology are parts of psychology or independent fields of inquiry and knowledge.

Logical psychologism, as described by Richards (1980), is "the position that logic is a special branch of psychology, that logical laws are descriptions of experience to be arrived at through observation, and are *a posteriori*" (Richards, 19). In contrast, logical realism, as described by Brockhaus (1991), holds that "logical laws describe objective, necessary connections between abstract entities" (Brockhaus, 494).

Łukasiewicz, in his discussion of Aristotle's argument for the psychological principle of contradiction, takes a decidedly anti-psychologist, logical realist position. He points out that even though Aristotle does distinguish between convictions and statements, he does not fully recognize the psychical nature of convictions. In Łukasiewicz' view, the question about an individual's ability to hold opposed convictions at the same time is a psychological issue, but Aristotle treats this issue as as if it was a purely logical problem about the relation between opposing statements. According to Łukasiewicz, Aristotle makes the mistake of interpreting the psychological problem as a logical one and, without justification, attributes the same (logical) relations, which hold between statements, to beliefs. Thus, Łukasiewicz concludes, "Aristotle illegitimately transposes the relation of dependence between statements into the sphere of psychical phenomena" (IV, 105).

In Łukasiewicz' view, the difference between statements and beliefs is characterized by the feature of meaning, which he considers to be unique to statements. It is because statements mean something, i.e., that they present a state of affairs, that statements acquire a truth-value. A statement, in Łukasiewicz' account, expresses "that something is or is not, that some object contains a property or does not contain it" (IV, 106). It is because a statement has a definite meaning that it is in a "relation of *agreement* or *disagreement* with the facts of containing or not containing of a property by an object" (IV, 106) and it is this relation of agreement or disagreement that generates the truth-value of a statement.

Beliefs, on the other hand, are not characterized by such a relation of agreement or disagreement with a state of affairs and, thus, are not proper bearers of truth-values. Instead, following Meinong's account, Łukasiewicz argues that beliefs are characterized by an intentional relation towards a content, which in turn may be expressed in propositional form, but the intentional directedness is distinct from the content to which it is directed. Thus, in Łukasiewicz' analysis, beliefs or convictions "do *not* mean that something is or is not" and "are to be considered as certain feelings that are not to be determined but to be experienced" (IV, 106). A belief, then, is neither true nor false in a strict sense, since it does not represent some state of affairs, but consists of a psychical directedness or attitude towards a content.

According to Łukasiewicz, these considerations show that beliefs are neither true nor false in the relevant (logical) sense and, thus, that beliefs cannot stand in opposition to other beliefs in the sense required by Aristotle's argument. Consequently, Aristotle's argument and proof is insufficient in establishing its conclusion, the psychological formulation of the PC (IV, 106).

If Łukasiewicz' analysis of beliefs is correct, then Aristotle's argument not only fails to demonstrate the psychological PC—the psychological principle of contradiction as such cannot be true. If beliefs are psychological phenomena that primarily indicate a certain intentional directedness or attitude towards a given content that is expressed by a statement, and if beliefs, as psychological phenomena, do not and cannot enter a logical or ontological relation of opposition to each other, then a person may very well hold contradictory beliefs at the same time. (Whether the contradictory statements, which are believed to be true, are in fact true is a separate issue and independent of the ability to hold such beliefs.) Thus, if Łukasiewicz' analysis is right, then it is possible "to believe the same thing to be and not to be."

Commentary – Chapter V
Critique of the Psychological Principle of Contradiction

- Contrary vs. Exclusive Properties
- *A Priori* Proof of the Psychological PC is Impossible
- The Psychological PC as Empirical Law
- Empirical Investigations of the Psychological PC are Incomplete and Inconclusive
- Explicit Denials of the Psychological PC
- The Psychological PC and Religious-Aesthetic Experience

Contrary vs. Exclusive Properties

The failure of an argument to establish its conclusion is not sufficient to show that the conclusion is false. It only shows that the conclusion is not a logical consequence of the premises of the argument. Recognizing this, Łukasiewicz examines the possibility that a different set of premises may be sufficient to establish Aristotle's psychological formulation of the PC. It would be sufficient to establish the psychological PC by showing that beliefs in contradictory statement are exclusive of each other, rather than attempting to demonstrate that they are contrary to each other, which is the crucial claim in Aristotle's argument.

In shifting the distinction towards incompatibility instead of contrariety, Łukasiewicz follows Christoph Sigwart's analysis, who rejected the notions of "opposition" and "opposed" as "almost useless" for logical purposes because of "the different meanings given to them and . . . the frequently vague relation between what was called opposition and negation on the one hand, and difference on the other" (Sigwart, 131).

However, in place of contrariety, Sigwart considers the relation of incompatibility as logically useful.

> Incompatibility has no degrees; and when we are dealing merely with the ground of the negation, the relation between black and invisible does not differ from that between black and blue, nor the relation between black and blue from that between black and white (Sigwart, 133).

As Sigwart points out, it was noticed by first by Aristotle (in *Categories* 6a 12)) and later by Trendelenburg, in his critique of Hegel's dialectic, "that the increase of difference in such an ordered series of ideas, and the position of the extremes of the series, is represented to us by a spatial image" (Sigwart, 134). Sigwart claims that it was Trendelenburg who, citing Aristotle's account in the *Categories* (6a 17), argued that the term "contrary opposition" should be confined

> to those terms in such a series of differences which are furthest apart; thus, in the case of colours, only black and white are said to be in contrary opposition, while red and yellow are merely disjunct, not contrary (Sigwart, 137 n.1).

Sigwart points out that Aristotle introduces the same distinction between contrary and contradictory opposition in the *Categories* (10, 11b 33). However, in Aristotle's account, the colors black and white are considered as opposites that admit of intermediates, in contrast to

> opposites which admit of no intermediaries, such as even and uneven in the case of whole numbers, illness and health in a living being (Sigwart, 137).

Thus, Sigwart continues,

> contradictory opposition is found where only two determinations are opposed to each other; where therefore the negation of the one definitely implies the other . . . while contrary opposition is found where several determinations appear on an equal footing, as in the case of colours (Sigwart, 137).

Łukasiewicz adopts Sigwart's preference of exclusivity in favor of contrariety and argues that "the concept of mutually exclusive properties has a greater scope than that of opposing ones" (V, 107). Łukasiewicz offers a definition of exclusive properties in terms of class membership: two properties are "mutually exclusive of each other with respect to a class of objects, if they cannot simultaneously belong to the objects of this class" (V, 107).

Thus, two properties F and G are mutually exclusive with respect to the objects in a class C iff

$$\forall xy\ (Fx \wedge Gy) \rightarrow [(x \notin C) \vee (y \notin C)]$$

Or, perhaps closer to the intent of Łukasiewicz' proposed definition of exclusive properties:

$$\forall xy\ (Fx \wedge Gy) \rightarrow \neg\ [(x \in C) \wedge (y \in C)]$$

However, considering only a single object *x*, which is a member of C, the exclusivity of F and G can be expressed as a consequence of the definition(s) above:

$$\forall x\ [(x \in C) \rightarrow \neg(Fx \wedge Gx)]$$

which is equivalent to

$$\forall x\ (x \in C) \rightarrow (Fx \rightarrow \neg Gx)$$

If the class C is considered as a class of objects that belong to a specific category, then the attribution of property G to any object not belonging to C would constitute a category error, i.e., the attribution of a property to an object that is not a member of the class of objects to which that property is applicable. Thus, the scope of exclusive properties includes cross-categorial properties, which do not enter Aristotle's relation of opposition and, thus, the scope of exclusive properties is greater than that of contrary properties.

Łukasiewicz' suggestion of replacing contrary with exclusive properties in Aristotle's argument has the advantage that the relation of exclusivity allows for a more precise formal presentation than Aristotle's relation of contrary opposition, which must rely to a larger extent on exegetical considerations and which, consequently, allows for a larger range of disagreement. However, Łukasiewicz' main point and most decisive criticism of Aristotle's argument in favor of the psychological PC is not grounded in considerations of the scope and specifications of suitable classes of admissible predicates, but it is based on a distinction between the methods by which the truth of a claim that asserts the exclusivity of beliefs in contradictory statements is established. Łukasiewicz argues that any demonstration that two properties are exclusive of each other, must take one of two forms: it is either based on *a priori* considerations or on empirical observation. And, furthermore, the exclusivity of beliefs in contradictory statements, Aristotle's psychological PC, cannot be proven based on *a priori* considerations (V, 107 f.).

The Psychological PC cannot be demonstrated on *A Priori* Grounds

Łukasiewicz' argument relies on a distinction between *real* or *reconstructive* concepts, which aim to describe and distinguish actual objects and phenomena in the world, and purely abstract concepts that are derived from *a priori* considerations, that is, independently of experience, and which characterize ideal objects and their features. A re-constructive concept is based on the observable features of an object or phenomenon. Its correctness and utility depends on the scope and acuity of the correspondence between the concept and the objects that that the concept aims to describe and distinguish. It is not exclusively based on definitions and *a priori* stipulations, as concepts of abstract objects are, but on a correspondence to the real objects and phenomena in the world, and this correspondence "is always merely a more or less likely *hypothesis*" and "conclusions that rely on such concepts can also always merely be *probable* and ultimately belong to *experience*" (V, 108). Beliefs and convictions, however, are real phenomena and the adequacy of their conceptual reconstructions is always open to revision. Thus, the psychological formulation of the PC, which is a claim about beliefs, is also susceptible to revision because it must employ a re-constructive conception of the real phenomenon of belief in its formulation. Consequently, Łukasiewicz concludes, the truth of the psychological PC cannot be ascertained based on *a priori* considerations.

The Psychological PC as Empirical Law

Łukasiewicz' distinction between constructive and re-constructive concepts shows that the psychological PC does not articulate an *a priori* claim and, consequently, that it cannot be established through purely *a priori* considerations as Aristotle's argument attempts to do. However, this nevertheless leaves the possibility that the psychological PC might be an empirical law. Empirical laws are based on induction and, as such, they do not exhibit the necessity of statement that are demonstrated by *a priori* considerations and deductions, but only a high degree of probability. However, as Łukasiewicz continues his argument, even if considered as an empirical law, it is not even clear to what extend the psychological PC has been confirmed by inductive and empirical investigations.

Łukasiewicz' cites a passage from Volume 1 of Husserl's *Logical Investigations*, (Husserl 1900) in which Husserl expresses his concern that a thorough empirical investigation of the psychological PC has remained incomplete and inconclusive, if it has been undertaken at all. Łukasiewicz sides with Husserl in his critique of psychologistic misrepresentations of the PC and its validity, charging that psychologists "do not know how to distinguish the psychological principle of contradiction from the logical one–and they do not doubt the truth of the logical principle" (V, 109). As long as empirical research has not established that the psychological PC is a "law of thought", the scope of its validity remains extremely doubtful and unacceptable in Łukasiewicz' analysis.

Some twenty years later, Conze (1932) presents a long list of examples that document experimental investigations into violations of the PC in the reasoning of a diverse group of study participants. The results of one study show that violations of the PC occur frequently in situations that involve strong personal interests, for instance, the desire for financial gain that prevented individuals from noticing the contradictions in the statements made by them in support of fraudulent insurance claims (Conze 1932, Sec.48). Another study details various failures by test subjects to detect and comprehend hidden contradictions, for example, in their responses to the question: Is infertility inheritable? (Conze, Sec.54) According to Conze, the occurrence of actual contradictions between the beliefs articulated by the respondents in these studies is the result of either a diminished unity of thought or a failure to comprehend the content of what is thought and believed. (cf. Conze, Sec.42 ff). However, in all the examples Conze presents, the occurrence of (erroneous) contradictory beliefs is clearly established and, thus, the psychological formulation of the principle of contradiction is shown to be incorrect even if it is considered merely as an empirical generalization.

Still, a defender of the psychological PC is likely to point out that erroneous violations of the PC do not refute the principle's validity, even though they may compel the addition of qualifications to its formulation, i.e., conditions like a complete and conscious determination of the content asserted, a robust unity of consciousness on the side of the asserting subject, a disinterested attitude towards to the content that is asserted. Given such amendments to the original, Aristotelian formulation, even empirical violations of the principle may be interpreted as evidence that the psychological PC is recognized as a valid principle governing proper reasoning. This would be the case if it can be shown that the violations of the PC are recognized as erroneous once examined and analyzed properly, that they constitute mistakes and, if pressed on the matter, the subjects how initially asserted them will admit that they are instances incorrect reasoning and the result of insufficient determinations of the content that is asserted, or of a lack of unity of the subject's consciousness, or of an overriding interest connected to a denial of the incommensurability of the contradictory statements that had been asserted (as in the case of the insurance claims mentioned above).

However, even if most instances of an assertion of contradictory beliefs turns out to involve some erroneous omission, there still are instances in which a few philosophers have asserted their beliefs in true contradictions and have done so not in a careless or *ad hoc* fashion but as the result of careful and detailed analysis and reasoning. The prime example of such a position that wielded considerable influence on philosophical debate at the turn of the twentieth century was the work of Hegel's dialectical philosophy and the unresolved questions that it posed.

Explicit Denials of the Psychological PC and Auxiliary Hypotheses

Hegel most famously argued for the truth of statements that clearly assert the actual existence of contradictory situations and states of affairs. Łukasiewicz cites one of the more famous passages from Hegel's *Science of Logic* in which Hegel states that "movement is the *being-present* of contradiction" (Hegel 1834, 69). This statement encapsulates the result of Hegel's preceding analysis of motion, where he argues that if an object is in motion, then "it is in one and the same now [instant] here and not here . . . it is and simultaneously is not in this here" (Hegel, 69).

Łukasiewicz returns to Hegel's account of motion (and this citation) later in his work as part of his discussion of the possibility that the actual, observable world may contain occurrences of contradictory phenomena. At this point, however, the citation merely serves to establish the point that there are considered and deliberate articulations of claims that do violate and PC. Their author, Hegel in this case, deliberately expresses his belief that there are contradictory states of affairs—thus, such carefully stated beliefs provide indisputable evidence of exceptions to the psychological formulation of the PC. Consequently, in terms of purely empirical evidence, the psychological PC does not universally hold.

In light of this, defenders of the psychological PC seem to run out of viable options of reply. Łukasiewicz considers one the few remaining strategies, which is to claim–just as Aristotle did with respect to Heraclitus–that Hegel (or any other philosopher that endorses true contradictions) did not really mean what he wrote. But such a strategy requires elaborate auxiliary explanations, including Aristotle's own defense and argument in favor of the psychological PC, which attempts to explain the impossibility of a person's holding of contradictory beliefs by erroneously translating psychological phenomena into logical facts that are assumed to present objective equivalents to subjective states of affairs. Other attempts at explaining the deliberate and reasoned expression of contradictory beliefs take the form of claiming that the person holding such beliefs failed to realize the full content of their beliefs. In other words, the argument rests on the claim that the person holding contradictory beliefs does not fully understand the full content of what he or she is asserting to be their beliefs, that the contradiction contained in their beliefs remains hidden to themselves. However, this line of critique flies in the face of the undeniable care and reflection that is found in the expressions of thinkers like Hegel and, arguably, Heraclitus. A more recent defender of true contradictions, Priest (1987, 2008 [2006]), not only shares Łukasiewicz' objections against attempts to reinterpret the claims of thinkers like Hegel, he also pre-emptively addresses such challenges to his own views by explicitly declaring in advance of any such attempts at reinterpretation that he does believe that there true contradictions and that he does so based on careful and reasoned deliberation and argument, which he offers for inspection and analysis.

To further strengthen his account, Aristotle later goes on to argue that the truth of the psychological PC shows itself in the behavior of persons that do deny the validity of the principle, i.e., that they act in accordance with it, while denying it only verbally. However, Aristotle's argument trades on a misrepresentation of what is asserted and violated by such individuals. The universal validity of the PC is denied by the claim that there are *some* true contradictions (or even just one), not by the much larger claim that *all* contradictions are true.

Attempts to reinterpret deliberate assertions of contradictory beliefs by alleging that the holder of such beliefs somehow does not fully comprehend the content of his or her beliefs remain hopeless and utterly unconvincing. Not only is the psychological PC unsupported by a priori reasoning, as attempted by Aristotle's argument, it also remains unsupported as a universal law by empirical observation. In fact, as an alleged empirical law, it is refuted by evidence in the form of testimony.

The Psychological PC and Religious-Aesthetic Experience

Łukasiewicz closes his discussion of Aristotle's psychological formulation of the PC with a narrative about his personal experience of acceptance of contradictory statements in the context of religious ceremonies and meditations. The symbol of the Holy Trinity of the Father, Son, and Holy Spirit, which lies at the heart of the Christian faith, appears to present an irresolvable contradiction. It asserts the identity and unity of three distinct and separate entities, but from within a spiritual state of mind, the distinctions are preserved *and* united regardless of their apparent incompatibility. Łukasiewicz offers the religious experience of their unity in difference as an example of a (personal and subjective) state in which the psychological PC is violated and the apparent contradiction is no longer rejected. In the poetic description of the Holy Trinity by St. Athanasius,

> a *clear* contradiction is no more to be found than a latent one (in a corresponding theological interpretation). But whomever surrenders to the religious-aesthetic effect of this poetry, by leaving out theological problems, will experience for a

> moment that he believes two statements that appear contradictory (V, 110).

Conze (1932) includes an analysis of mystical and trance experiences as instances in which the psychological principle of contradiction loses its validity (Conze 1932, Sec.15 ff). Conze limits the validity of the psychological PC through certain conditions that an individual consciousness must meet for the psychological PC to govern its operations, including the formation of perceptions and beliefs. Crucial among these conditions is the unity of consciousness in the form of a unified 'self' that is set in opposition to all that is 'not-self'. However, Conze argues, by entering a meditative or mystical, spiritual state,

> the self gives itself up only in order to find itself; since what appeared as the self was only apparently the self; the true self, that is Brahman, God, the "wisdom of Buddha," Dao (Conze, Sec.16).

In the state of meditative or 'mystical' consciousness, which Łukasiewicz describes as a "religious-aesthetic effect", the limited self dissolves and with this dissolution and disappearance of the 'self' or unified consciousness, the principle of contradiction loses the foundation on which it maintains itself as a psychological phenomenon. In its place emerges a self that is no longer based on limitation and separation, and for this 'unbounded self', the psychological PC does not hold.

The conclusion of Łukasiewicz' analysis of the psychological PC is that it is not a principle that permits of demonstration on a priori grounds. Further, it is not sufficiently supported by empirical evidence as *a posteriori* law. Thus, it has no relevance for his investigation into the logical foundations and reasons for its validity of the PC as a logical and ontological principle. For Łukasiewicz, the psychological formulation of the PC is a strictly psychological and, thus, empirical claim that has no bearing on logical facts.

Commentary – Chapter VI
The Unprovability of the Ontological and Logical Principle of Contradiction

- PC as a First or Ultimate Principle
- Aristotle's Dual and Unprovable Claims about the PC

After the rejection of the psychological formulation of the PC as irrelevant to his logical and ontological analysis, Łukasiewicz returns to issues surrounding the ontological and logical PC. The focus of his investigation is the examination of the reasons and arguments that would compel an acceptance of the PC in its ontological (object-theoretical) formulation and, more specifically, its acceptance as a first principle.

In Aristotle's conception of scientific knowledge, first principles constitute the foundation of a hierarchical structure. They are *universal statements* that furnish the starting points of chains of inferences that generate the content of a science. The broadest and most general of all sciences is the science that investigates being *qua* being. The first principle, the πρώτη ἀρχή (first *arche*), of this science is the ontological formulation of the principle of contradiction, which expresses the principle κατ' ἐξοχήν.

According to Aristotle, the ontological PC is the foundational or grounding statement of this science because there are no other, prior, and more fundamental statements (about the nature of being) from which it could be derived. However, there are other, qualifying attributes that, in Aristotle's view, establish that the ontological PC is also "the *most certain* of all principles" (1005b 22, Ross translation, *italics* added).[53]

In Aristotle's account, the ontological formulation presents the most certain or firmest of principles because it satisfies the criteria that a principle must fulfill to be a *first* principle of the science that investigates being *qua* being. The criteria are the following:

1) it is "impossible to be mistaken" about it
2) it is "best known"

3) it is "non-hypothetical"

4) it is a principle that "every one must have who *knows* anything about being" (1005b 12-17, italics added).

However, while the list of criteria may be sufficient to determine whether the ontological formulation has all the attributes that Aristotle expects the first principle of the science that investigates being *qua* being to have, the list itself does not constitute proof that the ontological principle is in fact a first principle.

In his defense of the principle of contradiction, Aristotle shows signs of irritation when pressed to offer a proof for the principle and the claim that it constitutes a first principle. Łukasiewicz interprets Aristotle's polemics as an indication that Aristotle is aware of the weakness of his position and sets out to investigate the logical reasons that would be sufficient to establish the ontological PC (or any other foundational statement) as a first principle or axiom.

Łukasiewicz accepts several key aspects of Aristotle's description of the axiomatic features of a first principle. First principles are true by and through themselves. They do not allow of proof in the form of inference since they are *τὰ ἄμεσα,* statements without a middle term. As such, they are unprovable and final. However, Łukasiewicz adds an important qualification: first principles do not necessarily have to take the form of a *universal* statement but, as will be seen later, may also take the form of a definition. With this qualification added, Łukasiewicz agrees that there may be ultimate principles in the sense that they are "*statements, which cannot be proven based on other statements, but which are true by themselves*" (VI, 116).

Aristotle takes it for granted that the PC does fulfill the four criteria he listed and does not seem to perceive any need to offer a proof for the claim that it is indeed a first principle. Łukasiewicz takes issue with this and objects that, without any proof of the status of the PC as a first principle, there may be other—and still to be determined—candidates that not only satisfy the required criteria of a first principle, but that satisfy the criteria more completely and convincingly than the ontological PC.

Thus, Łukasiewicz concludes, Aristotle does not assert just one claim without offering proof, but two. The first claim is that the PC is true. The second claim is that the PC is a first principle. But the principle can only be considered true through and by itself (without proof), if it is in fact a first principle. If a competing statement can be found that fulfills the criteria of a first principle better than the PC, then the second of Aristotle's claims, i.e., that no proof for the PC can be given, no longer holds and the PC will require a proof of its truth to be accepted.

Commentary – Chapter VII
The Principle of Contradiction and the Principle of Identity

The principle of identity (PI) presents a compelling alternative for a simpler and more basic first principle than the principle of contradiction (PC). It is introduced as the initial axiom in the propositional logic that Łukasiewicz presents in the Appendix and, furthermore, it provides the foundation for a challenge to Aristotle's claim that the PC cannot be derived from another, simpler principle.

In standard formal logic, the PC is a direct consequence of the PI. The propositional PC, $\sim(\alpha \wedge \sim\alpha)$, follows through a single application of the rule of inference, $(\alpha \rightarrow \beta) \vdash \sim(\alpha \wedge \sim\beta)$, from the conditional representation of the PI as $(\alpha \rightarrow \alpha)$. Aristotle never formulated the principle of identity as a specific logical or metaphysical principle, as Łukasiewicz notes, but the principle does present a simpler, universal statement from which the PC is derivable by a deductive argument, that is, in a manner that corresponds to Aristotle's concept of a direct demonstration.[54]

Łukasiewicz begins his discussion of the PI and its relation to the PC by offering not one but two ontological formulations of the principle, one affirmative, one negative. Furthermore, in preparation for his subsequent discussion of logical equivalence between categorical and conditional universal statements, he additionally presents each of the two formulations as conditional statements. All the formulations characterize the PI in terms of the presence or absence of an inherence relation between objects and properties and, as Łukasiewicz points out, the proposed formulations are ontological, because "they contain the concepts of object and property" (VII, 118).

The inclusion of the second, negative formulations of the PI are of particular interest because they appeal to negative facts or states of affairs: "*no object contains the property that it does not contain*" and, in conditional form, "*if an object does not contain a property, then it does not contain it*" (VII, 118). The inclusion of statements of the PI in the form of negations without any further commentary suggests that Łukasiewicz does not consider negative facts or states of affairs as problematic in terms of ontological commitments or in terms of the cognitive and epistemological issues that are commonly raised about negative statements—issues that were of great concern to Łukasiewicz' teachers and mentors, Meinong and Twardowski, and which still are subject to considerable debate. However, the main reason for their inclusion among the formulations of the PI in this section is Łukasiewicz' account of the logical equivalence between universal categorical and conditional statements, which he develops for both affirmative and negative formulations.

Łukasiewicz' initial concern is to point out and clarify common misrepresentations of the relationship between the PC, the PI, and the principle of double negation (PDN) in the writings of contemporary logicians and theorists, in particular, Sigwart (1889), Trendelenburg (1870), and Überweg (1882). Against the various accounts and positions articulated by these theorists, Łukasiewicz argues that the PC, PI, and PDN are independent and distinct principles. The formulations of these principles do not express "the same thought" and "do not have the same meaning" (VII, 120).[55]

In support of his argument, Łukasiewicz' returns to the distinctions between logical equivalence, meaning, and sense of sentences, which he introduced in Chapter II. No affirmative statement has the same meaning as a negating one; however, an affirmative statement and a negation may be logically equivalent as, for example, in the formulae "*a* is *a*" and "*a* is not non-*a*." The two statements are logically equivalent with the first expressing the principle of identity and the second the principle of double negation. However, the two statements differ in meaning and, thus, do not present the same statement, because the meaning of a negation is always different from that of an affirmative statement. Furthermore, Łukasiewicz continues, both statements are different in meaning from the principle of contradiction (VII, 119).

Łukasiewicz then presents the three principles in the form of conditional statements, because the conditional form makes it easier to detect the differences between statements (VII, 120). The conditional statements are logically equivalent to their categorical counterparts, i.e., the pairs of categorical and conditional statements for each principle mutually entail each other. Further, the pairs of statements are not only logically equivalent, they also have the same meaning. This identity of meaning, Łukasiewicz argues, is a consequence of the correct formulation of the meaning of "all *x*" and "no *x*", which is hidden in the categorical formulations but explicated and revealed in its logical structure (as an inference relation) by the combination of antecedent and consequent in the conditional formulations (VII, 120).

The logical equivalence between universal categorical and hypothetical statements was first anticipated in the writings of Bain (1870, I, 117) and J.S. Mill (1843, I, 92). According to Stcherbatsky (1930), it was Mill who "seems to have been the first to express the opinion that the hypothetical judgment does not differ very substantially from the categorical one" (Stcherbatsky, I, 313 n.3). However, Stcherbatsky credits Sigwart with the first complete articulation of this idea and it was Sigwart's account in his *Logik* (1889, I, 213, 224) that exerted the strongest influence on both German and English logicians at the end of the nineteenth century (ibid; for more on the reception of Sigwart's account, see Introduction, 51).

Sigwart distinguishes between unconditionally universal plural judgments and empirically universal ones. In empirically universal judgments, 'all' denotes a limited and definite number of objects whereas in unconditionally universal judgments, 'all' denotes an unlimited number (Sigwart 1895 [1873], 160). However, the crucial point in his analysis of universal judgments, that is, judgments of the form "all *A*'s are *B*", is that he interprets the meaning of judgment of this form as equivalent to "if anything is *A*, it must also be *B*" (Sigwart, 160). Furthermore, Sigwart points out,

> if a judgment concerning 'all' is unconditionally universal, then it is clear that no direct statement is made about the actual existence of the subjects, though this is most certainly presupposed by empirical judgments if they refer to actual things at all. 'All A's are B' means only 'what is A is B'; or 'if anything is A it is B.' It is, indeed, indefinitely presupposed that some existing particular thing is recognized and called by the name A, but this is not stated in the judgment (Sigwart, 163).

Łukasiewicz certainly was familiar with Sigwart's *Logik* (he cites the work at three locations in his monograph). However, another direct line of influence for this account goes back to his teacher in Lwóv, Kazimierz Twardowski. Twaradowski's lecture notes for his logic courses contain the following remarks:

> All categorical judgements are judgements about a relation; moreover, also hypothetical judgements are categorical, and therefore relational judgements (Twardowski 1894/5, 124; as cited in Betti 2004, 9).

No matter what the ultimate source of Łukasiewicz' acceptance of the logical equivalence between categorical and hypothetical statements was, Łukasiewicz employs the conditional formulations of the three principles in his discussion because the main features that reveal the differences in meaning between the three principles are easier to detect in the consequents of the conditional formulations. However, Łukasiewicz adds a cautionary note, which suggests that he is not fully convinced that his proposed account of the meaning of the particles "all" and "none" is fully adequate.

> The same differences, however, are also decisive for the *categorical* form of the principle of contradiction, so that the following examination will still remain correct even if the conditional form were to reveal itself as not identical in meaning with the categorical one (VII, 121).

This is so, Łukasiewicz argues, because the decisive differences between the meanings of the formulations of the three principles, PI, PDN, and PC, arise from the different meanings of the logical terms, i.e., logical constants, which are employed in their articulation. These differences are preserved in both the categorical and the conditional formulations. The PC is the most complex of the three principles and requires both logical multiplication and negation for its formulation. Logical multiplication is expressed by joint occurrence of the terms "and" and "simultaneously" and requires two distinct statements for a meaningful articulation. (The multiplication of the same statement simply returns the truth-value of that statement, as already found in Boole's algebraic logic.) As mentioned, Łukasiewicz considers the negation of a statement to have a different meaning from the affirmative statement and argues that, in addition, the formulation of the PC requires the multiplication of two statements, whereas the PI and PDN do not involve logical multiplication. The simplest of the principles, the PI, does not even require negation for its formulation. Thus, Łukasiewicz concludes:

> As long as negation and logical multiplication mean something different from the absence of negation and logical multiplication, so long *the principle of identity will be different from the principle of contradiction* (VII, 122).

Commentary – Chapter VIII
The Ultimate Principle

Łukasiewicz argues that the principle of identity (PI) is not an ultimate principle either. The definition of a true statement, on the other hand, presents the most convincing candidate for an ultimate principle because it is possible to prove the PI based on a (suitable) definition of truth. However, the definition of a true statement, Łukasiewicz claims, does constitute an ultimate principle.

The definition of a true statement is a necessary part of all other principles, since they must be true to be principles. Further, as already mentioned, the PI is a consequence of the definition of truth. Finally, and most importantly, the definition of truth does not (and cannot) depend on any other, prior principle. This crucial feature of Łukasiewicz' proposed definition of truth is a consequence of the unique performative or generative property of the definition of truth: it is exclusively and independently true through itself.

The implication of this finding marks the conclusion of the first part of Łukasiewicz' investigation of the PC and fundamental logical principles like the PI: they are not ultimate and immediate principles and thus, the PC (as well as the other principles) require proof for their acceptance. The broad outline and thrust of this argument agrees to a considerable extent with Ueberweg's critique of the priviledged status of the three fundamental principles of logic (PI, PET, PC) in his *System of Logic* (Ueberweg 1857). However, Łukasiewicz considerably extends and refines Ueberweg's initial attempt (for a discussion of Ueberweg's critique, see Introduction, 45 above).

Łukasiewicz proposes a definition of truth that articulates the basic features of a classical correspondence theory. In his definition, truth is the property of certain declarative sentences or statements, which play the role of truth-bearers. Thus, Łukasiewicz' definition addresses the issue of truth exclusively in terms of declarative statements. The truth (or falsity) of a statement is the result of a relation of correspondence (or lack thereof) between the presentation contained in a declarative statement and the state of affairs that obtains (or does not obtain) in an extra-linguistic domain which is depicted and referred to in the statement. Put simply, truth consists in a relation of correspondence between a symbolic presentation of a state of affairs or fact with the existence of that state of affairs or fact in a non-symbolic, real domain—it is the successful and accurate rendering or depiction of a real state of affairs or fact that obtains in an independently existing domain.

> An affirmative statement is to be designated as true if it attributes a property to an object that the object contains. A negative statement is to be designated as true if it denies a property of an object that the object does not contain (VIII, 124).

Łukasiewicz does not offer a discussion of competing theories of truth, for example, coherence theories of truth or pragmatic accounts of truth. He also does not address the ontological issues that arise with respect to the reference to an obtaining fact or states of affairs that functions as the grounding truth-making factor in his definition.

In Łukasiewicz' view, logic is a scientific method and tool that guides the investigation and cognition of reality. A classical correspondence theory of truth establishes an account of the fundamental connection between symbolic representation and reality. It is a theory that follows the classic Aristotelian account in which *logos*, in the sense of a description or account, follows *being*, which consists of substances, their features, and their relations. However, the definition proposed by Łukasiewicz is strictly a definition of a true statement. It is much narrower in scope (minimal, in a sense) and does not include any commitments regarding the specific domain(s) in which an object has a property or does not have a property. At other locations, Łukasiewicz distinguishes the domain of the physical, empirically observable world and the ideal or abstract domain of mathematical objects and their relations. The proposed definition may even be able to accommodate fictional domains like the worlds described in novels or mythologies. However, all that the proposed definition requires is that there is a domain of facts or states of affairs that is constituted by objects and their properties, which in turn grounds and determines the relation of correspondence between these objects and their properties and their presentations in declarative statements. Whatever the exact domain is, it is the ground or foundation of the truth or falsity of presentations, which is articulated in the form of object/property statements. As Łukasiewicz argued earlier in Chapter II, for Aristotle, this domain of facts or states of affairs is being, which

> is the logical reason for the truth of statements, just as it is a real cause for their assertion. The truth of statements, on the other hand, is merely a logical reason, but not a real cause of being (II, 94).

The focus of Łukasiewicz' discussion is not epistemological or ontological, it is meta-logical; it is *about* logic and the structure of axiomatic logical systems. Łukasiewicz aims to show that the definition of truth is the ultimate principle from which all other principles of logic originate. Of course, a definition based on a correspondence theory of truth does connect logic with a domain that is real *and* with the *telos* or aim of an accurate cognition of reality. However, meta-logically, the central claim and insight is that it is the definition of truth, which constitutes the ultimate grounding principle of (a) logic. One implication, not articulated by Łukasiewicz at this point, is that different correspondence theories of truth, for instance, theories that include additional assignments of truth-values to statements, generate a different system of logic (in the sense of a system of inference). However, Łukasiewicz' principal concern at hand is to show that the proposed definition of truth is an ultimate principle—it is the only principle that is true in virtue of itself and, consequently, any subsequent principles require proof and demonstration.

Łukasiewicz constructs his argument for the definition of truth as the ultimate principle on four considerations:

(i) The definition of truth is a singular and not a universal statement (VIII, 124).

(ii) As a singular statement, a definition has the unique property of asserting a property about its author which is performatively true (VIII, 125).

(iii) The definition of a true statement generates its own truth-maker and does not rely on any other principles (VIII, 126), and

(iv) No other ultimate principles exist (VIII, 127).

(i) The first point is motivated by the following considerations: Definitions are distinct from the principles that follow from them. A definition is a singular statement since it contains, explicitly or implicitly, a performative declaration that identifies a statement as a definition (as distinct from other performative statements like a promise or a vow, a legal verdict, or a prayer). For Łukasiewicz, this declaration is singular and explicitly or implicitly performed by the author of the definition, i.e., it takes the form of a prefix that states: 'I define (or designate, name, delimit) *x* as follows …' Łukasiewicz' emphasis on the first person singular denotation seems needlessly restrictive. The same idea holds for a collective of authors, who jointly declare what the object of their assertion is, and which thereby establish it as such. Examples for such collective performatives abound, most famously, perhaps, the second paragraph of the United States' *Declaration of Independence*, which begins with the iconic announcement that was to become the rallying call of the American revolution: "*We* hold these truths to be self-evident …"[56]

The point of Łukasiewicz' observation is that definitions (and similar performative statements) are generated and accepted on an individual basis and that their acceptance is voluntary. They neither require nor compel a universal acceptance and are singular in precisely this sense. Furthermore, a singular statement of a definition has a unique performative property, which Łukasiewicz emphasizes in his second point of discussion: it asserts a property about its author(s) which is true through its statement.

(ii) By including a declaration of the appropriate kind, i.e., "I define *x* as such and such", the statement of the definition asserts and instantiates a property of the author of the statement. The utterance or declaration of such a statement of a definition generates the truth of the utterance because it attributes a property to the speaker which the speaker obtains by the utterance of the statement. First person uses of verbs like "define" or "declare" that take a direct object are intrinsically factitive. Thus, as early as 1910, Łukasiewicz articulates a pragmatic, performative statement theory that not only includes an account of how a statement can bring about a certain state of affairs, but how certain statements can make themselves true through being asserted. In its broad outlines, Łukasiewicz' theory anticipates certain aspects of J. L. Austin's pioneering work on speech acts and ordinary language philosophy, which Austin presented in his *William James Lectures* at Harvard University in 1955 and subsequently published in his by now classic work *How to do things with words* (Austin 1975 [1955]). It was Austin, who famously coined the term "performative utterances" or "performatives." It is a striking fact that key features of Austin's speech act theory are already developed in outline within Łukasiewicz' analysis of the pragmatic truth-making features of Łukasiewicz' definition of a true statement.

More specifically, Łukasiewicz' analysis of definitional verbs anticipates their classification as locutionary performatives, that is, verbs that according to Bach and Harnish "are performative in that sentences in which they occur in the first-person present can be true of their very utterance" (Bach 1979, 209).

> Locutionary performative utterances are true just in case what the speaker says in issuing them is what he predicates of himself. ... Unlike conventional illocutionary acts no special nonlinguistic convention is involved. That the speaker is mentioning something, repeating himself, or listing items depends merely on what he says and is identifiable thereby (Bach 1979, 209).

One particularly interesting feature of Łukasiewicz' account, which distinguishes it from the theory advanced by Austin some forty years later, is that in Łukasiewicz' view, the performative truth of a definition arises independently of the author or speaker's intention, that is, the statement of the definition generates its own truth independently of whether the author is sincere in the declared intention of providing a definition. The truth of the statement is established inferentially from the meaning of the words of the statement alone (the statement still needs to be made in some form by an individual, i.e., there must be a performative action, but the individual's intention is largely irrelevant to the performative success of the statement).[57]

This particular aspect of Łukasiewicz' account illustrates again one of the larger issues that Łukasiewicz addresses throughout his monograph, a clear distinction between what is properly part of psychology (psychological phenomena) and what belongs to logic (logical facts). In the evaluation and interpretation of performative expressions that indicate a definition, for example, verbs like 'understand', 'designate', 'determine', Łukasiewicz argues, "one should always relate to *signs*, that is, to sentences in which they occur, and not to *psychical acts*" (VIII, 126). Thus, a definition, which has the form of a first person (singular) statement and is prefaced by an appropriate declaration by the author, i.e., a declaration that indicates that what follows is a proposed definition, "stands in relation to a fact, which comes about together with it and which is contained in it. It is because of this, that every definition is true" (VIII, 126).

This is the case not only independently of the author's intention, but also independently of the usefulness or appropriateness of a proposed definition, which are factors that do not affect the performative success of such a statement. In addition, as Łukasiewicz points out, whether or not the concept articulated in a particular definition corresponds to anything in reality is also irrelevant with respect to the performative aspect of definitions (in a sense, it is posterior to the statement of a definition); for Łukasiewicz, the question whether or not anything falls under a proposed definition is a separate and independent question that calls for its own investigation (VIII, 126).

(iii) According to Łukasiewicz, the two crucial features of a definition of a true statement are (1) it does not rely on any other principles for its truth and (2) it is true in virtue of its own articulation. Thus, the definition of a true statement satisfies the conditions of an ultimate principle. However, the feature that the definition is true through itself is restricted to individual statements (performances) of the proposed definition of a true statement. Łukasiewicz describes this situation as follows:

> If somebody says: "Under a true statement I understand a statement that attributes a property to an object that the object does possess", then he attributes to himself the property of "understanding-something-by-a-true-statement". He indeed does possess this property because he just asserted it in the utterance of this definition (VIII, 126).

In its performative aspect, Łukasiewicz' identification of the definition of a true statement as an ultimate principle is reminiscent of Descartes famous dictum "*cogito ergo sum*", which also was introduced as a first principle. In both cases, the truth of the statement is established by its performative component, that is, by the execution of what is stated, i.e., the activity of thinking or defining. Thus, Łukasiewicz' ultimate principle presents something of a Cartesian moment in his meta-logical search for a first principle of logic. However, it also restricts the principle to individual, performative statements—certainly not an ideal foundation for a system of logic. As mentioned, Łukasiewicz attempts to separate his proposed ultimate principle as much as possible from potential psychologistic snares by arguing that, even though the definition of a true statement must be stated in some performative manner by some individual, its truth is generated through a combination of the act of stating it and the meaning of the statement itself, not from any psychological state or experience on the part of the person stating the definition.

How to connect the singular statement of a definition with the universal statement of a principle? Łukasiewicz argues that the first step is to

> distinguish the definition from the principle that follows from it. A definition is always a *singular statement*, which states that someone determines, designates and names an object in a certain way. A principle that rests on a definition is always a *universal* statement, which asserts a property about the defined object that the definition attributes to it (VIII, 125).

An ultimate principle cannot be a universal statement because universal statements are equivalent to conditional statements. The truth of a conditional statement is not immediate since it is a consequence of the combination of two separate statements and their respective truth-values. Łukasiewicz argued for the equivalence between universal categorical and conditional statements in Chapter VII, and he applies his finding again in his conclusions of point (iv) as part of his argument that no principles other than the definition of truth qualify as immediate and ultimate principles.

iv) There are no ultimate principles except the definition of a true statement. (VIII, 127). Łukasiewicz considers the alternatives: other definitions, other immediate truths (Brentano) that arise from internal or external experiences, and universal statements, like the axiomatic principles of logic, i.e., the PI, PC, or PET. However, none of these alternatives proves viable compared to the definition of a true statement based on a correspondence theory of truth.

One of the functions of a correspondence theory of truth is to provide an account of the connection between the meaning of a (logical) statement and the state of affairs that it describes. A theory of truth determines the relation between symbolic representation and what is represented. It connects abstract depiction with the entities that constitute the ground of the truth or falsity (or other qualities) of the depiction.

In a correspondence theory of truth, it is sentences, declarative statements, or the statement articulated by sentences, that are the bearers of truth. Truth or falsity are the values that a statement may have. Truth is the quality of certain statements; it is a property.

Alternatively, for example in Brentano's account, it is a quality of the disposition of a subject towards (the content of) a presentation. For Brentano, this disposition is characterized by the polarity of acceptance or rejection. It is psychological in nature and a quality of the judgment that consists in acceptance or rejection.

Correspondence theories do not require a commitment to a realist or anti-realist position. They can be incorporated into both views. Realism is the position that reality exists independently from abstract, theoretical descriptions. Anti-realism, on the other hand, is characterized by the view that such an independent reality remains outside of what can be presented in an abstract description and, further, that any form of symbolic or theoretical representation imposes its own structure on what it presents. The difference between realism and anti-realism arises from differences in the account of how symbolic representations connect what they represent.

Łukasiewicz' theory of truth is a correspondence account that is based on a comparison between the state of affairs presented by a statement (its content) and the state of affairs that obtains in the domain that is addressed by the statement (cf. Łukasiewicz' proof of the equivalence between the ontological and logical formulations of the PC in Chapter II, 91 ff., which relies on a t-schema that appeals to a correspondence between statement and being, and the Commentary to that section, 293 ff.). As such, Łukasiewicz' definition of truth does not require any commitments with respect to a particular ontological mode in which an object has or does not have a property. It requires only that there are objects and properties. An object can be a physical object, like a table or a rock, or it can be an abstract or ideal object, like a number or a relation.

Łukasiewicz concludes that, as a definition, a definition of truth is true in virtue of itself. It is true through its own articulation. It is performative in that it establishes itself as true through its formulation and it is self-reflexive: its content is applicable to itself. As such, the definition of a true statement presents the most fundamental of first principles.

Commentary – Chapter IX
Aristotle's Elenctic Proofs

- *Elenchus* or Demonstration by Refutation
- *Apagoge* or Direct Demonstration
- Inferential Structures of Elenctic and Apagogic Demonstrations
- Summary of Results

Łukasiewicz points out that Aristotle appears to contradict himself when he asserts that the PC, as a first principle, cannot be proven directly but then nevertheless proceeds to present a series of arguments that aim to offer explicit proofs the PC. To resolve the issue, Łukasiewicz sets out to determine whether Aristotle's account presents (or intends to present) a direct demonstration or proof of the principle, which would mean that Aristotle does contradict himself, or whether Aristotle's account presents a collection of reasons or considerations that support the PC in some other fashion. The focus of Łukasiewicz' discussion in this chapter is on the formal structure of Aristotle's demonstration by refutation and subsequent arguments that Aristotle presents in favor of the PC.

Elenchus or Demonstration by Refutation

According to Aristotle, the first and longest of these demonstrations is not a direct demonstration of the principle, but an *elenchus*, a demonstration by refutation or indirect demonstration. A direct demonstration of the PC will be liable to assume what it sets out to prove, as Aristotle himself points out, and thus, it would appear to commit the fallacy of a *petitio principii*. An elenctic demonstration, on the other hand, does not run this risk because "another person is responsible for the assumption" (1006a 18). This assumption (which, in Aristotle's view, entails the validity of the PC) is provided by the opponent of the PC once he says "something which is significant both for himself and for another" (1006a 22). If the opponent complies and makes a significant utterance, then "demonstration will be possible; for we shall already have something definite" (1006a 24).

Łukasiewicz is critical of Aristotle's distinction between an indirect proof by refutation and a direct, syllogistic demonstration. He argues that an *elenchus* or indirect proof by refutation, in terms of Aristotle's own account in the *Prior Analytics II* (66b 6-13), constitutes a deductive demonstration and, thus, presents a proper proof of its conclusion.[58] In Aristotle's account, one of the characteristic features of an elenctic syllogism is that it requires and proceeds from a positive thesis, that is, from a complete declarative statement that, as Aristotle emphasizes, may not be a negation. From this thesis and an additional premise, the syllogism derives a conclusion (by direct derivation) which contradicts the opponent's main position. The opponent's main position, which the elenctic refutation aims to defeat by the derivation of its contradictory, is distinct from the premises of the elenctic syllogism that are accepted by the opponent.

A further distinguishing feature of the elenctic refutation, emphasized by Aristotle in both the *Prior Analytics* and the *Metaphysics*, is that the theses and syllogistic form through which the conclusion is derived must be asserted, endorsed, or otherwise accepted by the opponent. Since the conclusion of the syllogism contradicts the opponent's main position and the opponent at the same time accepts the premises, deductive form, and conclusion of the syllogism, the syllogism provides a refutation or indirect demonstration which shows that the opponent's position is false or, at least, that the theses accepted by the opponent and his or her main position cannot be both true (since it is contradicted by the conclusion derived by the syllogism).

The requirement that the opponent endorses or—even better—asserts the starting premise(s) suggests that an *elenchus* constitutes an *ad hominem* argument. An elenctic refutation is an *ad hominem* argument in the sense that it requires and is directed against an individual opponent, who is willing to assert a positive statement, i.e., it takes aim at an opponent who is willing to state that something is the case. If an opponent does make such a statement, then a successful elenctic syllogism delivers a refutation specifically targeted against the opponent's main position through "a deduction which establishes the contradictory" (66b 11).

The conclusion of the direct demonstration contradicts the opponent's main position based on premises (and inferential forms) accepted by the opponent. As such, an elenctic refutation, provided it is successful, defeats only an individual opponent against whom it is directed (and like-minded individuals who also accept the same position and theses that opponent admits during the argument). Furthermore, an elenctic refutation proceeds not only *ad hominem* but, crucially, it is also based on the derivation of a contradiction. Thus, it may very well be insufficient and lacking in persuasiveness against an opponent who denies the universal validity of the principle of contradiction in the first place.

More importantly in the current context, one of the crucial stipulations in the elenctic refutation of an opponent of the PC in the *Metaphysics* is that the opponent is not required to "say that something either is or is not" (1006a 21). Thus, the opponent is not required to endorse any declarative and affirmative statement about a relation between terms (to avoid a *petitio principii*), as stipulated in the description of elenctic refutations in the *Prior Analytics*. Instead, Aristotle's elenchus in the *Metaphysics* aims to refute the opponent of the PC based on a speech act that is performed by the opponent and that successfully produces the determinate signification of an item. Thus, the elenchus in defense of the PC in the *Metaphysics* is significantly different from the elenctic refutation described in the *Prior Analytics*.

Once the opponent has produced the required utterance, the argument proceeds without any specific reference to the opponent's position and does not require any additional participation by the opponent except to listen to the refutation as it unfolds. As Aristotle puts it, "the person responsible for the proof, however, is not he who demonstrates but he who listens; for while disowning reason he listens to reason" (1006a 26).

Aristotle's indirect demonstration relies on two underlying hypotheses: 1) any successful and determinate signification of an item by a meaningful expression, even by a single word, requires the validity of the PC as a necessary condition, and 2) the successful performance of a determinate signification somehow provides a foundation on which the universal validity of the principle can be demonstrated. The moment of definite signification marks the crucial difference that distinguishes Aristotle's indirect demonstration of the PC from a direct one. If determinate signification is admitted, Aristotle argues, then it is also the case that "something is true apart from demonstration" (1006a 28) and the foundation on which a demonstration of the PC (by deductive argument) can be accomplished has been established.

However, the actual premises which constitute Aristotle's elenchus are not directly provided by the opponent, but derived from the fact of his determinate signification of an item. By signifying an item, the opponent endorses the view that a given word, e.g., "man", has at least one definite meaning—it permits the signification of exactly one thing. Aristotle's elenchus derives a formulation of the PC from the acceptance of this premise (a definition of the meaning of the word "man") and, thus, generates a contradiction between the opponent's acceptance and endorsement of determinate signification and the opponent's rejection of the PC.

Apagoge or Direct Demonstration

Łukasiewicz concludes that the elenctic argument, which commences following the meaningful utterance by the opponent of the PC, constitutes an attempt to prove the PC. In addition, Łukasiewicz points out, Aristotle not only provides an elenctic or indirect proof but also several direct demonstrations of the PC in several shorter arguments and considerations that follow the longer, indirect demonstration. Łukasiewicz emphasizes that Aristotle himself considered his arguments to constitute a proof that "contradictory statements cannot be simultaneously accepted" (1007b 18; Łukasiewicz translation).[59] If this is correct, then Aristotle does indeed contradict himself in his account of the PC when he claims that the PC cannot be proven and then nevertheless proceeds to offer multiple arguments that aim to prove the truth and universal validity of the PC. However, to clarify that Aristotle does present proofs of the PC, Łukasiewicz moves on to examine the logical differences between an elenctic and apagogic (direct) demonstration.

Inferential Structures of Elenctic and Apagogic Demonstrations

According to Łukasiewicz, an elenctic demonstration is a valid syllogism that instantiates the formal inference schema of *modus ponens* or detachment: $A \rightarrow B, A \vdash B$. With respect to the elenchus presented by Aristotle in the *Metaphysics*, the inference proceeds from the performatively established fact of determinate significa-tion to a conclusion that states the PC. An apagogic demonstration or *reductio ad absurdum*, on the othe hand, is a valid syllogism that instantiates the inference schema of *modus tollens*, which Łukasiewicz presents in the form: $\neg B \to \neg A, \neg\neg A \vdash \neg\neg B$ (instead of the more commonly used formulation $B \to A, \neg A \vdash \neg B$). The two formulations are equivalent since the principle of double ne-gation holds in classical logic and the inference schema is valid in classical propositional calculus (it is also included and applied in the algebraic propositional calculus introduced by Łukasiewicz in Appendix I).

Łukasiewicz claims that *modus ponens* inferences do not rely on the PC in general, whereas *modus tollens* inferences always pre-suppose the PC. However, he postpones an argument in support of the latter claim to Chapter XII and, regarding the former claim, i.e., that the *modus ponens* inference schema generally does not rely on the PC, he unfortunately does not offer an explicit argument or ex-planation. Instead, he merely notes that this is the case if the infer-ence schema is not used to "to demonstrate the connection between premise A and conclusion B" (IX, 133). It is not altogether clear what to make of this claim, but it does not seem to concern nega-tion and its behavior.

From today's perspective, the acceptance of a rule inference like *modus ponens* in a given logic does not exclusively depend on criteria that rely on or appeal to the validity of logical principles like the PC. Instead, the understanding and interpretation of the logical structure of conditional sentences have been shown to have major consequences for the validity of *modus ponens* as a rule of inference within a given logic. For example, in modal logics, the accessibility relation of reflexivity directly affects the properties of the strict conditional. Without reflexivity, *modus ponens* does not hold for strict implication in modal logics (cf. Priest 2001, 65). *Modus ponens* also fails in certain conditional logics, as for exam-ple, the logic C, (cf. Priest 2001, 81) and—perhaps most relevant in a discussion related to the PC—*modus ponens* is not a valid form of inference in the three-valued logic LP. In LP, the premises p, $p \to q$ do not necessarily entail q since the inference fails in the case in which p is assigned the value i and q the value 0 (cf. Priest 2001, 122).

However, these observations neither support or refute Łukasiewicz' claim about the relation between *modus ponens* and the PC. While most applications of *modus ponens* may not aim to demonstrate the conditional relation between two claims, as Łukasiewicz puts it, a *modus ponens* inference certainly appeals to the conditional relation as a necessary premise for its conclusion. Furthermore, within classical logic, the material conditional $A \rightarrow B$ is equivalent to the disjunction $\sim A \vee B$. If A is added as premise to this disjunction, the two premises entail B via disjunctive syllogism. The conclusion of a disjunctive syllogism, however, derives its necessity through an application of the PC.[60] Based on this interpretation, then, and contrary to Łukasiewicz' claim, the *modus ponens* inference schema is logically equivalent to the disjunctive syllogism and, thus, relies on and presupposes the PC for its validity without exception.

In light of these considerations, it remains unclear what Łukasiewicz' might have meant by his claim. One possibility is that he did not think that the conditional is a material one. The conditional that he introduces in the propositional calculus outlined in Appendix I, is not a material conditional. In the Appendix, Łukasiewicz describes the relation expressed by a conditional as a "fundamental logical relation" that expresses a consequence relation between two statements as a necessary relation, which suggests that he thought of the conditional as a strict conditional: "from statement *a* follows statement *b*, if *b* has *always* to be given in case *a* is given" (Appendix I §2, 226; italics added). However, Łukasiewicz does not further specify the sense of necessity that he employs in his description the relation that is expressed by a conditional statement, but he does point out that the consequence relation is reflexive, transitive and asymmetric (Appendix I §2, 226 f), which means that even if interpreted as a strict conditional, *modus ponens* holds, since the relation is reflexive (as pointed out above). It should be noted, though, that the fact that the conditional connective is reflexive does not mean that the inference relation expressed by it is reflexive as well.

For Łukasiewicz, one of the key differences between *modus ponens* and *modus tollens* is that *modus ponens* does not require the concept of negation for its formulation whereas both *modus tollens* and disjunctive syllogism do. In this context, it may not be without significance that Łukasiewicz' formulation of *modus tollens* employs the negations of all constitutive propositions that appear in the premises (except the conditional). Thus, his formulation employs negation far beyond the two negations that are needed to uniquely characterize the inference schema. Even the conclusion takes the form of a negation in his formulation (a double negation, to be sure, but a negation nevertheless). But no matter how *modus tollens* is formalized, *modus ponens* is the structurally simpler rule of inference since it involves fewer logical constants in its formulation. Further, and perhaps most important to an understanding of Łukasiewicz' claim, the formulation of the *modus ponens* scheme of interence does not include negation at all. Negation, however, is necessary for the formulation of the PC. Thus, apart from the difference in their inferential form, there is a definite semantic difference between *modus ponens* and *modus tollens* inferences. However, this difference is insufficient to show that the inference schema does not rely or appeal to the validity of the PC.

Be that as it may. Łukasiewicz' conclusion is that an apogetic proof or *reductio* argument for the PC, which is a *modus tollens* inference and relies on the PC for its validity, will beg the question and commit a *petitio principii*, as Aristotle suggests. On the other hand, Łukasiewicz concludes that an elenctic argument that relies on *modus ponens* as its principal rule of inference provides a formal structure that does not include an appeal to the PC and, consequently, constitutes an argument that does not formally beg the question. However, as argued above, Łukasiewicz is mistaken about the latter point. Any (classical) argument that relies on a *modus ponens* inference also relies on and presupposes the PC. Thus, either rule of inference, if employed by Aristotle in his arguments in defense of the PC, includes a *petitio principii*. As a result, the situation for Aristotle is far worse than what Łukasiewicz' critique asserts.

Chapters I to IX Summary of Results

In the final part of the chapter, Łukasiewicz presents a summary of the main findings of his discussions in Chapters I to IX. Distinguishing between the PC as a law of thought and the PC as a law of being, he aimed to show that it is doubtful that the PC is a law of thought by showing that the psychological formulation is, at best, an inductive generalization from empirical evidence and, even as such, incomplete and far from certain. The PC as a law of being, on the other hand, was shown not to be an ultimate principle and in need of proof. Finally, he showed that Aristotle did try to prove the principle in chapter 4 of *Metaphysics Γ*. A careful analysis of Aristotle's proofs is the next task in Łukasiewicz' investigation.

Commentary – Chapter X
The Principle of Contradiction and the Principle of Double Negation

Łukasiewicz distinguishes two proofs in Aristotle's elenctic demonstration by refutation. Fhe first and simpler proof relies on the Principle of Double Negation (PDN), the second and more complicated one is based on the Aristotelian concepts of essence and substance. Both proofs are based on the consequences that follow from the acceptance of a definition and, more specifically, the consequences that follow from the determination of the meaning of a term based on its definition.

Interestingly, Łukasiewicz' distinction of two proofs within Aristotle's *elenchus* foreshadows and identifies some of the key points of contention in the recent debate about the Anscombe/Cresswell interpretation of Aristotle's elenctic argument in terms of the distinction between essential and accidental predication.

Max Cresswell (2003), expanding on the analyses of Aristotle's argument developed by G. E. M. Anscombe (1961, 39-43) and Łukasiewicz' comments in his companion article to the monograph (1971 [1910]), argues for an interpretation of Aristotle's argument as primarily concerned with establishing the PC for Aristotelian substances. Thus, in the Anscombe/Cresswell interpretation, Aristotle's elenchus aims to establish the PC not as a logical principle but as a metaphysical principle that describes substantial being. As Cresswell notes, substances are the ontologically most real objects in the universe for Aristotle. "A substance is an independently existing thing which has an essential nature" (Cresswell 2003, 166). The central claim of the Anscombe/Cresswell interpretation of Aristotle's argument is that

> the law of non-contradiction is concerned with the application of a predicate to a substance. On the Anscombe interpretation we must make a distinction between predicates which say what a substance *is* (substantial predicates) and predicates

> which say something about a substance (Cresswell 2003, 167)

Cresswell's interpretation emphasizes what Łukasiewicz identifies as the second proof contained in Aristotle's account and is discussed separately by Łukasiewicz in the next chapter. Without going into the details at this point, it is sufficient to note that in the Anscombe/Cresswell interpretation the validity of the PC is restricted to substantial predication, which in turn depends on the metaphysical concept of substances as a fundamental ontological entity. Łukasiewicz discusses the substantial predication argument for the PC in the next chapter. In the current chapter, the focus is on Aristotle's argument for the PC as a logical principle and, specifically, on the question whether the PC is derivable from the principle of double negation.

In Łukasiewicz' analysis, this subordinate argument, which attempts to derive the PC as a consequence of the PDN, is inserted into the larger (elenctic) argument that aims to prove the PC as a metaphysical principle with respect to the Aristotelian concept of substance, but the subordinate argument does not appeal to or rely on the metaphysical concept of substance. Instead, the argument aims to show that the PC is a logical (or semantic) consequence of the PDN.

In his previous discussions, Łukasiewicz had argued that the PDN and PC differ in meaning (since they require the employment of different logical constants for their expression). Despite the difference in meaning, it is possible that the two principles are logically equivalent, that is, each of the principles entails the other. However, Łukasiewicz argues, the application of the two principles to contradictory objects shows that the PDN does not entail the PC. In his analysis, the principle of double negation holds for contradictory objects whereas the principle of contradiction does not. Thus, the PC is not a consequence of the PDN and Aristotle's proof of the PC based on the PDN fails.

The crucial point in Łukasiewicz' analysis is the claim that the PDN holds true for contradictory objects. However, it is questionable whether this is the case. A round square is square and, according to the PDN, it is not the case that it is not square. However, a round square is also round and, thus, it is not square, which negates what the PDN asserts (i.e., that it is not the case that it is not square). The PDN, applied to a contradictory object, is both true and false. At least, it is not true *simpliciter*, as claimed in Łukasiewicz' argument.

Translated into object-theoretical terms, the PDN (of a bivalent logic with Boolean negation) asserts that if an object x has a property F, then it does not not have that property. The PDN denies the lack of a property that an object does possess. However, it is precisely the joint absence and presence of a property that makes an object contradictory. Thus, with respect to a contradictory object x for which F_x and not F_x both hold for some property F, it is true that the object does have the property F and it is true that it does not have that property. The PDN fails because it is not the case that x does not not have the property F as asserted by the PDN. A round square is square *and* it is not square. Contradictory objects violate the PDN just as much as they violate the PC.

Łukasiewicz' attempt to show that the two principles are not logically equivalent is unsuccessful. It appears that Łukasiewicz attempts to expand and develop Sigwart's analysis of the relationship between logical principles, which considers them as related through a hierarchical progression and dependence (cf. Sigwart 1895 [1873], Ch.4, and the discussion of Sigwart's influence in the Introduction, 50).

Commentary – Chapter XI
The Principle of Contradiction and the "Essence" of Things

Aristotle's elenctic proofs, as Łukasiewicz points, trade on definitions and the determination of the meaning of a word. Further, a crucial point in both arguments is that whatever the word under consideration is, it must designate one and exactly one thing. Thus, the meaning of the word must be determinate and unique for the arguments to proceed.

However, whereas the first proof does not place any constraints on the meaning of the word that the opponent is expected to introduce, the second and more elaborate proof requires that the word used as the starting point of the elenctic proof designate a substance, the essential being of an object. In Łukasiewicz' reading of Aristotle, the essence or substantial being of an object has the following properties: it is fixed, immaterial and cognitively accessible only by the intellect in the form of a concept. It cannot be changed. If it were to change, it would be a different essence belonging to a different kind of object. It is ideal and, thus, not perceptible through the senses. Aristotle distinguishes two modes in which something may be a substance in his fourfold distinction of things that are (*ousia*) at the beginning of the *Categories*:

> Some are *said of* a subject but are not *in* any subject. For example, man is said of a subject, the individual man, but is not in any subject (*Cat.* 1a 20-21).[61]

and

> Some are neither in a subject nor said of a subject, for example, the individual man or the individual horse—for nothing of this sort is either in a subject or said of a subject (*Cat.* 1b 4-6; cf. 1b 7-8, 2a 13-18, 3a 8-21).

The key contention in Łukasiewicz' interpretation of Aristotle's second elenctic proof is that a word has meaning iff it designates what is *one* in its essence, that is, that a word is suitable as the starting point for the argument iff it denotes a thing that is individual and numerically one. For Aristotle, Łukasiewicz argues, "the essence of every object is some one thing" (XI, 141).

Semantic Interpretation of the Argument

Łukasiewicz identifies the second elenctic argument in a specific passage from *Met.Γ* 4, 1006b 11-22. He formally represents the argument as consisting of two premises and a conclusion, which, if an assumption is added, results in the conclusion that the PC holds for essential being, i.e., substances do not contain contradictory properties. In Łukasiewicz' analysis, Aristotle's argument exhibits the formal structure of a hypothetical syllogism combined with an additional application of a *modus ponens* inference. The two premises and their respective proofs as offered by Aristotle, are as follows:

> First premise: The word necessarily signifies an essence, that is, it signifies "something that is one thing according to its essence" (XI, 142).
>
> Second premise: If the word is significant, that is, if it signifies the essence of a thing, then it cannot signify a thing that contains a contradiction in its essence, that is, it does not signify something that both has and does not have a given property. In other words, the properties that define the essence of an object are such that they do not include any property *F* such that the object both is *F* and simultaneously is not-*F*. Essences are consistent (XI, 142).

Łukasiewicz considers two objections to Aristotle's argument.

Objection (a)

Łukasiewicz claims that Aristotle's argument mistakenly relies on the claim that a word has meaning only in case it signifies an item that is an individual and unified entity, something that is one in its essence. Instead, Łukasiewicz argues that "words may have meanings without signifying something that is one thing according to its essence" (XI, 143). He offers the counterexample of hippocentaur, a mythical beast that consists of the body of a horse combined with a human head and torso in place of the horse's neck and head. Łukasiewicz argues that even though 'hippocentaur' refers to a non-existing object, it is nevertheless a meaningful word and indicates an object that is both man and not-man. This challenges the assumption that a meaningful word cannot denote a contradictory object because such an object, to be determinately signified by a word, must be "determined unequivocally" (XI, 143).

However, it is not altogether clear whether this reflects Aristotle's views accurately. Aristotle himself admits at other locations that words may signify contradictory objects. For instance, in *De Interpretatione* Aristotle notes in passim that "even 'goat-stag' signifies something" (16a 16; Ackrill translation). The crucial point with respect to Aristotle's argument is not that a word cannot successfully signifiy a contradictory object, but that contradictory objects cannot be items that exist and, further, that only substances, that is, things that are, have essences that can be unequivocally determined in a definition. For Aristotle, it is certainly possible to give an account (in the sense of a description) of what the word goat-stag means and what it signifies. However, the existence and intelligibility of a description of a contradictory object is no warrant that the object exists. As Aristotle points out in *Posterior Analytics* II, "one can signify even things that are not" (92b 29; Barnes translation).

Further, if a description attributes contradictory properties to an object, then the description fails to demarcate a unified entity, something that is one in Aristotle's sense, and whatever is not one thing in its essential properties, Aristotle argues, cannot and does not have being. Consequently, it also cannot be an object of knowledge since, for Aristotle, what is not is not knowable. The difference is between the account of *what* something is, i.e., the definitional statement of its essence, and the actual being of that object. Aristotle discusses this issue in *Posterior Analytics* II, where he notes:

> It is necessary for anyone who knows what a man or anything else is to know too *that* it is (for of that which is not, no one knows what it is—you

> may know what the account or the name signifies when I say goatstag, but it is impossible to know what a goatstag is) (92b 4-8; Barnes translation).

Aristotle's distinction suggests that there are two different senses of "signification". First, a primarily semantic sense of signification that plays the role of an explication of the meaning of a term by giving a list of the properties that the item that is signified by a term is understood to possess. Second, a primarily metaphysical sense of signification, in which the essential properties of an object are determined in a definition and which additionally includes the knowledge that the object signified exists. In the first sense, signification amounts to knowledge of a description, that is, knowledge of a statement that determines the properties some thing must have to be a certain thing; the second sense of signification consists in a definition of the essential properties of a thing that is grounded in the existence of the thing signified, in its actual being.

What Aristotle argues is that while it is possible for a word to signify contradictory items, what is required for his argument is that a word is selected that signifies the essence of a substance (substantial signification), and the essence of a substance presents a unified and non-contradictory entity. The properties that define the essence of an object that a word can meaningfully and determinately signify must be one. Thus, even though it is possible to combine properties to specify the meaning of words that signify contradictory objects, as for example, the meaning of hippocentaur, wooden iron, or square circle, the properties that make up the essence of a substance must compatible, i.e., consistent, to describe an essence in Aristotle's sense.

Objection (b)

Łukasiewicz' second objection raises the point that even if it is admitted that words "signify something that is one thing according to its essence, it would not follow from this that *reality does not* contain a contradiction" (XI, 144). Aristotle's account of essential signification generates a linguistic structure that favors and promotes consistency in its representations of the world and at the same time obscures or misrepresents contradictory items that may very well be part of the actual world. Thus, even if it were the case that linguistic representations of the world are inadequate to signify or meaningfully articulate contradictory objects or states of affairs, this does not entail that contradictions do not exist in reality—it only means that language, under the constraint of Aristotle's requirement of substantial signification as a condition of meaning, does not have the resources to capture and represent contradictory objects in its depictions of the world. Language includes its own, semantic consistency filter, as it were, which limits meaningful discourse to discourse about consistent objects and situations.

However, as Łukasiewicz points out, Aristotle is not primarily concerned with semantic considerations alone. At the center of his argument is the question whether contradictory objects do exist. Thus, the argument's key concern may not be the semantic nature of signification but the ontological nature of objects. Consequently, Łukasiewicz modifies his formal presentation of Aristotle's argument and reconfigures it with a focus on ontological features and logical structure of the objects that are signified by words. He represents the argument as an ontological, object-theoretical argument.

Ontological Interpretation of the Argument

In this version, Łukasiewicz replaces the parts that indicate the signification of an object with expressions that indicate the being of an object. The argument no longer is about words and signification but objects and their essential properties.

The first premise specifies the condition that an item must meet to be an object: "If *x* is an object, it must be one thing according to its essence" (XI, 144). However, in the ontological interpretation of the argument, this condition is no longer a semantic condition that a word must satisfy to successfully signify an object, but a metaphysical condition that an item must satisfy to be an object—its essential properties must determine it as a unified and individual entity, that is, it must be a substance.

The second premise introduces a stipulation about the logical and ontological structure of a substance. It states that if something is a substance, that is, if it "is one thing according to its essence, then it cannot be *F* and not be *F* according to its essence" (XI, 144).

Thus, the pivotal term in Aristotle's argument in this interpretation is no longer the concept of signification, but the concept of an object and, crucially, of essences and their ontological and logical structure. Łukasiewicz does not endorse one or the other interpretation as *the* correct rendering of Aristotle's argument. Rather, Łukasiewicz' exposition aims to show how Aristotle's argument attempts to establish the validity of the PC on dual grounds: In its semantic formulation, it traces the symbolic representation of the world in language (*logos*) back to the world as it is (*to ov* and *ta onta*, being and the things that are). In its ontological formulation, the direction of Aristotle's argument is reversed. It starts with the items that have being in its primary sense, *ta onta*, the things that are, substances and their essences, and derives the correct presentation of their being in language.

In Łukaisewicz' analysis, the second, ontological version is just as flawed and unconvincing as the first, semantic version. He introduces two additional objections that are specifically directed against the ontological interpretation of Aristotle's argument.

Objection (c)

Łukasiewicz argues that, even if Aristotle's argument in its ontological interpretation were to be sound, it would establish the validity of the PC only for a limited domain of objects. If accepted, the argument establishes the PC only for the essences of substances. More specifically, it is the properties that constitute the essence of a substance that are shown to be necessarily consistent, if the argument is correct. Thus, the PC is restricted to a very specific subset of all properties, a subset that is furthermore deeply embedded within the Aristotelian metaphysics of being and its ontological foundation, the concept of substance. The argument does extend to accidental properties or the properties on non-substantial items (i.e., contradictory objects in Aristotle's account). At the very least, Aristotle's argument leaves the non-essential properties of an object undetermined with respect to the PC. Thus, there is no proof that properties that are not a constitutive part of the essence of an object may not be inconsistent in their inherence relation to substances. Such properties may belong and not belong to an object simultaneously, albeit as accidental properties.

If Łukasiewicz' analysis is correct, the argument falls short of Aristotle's intention to establish the universal validity of the PC, that is, he wants to prove that the PC is valid for everything that has being. Thus, if the ontological version is accepted and the PC is valid for essential properties that define substances, Aristotle's account either fails in this attempt and there are things that may be contradictory, or Aristotle holds the view that substances are the only items that exist or have being in the requisite sense.

Objection (d)

Łukasiewicz takes up the second possibility, i.e., that Aristotle holds that the only items that have being in the requisite sense are substances and that, consequently, his argument establishes the universal validity of the PC since his argument demonstrates its truth for all substances and substances are the only items that have being.

Łukasiewicz does not address the arguments that Aristotle offers in support of his core metaphysical claim, the existence of substances and their essences. Instead, he argues that essences are conceptual and ideal in their nature, not empirically observable as such, and that because of this, the assumption of their existence necessarily remains a hypothesis and not an issue that could be decided on *a priori* grounds.

However, a further objection against Aristotle's account can be brought. It is not at all clear why the essence of a substance, granted that there are such items, must be free of contradiction. It is certainly a unity, a nexus that holds properties together, as it were, and fuses them into one thing. The *hypokeimenon* is that which underlies a thing and gives it its unity. But why would a contradictory object not have a *hypokeimenon*? And, further, Aristotle's own account of substances and their specifications, terminates in what he called prime matter, which—like the *hypokeimenon*—is an inconsistent object.

The *hypokeimenon* itself is not anything at all. It does not have any intrinsic properties, but constitutes the nexus or connecting point that holds the properties that make up an object (a substance). But, if it is nothing, how can it be the center piece, as it were, of a substance? Structurally (both logically and ontologically), the notion of a *hypokeimenon* is similar (isomorphous) to the Aristotelian notion of prime matter. Just like prime matter, the concept of *hypokeimenon* is inconsistent. It includes a contradiction at the very heart and foundation of the theory.

But even further, there is no argument to show that the essential properties, which determine the "what it is" of a substance, must be consistent. A contradictory object is a unity simply in virtue of being *one* object. Its properties are inconsistent, but that does not prevent it from being unified—having those properties bound together by one nexus (*hypokeimenon*) is precisely what makes it *one* object, regardless of the consistency or inconsistency of those properties with each other.

Objection (e)

In both interpretations, Aristotle's argument is exposed to serious objections, which are not easily rebutted. Before closing his discussion of Aristotle's main argument in support of the PC, Łukasiewicz adds one further objection which applies equally to both two interpretations discussed. The objection is that Aristotle's arguments in support of the two main premises rely on *modus tollens* inferences and *modus tollens* is a form of inference that presupposes the validity of the PC. Thus, even if Aristotle's main argument for the PC were sound, the arguments he advances to establish the two crucial premises of the main argument contain a *petitio principii.*

Commentary – Chapter XII
Apagogic Proofs of the Principle of Contradiction

- *Modus Tollens* and the PC
- All is One
- All is True and False
- Rational Choice and the PC

Łukasiewicz discusses three shorter arguments that Aristotle presents after the main elenctic demonstration by refutation. In Łukasiewicz' analysis, the arguments present three indirect demonstrations (*apagoge*) of the principle of contradiction. Further, all three arguments rely on *modus tollens* as their primary scheme of inference. However, in Łukasiewicz' earlier discussion of apagogic and elenctic demonstrations in Chapter IX, *modus tollens* inferences presuppose the principle of contradiction. Thus, all three arguments are flawed as proofs of the PC since they assume what needs to be demonstrated, i.e., the universal validity of the PC. Łukasiewicz concludes that the three apagogic arguments are inconclusive and fail to prove the principle of contradiction.

Łukasiewicz' criticism of Aristotle's apagogic arguments depends on a reading of Aristotle's account that fails to fully capture Aristotle's goals in the relevant passages. In the following, two objections are introduced that arise from an alternative reading of Aristotle's account and the goals of his apagogic arguments. In this interpretation of the text, Aristotle's aim in presenting the apagogic arguments is not to offer a proof of the principle of contradiction but, instead, his primary goal is to refute the claim associated with Protagoras, that is, to refute the claim that "all contradictory statements about the same object are simultaneously true" (1007b 19). Based on this interpretation, Aristotle's arguments gain in strength and Łukasiewicz' criticisms, including his charge that Aristotle repeatedly commits the fallacy of *ignoratio elenchii* in his arguments, are shown to miss their mark.

Modus Tollens and the PC

Łukasiewicz continues his earlier discussion begun in Chapter IX about the difference between *modus ponens* and *modus tollens* forms of inference and the logical consequences of their application in arguments that aim to establish the principle of contradiction. He further develops and strengthens his claim that *modus tollens* inferences depend on the principle of contradiction by presenting a *reductio ad contradictionem* proof that demonstrates that *modus tollens* is a valid form of inference in classical logic.

The proof follows the basic *reductio* format. It assumes the negation of the claim that is to be demonstrated and then derives a contradiction from this assumption and the other premises of the argument. The derivation of a contradiction, in turn, establishes that the assumption that led to it is false (provided all other premises that enter the derivation are true). In a classical, bivalent logic, if the assumption is shown to be false, the negation of the assumption (the claim to be demonstrated) must be true, which is what the *reductio* proof aimed to demonstrate.

Since a *reductio ad contradictionem* proof depends on the rejection of an assumed premise because that premise entails a contradiction, it appeals to and relies on the principle of contradiction. Consequently, *modus tollens* presupposes the principle and cannot be used in an argument that aims to demonstrate the validity of the principle of contradiction. Thus, Łukasiewicz concludes, it is possible to "claim in advance that the apagogic proofs have no force to convince" (XII, 149).

A first objection to Łukasiewicz' analysis arises at this point. It is not altogether clear that Aristotle's understanding of an *apagoge* requires or relies strictly on *modus tollens* as an inference schema. In his *apagoge* proofs, Aristotle does not explicitly claim that the consequences that he derives from Protagoras' thesis, i.e., that all contradictories are true, are contradictions, which would seem rather unsatisfactory given that the existence of contradictions is already admitted in the assumption of Protagoras' claim. Rather, what Aristotle's argument aim to establish is that the consequences that follow from Protagoras's thesis are unacceptable because they are utterly absurd—at least in Aristotle's view. Interpreted this way, Aristotle's approach is better described as a dialectical or transcendental rebuttal of Protagoras' position. This claim contains the key point of the second objection to Łukasiewicz' interpretation: in the arguments under consideration,

Aristotle is not trying to prove the principle of contradiction. Aristotle believes that the principle is true and that it cannot be proven. His apagoge arguments try to establish that a denial of the principle of contradiction has unacceptable consequences, just as he did in his elenctic demonstration by refutation. If this is correct, then Aristotle's apagogic arguments do rely on the PC, but not exclusively in the logical sense in which a *reductio ad contradictionem* demonstration presupposes the principle. Instead, it would be better to describe Aristotle's strategy as a *reductio ad absurdum* of the views associated with Protagoras.

All is One

The first of Aristotle's apagogic arguments that Łukasiewicz examines is the following:

> If all contradictory statements about the same object are simultaneously true, then of course all is one. Then, the same will be ship and wall and man (*Met.* 1007b 19-21, Łukasiewicz translation).

Łukasiewicz is highly critical of Aristotle's attack on the view that *all* contradictions are true since it presents an unwarranted shift from the much narrower claim that *some* contradiction are true, which—if shown to hold even for a single instance—is sufficient to deny the universal validity of the PC. The claim that all contradictions are true is not a claim that an opponent of the PC must endorse. However, it does present the view Aristotle attributes to Protagoras, and it is the relativistic doctrine associated with Protagoras that is one of the crucial positions that Aristotle aims to refute with his argument.

Prima facie, Aristotle's argument claims that if it is assumed that all contradictory pairs of statements about one object are true, then this premise entails that the same object will be equally a man, a wall, a ship, or anything else for that matter. This is so because it is no longer possible to distinguish one object from another, since each object will have and not have any property whatsoever (all contradictory statements are true). Thus, no object is distinguishable from another and "all is one" (in the sense that each object has and does not have the same set of properties). If the argument is a *reductio ad contradictionem* and employs *modus tollens* as its main inference, as Łukasiewicz suggests, then Aristotle must reject the claim that "all is one" and its incidental consequences because it entails a contradiction. Aristotle does not explicitly state a claim that would engender a contradiction to the conclusion of his argument, but a plausible candidate is the claim that all things are not the same (all is not one), that is, whatever a man is, is different from what a wall is, and what a wall is, is different from a ship is and, thus, that they are not one thing. It is safe to assume that Aristotle holds that this is an accurate picture of the way things are, but is it because this claim is the contradictory to the arguments conclusion, i.e., that all is one, that he rejects that conclusion? It seems highly unlikely that this is the reason underlying Aristotle's apagoge.

The following considerations support the view that Aristotle is not trying to show that Protagoras' thesis ought to be rejected because it entails a contradiction to what Aristotle considers to be an obvious and undisputable fact (i.e., that the world contains different and distinguishable things).

Protagoras' thesis (as expressed by Aristotle) unequivocally states that there are true contradictions and, even further, it states that all claims and their negations are equally true. Everything is contradictory. Why should the contradiction in one claim provide more of a reason to reject it than the contradiction contained in the other claim? Aristotle's *apagoge* does not aim to show that one contradictory claim follows from another contradictory claim or that one contradiction must be rejected because it entails another contradiction. There is no point in applying a *reductio ad contradictionem* to a contradiction—it already is a contradiction.

Rather, the conclusion (all is one) is unacceptable because of its sheer absurdity and thereby presents a sufficient reason to reject the premise (all contradictions are true) from which it is taken to follow. Protagoras and his followers may not think that the conclusion is absurd. It is just one more claim that—together with its contradictory—is true. However, in Aristotle's view, the conclusion is obviously false and, thus, the pemise that led to this conclusion must be rejected. Aristotle's argument is a *reductio* (albeit as a *reductio ad absurdum*), and the conclusion of the argument is the negation of the claim that all contradictory pairs of statements about one object are true at the same time, which—according to Aristotle's own square of opposition—is that some contradictories are not simultaneously true.

However, the contradictory claim to Aristotle's premise, i.e., the claim that some contradictories about the same object are not true simultaneously, is not a formulation of the principle of contradiction. This is one of the reasons why Łukasiewicz and like-minded interpreters reject Aristotle's argument as insufficient to establish the principle of contradiction. True enough—the argument most certainly does not demonstrate the principle. The conclusion of the argument, if accepted, merely establishes that there are some pairs of contradictory claims that are not simultaneously true. However, and more imporantly, it refutes Protagoras' thesis as a universal claim with a *reductio ad contradictionem* and through an application of *modus tollens*. The extent to which an argument that appeals to and relies on the principle of contradiction can succeed against an opponent who denies the principle is a separate question. Furthermore, it does not exclude the possibility that some contradictory pair of statements is true, a claim that, if found to be true, would be sufficient to refute the principle of contradiction. And furthermore, as Łukasiewicz points out, the claim seems to suggest that there may be such instances in which pairs of contradictories are in fact true.

However, and most decisively, there is no reason to assume that Aristotle does not realize that the contradictory of the assumed premises (all contradictories are true) does not establish the principle of contradiction. So, if Łukasiewicz is nevertheless right and Aristotle's argument is a *reductio* that aims to prove the principle (and not merely an attempt to show that Protagoras' views have absurd and unacceptable consequences), what is Aristotle trying to do with this argument?

A plausible explanation emerges from the following considerations: the interpretation and Łukasiewicz' criticism is based on a modern understanding of the formal meaning of a universal claim, its negation, and the inferential structure of a *reductio* argument. In this understanding, the derivation of a contradiction from a claim establishes that the claim must be false and, thus, warrants the assertion of the contradictory to the claim, which, as the contradictory of a false claim, must be true. This is also the case in Aristotle's account of the logical relation between contradictory statements—one of the pair must be true, the other false. Further, contradictory pairs are the most opposed statements in Aristotle's theory of opposition. However, a central but not completely resolved question for Aristotle is the determination of the statement that is most opposite to a universal claim (A: all *S* are *P*), i.e., whether the most opposite claim is its contradictory (O: some *S* is not *P*) or its universal contrary (E: no *S* is *P*). For Aristotle, this is a problem especially with respect to opposed beliefs, but it also enters his discussion of opposition between statements.

In *De Interpretatione* 14, Aristotle argues that the most opposite belief to a belief in a universal claim is the belief in the corresponding universal contrary statement, not the belief in the corresponding contradictory one (*De Int.* 24a 5-6). According to Whitaker (1996), Aristotle's view is based on the consideration that in the case of universal contrary claims, "one contrary asserts that subject and predicate are completely combined, the other that they are entirely separate" (Whitaker 1996, 175). Since these two states, i.e., full combination and full separation, are the two most opposed states of relation between terms, Aristotle holds that the person who believes in the false contrary of a true universal claim, is the person

> who is most deceived with regard to anything, since contraries are among things which differ most with regard to the same thing (*De Int.* 23b 22-23, Ackrill translation).

Aristotle's point is not just that a belief in the false universal contrary of a true universal statement entails (quantitatively) more false beliefs than a belief in the corresponding, non-universal (and also false) contradictory statement. His point is that a belief in a false contrary universal represents a far more severe misconception of the relation between the items under consideration. For example, to believe the false contrary to "no cats are reptiles", i.e., to believe that "all cats are reptiles", presents a significantly more radical error than to believe the false contradictory that "some cats are reptiles." Łukasiewicz and like-minded commentators will insist that both statements are equally false and that their respective consequences to a person's overall understanding or representation of the world are not an immediate concern of logic.

In Aristotle's view, however, it is significant that a belief in a false contrary universal claim is more opposed to the belief in the corresponding true universal claim than the belief in its (equally false) contradictory. The more opposed a pair of beliefs is, the more contrary the beliefs are to each other and, in Aristotle's view, the most contrary beliefs are the beliefs *par excellence* that cannot be held simultaneously by an individual. This, of course, is what

Aristotle claims in his psychological formulation of the principle of contradiction.

However, Aristotle does consider whether his analysis of the opposition between beliefs in universal assertions, their contradictories and their contraries extends to the relations of opposition between statements as such:

> If then this is how it is with beliefs, and spoken affirmations and negations are symbols of things in the soul, clearly it is the universal negation about the same thing that is contrary to an affirmation; e.g. the contrary of 'every good is good' or 'every man is good' is 'no good is good' or 'no man is good', while 'not every good is good' or 'not every man is good' are opposed contradictorily (*De Int.* 24b 2 – 8, Ackrill translation)

Thus, with respect to statements, Aristotle holds that it is always the pairs of contradictory claims that are (logically) most opposed to each other. Accordingly, contradictories also are the preferable type of claim to be used in demonstrations since the logical behavior of contradictories generates the necessity required for proofs (cf. *Prior Analytics* I, 62a 11 – 62a 19). However, in the present context, it is important to note that Aristotle also admits refutations (indirect demonstrations, i.e., *reductio* type arguments) that include the introduction of a contrary claim in certain syllogisms. In the *Prior Analystics*, Aristotle distinguishes between contrary and opposite (i.e., contradictory) refutations. A refutation proceeds contrarily, "if the conclusion is converted into its contrary" and by contradiction, if the conclusion is converted into its contradictory (*Prior Analytics* I, 60a 21, Jenkinson translation).

Based on these considerations, the following view of Aristotle's refutation of Protagoras' views emerges: Aristotle's argument does not only aim to refute the assertion that all contradictories about one object are true—it also attempts to show that holding the belief that this claim is true means holding a belief that is most opposite to and, thus, the furthest removed from the truth. Aristotle's refutation resembles a *reductio* argument but the conclusion of the argument is not the contradictory negation of the universal premise (as is commonly assumed by commentators who consider Aristotle's argument to be a proper *reductio*) but the denial of a universal premise by its universal contrary. If this is correct, then the conclusion of Aristotle's *reductio* (via contrary) is: No pair of contradictory statements about one object is true at the same time—Aristotle's (narrow) logical formulations of the PC!

Of course, the rejection of one claim of a pair of contraries does not entail the truth of the other. Aristotle repeatedly argues that two contrary claims cannot be both true, but also that—other than contradictories—both may be false. Thus, the rejection of one statement of a pair of contraries is insufficient establish the truth of the other—at least not without further argument.

If both are false, Aristotle's attempt of an apagogic argument is support of the principle of contradiction via rejection of its contrary, Protagoras' thesis, fails. However, the truth of one contrary entails the falsehood of the other and, at least, Aristotle's argument succeeds in strengthening the principle of contradiction by eliminating its contrary. Protagoras' thesis asserts that all contradictory pairs are true, Aristotle's thesis (PC) asserts that no contradictory pairs are true, that all contradictory pairs are-not true. Protagoras' thesis holds that there is a complete and exceptionless combination of the two terms (contradictory pairs of statements and truth), Aristotle's thesis holds that there is complete and exceptionless separation between the two terms. The question remains: does one entail the falsehood of the other, or is it possible for both to be false? A (modern) dialetheist will reply that the latter case is exactly right. Both theses are false. *Some* but *not all* contradictory pairs are true and, consequently, it is not the case that all contradictory claims are true *and* it is not the case that all contradictory claims are not true. Protagoras and Aristotle are both wrong.

Aristotle, of course, holds that the PC is true and if the PC is true, its contrary—Protagoras' thesis—must be false. On the other hand, while the derivation of absurd consequences from Protagoras' thesis may be sufficient to reject it as false, but this does not establish the truth of the PC. Aristotle may have been satisfied with showing that Protagoras' thesis leads to a conclusion that he considered utterly unacceptable. However, if Łukasiewicz is right and Aristotle's argument is not merely intended as a refutation of Protagoras' thesis but as a *reductio* to demonstrate with logical necessity that the PC is true (and not merely that some contradictions are not true), Aristotle would have to show that the PC and Protagoras' thesis are contraries that cannot both be false—and this, Aristotle does not do.

Łukasiewicz charges that Aristotle's reasoning in response to Protagoras' thesis frequently disregards or violates common rules of inference (XII, 149). In particular, he rejects an additional consequence that Aristotle derives from Protagoras' thesis. If all is one, Aristotle argues, and all contradictories are true at the same time, then it follows that the doctrine of Anaxagoras, i.e., that "all things are mixed together" is also true and this, in turn, entails that "nothing really exists" (1007b 26, Ross translation) or that "nothing is truly one" as Kirwan translates Aristotle's conclusion (1993, 12).

Aristotle's argument draws on the following considerations: if it were the case that all contradictories are true, then all objects are completely indeterminate. However, whatever is indeterminate does not have being in the requisite Aristotelian sense of being, i.e., it is not *one* thing—it is not anything (determinate) at all.

Nevertheless, in Aristotle's metaphysics there is a domain of being in which *all* things that belong to this domain are necessarily indeterminate: the domain of potential being. This domain includes cases in which an object potentially has a property and at the same time potentially does not have that property. As Aristotle puts it in Book 9 of the *Metaphysics*,

> every potentiality is at the same time a potentiality for the opposite … that which is capable of being may both be and not be. Therefore, the same thing is capable both of being and of not being (1050b, Tredennick translation).

Thus, reminiscent of Protagoras' thesis, contradictory claims appear to be simultaneously true about one thing. In Protagoras' view it is the actual world that is indeterminate, in Aristotle's account it is the domain of potential being that is indeterminate. But, for Aristotle, what is indeterminate is "that which exists potentially and not actually" (1007b 28). Consequently, if something is indeterminate, then it does not exist actually but only potentially. Thus, Aristotle concludes, those who take Protagoras' view (that all contradictories are true) "while fancying themselves to be speaking of being, they speak about non-being" (1007b 28-29, Ross translation) and nothing truly is, since all is merely potentially but not actually.

Łukasiewicz objects to Aristotle's argument by appealing to Aristotle's own account of truth: For a contradiction to be true means precisely that there is a contradiction in the actual world—something does and does not have a certain property and this state of affairs does obtain in the actual world. "This, after all, follows from the definition of a true statement," Łukasiewicz notes (XII, 149). Aristotle's assumption that the actual is consistent throughout, which he smuggles into the debate, either begs the question or needs additional argument in support. By itself, it does not license the inference that, if there is a contradiction, then the contradiction addresses and represents a state of affairs that belongs to the domain of potential being. If Protagoras' thesis is true, then the actual world is completely indeterminate and contradictory. Nevertheless, it would still be the actual world.[62]

All is True and False

The second of Aristotle's apagogic arguments that Łukasiewicz takes into consideration concludes that a further, and equally undesirable consequence of Protagoras' thesis is that no statement could be asserted as simply true since every assertion will be simultaneously true and false. An additional consequence is that those who share the views of Protagoras must admit that everything that they assert is both true and false and, consequently, that despite being right about everything, they are also just as much in error about everything as well. As Kirwan points out, this argument became known as a *peritropē*, a "turning around" or "turning the table" type of argument (Kirwan 1993, 104). It targets the self-refuting aspect of a strong or global relativistic claim as articulated, for example, by the thesis that all contradictory assertions are true and false simultaneously by showing that the assertion of the thesis itself also must be both true and false at the same time and, therefore, includes the admission of its own falsity.

Socrates' critique of Protagoras' views in Plato's *Theaetetus* (170-1) contains a predecessor to Aristotle's peritropic refutation of the teaching of Protagoras. In Plato's dialogue, Protagoras' view is encapsulated in the thesis that "man is the measure of all things: of things which are, that they are, and of the things, which are not, that they are not" (*Theaetetus* 151 a, Levett translation). Socrates interprets this thesis as a relativistic claim which obliges anyone who asserts it to accept also the opposite claim, which denies this thesis, as equally justified and true. Thus, Socrates concludes, if Protagoras endorses this claim then he also has to admit "that the contrary opinion about his own opinion (namely that it is false) must be true" and, consequently, he has to admit "the falsity of his own opinion" (*Theaetetus* 171 a-b).

In response to Aristotle's peritropic refutation of the claim that all (contradictory) statements are true and false, which Aristotle derives as a consequence of Protagoras' views, Łukasiewicz points out again that an opponent of the PC does not need to commit to a strong, relativistic thesis as the one advanced by Protagoras (XII, 151). The claim that all contradictories are true and, thus, the claim that all statements are both true and false, is not the thesis that an opponent of the PC must endorse. Instead, all that is necessary to defeat the PC is to show that there are *some* contradictions that are true. With regards to such true contradictions—if they were to be established—it would then be correct to say that they are true and not true simultaneously but, more importantly, many other statements will still be simply true or simply false in agreement with Aristotle's account of the truth a falsity of a statement. Thus, Łukasiewicz concludes, "whoever does not accept the principle of contradiction is not immediately forced to attribute contradictory properties to *all* objects and to consider *every* statement as simultaneously true and false" (XII, 151). A denial of the PC does not require the acceptance of a strong relativism.

Rational Choice and the PC

Aristotle's third *apagoge* argument against Protagoras and his followers holds that the actions that individuals take offer conclusive evidence that no one believes that all contradictories are true. The underlying assumption of this argument is that the actions of individuals reveal preferences and purposes but—in Aristotle's view—such preferences and purposes cannot arise unless the individuals make distinctions between the truth and falsity of statements, distinguish between different courses of action, and form preferences regarding the anticipated consequences of distinct actions. In other words, efficacious rational deliberation and action require and presuppose the acceptance and application of the PC.

In his critique of Aristotle's argument, Łukasiewicz' argues that "there is no connection at all between acting and recognizing, or not recognizing, the principle of contradiction" (XII, 152). Actions come about in various ways and not all of them require any kind of deliberation. Even if they do, only a preference is needed to act and this preference may arise and be acted upon without considerations of the truth or falsity of any statement. As Łukasiewicz points out, since everything is supposed to be contradictory, a person is free to simply prefer one possibility over the other and act accordingly.

Secondly, Łukasiewicz points out that a person who denies the truth of the PC does not therefore have to believe that the affirmation and denial of a claim are the same or that they mean the same thing. A person may believe that an object is both moving and not moving, but from this it does not follow that moving is the same as not moving.

However, the main point of Łukasiewicz' criticism of Aristotle's third apagoge is that it, just like the previous two arguments, is based on the claim that all contradictories are true and, thus, that it postpones and fails to address what is really at issue—the truth and universal validity of Aristotle's principle of contradiction. A single exception to the PC is sufficient to reject its universal validity and an opponent of the PC needs to hold only that there are some (at least one) true contradictions and not that all contradictions are true.

In conclusion, Łukasiewicz notes that his analysis shows that all of Aristotle's elenctic and apagogic arguments discussed so far fail to establish the truth and validity of the PC. Furthermore, wheras Ross (1924) and other commentators (for example, Kirwan 1993; Priest 2008 [2006]) distinguish a total of seven or more arguments in the text, Łukasiewicz does not identify any additional arguments in Aristotle's account that, in his interpretation, directly aim to demonstrate the principle of contradiction and, given the results of his analysis, concludes that Aristotle was unable to prove the principle of contradiction (XII, 153).

As argued above, it is rather doubtful that Aristotle was trying to offer a proof of the principle in the form of a deductive argument. According to Aristotle, it is impossible to construct such a proof and not one of the three arguments considered can be construed as an attempt to prove the principle of contradiction. What Aristotle does offer are three dialectical or transcendental arguments that aim to show that Protagoras' view has absurd and unacceptable consequences. To what extent these arguments are successful is a matter of debate. But Łukasiewicz' claim that Aristotle commits the fallacy of *ignoratio elenchii* in all three cases is unjustified since the arguments are directed against Protagoras' view and not meant to prove or demonstrate the principle of contradiction.

Commentary – Chapter XIII
Ignoratio Elenchi in Aristotle's Proofs

- Some Objects are Consistent
- There is One Non-Existent Consistent Object
- Degrees of Truth Presuppose Truth *Simpliciter*
- The Case for *Ignoratio Elenchii*

Łukasiewicz considers the reasons for Aristotle's failure to provide a sound proof of the principle of contradiction in *Book Γ* of the *Metaphysics*. At the beginning of Aristotle's account, the aim is to prove the PC in its full universal validity. The elenctic demonstration offered by Aristotle—despite its shortcomings—exhibits "a tendency to prove the principle in its entire breadth" (XIII, 154). However, Łukasiewicz notes, this initial goal changes dramatically in the subsequent shorter, apagogic proofs presented by Aristotle. "In the end," Łukasiewicz argues, "the Aristotelian proofs strive towards the justification of the thesis that *not all objects contain a contradiction*" (XIII, 155).

Thus, if Łukasiewicz is right, Aristotle's aim shifts from attempting to provide a demonstration of the universal validity of the PC, i.e., no object contains a contradiction, to an attempt to establish a much weaker claim, i.e., some objects do not contain a contradiction—a claim that would limit the validity of the PC to a class of objects.

Łukasiewicz suggests that the latter claim "contains the acknowledgement of the existence of contradictory objects" (XIII, 155), but this seems to go beyond what Aristotle asserts in the text. Still, the weaker claim that some objects do not contain a contradiction includes at least two possibilities:

a) there are other objects that do contain contradictions and, more cautiously,

b) there are objects that cannot be shown to be free of contradictions, objects that are indeterminate with respect to the PC.

Łukasiewicz admits that his interpretation attributes a "strange and unexpected thought" to Aristotle (XIII, 155), a thought that seems to contradict Aristotle's explicit aim of his discussion of the PC. Nevertheless, Łukasiewicz holds that a careful analysis of the text does reveal that Aristotle's account retreats from its initial goal to an attempt to defend this weaker and much more limited claim about the validity of the PC.

The first indications of this shift, Łukasiewicz argues, appear already during the initial elenctic demonstration, at 1006a, where Aristotle argues that, at the very least, it should be accepted "that the word 'be' or 'not be' has a definite meaning, so that not everything will be so and not so" (Ross translation). Even though this conclusion anticipates the weaker claim, i.e., that not all objects contain a contradiction, Łukasiewicz admits that at this early stage of Aristotle's account, the conclusion that "not everthing will be so and not so" is best interpreted as a preliminary step towards a demonstration of the universal validity of the PC. At this stage, the claim that at least some objects are not contradictory clears the path "for a universal statement that no object contains a contradiction" (XIII, 156).

Some Objects are Consistent

However, in the subsequent apagogic demonstrations, the attempt to demonstrate a claim that establishes only a limited validity of the PC takes on a more pronounced role in Aristotle's arguments. Łukasiewicz cites a longer passage of Aristotle's critique of Protagoras' thesis, i.e., the claim that all contradictory statements are true.

> Again, either the theory is true in all cases, and a thing is both white and not-white, and being and not-being, and all other contradictories are similarly compatible, or the theory is true of some statements and not of others. And if not of all, the exceptions will be agreed upon (1008a 8-12, Ross translation).

In this passage, Aristotle distinguishes between the following possibilities:

1) Protagoras' thesis is correct and all contradictory statements about any object are simultaneously true, then all objects are contradictory, or
2) Protagoras' thesis is false because only some objects are contradictory and others are not.

For Łukasiewicz, Aristotle holds the view that if the latter claim is accepted, then "the existence of non-contradictory objects besides the existence of contradictory objects" must also be assumed (XIII, 156). This is a plausible goal of Aristotle's critique of Protagoras' thesis. After all, if demonstrated, it is sufficient to prove that Protagoras's thesis is false or, at least, that it is not true in its universal scope.

One Non-Existent but Consistent Object

Aristotle's argument continues and aims to show that even if Protagoras thesis (all contradictions are true) is accepted, it is still possible for there to be at least one non-contradictory object, albeit a consistent object with a unique ontological and logical constitution. If Protagoras' thesis holds in all cases and all contradictory statements are true, then

> either the negation will be true wherever the assertion is, and the assertion true wherever the negation is, or the negation will be true where the assertion is, but the assertion not always true where the negation is. And in the latter case there will be something which fixedly *is not,* and this will be an indisputable belief (1008a 12-16, Ross translation).

Aristotle's argument can be paraphrased as follows: if Protagoras' thesis is right, then there are at least two possibilites:

(i) it is possible with regard to every object to (truthfully) affirm anything about it and it is simultaneously possible to (truthfully) deny anything about it or

(ii) it is possible with regards to every object to (truthfully) deny anything about it, but it is not possible with regards to every object to (truthfully) affirm what is (truthfully) denied about it.

There should be two more possibilities, if the first two are admitted:

(iii) it is possible to affirm anything about all objects, but it is not possible with respect to all objects to deny what has been affirmed and, finally,

(iv) with respect to all objects, it is not possible to affirm and it is not possible to deny anything.

However, Aristotle does not introduce either one these two additional options.[63] Arguably, only option (iii) could do the same work as (ii) in an attempted refutation of Protagoras' position—but first a closer look at the argument that Aristotle does present and which appeals to option (ii).

Łukasiewicz interprets Aristotle's argument as aiming to show that even if Protagoras' thesis is admitted, it does not exclude the possibility that there is at least one object that is determined exclusively by negations, i.e., an object of which it is denied that it has any property whatsoever and none of the properties that are denied of it can be (truthfully) attributed to that object. According to Aristotle, if there is such an object, then there would be something that "fixedly *is not*" (Ross), something that "would be securely *not* a thing-that-is" (Kirwan). This something, as Łukasiewicz notes,

> would most certainly be a non-existing object, but it would not contain a contradiction. Contradictions only arise if *affirmation* and *denial* were to take place simultaneously (XIII, 157).

Thus, if this object can be shown to exist in the Protagorean universe, then it contradicts Protagoras' thesis and provides proof that Protagoras' thesis is false.

Such a non-existent but consistent something, which in Aristotle's view is not excluded by Protagoras' thesis, closely resembles Hegel's notion of pure non-being and—in terms of the initial unfolding of the Hegelian dialectic—it also resembles pure being as well (cf. Introduction, 37 ff.). Pure non-being has only a single content; it *is* not. This purely negative content is the complete absence of any determinate mode of being. It is the result of a complete and exhaustive process of abstraction. Therefore, all negations, all denials are true of pure non-being, and no positive affirmation is true—exactly as it is in the case of Aristotle's object that is exhaustively determined by negations. The Hegelian dialect of being and non-being begins precisely at this point. Pure being and pure nothingness are and are not one and the same. It is in this sense that possibility (iii) mentioned above, i.e., the possibility of an object such that all affirmative statements about it are true, but no negation of any affirmative statement about this object is true, may also be sufficient to establish an object that does not contain a contradiction. Pursued in this direction, the object that is exhaustively determined exclusively by affirmative statements quite plausibly resembles (the content of) Hegel's pure being. The lack of any negations, at any rate, just like the lack of any affirmations in case (ii), makes contradiction impossible. Thus, considered as fully and exhaustively abstracted objects, neither Hegel's notion of pure being nor his notion of pure non-being contains a contradiction and each presents exactly the kind of object that Aristotle needs to refute Protagoras' thesis.

Łukasiewicz argues that Aristotle's attempt to establish that there must be at least one object that does not contain a contradiction presents a postponement of the question of the validity of the PC. While Aristotle's arguments aim to refute the view attributed to Protagoras, i.e., all contradictory statements are simultaneously true, they fail to demonstrate the truth of the PC and, further, they do not address the additional problems for a defense of the PC that emerge in the attempted refutations of Protagoras' thesis. Thus, in Łukasiewicz' view, Aristotle's arguments against Protagoras engender an *ignoratio elenchi*.

Degrees of Truth Presuppose Truth *Simpliciter*

According to Łukasiewicz, Aristotle's avoidance of the real problem, the demonstration of the universal validity of the PC, comes even more to the fore in the final argument that Aristotle presents at the end of Chapter 4 of *Book Γ* at 1008b 31 – 1009a 5.

Aristotle's argument begins by drawing out some of the consequences of Protagoras' claim that all objects are contradictory in all respects and, thus, that all contradictory statements are true. Even if this were to be true and "however much all things may be so and not so," Aristotle argues, "still there is a more and a less in the nature of things" (1008b 32-33, Ross translation). False statements contain errors of different magnitude, i.e., the person who thinks that four is equal to five is less in error than the person who thinks four is equal to thousand. But if there are statements that are "less false" than others, these statements are also "more true" than others. What Aristotle is driving at is that once it is admitted that there are "more" and "less" true statements, then there has to be—

at least in principle—a statement that is completely true (and not also false), a truth *simpliciter*, a statement that exactly asserts what is in fact the case and nothing else. Thus, Aristotle's argument—just as his *elenchus* for the truth of PC— has a strong transcendental tendency.

The argument aims to show that there is a necessary and prior condition to any meaningful assertions that a statement may be "more true" or "less true" than another statement. This condition is the existence of truth *simpliciter*. "There must be some truth to which the more true is nearer," Aristotle concludes (1009a 2) and, consequently, if there is truth in this sense, or even just "something more certain and true" (1009a 4), then Protagoras' thesis is refuted since then there are at least some statements that are simply true and not also false or, in the weaker case, there are statements that are at least not equally true and false.

Łukasiewicz does not offer any critical objections to Aristotle's argument at this point. He did so earlier, where he rejected the notion of degrees of truth (IV, 103 ff. and Commentary to Chapter IV, 304 ff.). In the current context, he emphasizes what he perceives as Aristotle's despair in the face of Protagoras' claim that all contradictory statements are equally true and Aristotle's desparate attempt to salvage at least one secure and firm resting point that would abide by the principle of contradiction.

The crucial premise of Aristotle's argument is that there is "a more and a less" that is determinable in a meaningful way once Protagoras' thesis is admitted. It is highly doubtful that a Protagorean could be convinced to accept this premise by itself, that is, without also accepting its negation, i.e., that there is no such thing as "a more and a less" in the nature of things. Aristotle, on the other hand, clearly thinks that there are differences in the degrees of error contained in statements (and, correspondingly, degrees of truth) and that these differences are, at least in principle, of a determinable scope or magnitude because, as articulated in his definitions of true and false statements, there are statements that are simply true and not also false, and statements that are simply false and not also true.

The Case for *Ignoratio Elenchii*

Earlier (IV, 103 ff.), Łukasiewicz strongly rejected the idea of degrees of truth or falsity for both statements and beliefs (cf. Commentary to Chapter IV, 304 ff.). In the current context, however, he does not consider Aristotle's argument as an argument that can be interpreted as supporting and presupposing this view but as an act of despair in the face of insurmountable challenges in the attempt to prove the PC and refute Protagoras' thesis. According to Łukasiewicz, Aristotle's argument is reduced to a desperate attempt to salvage the idea of at least one, non-contradictory truth—a result that falls far short of a demonstration of the universal claim that all being *qua* being does not contain contradictions. In Łukasiewicz' interpretation, Aristotle finds himself close to defeat in the face of Protagoras' thesis and its defenders. Aristotle's effort is reduced to attempting to show that

> If only one could find truth, even *a single one*, secure, unspoiled by any mistakes, and free of contradiction! Or, at least, if one could win the certainty that there are some probable statements, statements that are approaching the truth! (XIII, 159)

Łukasiewicz' charge that Aristotle's account contains a repeated *ignoratio elenchi* depends on reading Aristotle's *apagoge* arguments as proofs that aim to establish the PC. However, it seems more plausible to consider Aristotle's arguments primarily as refutations to Protagoras' claim. If this is their main objective, the conclusions that Aristotle aims to establish do not prove the universal validity of the PC but refute the universal claim of Protagoras' thesis.

Aristotle is convinced that the PC is true. He is also convinced that no direct demonstration of the PC is possible. Instead, he presents an elenchic proof, which consists of a transcendental argument or demonstration by refutation that aims to establish that the PC must be assumed for meaningful speech, rational deliberation and reasoning. Protagoras' challenge, and related accounts that violate the PC from a sensualist perspective, are the main targets of Aristotle's apagogic arguments. Łukasiewicz, too, argues that Aristotle perceived the greatest threat, the most persuasive arguments and strongest objections against the universal validity of the PC, as springing from Protagoras and the sensualist Megarian philosophers (cf. Chapter XIV, 161 f.). And it is because Aristotle perceives that the strongest objections to his own account come from this corner that he engages with the main position and epistemological underpinnings of the sensualist position in such detail.

Protagoras' thesis is the universal contrary to Aristotle's principle of contradiction. Contraries cannot both be true but they can both be false. By showing that Protagoras' thesis is false—or, at least, that it entails unacceptable consequences—Aristotle strengthens his account in defense of the principle of contradiction. And all he needs to defeat Protagoras' universal claim is at least one object that does not contain contradictions. Aristotle's apagogic arguments not merely aim to show that there is such an object but also to persuade or convince the adherents of Protagoras' thesis that this is so—a far more difficult task. If Aristotle does show signs of despair or exhaustion in his argumentation, it is because he senses the lack of persuasiveness of his arguments and apagogic refutations of Protagoras' thesis in the eyes of the adherents of a Protagorean viewpoint. Aristotle does not retreat or admit failure in an attempt to prove the principle of contradiction. In Aristotle's view, the principle cannot be proven (since it is a first principle or *arche*).

Łukasiewicz misinterprets Aristotle's arguments as arguments that aim to prove the principle of contradiction, but that is not what they are intended to do. Aristotle's apagogic arguments aim to show the inadequacies of a Protagorean position and it is this effort that brings out Aristotle's difficulties. More light on this is shed in the next chapter, where Łukasiewicz continues his investigation of the discussion of the sensualist position and Aristotle's response is the topic.

Commentary – Chapter XIV
Characteristics of Aristotle's Proofs

- Aristotle's Opponents
- Antisthenes
- The Megarian School of Philosophy
- Protagoras and the Sensualist Philosophers
- Potential and Actual Being

At the center of this chapter is an investigation into the key tenets of the sensualist accounts associated with Protagoras and his followers which, in Łukasiewicz' analysis, generate the strongest objections to Aristotle's account of the principle of contradiction. Łukasiewicz examines Aristotle's response to the sensualist position in Aristotle's earlier attempt to offer decisive reasons in support of the PC in his elenchic demonstration by refutation. Aristotle's solution to the problems posed by the sensualist-based accounts relies on a distinction between actual and potential being and an increased emphasis on the concepts of substance and substantial being. The distinctions introduced by these primarily metaphysical concepts preserve a domain in which Aristotle can defend the validity of the PC as the principle of being *qua* being against the sensualist challenges. Łukasiewicz' analysis of Aristotle's responses to the sensualist challenges leads him to the conclusion that Aristotle's principle of contradiction is most of all a metaphysical principle associated with the concepts of substantial being and essential predication. Thus, in Aristotle's account, the principle of contradiction is not a logical principle per se, but a metaphysical one that entails significant logical, ontological, psychological and ethical commitments.

Aristotle's Opponents

Łukasiewicz points out that Aristotle's arguments and discussions in defense of the PC exhibit a markedly polemic character. The peculiar nature and style of Aristotle's responses raises a cluster of interrelated questions. What are the reasons for Aristotle's hostile and dismissive comments? Who were the philosophers that managed to attract Aristotle's ire and what was the specific content and scope of their positions? Thus, the investigation turns to the opponents of Aristotle's account of the principle of contradiction and their arguments.

At the beginning of his discussion, Łukasiewicz briefly mentions the Megarian philosophers on the one hand and Antisthenes and his followers on the other. Both groups are associated with an eristic and combative style of philosophical debate and, in Aristotle's view, both advance arguments against the principle of contradiction merely for the sake of argument and not because of any genuine, philosophical concern about the truth of the principle (cf. 1009a 22-28).

Łukasiewicz does not further elaborate on the philosophical positions presented by these two groups, except by noting that the Megarian philosophers rejected Aristotle's distinction between substance and accident and, in agreement with Maier (1896), that Aristotle's elenctic demonstration by refutation and, possibly, the third apagoge, which includes the example of "walking to Megara", were directly aimed at the Megarian challenges to the principle of contradiction (XIV, 161).

Łukasiewicz observes that Aristotle perceived the "sensualist epistemology of Protagoras and related currents" as the more serious threat compared to the objections that were raised by the Megarian philosophers or by the followers of Antisthenes. Consequently, Łukasiewicz focuses his inquiry on Aristotle's responses to the objections against the principle of contradiction that were brought from the first group, Protagoras and his followers. In Łukasiewicz' reading, the crucial tenet of the views held by this group of philosophers with respect to the PC is that "all … knowledge rests on sense perception" (XIV, 161). The protagonists of this sensualist epistemology argue that both the process of sense perception and the objects that are perceived by the senses contain contradictions. These contradictions arise, one the one hand, from the differences between the observations made by different individuals and, on the other, from the continuous change—the Heraclitean flux—that characterizes the objects of sense perception. Thus, for philosophers who hold views of this type, the sensible world is filled with contradictions.

Aristotle's responses to this group of philosophers and their arguments are the focus of Łukasiewicz' discussion in this chapter. However, it is worthwhile to begin with a closer look at the philosophical views that are mentioned but left without rebuttal, as it were, by both Łukasiewicz and Aristotle. As will be seen, some of these views do present substantial challenges to Aristotle's account in their own right, whereas others are based on a sensualist epistemology close to the position presented by Protagoras. The paradoxes associated with the Megarian philosopher Eubulides, especially, introduce objections to the principle of contradictions based on semantic and truth-theoretical considerations that are largely independent of the sensualist challenges to Aristotle's account. On the other hand, a closer look at both the rejection of Aristotle's distinction between actual and potential being by the Megarian School of philosophers and the objections to the principle of contradiction raised by Antisthenes and his followers will show these challenges to be closely related to the sensualist views attributed to Protagoras and his followers.

Anthisthenes and the Single *Logos* Thesis

Antisthenes (c. 445 BCE – c. 365 BCE) was an Athenian philosopher and a contemporary of Plato. Diogenes Laertius reports that Antisthenes began his study of philosophy with the rhetorician Gorgias. Subsequently, he became a close and dedicated follower of Socrates. According to Laertius, Antisthenes was a prolific writer and the author of numerous works including a handbook on debating strategies and techniques titled *Of Discussion*, a work titled *On Names* (consisting of five books), a "controversial" work *On the Use of Names*, a book titled *Truth*, and a work on *Contradiction* (consisting of three books) (Laertius, VI, 15-18). The last title may have consisted of Antisthenes' critique of Plato's views on contradiction and may or may not be the same work by Antisthenes disparagingly titled *Sathon* (*Little Dick* or *Tiny Weeney*). The Greek word "sathon" sounds similar to Platon and, as Nicolas Denyer reports, was a name that Antisthenes used for Plato (Denyer 1991, 27; cf. Guthrie 1979, 310).

Unfortunately, none of Antisthenes' works have been preserved and the exact nature of his philosophical views is difficult to ascertain. Based on existing fragments, Antisthenes' philosophical position is traditionally associated with the following claims:

(1) There is only one proper description or *logos* of each thing.
(2) It is impossible to make a false statement.
(3) Contradiction is impossible.

Aristotle attributes each of these claims directly to Antisthenes and offers a cursory discussion of their respective philosophical merits at two locations in the *Metaphysics* (1024b 28 – 1025b1 and 1043b 24 – 32). The focus of Aristotle's remarks is Antisthenes' claim that each thing has exactly one *logos* —a claim that Aristotle swiftly, but without much argument, dismisses as "foolish" (1024b 31). However, before examining Aristotle's rather brusque response to Antisthenes' views, it is worthwhile to attempt a reconstruction of Antisthenes' core philosophical position in order to gain a better understanding of the full scope and impact of his critique of the principle of contradiction.

The Megarian School of Philosophy

As in Antisthenes' case, original documents or texts with detailed accounts of the philosophical positions held by members of the Megarian School are not available. Still, a general sense of their philosophical views and temperament, and their criticisms of Aristotle's PC and his proposed science of being *qua* being can be gained from existing fragments and historical accounts. Diogenes Laertius provides a comparatively detailed description of the history of the Megarian school of philosophy (Laertius, II, 106-120). However, Laertius' account tends to stay on the surface of the philosophical doctrines that he sketches out and, in general, his descriptions do not exhibit much philosophical acumen. Furthermore, in considering Laertius' accounts, it should be kept in mind that he wrote some five centuries after the days of Aristotle and his Megarian opponents. As Herbert Long observes in his "Introduction" to Laertius' *Lives of Eminent Philosophers,* it is by sheer accident that Laertius "acquired an importance out of all proportion to his merits" (Long 1972, xix). According to Long, Łaertius became the primary source on the history of Greek philosophy only because many of the primary and early secondary sources have been lost (Long 1972, xix). Still, whatever their shortcomings, Laertius' accounts do offer at least a glance at the broad features of the philosophical views and disputes of the time.

Laertius reports that the Megarian school was founded by Euclid of Megara (c. 435 BCE – c.365 BCE) and "his followers were called Megarians after him, then Eristics, and at a later date Dialecticians ... because they put their arguments into the form of question and answer" (Laertius, II, 106). Laertius describes Euclid of Megara as a philosopher who had studied the writings of Parmenides and, like Antisthenes, had been an avid follower of Socrates.[64] Thus, it is likely that Euclid of Megara's philosophical views articulated an ethical monism that combined the teachings of Parmenides and Socrates. In addition, Laertius notes that Euclid of Megara had a strong interest in logic and, in particular, in the structure of arguments and different strategies and methods of refutation (Laertius, , II, 106-107). According to Timon of Phlius (c. 320 BCE – 230 c. BCE), it was Euclid of Megara who "inspired the Megarians with a frenzied love of controversy" (as cited by Laertius, II, 107).

Laertius reports that in the aftermath of Socrates' execution in Athens in 399 BCE, many of the followers of Socrates, including Plato, "being alarmed at the cruelty of the tyrants", sought refuge in Megara, where they stayed with Euclid of Megara in an effort to avoid repercussions or persecutions because of their association with Socrates and his teachings (Laertius, II, 106). For Plato, Euclid of Megara's home was the first stop of a long exile until his return to Athens in 387, some twelve years after Socrates' execution.

In this context, Aristotle's use of the example of "going to Megara" in his argument for the validity of the PC in the domain of action takes on an important additional significance. Instead of interpreting it as a mere allusion to the philosophical positions of the Megarians—views that Aristotle broadly dismisses as "crazy teachings" (*λόγος ἄκρατος*)—the expression "to go to Megara" may also evoke the memory of the city of Megara as a place of refuge for the Socratic philosophers that were driven out of Athens in fear of reprisals, a place where the teachings and inquiries of their master could continue and flourish.

Among the initial members of the Megarian school, Laertius mentions two students of Euclid of Megara, Clinomachus of Thurii and Eubulides of Miletus, (Laertius, II, 108, 112, 113). Both Clinomachus and Eubulides continued the logical interests of their teacher. Clinomachus "was the first to write about propositions, predications and the like" (Laertius, II, 112) whereas Eubulides is well known for his delight in paradoxes, including the Sorites, Liar, Electra, Masked Man, and Horned Man paradoxes. All the paradoxes arrive at conclusions that violate the PC in some form and, consequently, present a direct challenge to Aristotle's metaphysics, his ontology and logic of being *qua* being, and—perhaps most crucially—his theory of truth.

While Aristotle does not explicitly mention Eubulides and his paradoxes anywhere in the corpus, he discusses what appears to be a version of the Liar paradox in *Sophistical Refutations* (180a 32 – 180b 40). After listing a set of arguments that bear considerable similarity to the Masked Man and Horned Man paradoxes, Aristotle notes that the latter arguments all appeal to the same problem: "Is it possible for what is not to be?—But it *is* something, despite its not being" (*Soph. Ref.* 180a 32-33). In Aristotle's analysis, the arguments based on this problem are similar to an argument that raises the question

> whether the same man can at the same time say what is false and what is true; but it appears to be a troublesome question because it is not easy to see whether it is saying what is true or saying what is false which should be stated without qualification (*Soph. Ref.* 180b 1-4).

As Kneale and Kneale (1962) point out, the passage does not exactly state the Liar paradox and, furthermore, Aristotle does not state the Liar paradox anywhere else in his extant writings. In their estimate, the above passage from *Sophistical Refutations*, even though it may possibly be a reference to Eubulides' Liar paradox, is "not enough to enable anyone to reconstruct the paradox without a good deal of fresh ingenuity" (Kneale 1962, 228).

The fact that this brief passage in the *Sophistical Refutations* constitutes—at best—the only allusion to the Liar paradox in the Aristotelian corpus, as well as Aristotle's silence about Eubulides and his paradoxes, raises intriguing questions. It would go beyond the scope of this commentary to address in detail the challenges that Eubulides' paradoxes present to Aristotle's philosophical views in general and his defense of the principle of contradiction in particular. However, even a cursory glance at the dialectical thrust of the consideration that lead to the paradoxical conclusions, i.e., that the liar sentence is both true and false, that Electra does and does not know her brother, or that a collection of grains is and is not a heap, reveals that the paradoxes are not merely the result of some equivocation or sophistical argumentation, but that they do present a direct and serious challenge to Aristotle's theory that being *qua* being does not and cannot contain contradictions. As Pieter Seuren argues, Eubulides' paradoxes reveal "the main weaknesses of the Aristotelian paradigm" (Seuren 2005, 75). The question remains—why does Aristotle not respond to these challenges?

Aristotle's defense of the PC in the *Metaphysics* would be the natural place to address these challenges, but Aristotle does not even mention Eubulides. Nor does he mention Eubulides anywhere else in the existing corpus. Aristotle's silence is even more puzzling in light of Laertius' cryptic remark that "Eubulides kept up a controversy with Aristotle and said much to discredit him" (Laertius, II, 109). Laertius does not provide any details regarding the controversy between the two, but if his report is correct, Aristotle must have been aware of Eubulides and his paradoxes, which were closely associated with the Megarian School of philosophy.

Aristotle does mention the Megarian philosophers in *Metaphysics* Book Θ, where he discusses the Megarian denial of his distinction between potential and actual being. The Megarian school holds "that a thing can act only when it is acting, and when it is not acting it cannot act" (1046b 29 – 30). Aristotle is quick to dismiss this objection to the existence of potential being because "it is not hard to see the absurdities that attend this view" (1046b 33). Nevertheless, the Megarian point of view gains in strength if it is taken into consideration that potential being as such is not perceptible through the senses. Further, if sense perception is considered as the only foundation and source through which being is encountered and comes to be known, then potential being does not exist. Instead, only what is perceptible by the senses does exist. Furthermore, based on Aristotle's paraphrase of the Megarian position, it seems that the Megarian philosophers held a kind of epistemological presentism so that whatever exists is known to exist only when and if it is perceived.

Aristotle argues that it is an important consequence of this reconstruction of the Megarian position that "nothing will be either cold or hot or sweet or perceptible at all if people are not perceiving it" (1047a 1–2) and, consequently, that the Megarians or any other philosophers who hold this view "will have to maintain the doctrine of Protagoras" (1047a 3). Aristotle concludes that the Megarian position reveals their commitment to views that "do away with both movement and becoming" (*Met.* 1047a 11) and, consequently, the Megarian position is absurd or silly (ἄτοπον).

However, Aristotle's response, as Brian Calvert (1976) points out, does not address the core claim that underlies the Megarian position, i.e., that motion and change are logically impossible, but instead focuses on the unacceptable and absurd consequences that follow from this claim (Calvert, 34).

While the exact positions defended by the Megarian school remain a matter of conjecture, Łukasiewicz sides with Maier's claim that the Megarians denied the Aristotelian distinction between substance and accident and advanced their criticisms for the sake of debate alone. However, Antisthenes and his followers are the more likely representatives of a position that denies the existence of universals as actual, existent entitities that are the referents of Aristotelian secondary substances and essential qualitities (or, depending on the variety of denial, the existence of universals denoting any qualities).

Protagoras and the Sensualist Philosophers

Łukasiewicz argues that while Aristotle simply dismissed the challenges by the Megarian school and by Antisthenes and his followers without addressing their arguments, he did respond to the challenges advanced by Protagoras and sensualist philosophers (XIV, 161 ff.). In Aristotle's view, the most serious challenges to his account of the PC result from arguments and observations that are based on a sensualist epistemology. "Those who really feel the difficulties have been led to this opinion by observation of the sensible world" (1009a 22-23, Ross translation).

Laertius reports that

> Protagoras was the first to maintain that there are two sides to every question, opposed to each other, and he even argued in this fashion, being the first to do so. Furthermore he began a work thus: 'Man is the measure of all things, of things that are that they are, and of things that are not that they are not.' He used to say that soul was nothing apart from the senses, as we learn from Plato in the *Theaetetus* [152 a], and that everything is true (Laertius, IX, 51).

The main argument of these opponents of the PC applies an Eleatic logic of being to the observation of change in the sensible world. "They think that contradictions or contraries are true at the same time, because they see contraries coming into existence out of the same thing" (1009a 24-25, Ross translation). However, in the Eleatic conception of being, anything that is not, non-being, is *eo ipso* ineligible to undergo change and, even less, unable to become something that has being. Whatever is not cannot bring forth anything—nothing comes from nothing. Non-being cannot have agency or potency, or any other property or capacity, since it lacks being and only what has being is able to have or receive properties; thus, non-being cannot generate being.

If this Eleatic account is accepted, then contrary properties that are observed in a changing object, for example, the heat of a hot piece of iron and its coolness after being dipped in water, "must have existed before as both contraries alike" (1009a 27, Ross translation). Thus, Aristotle's opponents conclude that the observation of change shows that contrary properties exist simultaneously in one and the same thing and, consequently, that contradictions exist and the PC does not hold for sensible objects that undergo change.

Aristotle pays considerable respect to the advocates of this position and notes that "in a sense they speak rightly and in a sense they err" (1009a 30, Ross translation). Aristotle's solution to the problem is a distinction between two senses of being, a distinction that separates and delimits two modes or two domains of being, *potential* being and *actual* being. This distinction between potential and actual being provides Aristotle with a conceptual apparatus that allows him to explain and resolve the issue of apparently real contradictions that is raised by the Eleatic analysis of sensible change. Aristotle presents his solution as follows:

> 'that which is' has two meanings, so that in some sense a thing can come to be out of that which is not, while in some sense it cannot, and the same thing can at the same time be and not be—but not in the same respect. For the same thing can be potentially at the same time two contraries, but it cannot actually (1009a 32-36, Ross translation).

For Łukasiewicz, this passage signals a crucial change in Aristotle's account of the PC. Aristotle's statement appears to assert that there is a limitation on the PC's domain of validity. What Aristotle admits in this passage, Łukasiewicz' claims, is that

> *potential being, τὰ δυνάμει ὄντα,* does not fall under this principle [the PC] because it may contain simultaneously opposite and, therefore, also contradictory properties. *The principle of contradiction applies only to actual being, τὰ ἐντελεχείᾳ ὄντα.* (XIV, 163).

Thus, Łukasiewicz concludes, objects potentially possess contradictory properties and Aristotle's domain of potential being presents an exception to the validity of the PC. The crucial question is whether Aristotle's domain of potential being includes the simultaneous presence of contradictory properties.

Potential and Actual Being

In the passage cited above (1009a 32-36), Aristotle presents three distinct claims that illustrate the relation between potential and actual being.

(1) A thing can come to be from what is not, and it cannot come to be from what is not, each in a different domain of being.

(2) A thing can simultaneously be and not be, but only in different domains of being.

(3) A thing can simultaneously have contrary properties, and it cannot simultaneously have contrary properties, each in a different domain of being.

Beginning with claim (2), i.e., that "the same thing can at the same time be and not be—but not in the same respect" (1009a 34), the statement suggests that even though there appears to be a contradiction, the contradiction is not real but arises from an equivocation of two senses of being, potential and actual. In the terms of Aristotle's distinction between these two domains of being, an object *x* may potentially have the property *F*, i.e., it *is* potentially *F*, while at the same time it *is not* actually *F*.

For Aristotle, both potential and actual being are equally modes of being. A statement that asserts that something is possible is "affirmative in form"; it affirms that a relation between the terms of the statement has being, just as a statement that asserts that something is does and, consequently, "'to be possible' is in the same rank as 'to be'" (Prior Analytics I, 25b 22-24, 32b 3; Jenkinson translation). Thus, something can simultaneously be and not be, albeit in different modes of being. Formally, this situation may be expressed as:

$$\exists_x (\Diamond F_x \wedge {\sim}F_x) \vee (\Diamond{\sim}F_x \wedge F_x)$$

The conjunction does not present a contradiction since the two conjuncts are not negations of each other. The contradiction-forming negation of ${\sim}F_x$ is F_x, which is not equivalent to $\Diamond F_x$.

Arguably, the disjuncts $(\Diamond F_x \wedge {\sim}F_x)$ and $(\Diamond{\sim}F_x \wedge F_x)$ present the characteristic feature of the objects that Aristotle refers to as "changeable things" in *De Interpretatione* (23a 11). Changeable things are precisely the objects observable by the senses and, in the current context, their pertinent characteristic is that they manifest some but not all their potential properties. In other words, a changeable object has simultaneously actualized and unactualized potential properties. But it is through the being of unactualized, potential properties (including potentially not having a specific property that an object currently does possess) that they are changeable objects.

On the other hand, "unchangeable things" are characterized through the actualization of all their potential properties. In their case, "what is called capable already is in actuality" (*De Int.* 23a 10, Ackrill translation). Consequently, things of this kind are incapable of change since they do not possess any potential properties that are not already actualized.

However, the formulations for changeable and unchangeable objects both do not fully capture Aristotle's intent since they fail to block the realization of potential properties that would be incompatible or contrary to each other if realized. Since Aristotle holds that actual being does not contain contradictions, there must be some restriction of the range of potential properties that are realized in either type of object.

Change is constituted by acquiring a property that the object does not already have. This is possible only if that property is a property that the object does have potentially. If it does not have the property potentially, then it does not have the potential to acquire that property and, consequently, it is unable to undergo change.

Aristotle began his outline of the modalities of change with his first claim in the passage cited, the claim that "in some sense a thing can come to be out of that which is not, while in some sense it cannot" (1009a 32-33). This claim restricts change from what is not to something that is to only one of the two domains and, as will be argued in the following, the domain where this type of change happens is the domain of actual being. Aristotle's domain of actuality includes, but is not limited to, the sensible world and the changes that are observable in it.

Object x does not have property F in actuality at t_1 but does so potentially and, furthermore, x does acquire that property in actuality at some later point t_2. Thus, x changes from what is not (from $\sim F_x$) to what is (i.e., to F_x).

On the other hand, it is a feature of potential being that makes it impossible for something to come to be out of anything that is not have potential being, i.e., to come to be out of anything that is not. It is a condition for anything that comes to be in actuality that is had to have potential being prior to its manifestation. Thus, if something *is not potentially F,* it cannot become F in actuality.

Thus, according to Aristotle's theory of the relation between actual and potential being, an object x cannot come to be (actually) F from a state in which x is not (potentially) F. Aristotle's theory endorses the familiar modal claim $\sim\Diamond F \rightarrow \Box\sim F$.

Finally, Aristotle's third claim asserts that "the same thing can be potentially at the same time two contraries, but it cannot actually" (1009a 35-36). Łukasiewicz (XIV, 163; Commentary, 383) takes Aristotle's claim to imply that, since objects may potentially have contrary properties simultaneously, they thereby potentially have contradictory properties, i.e., $\Diamond(F_x \wedge \sim F_x)$ and, therefore, that the domain of potential being is not governed by the PC. However, what Aristotle does endorse is $\Diamond F_x \wedge \Diamond\sim F_x$.

For the domain of potential being to be inconsistent, that is, for potential being to contain contradictions, it must admit of a positive determination of a potential property and the denial of the being of that potential property. Thus, a contradiction in the domain of potential being would have the following form: $(\Diamond F_x \wedge \neg\Diamond F_x)$. This is exactly what Aristotle concludes: "The negation of 'possible to be', therefore, is 'not possible to be'" (*De Int.* 24b 24) and "the negation of 'possible not to be' is 'not possible not to be'" (*De Int.* 24b 34, Ackrill translation).

Contradictions, in Aristotle's account, simultaneously assert the being and the not-being of a relation between the subject and predicate terms. Translated into the language of potential being, a contradiction consists of a property being potentially the property of an object and at the same time not being potentially the property of that object. This is so because, as Whitaker (1996) points out, in Aristotle's interpretation of modal sentences, being "becomes a kind of 'underlying thing' or 'subject' (*ὑποκείμενον*) itself, along with subject and predicate, and the modal word is now the addition (*πρόσθεσις*)" that indicates the existence of a relation between the underlying subject term (being) and a modal property; thus, it is the negation of the addition expressed by the modal words that generates the proper negation of a modal sentence (Whitaker, 159).

The question remains whether simultaneous contrary potential properties, as Łukasiewicz claims, might also generate a contradiction? In Aristotle's conception of potential being they do not. While "it seems that for the same thing it is possible both to be and not to be" (*De Int.* 21b 12), two such statements are not contradictory to each other. According to Aristotle, the reason why they are not contradictories is that "whatever is capable in this way *is not always actual*, so that the negation too will hold of it: what can walk is capable also of not walking, and what can be seen of not being seen" (*De Int.* 21b 14-16, *Italics* added). Aristotle is concerned only with changeable things, i.e., objects that can be observed through the senses, and a characteristic feature of such objects is that their potential properties are never all actualized. In fact, this is impossible for at least two reasons:

(1) if all potential properties are actualized at the same time, the object is no longer a changeable object and

(2) given that the properties of changeable objects include ranges of properties that are contrary to each other in actuality and actual being does not admit of contraries, it is impossible for a changeable object to actualize all of its potential properties.

Finally, changeable objects may lose an accidental property so that for any actualized accidental property that a changeable object does have, it potentially also does not have that property. As a result, there are always some properties of changeable objects which are in opposite states in either one of the two domains of potential and actual being. Thus, "it is possible for the same thing to be and not to be" but "such statements are not contradictories of one another" (*De Int.* 25b 35).

Commentary – Chapter XV
The Principle of Contradiction and the Syllogism

- Logical, Ontological, and Metaphysical Principles
- The Condition for All Other Principles
- Syllogistic Inference and Contradictory Premises

In the *Metaphysics*, Aristotle argues that the principle of contradiction is the foundation of all other principles of reason and inference. However, in the *Analytics*, Aristotle observes also that there are certain syllogisms that remain valid even though the minor premise includes a contradictory middle term. Łukasiewicz argues that this offers proof that there are modes of deductive reasoning that do not rely upon or presuppose an acceptance of the PC. The principle of contradiction, Łukasiewicz claims, "is not a necessary condition for one of the most significant rules of inference, syllogistic reasoning" (XV, 170).

Logical, Ontological, and Metaphysical Principles

Łukasiewicz argues that logical and ontological principles have a broader scope and range than metaphysical principles. They are also known with more certainty. The logical and ontological principles range over the metaphysical modes of being, which—according to Łukasiewicz—comprise "the essence of the world" and encompass both concrete objects of experience and ideal objects of abstract reasoning. For Łukasiewicz, logical and ontological principles address "all that is something and not nothing" (XV, 169).

Łukasiewicz identifies the proper domain of metaphysics with the Aristotelian inquiry into the nature of being and its analysis and cognition in terms of substances and essential properties. The domain of logical and ontological principles, on the other hand, is broader in range and scope in that the subject matter of its inquiries and investigations is constituted by whatever satisfies the intentional definition of object.

Łukasiewicz' distinction suggests that he considers the principles of logic and ontology as the fundamental principles of a comprehensive theory of objects in Meinong's sense. Given the central role and position of the (Meinongian) intentional definition of an object in Łukasiewicz' analysis, his investigations squarly address what—according to Cocchiarella (1987)—was one of the central concerns of early twentieth century logic, the correct analysis of what constitutes a "logical object".

Aristotle's syllogisms address and illumate relations between classes of objects and their members. Given Aristotle's insistence on the non-contradictory nature of all that has being in the *Metaphysics*, it is surprising to see that he includes a syllogism in his discussion in the *Analytics* that—in Aristotle's analysis—would still be valid even if they were to contain a contradictory term in the minor premise (*An. Post.* I, 77a 10-22). To be sure, Aristotle's considerations about the consequences (or lack thereof), which result from the introduction of a class of inconsistent objects to a syllogistic demonstration, is strictly hypothetical—he does not state that there are such things—but Aristotle's considerations nevertheless raise questions about the status of the principle of contradiction as the ultimate arche of all principles, including the principles of syllogistic demonstration.

The Condition of All Other Principles

According to Aristotle's account in the *Metaphysics*, all other logical principles ultimately derive their justification through an appeal to the principle of contradiction: "all who are carrying out a demonstration refer it to this as an ultimate belief; for this is naturally the starting-point even for all the other axioms" (1005b 33-34).

Łukasiewicz raises the issue anew by asking if the PC is a necessary or a sufficient condition for other principles, including the principles of syllogistic reasoning? Aristotle's answer must be that the ontological and logical structure of being constitutes the necessary reason for both the truth of the PC and for the truth of syllogistic deductions. In Aristotle's conception, the PC expresses the most fundamental principle of being, whereas the syllogistic principle expresses the most fundamental principle of the relations between beings. As such, both are grounded in being, but the two principles appear to address different aspects of being—the PC presents primarily the ontological ground of being *qua* being, the syllogistic principle states fundamental logical relations that hold between items (and collections of items) that have being in one of the senses admitted by Aristotle.

However, in his discussion of a syllogistic deduction that (hypothetically) includes a premise with a contradictory middle term in the *Posterior Analytics*, Aristotle concludes that even this type of syllogism would stay valid and establishe its conclusion. According to Łukasiewicz, this suggests that the principle of syllogistic inference is independent of the PC and thus, that the PC is not the ultimate foundation of all logical principles as Aristotle seems to suggest in the *Metaphysics* (1005b 32—34).

The question is what exactly does Aristotle mean when he asserts that "this is naturally the starting-point even for all the other axioms" (1005b 34)? Aristotle makes this claim at the conclusion of his arguments in support of the psychological version of the principle of contradiction and it is far from certain that Aristotle is referring to the logical or metaphysical principle in this passage, as Łukasiewicz and many other commentators claim. It is—at least *prima facie*—equally plausible that Aristotle is referring to the psychological formulation of the PC as the ultimate *arche* of all other principles. The immediate context, the passages immediately before and after, support a reading in which Aristotle is using the indexical "this" to refer to the content of the psychological formulation of the PC, namely, that it is impossible for a person to simultaneously believe that something is and is not. If Aristotle considered the psychological formulation of the PC as the "starting-point even for all the other axioms", then Aristotle is concerned with the persuasive force of arguments as a psychological effect, not with logical facts as such. Thus, in this interpretation of Aristotle's account, it is the realization of the PC as psychological principle that compels the recognition and acceptance of the truth of the logical and ontological PC. Such a reading, of course, presents a complete reversal of the line of dependence that is claimed in interpretations that take Aristotle's argument as an attempt to derive the psychological formulation from the logical and ontological ones, as argued by Łukasiewicz in Chapter III (100 f.).

The crucial point, however, is what the indexical "this" in the passage refers to. Dancy and Priest interpret it as a reference to the PC as a logical or ontological principle. Priest cautiously entertains (and ultimately rejects) the possibility that what Aristotle may have meant by the claim that the PC is the natural starting point for all other axioms "is not that each of the others presuppose it, but that the very notion of (deductive) inference presupposes it" (Priest 2008 [2006], 10).

What, then, did Aristotle mean when he declared that the PC is the ultimate *arche* of all other logical principles? Did he think of the (ontological or logical) principle as an implied premise that is part of all deductive reasoning? This position seems rather unconvincing. As Lear (1980) in his discussion of Aristotle's argument in support of the psychological PC points out, Aristotle's argument assumes that the PC is true, but the argument does not include the principle as a premise. Instead, Lear argues, the argument "works *by means* of the law of non-contradiction" (although in some unspecified way) (1980, 101).

The point is taken up by Dancy (1975), who notes that Aristotle himself mentions in the *Analytics* (77a 10-21), in his discussion of a syllogism with a contradictory minor premise, that the PC appears as a premise only in a limited number of cases. Further, only a few lines earlier, at 76b 10-11, Aristotle states that in general "proofs are conducted *by means of* (*διά*) the axioms" (Dancy, 8). According to Dancy, this suggests that Aristotle may have considered the PC as something similar to a rule of inference (as well as a first principle). One immediate difficulty with this view, as Dancy notes, is that it is not altogether clear how the principle would be expressed as a set of instructions. Nevertheless, Dancy suggests, "the law of non-contradiction ... is somehow presupposed by every demonstration" (Dancy, 8).

Of course, this is exactly what Łukasiewicz, following Husik (1906), denies. Husik argues that "the syllogism does not presuppose the law of contradiction" and, furthermore, that this view "is held by no less an authority in logic than Aristotle. In a passage in the *Posterior Analytics* [77a 10-22]... Aristotle states the thesis and proves it" (Husik, 217).

According to Husik, the syllogism is unaffected by contradictory terms in the minor premise because

> Aristotle bases the syllogism upon the *dictum de omni et nullo*, which is a definition and has nothing to say about the compatibility or incompatibility of the positive and its negative (Husik, 221).

Aristotle's defines the concept of *de omni et de nullo* predication at the beginning of the *Prior Analytics*, where he states the principle as follows:

> one term is predicated of all of another, whenever nothing can be found of which the other term cannot be asserted; 'to be predicated of none' must be understood in the same way (24b 28-30; Jenkins translation).

In Husik's analysis, the validity of the syllogism that Aristotle discusses is preserved by the range of the major term. The contradictory predications attributed to the middle term have no effect on the conclusion (Husik, 220). This result does not reject the results of Aristotle's defense of the principle of contradiction in the *Metaphysics*, Husik points out, because

> In the *Posterior Analytics* he [Aristotle] is dealing with the purely formal process of evolving the conclusion out of the premisses, or, more strictly speaking, out of the major premiss. In so far as we merely do this, the law of contradiction is not involved (Husik, 222).

Łukasiewicz, who agrees with the core ideas underlying Husik's analysis (XV, 170 n.111) and develops it further in his own discussion, reaches the same conclusion:

> The syllogism principle maintains its validity even though the principle of contradiction has ceased to be true. Thus, it has been shown that the principle of contradiction *is not a necessary foundation of syllogistic reasoning* (XV, 174).

This result, as Łukasiewicz points out, is less surprising that it may appear at first sight. Modern formal logic has shown that "there are numerous other rules and principles of demonstration, which do not depend on the principle of contradiction" (XV, 174). The question now is whether it is possible to reason rationally and successfully about the world without any use or appeal to the principle of contradiction. Łukasiewicz sets out to resolve this question in the next chapter.

XVI. Non-Aristotelian Logic

To support his claim that the principle of contradiction is independent of many other logical principles and, specifically, that it is possible to reason without any reliance on the PC, Łukasiewicz proposes the idea of a logical fiction. Łukasiewicz invites his readers to imagine a world that is characterized by a unique socio-logical feature—all and any negations are always true for the denizens of this world. The consideration underlying this unusual valuation is that there is always some property that justifies the denial of some other property because it is different from that property. For example, the negation "the sun is not shining" is always true since there are always properties of the sun that differ from "shining" and which, because they are different from the property "shining" fall under the range of the properties delimited by the negation "not shining".

Thus, the meaning of negation applied here is that of a negation that includes everything except what it excludes. Łukasiewicz' implements this rather unorthodox use of negation in his fictional world to show that reasoning is possible without use or appeal to the PC. In his view, the denizens of this logical fiction would not be concerned with negations. It would be common knowledge that negations are always true and, furthermore, that all that exists is contradictory since all negations are true. Only "certain non-existent and unlikely objects, about which nothing positive could be asserted, would contain no contradictions" (XVI, 176). Łukasiewicz wants to investigate whether it is possible for a society that accepts and adopts this view of a world, which is characterized by a ubiquity of contradictions, would be able to reason and act rationally (XVI, 176).

The method of investigation is by example. Łukasiewicz considers the case of a doctor treating a patient that exhibits (and, of course, also is held not exhibit) the symptoms of diphtheria. In developing this diagnosis, the doctor "ascertains that which is and not that which is not" (XVI, 176). In other words, all facts are empirically derived from sense experience and in this processe,

Łukasiewicz asserts, "the principle of contradiction is completely useless" for the doctor (XVI, 176).

Based on the positive facts derived from empirical observation, the doctor completes the diagnosis by inductive inference, which—according to Łukasiewicz—does not involve negations and, thus, cannot involve any appeal to or reliance on the PC. "Where there are no negating statements, the principle of contradiction cannot find application" (XVI, 177). Finally, in the prescription of treatment, the physician employs deductive reasoning as well and, again, without appeal to the PC. Łukasiewicz convinced himself in Chapter XV that some syllogistic inferences are independent of the PC. An important characteristic of these syllogistic inferences in this context is that they do not contain negations among their constitutive statements and, without negations, the PC cannot be articulated (or applied). Further, Łukasiewicz argues that the derivation of *A* is *C* from *A* is *B* and *B* is *C* not only does not contain negations, the derivation itself does not require any appeal to the PC (XVI, 178).

Łukasiewicz concludes that his example has shown that the denizens of his fictitious world, who "do not recognize the principle of contradiction, that ascertain matters of experiential fact, are able to reason inductively and deductively and are able to act effectively based on such conclusions" (XVI, 178). Furthermore, since it was possible for the hypothetical physician in this fictitious world to successfully reason and act rationally, it is in principle possible to do so for all denizens of that world (XVI, 178). Despite the inconsistencies in the descriptions of the world, which are accepted and endorsed by its denizens, the world has a logical and ontological structure that permits rational cognition, deliberation, and action.

Given additional similarities in the intellectual organization of Łukasiewicz' fictional rational beings and actual human beings, Łukasiewicz goes on to describe a development of scientific thought and discovery in this fictional world that is populated by contradictory objects and phenomena, which that parallels the evolution of human scientific knowledge. If this society were to develop a theory of logic, Łukasiewicz suggests, it might very well produce a second Aristotle. This fictional Aristotle, Łukasiewicz argues, would develop the same logical principles of syllogistic reasoning as did the historical Aristotle, but he would not formulate those logical principles that express and rely upon the metaphysical principle of contradiction. “If one may call a system of logical laws, in which the principle of contradiction is not valid, non-Aristotelian logic,” Łukasiewicz concludes, “then this society would commit to *non-Aristotelian* logic” (XVI, 179).

Łukasiewicz’ discussion of an imaginary society of rational beings that accept any negation as true presents the final chapter of critical consideration of Aristotle’s principle. Łukasiewicz’ imaginary world recalls Vasil’év’s attempts to show that the PC may not be necessarily a universal truth and that it is possible to imagine a world in which the Aristotelian PC fails.

In his article titled “Logic and Metalogic”, which was published in 1910—the same year Łukasiewicz’ work on the principle of contradiction and Meinong’s second edition of *Über Annahmen* were published (see and note above)—Vasil’év sets out to develop a solution to the dispute between Benno Erdmann and Eduard Husserl regarding the nature and foundation of logical principles (with Erdmann representing the psychologism side of the argument and Husserl, the anti-psychologist and logical realist side). At issue was whether logical laws are empirically derived, psychological principles that are subject to change and modification (Erdmann) or whether they constitute transcendent and immutable principles that express necessary truths (Husserl).

The dispute between Erdmann and Husserl exemplifies the main problematic and positions that characterized the psychologism debate. In his discussion of the psychological formulation of the principle of contradiction, Łukasiewicz takes a decidedly anti-psychologist, logical realist position. Even further, he identifies an early instance of psychologism in logic back to of Aristotle’s arguments in support of the psychological principle of contradiction (IV, 105; Commentary to Ch.IV, 304).

Vasil’év argues that both the positions, Erdmann’s insistence on the fluid nature of human reasoning and understanding of logical principles and Husserl’s insistence on an objective reality of abstract, ideal objects and their properties and relations, contain elements of truth. His proposed solution was an attempt to vindicate those parts of each position, which he considered to be accurate. Furthermore, the key ideas contained in each of the two positions are not incommensurable but can be reconciled once it is recognized that each the principles of logic is derived from one of two distinct sources, one is empirical in its origin, the other rational. The purely rational principles, in Vasil'év's account, form an indispensable and unalterable core of logical thought. However, the principles that are derived from experience are, in a sense, additions to the rational core of logic. As such, they belong to a group of logical principles that may be omitted, altered, or added to the necessary core principles. The resulting combinations, in turn, give rise to different, imaginary, systems of logic, which offer suitable descriptions of the ontological structure of corresponding, imaginary worlds.

The logical principle that may be removed from the traditional principles of logic is the principle of contradiction. "There are possible logics without the the law of contradiction," Vasil'év argues and one such logic is his proposed imaginary logic (1993b, 336). This imaginary logic includes three types of propositions which are distinguished by the three truth-values that propositions may have—true, false, and indifferent. In addition, Vasil'év proposes a distinction between two principles of contradiction based on two different types of foundation: one that agrees with the Aristotelian object-theoretical or ontological formulation principle of contradiction but which is not grounded in *a priori* considerations. Instead, this principle of contradiction is the result of inductive generalizations based on empirical observations (as argued, for example, by J.S. Mill, which led him to be charged with psychologism).[65] The second, over-riding and (proto) metalogical principle of contradiction asserts the impossibility of a joint assertion of contradictory propositions as a necessary condition of all logical reasoning and inference. It is the first, empirically grounded principle, Vasil'év proposes, which is not a necessary principle of logic and which may be altered or omitted in a non-Aristotelian, imaginary logic.

For example, an imaginary world, which does contain contradictory states of affairs as empirically observable phenomena, would require propositions that are not simply true or false, but which are "indifferent" or "contradictory" for a complete or, at least, more accurate logical description. The Aristotelian formulation of the principle of contradiction obviously does not hold in a world that does contain actual contradictions. The second principle, however, belongs to the unalterable conditions and principles of logical though. It is the warrant of inner, subjective consistency and must be upheld in any logical system whatsoever.

It is interesting to note that Husik (1906) also argues that there may be certain empirical factors that underlie the belief in the truth of the principle of contradiction. He argues that it is impossible to determine by *a priori* considerations which properties of (concrete, physical) objects are contrary (or incompatible) with each other. In Husik's analysis, "experience alone can tell us what attributes are, and what are not, incompatible" (Husik 1906, 215-6). But if this is the case, then the opposition and mutual exclusion of contraries is not a pure *a priori* principle, but a principle that is primarily based on observation and experience.

Husik proposes that the empirical content of incompatibility may be altered in an imaginary psychological state in which incompatible properties no longer exclude each other in experience—a proposal that, in its effect on the logical representation of what is empirically given, is not unlike Vasil'év's proposal of an imaginary world that contains contradictory states of affairs. According to Husik,

> it is conceivable that there might be a state of experience even if our present regions of incompatibles were dissolved. By this is not meant a chaos in which all things are and are not at the same time. All it involves is a state of thinking with the *a priori* element reduced to a minimum (Husik, 216).

The logic of such a world (based on the way that world presents itself in experience) would differ from Aristotle's logic. The attribution of a property to an object no longer excludes the simultaneous attribution of a contrary property to the same object, at least not on *a priori* grounds.

> If we were to construct a logic on this hypothesis, the implication of the assumption would be that the judgment A is B is to be taken at its face value, and no inference be allowed regarding not-B. Similarly the negative judgment A is not-B should be limited to its direct and explicit statement, and all *a priori* inference as to B be excluded. B and not-B, in other words, are to be treated, in accordance with this hypothesis, as B and C are in our actual logic. The psychological attitude of this hypothetical logic it is, of course, impossible for us to realise, as it is impossible to realise psychologically a fourth dimension or the meeting of parallel lines (Husik, 216).

The inference that Husik wants to exclude is the inference from 'A is B' to 'A is not not-B', i.e., the application of classical double negation. In his imaginary logic, double negation is not a valid form of inference; instead 'A is not-B' is treated as equivalent to 'A is C', that is, as equivalent to a predicate (or term) that has no immediate (a priori) relation to B other than that it is a different predicate (or term with a different extension). In this imaginary logic, which corresponds to and accurately represents an imaginary mode of experience, contrary properties may belong simultaneously to an object. Thus, according to Husik, it is possible to encounter simultaneous instances of B and not-B.

Husik introduces his account of an imaginary logic in order to set the stage for his discussion of Aristotle's account of a syllogistic demonstration that includes a contradictory minor premise (cf. Łukasiewicz' discussion of Aristotle's account in XV, 170; also Commentary, 388). Husik's imaginary logic "clears the ground" for the realization that syllogistic inferences are possible without appeal to the principle of contradiction—a result that Aristotle's account in the *Posterior Analytics* also demonstrated (Husik, 216).

Łukasiewicz, who agrees with Husik's result, presents his "logical fiction" as an example that illustrates Łukasiewicz' (and Husik's) finding that at least some syllogistic inferences are independent of the principle of contradiction. In Łukasiewicz' view, a society with an interpretation of the meaning of negations that prevents the articulation of an Aristotelian principle of contradiction would develop a logic that does not rely on the principle and, as Łukasiewicz concludes his account,

> If one may call a system of logical laws, in which the principle of contradiction is not valid, non-Aristotelian logic, then this society would commit to *non-Aristotelian* logic (XVI, 179).

Łukasiewicz concludes the chapter with a summary of the main results of his critical investigations of Aristotle's PC.

- It is (at the very least) doubtful that the PC is a psychological principle.
- The PC is not an ultimate principle, but requires proof to be accepted.

- Aristotle failed to provide proof for this principle and, thus, belief in this principle is unjustified.
- The Aristoelian PC is not universally valid since Aristotle restricted its validity to universal and essential being.
- The PC is not a necessary law of thought since, as Aristotle himself admitted, it is possible to make logical inferences without appeal to the PC.
- The PC fails with respect to contradictory objects.

Łukasiewicz summarizes his findings as follows:

> The principle of contradiction is *uncertain* in its psychological formulation, *unjustified* in its logical and ontological formulation, *superfluous* in many and *false* in some cases (XVI, 179).

The most important consequence of Łukasiewicz' results is that it is no longer possible to simply accept the PC without any further justification. The status of the principle of contradiction has become problematic again, the truth of the principle is clouded by doubts and a new analysis of its importance and domains of validity must be generated.

Commentary – Chapter XVII
Proof of the Principle of Contradiction

- Self-Evidence
- Psychological Necessity
- The Principle of Contradiction and Definitions of Truth and Falsity
- Formal Proof of the Principle of Contradiction

The critical part of Łukasiewicz' investigation into Aristotle's account of the PC has been completed. Aristotle's proofs and reasons for the PC fall short of their goal of establishing the universal scope and validity of the principle. Nevertheless, as Łukasiewicz points out, the principle has clearly shown its value historically, both in scientific pursuits and life in general. But the utility and success of the principle is not enough for its acceptance as a scientifically established truth. In order to settle the matter, Łukasiewicz returns to the demand made by Dedekind: "in science, whatever is provable ought not to be believed without proof" (Dedekind, 1888, vii), which constitutes the principal background claim of Łukasiewicz' "Introduction" (cf. 21, 271 ff.).

In the "Introduction", Łukasiewicz implicitly endorsed Dedekind's demand and applied it to logical principles in general and the principle of contradiction in particular—to be accepted as a scientific and logical truth, the principle of contradiction needs proof! As Łukasiewicz puts it at the end of his introductory discussion, one of the main goals of his work is to show that the principle of contradiction "presents a thesis that demands proof and that this proof . . . can be found" (Introduction, 82).

One key concern of Łukasiewicz' examination of Aristotle's account of the PC was to determine whether Aristotle presents a valid proof of the PC. Łukasiewicz' conclusion is that Aristotle fails to deliver such a proof. Further, due to the overwhelming acceptance of Aristotle's account of the PC as a secure truth beyond deductive proof in the history of Western philosophy, the lack of a proof of the principle remained largely unnoticed. It is precisely this task that Łukasiewicz sets his sights on: a deductively valid proof of the principle of contradiction.

The first step in developing such a proof is to determine the ground on which a proof of the PC could be developed. Łukasiewicz once again considers the appeals to (a) alleged self-evidence and (b) psychological necessity of the principle of contradiction, which he rejects as insufficient and tainted by the erroneous approach of a psychologistic interpretation of *a priori* principles of thought. In section (c), he argues that the PC must be grounded and proven based on objective, *a priori* considerations and considers to what extent the PC may be derivable from the definitions of truth and falsity. Finally, in the last section of the chapter (d), after a discussion of what Łukasiewicz terms a "characteristic" and "synthetic moment" in the principle of contradiction (XVII, 186), Łukasiewicz presents a "formal" proof of the principle.

(a) Self-Evidence

Łukasiewicz rejects all appeals to "immediate evidence" as basis for a proof of the PC. He considers the claim that a thesis is immediately evident or self-evident as a report of a subjective psychical experience. However, the psychical experience of the immediate truth of a claim by an individual is independent of the objective truth or falsity of the claim under consideration. Thus, Łukasiewicz argues, the experience of immediate evidence may be erroneous, and is inadmissible as a warrant of the truth of a claim. As an example, Łukasiewicz mentions Descartes' causal argument for the existence of God, which appeals to the immediate evidence of a clear and distinct idea of a "supremely perfect being". This clear and distinct idea, according to Descartes, warrants an inference to the existence of God, because his possession of this idea can only be explained as an effect of God's existence and "the total cause of something must contain at least as much reality as does the effect" (Descartes 1968 [1641], Meditation III).

While Łukasiewicz does not explicitly state this, his rejection of Descartes' argument suggests that he considers the (immediate) evidence afforded by a clear and distinct idea of a divine being to be insufficient for an inference from the existence of such an idea [in the sense of a subjective *Vorstellung* or presentation] of an object to the existence of that object. Such an inference is certainly invalid if Meinong's distinction between being and being-so is accepted together with Mally's assertion of the independence of being-so from being—a position that may be very close to Łukasiewicz' views in 1910.

Łukasiewicz' main point of criticism against appeals to immediate evidence is convincing: such appeals are inevitably purely subjective claims, relative to individuals who confirm that they perceive such evidence and opposed by others, who deny that they perceive such evidence. In Łukasiewicz' analysis, any appeal to immediate evidence is "a remnant of psychologism", which is closely connected to subjectivism and skepticism, and inadmissable as warrants for the truth of any claim within a scientific context (XVII, 181). For Łukasiewicz, the only proof that establishes the truth of an *a priori* claim is a valid deductive proof.

(b) Psychological Necessity

Next, Łukasiewicz returns to the idea that the principle of contradiction is a law of thought. Here, the belief in the truth and universal validity of the principle is explained as the result of a psychological necessity, which is assumed to underlie the operations of the human mind. In other words, the truth of the principle of contradiction is grounded in the fundamental structure and categories that determine the operations of the human mind, which generates the "psychological necessity" that "forces us to acknowledge this principle" (XVII, 182). Thus, the truth of the PC is not grounded in the logical and ontological relations that obtain or do not obtain between ideal and concrete objects.

Łukasiewicz points out that it is a consequence of this separation of psychological necessity and objective facts that if this were the case, the psychological necessity itself would be insufficient to warrant the truth and validity of the PC in the objective domains of concrete or ideal objects and their real, ontological, properties. According to Łukasiewicz, there is no "guarantee that the real external world follows the requirements of the inner organization of man" (XVII, 182).

Even Kant, who famously argued that the cognition of the objective features of the empirical world are conditioned by the structure and categories of the understanding, is unable to demonstrate the validity of the PC for the domain of the empirically observable world. In Kant's *Critique of Pure Reason* (1976 [1787]), the principle of contradiction is described as "the universal and completely sufficient principle of all analytic cognition" (A151/B191).[66] However, with respect to the crucial question of the conditions of *a priori* and synthetic cognition, the principle is primarily a negative principle, a *sine qua non*, that is, an analytic principle with the primary function of indicating or flagging any errors in any proposition (A152/B191).

According to Łukasiewicz, the extension of the validity of the principle of contradiction to the empirical domain would require the principle to be considered as a synthetic *a priori* claim, a view that Kant did not explicitly hold, as Łukasiewicz points out. However, if interpreted as a synthetic *a priori* claim, Łukasiewicz argues, the validity of the principle of contradiction

> in its application to the sensible world would be merely an assumption, because it would depend on a hypothesis which considers the world of appearances as a product of the human understanding (XVII, 183).

It would go beyond the scope of this commentary to develop a defense of the Kantian conception against Łukasiewicz' criticism. Nevertheless, it is worthwhile to point out that, in Kant's view, the acceptance of the PC as an analytic *a priori* truth is a necessary condition of the claim that every object must comply with the PC to be knowable as an object. In the Kantian account, intelligibility requires consistency. Interestingly, this point agrees with Łukasiewicz' own claim about the ontological and logical structure of what constitutes (or is admissible as) an object, namely, that it must be free of any contradictions, a claim that marks a crucial point in the formal proof of the PC that Łukasiewicz presents in section (d) of this chapter. Finally, in Kant's account, nothing definite can be known about the things-in-themselves (*Dinge an sich*) except that they must be there, underneath or behind the observable phenomena, as it were. In this sense, Kant's noumena are descendants of Aristotle's *hypokeimenon* or *substratum* and unknowable as such except for their cognitively accessible surfaces in the form of sensible phenomena shaped by the workings of the understanding). Consequently, it cannot be excluded that noumena may be inconsistent in some or all their (noumenal) aspects—a point seized upon by Hegel and his critique of Kant's transcendental philosophy.

This last point, too, could be interpreted as providing additional support to Łukasiewicz' main point of criticism, i.e., as providing support to the claim that even if it is admitted that the validity of the PC is grounded in the structure and functioning of the mind, it is not at all clear how, from a realist point of view, this validity could be extended to include the domain of objective (extra-subjective) being. Thus, the claim that the PC is a universally valid ontological and logical principle, both in its traditional Aristotelian or a modern realist interpretation, cannot be established on a psychologistic foundation. Instead, as Łukasiewicz' argues, any such attempt to ground the principle in experiential aspects of mental phenomena must fail and lead to subjectivist and skeptical accounts (XVII, 183).

(c) The Principle of Contradiction and the Definition of Truth and Falsity

For Łukasiewicz, the demonstration of the truth of an *a priori* claim must be derived through an objective argument, i.e., an argument that does not contain any appeals to (subjective) experience. An appeal to experience or observation renders the truth derived by a demonstration *a posteriori* and, thus, insufficient as a proof of an *a priori* claim. In Łukasiewicz' view, the strongest foundation of an argument that aims to demonstrate the truth an *a priori* principle is provided by definitions. Compared to arguments that appeal to the (subjective experience of) immediate evidence or psychological necessity of the principle of contradiction, arguments based on definitions are able to generate a proof of the principle in which "the truth of the matter would follow from it by *itself*, and not—at best—the truth of a statement that we have to accept this principle" (XVII, 183).

One might add, a proof of the principle of contradiction derived from definitions would also be more decisive compared to the results of Aristotle's attempts to establish the universal validity of the principle of contradiction through indirect demonstrations, which aim at the refutation of positions that deny the validity of the principle, and which—ultimately—rest on the assertion that the consequences of a denial of the PC are absurd and unacceptable, notions that are also infused with strong psychological components.

The definitions that Łukasiewicz has his sights on are the definitions of true and false statements. In Chapter VIII (124 ff.), Łukasiewicz argued that the definition of true statements provides the foundation for the principle of identity. He now considers the possibility that the definition of a false statement, either by itself or in combination with the definition a true statement, may provide the foundation for the principle of contradiction (XVII, 183). Taken together, the two definitions assert that contradictorily opposed statements have opposite truth values. If an affirmative statement is true (or false), its negation is false (or true). If a denial is true (or false), its corresponding affirmative statement is false (or true). No other possibilities are admitted.

Łukasiewicz observes that the conjoined definitions of true and false statements appear to firmly establish that "two contradictory statements cannot be simultaneously true and that the principle of contradiction, which rests on generally recognized definitions, is just as certain as the principle of identity" (XVII, 184). Furthermore, Łukasiewicz points out, Aristotle also seems to take a similar position. According to Aristotle, "if when the assertion is true, the negation is false, and when this is true, the affirmation is false, it will not be possible to assert and deny the same thing truly at the same time" (1008a 34 – b1, Ross translation).

Half a century before Łukasiewicz, Friedrich Ueberweg (1826—1871) also thought that the definitions of truth and falsity are fundamental notions from which the truth of the PC might be derivable (1857, 2001). As discussed in the Introduction to Łukasiewicz' work (45 ff.), Ueberweg was one of the first modern logicians to argue that the PC as a logical principle needs proof. Ueberweg doubted that the principle is a first and, therefore, underivable principle, and developed a proof of the principle in order to show that the PC is not an unprovable first principle but, instead, that it is derivable from other and more fundamental principles (Ueberweg 1857, 181). However, his proof does not derive the principle of contradiction, but a statement that is reminiscent of Aristotle's claim (1008a 34) cited above and which articulates a relationship between affirmation and denial and their respective truth values: "thus, if the affirmation is true, the denial is false, and if the denial is true, the affirmation is false, which was to be demonstrated" (Ueberweg, 178).

Łukasiewicz does agree with Ueberweg's conclusion about the truth-values of affirmations and denials and presents a similar argument to establish the point. However, like Brentano before him (albeit for different reasons),[67] Łukasiewicz points out that the argument does not prove the principle of contradiction. All that follows from the definitions of true and false statements is that contradictorily opposed statements have opposed truth values. This, however, is a statement that is very different from the principle of contradiction and—the two statements are not logically equivalent.

The difference between the two claims becomes clearer considering the following: Łukasiewicz argues that, based on the definitions of true and false statements, the falsity of a statement does not prevent that statement from also being true. This situation arises in statements about the properties of contradictory objects (XVII, 186). For example, it is false that a round square is round (since it is square and, thus, not round), but it is also true that a round square is round (since it is round). Thus, in statements about contradictory objects, Łukasiewicz concludes, "the definitions of truth and falsity can be satisfied, even though the principle of contradiction is rendered invalid" (XVII, 185).

The reason for this is that the definitions of truth and falsity that Łukasiewicz adopts appeal to the (real) existence or absence of an inherence relation between an object and a property. It is a consequence of this criterion of truth or falsity, that there are some statements about contradictory objects that are both true and false. Thus, with respect to contradictory objects, it is not only the principle of contradiction that fails, but also the principle of bivalence—a consequence that Łukasiewicz is unprepared to entertain and explore in 1910.

Still, Łukasiewicz is convinced that there is a close connection between the definitions of true and false statements and the principle of contradiction. A possible solution, a solution that preserves both the principle of bivalence and the failure of the principle of contradiction in statements about contradictory objects, may be found by modifying the definition of a false statement.

The purpose of statements is to represent reality, Łukasiewicz argues, and an alternative definition of a false statement may be constructed by shifting the decisive criterion from the presence or absence of an inherence relation between object and property to the criterion of a failure to correctly represent reality. The new definition of a false statement, which Łukasiewicz introduces, is the following: "a statement is false only if it does not agree with reality, that is, if it does not reproduce reality" (XVII, 185).

This definition allows Łukasiewicz to designate both consistent and contradictory statements as statements that are true (or false) *simpliciter*, that is, the statements have one and only one truth value; they are either true and not also false or they are false and not also true (XVII, 185). In other words, the new definition of a false statement introduced by Łukasiewicz allows him to preserve the principle of bivalence for all statements. This is particularly relevant with respect to contradictory statements. Neither one of a pair of contradictory statements (about contradictory properties of a contradictory object) is false since neither one of the pair of statements fails to reproduce reality (the actual features of the contradictory object). However, both contradictory statements are true simpliciter, which means that there are exceptions to the logical principle that correspond to the exceptions to the ontological principle that arise from the admission of contradictory objects. In comparison, the earlier definition of a false statement, which relies on the criterion of an inherence relation between property and object, is restricted in its applicability to objects that do not contain a contradiction. As Łukasiewicz puts it:

> Only if the object *x* does not contain a contradiction and contains a property or does not contain it, then the statement is false which denies it of it or attributes it to it (XVII, 185).

In Łukasiewicz' view, the new definition of false statements has at least two points in its favor: It agrees with the general conception that a false statement does not correctly represent reality and, furthermore, the new definition preserves bivalence, "it does not force us to call one and the same statement simultaneously true and false" (XVII, 186).

However, the main conclusion of Łukasiewicz' analysis of the connection between the definition of true and false statements and the principle of contradiction is that the two are independent or, at least, that the PC cannot be derived from the definitions of truth and falsity alone. This conclusion, Łukasiewicz adds, also shows that the theory of the principle of contradiction proposed by Sigwart fails to capture the concept expressed by the principle. As discussed in the Introduction (50 f.), Sigwart argues that Aristotle's formulation of the PC is "nothing but a statement concerning the significance of negation" (Sigwart 1895 [1873], 140). According to Sigwart, the principle of contradiction

> refers to a relation between a positive judgment and its negation; it expresses the nature and meaning of the negation by saying that the judgments '*A* is *B*' and '*A* is not *B*' cannot both be true together (Sigwart 1895 [1873], 139).

In Łukasiewicz' analysis, Sigwart's account—just like Aristotle's and Ueberweg's—is unable to demonstrate the truth of the principle of contradiction since Sigwart grounds his understanding of negation in the concept of a false statement. In Łukasiewicz' analysis, the definition of true and false statements is insufficient to derive the principle of contradiction and "the definition, which could support the principle of contradiction, must be found elsewhere" (XVII, 186).

After this section of Łukasiewicz' discussion, it is worth noting that Łukasiewicz' analysis of the connection between the definitions of true and false statements and the principle of contradiction illustrates and agrees with Priest's point (discussed earlier) that the issue and possibility of true contradictions is independent of theories of truth. In fact, Łukasiewicz' account offers a striking example of Priest's claim that a correspondence theory of truth does not foreclose the possibility of true contradictions but that in conjunction with paradoxes, it (naturally) lead towards a dialetheist position (cf. Priest 2000).

(d) Formal Proof of the Principle of Contradiction

For Łukasiewicz, the content of the principle of contradiction exceeds what is contained in the definitions of true and false statements. The principle expresses what he calls a "synthetic moment" (XVII, 186), an expression that evokes Hegel and his dialectical conception of logic. However, what Łukasiewicz has in mind in this section relates most of all to the principle of bivalence. The synthetic moment that Łukasiewicz identifies as a characteristic feature of the principle of contradiction is not so much a moment of combination and fusion, but of strict separation and exclusiveness:

> Affirmation and denial, truth and falsity cannot exist *next to each other*; they *cancel* and *exclude* each other. One and the same statement cannot be simultaneously true and false, one and the same object cannot have and not have one and the same property at the same time (XVII, 186).

Here, Łukasiewicz identifies the core meaning of the PC with the principle of bivalence in its logical and its ontological meaning. In the logical domain, truth and falsity are mutally exclusive and cannot coincide, in the ontological domain, only one of two states can obtain in the relation between an object and a property, either the object has the property or it does not.

However, this conception fails with respect to contradictory objects. They seem to present cases in which affirmative and negative claims do not cancel each other, but appear to be both true. If contradictory objects are admitted as objects, Łukasiewicz concludes, then "the principle of contradiction is not a universal law that governs all objects" (XVII, 186). But the principle is meant to be just such a universal law, a law that applies to and is instantiated by all objects and any of their properties. With his commitment to bivalence in place, Łukasiewicz sees only one solution:

> It has to be assumed that contradictory objects are no objects at all, that they are not something but nothing. Anything, however, that is an object and that, therefore, is something and not nothing, does not contain contradictory properties (XVII, 187).

Thus, the formal proof of the PC that Łukasiewicz constructs, requires a crucial restriction on what constitutes an object. No longer is an object anything that is something and not nothing—a description that does not warrant the exclusion of contradictory objects—but a candidate item now must be free of any contradictions; it must be consistent to be an object. With this new conception of what constitutes an object, a formal proof of the principle of contradiction is easily constructed. As Łukasiewicz points out,

> from this assumption, which one may take as the definition of 'object', it immediately follows based on the principle of identity that no object

> can contain and not contain one and the same property (XVII, 187).

Łukasiewicz is quick to acknowledge that this formal proof of the principle of contradiction falls short of the full *desideratum* of his inquiry. After all, if only consistent objects are admitted, it is not much of a surprise that the principle of contradiction holds in all cases—the principle encapsulates a theory of the logical features of consistent objects, their properties and relations. However, it fails and generates dialethias as soon as it encounters the inconsistent.

Łukasiewicz' formal proof shifts the focus of inquiry from the formal truth of the principle of contradiction (as a demonstrably true *a priori* statement of universal scope) to the question of the logical and ontological structure of an object. To prove the PC not only in a formal but also in a factual way, he argues that

> one would have to show that anything that is an object in the first sense, thus, everything that is something and not nothing, is also an object in the second sense, which is to say, that it does not contain a contradiction (XXI, 223).

Thus, a factual or material proof of the principle of contradiction requires a determination of the ontological structure of objects in the first sense. Such a determination requires the investigation of objects and the facts constituted by their actual being, it requires an investigation of the "real material of facts" furnished by ideal objects of theoretical thought on the one hand, and of concrete objects of sense perception on the other.

Commentary – Chapter XVIII
The Principle of Contradiction and Constructions of the Mind

- The Division of Objects
- Complete and Incomplete Objects
- Constructive and Reconstructive Objects
- Constructive Objects and Contradiction

Łukasiewicz turns to the question whether it is possible to determine that all objects in the intentional sense do or do not contain contradictions. To facilitate this task, Łukasiewicz focuses on the relation between object and property and, adopting a distinction developed by Meinong, divides objects into two groups, completely and incompletely determined objects.[68] According to this distinction, completely determined objects allow a positive or negative assessment for any property, i.e., a complete object either does possess a property or it does not possess it or, in the case of a contradictory object, there is at least one property that the object determinately does and does not possess at the the same time. Incompletely determined objects, on the other hand, feature gaps (and possibly gluts as well), that is, neither a positive nor a negative determination can be made with respect to certain properties.

Based on this distinction, concrete objects, for example, individual chairs or trees, are completely determined; they are complete objects because any statement attributing a property to such an object is either true or false. The latter claim is a universal assertion about inherently empirical facts. It is hard to see how this claim could be shown to be true on purely *a priori* considerations. In addition, predications involving category errors, like "the column is happy" may not be simply false, as Łukasiewicz suggests. In a classical, two-valued logic, the evaluation entails that the negation, "the column is not happy", is true. However, both assertion and denial seem equally non-sensical and, arguably, present a sentence construction that does not result in a statement that is either true or false, but a statement that does not have a truth-value at all. Łukasiewicz, in any case, adopts the claim and holds that concrete objects are completely determined with regard to any predicate.

On the other hand, abstract or ideal objects tend to be incompletely determined. For example, the abstract object denoted by "triangle" is neither equilateral nor not equilateral. It lacks a determination with respect to the property of equilaterality. The same is true for the property of "has a right angle" and other such attributes. "Triangle" denotes an incomplete object. Again, objection can be raised against the distinction. Arguably, the essential feature of an abstract object is precisely that it includes and is constituted by only a limited number of determinations (properties) and the designation of an abstract object as "incomplete" may be either meaningless or tautological.

Abstract and incomplete objects do not exist as actual, concrete objects in the world, Łukasiewicz points out. Instead, they are "products of the human mind" (XVIII, 190). In Meinong's theory of objects, the relations and properties that belong to them are said to subsist rather than exist (*bestehen* and *sein* in Meinong's terminology). However, each mode is a determinate mode of being. Thus, a relation that is stated to exist or subsist does or does not exist or, respectively, subsist. In other words, statements declaring existence or subsistence may be true or false by asserting a state of affairs [*Sachlage* in Meinong] that does or does not obtain.

As human products, abstract objects differ in their respective purpose, which leads to a secondary distinction among incomplete objects. The primary purpose of one group is to "grasp concrete objects." Łukasiewicz labels such objects "reconstruction objects" (XVIII, 191). They are ideal objects with concrete extensions.

A second group of incomplete objects are the objects that are determined by *a priori* concepts and which constitute the domain of objects that are "primarily the concern of mathematics and logic" (XVIII, 191). Łukasiewicz names these objects "construction objects" and notes that construction objects are constituted independently of experience, whereas reconstruction objects are dependent on experience (XVIII, 191).

Returning to the question of the consistency of intentional objects, Łukasiewicz now sets out to investigate whether it is possible to determine on *a priori* grounds whether construction objects do or do not contain contradictions. Citing Dedekind, Łukasiewicz considers that construction objects are "free creations of the human mind" and that, consequently, it "depends on us whether these objects turn out contradictory or not contradictory" (XVIII, 191).

However, the domain of construction objects seems to contain objects that are clearly contradictory, as for example, the objects denoted by the expression "the greatest prime number" or "square circle." An immediate objection is that these expressions do not actually denote an object at all; they refer to nothing and "have found their place among other constructions only erroneously and by accident" (XVIII, 191).

In Fregean terms, the expression "the greatest prime number" has a determinable sense, but no referent. No such prime number exists or, in Meinong's terminology, the greatest prime number has a determinate being-so, i.e., there is (*besteht*) an *Objektiv* that correctly presents the being-so (the properties) of the greatest prime number, but this being-so also shows that there can be no such object (cf. discussion of Meinong's distinction between modes of being and their presentation in an *Objektiv* in Commentary to Chapter I, 287).

The question remains, does the expression "the greatest prime number" denote an object in Łukasiewicz' first sense, an intentional object, a "something" that is able to present itself as an object to the mind? The expression "the greatest prime number" does denote such an entity. Not only can this "something" be brought before the mind, but it can be examined and recognized as an item that determinately contains a contradiction (in Meinongian terminology, an *Objectiv* presenting its contradictory being-so is the case). It is a further step to hold that because this item does contain a contradiction, it does not exist in the same way in which, for example, natural numbers do exist (have *Bestand* or subsist). And to claim that because of its unique mode of existence (subsistence), the item denoted by "the greatest prime number" is not an object at all but nothing requires additional argument.

Russell (1905), for example, rejects the idea that there are impossible or contradictory objects. The main objection, Russell argues in his review of Meinong's theory of objects, is that Meinong's account "involves denying the law of contradiction when impossible objects are constitutuents" (Russell 1905, 533). Russell suggests that Frege's theory of denoting and his distinction of *Sinn* and *Bedeutung*, avoids the problems that the admission of impossible objects as proper logical and ontological objects entail (Russell 1905, 533).

The main reason for his denial of contradictory objects, however, is that they lead to logical explosion. "If two contradictory propositions hold of an object, then all propositions concerning that object are true; for if *p* is any proposition, then every proposition is either implied by *p* or implied by *not-p*" (Russell 1905, 536; includes reference to PM, 18).

The problems surrounding items that are known to be contradictory are merely the tip of the proverbial iceberg. The real difficulty in the analysis of construction objects is the determination whether a constructed object contains a contradiction, whether it is or is not consistent. Łukasiewicz poses the question as follows: "how do we know that constructions, which are held to be not contradictory, do not contain a contradiction?" (XVIII, 192) According to Łukasiewicz, abstract objects are "only seemingly free products" of the human mind (XVIII, 192). Once created, they possess determinate features and relations that are independent of human will. Further, these features and relations are of a complexity that makes it difficult to determine conclusively whether a contradiction is hidden within them. The material presented by abstract objects exhibits its own resistance to a complete investigation and analysis of the properties and relations that belong to such objects. In Łukasiewicz' view, "this resistance proves that the properties of numbers, figures, functions, etc., in turn do not entirely depend on us" (XVIII, 192).

In his account, Łukasiewicz attempts to combine a realist position about the objective properties of abstract objects and, especially, mathematical and logical objects, with a moment of creative freedom, which is largely restricted to the initial determinations of an object. As discussed earlier (58 ff.), it is this tension between the objective necessity and determinacy that provides the ground of all *a priori* knowledge and reasoning and the moment of creative freedom that permits the assumption of an unlimited range of hypotheses, which informs Łukasiewicz' investigation of the principle of contradiction and motivates his continued search for a non-Aristotelian logic. In the discussion of the tension between determinacy and creativity in the analysis of abstract objects, Łukasiewicz gives first expression to the ideas that he develops in much more detail two years later in his article on "Creative Elements in Science" (Łukasiewicz 1970 [1912]).

However, in the current context, Łukasiewicz' focus lies on the analysis of the objective properties and relations that arise in the construction of abstract objects. He considers the possibility that even in the construction of just two abstract objects, "certain contradictory relations also co-arise immediately between them" and goes on to ask whether this contradiction might not "be an *essential* and *indispensable* characteristic of all construction objects?" (XVIII, 192)

The suggestion that it is not just a few construction objects that occasionally may be found to contain contradictions (and contain these contradictions accidentally, as it were) but, instead, that *all* abstract construction objects necessarily contain contradictions, is startling and provocative. On the one had, it has a certain Hegelian ring to it and it may seem as if Łukasiewicz is returning to his stated motive of completing the work that was left undone by Hegel. In the current context, however, Łukasiewicz' primary reasons for this provocative hypothesis are the deep uncertainties that arose from the investigations into the foundations of mathematics and logic at the end of the nineteenth and early twentieth century. In support of the possibility that contradictory moments are contained in all abstract objects, Łukasiewicz proceeds to explicate some of the set theoretic paradoxes that arise in the analysis of countable infinite sets, for example, the series of natural numbers, which lead to the conclusion that the set of natural numbers contains parts that are equal to the whole. In Łukasiewicz' analysis, this paradox is not resolved but re-emerges in Cantor's theory of transfinite numbers in the form of the Burali-Forti paradox—a circumstance that leads Łukasiewicz to consider the possibility that "Cantor merely repositioned the contradiction from one corner to another, but that the contradiction itself cannot be thought away from the foundations of mathematics" (XVIII, 194).

If Łukasiewicz is right and the foundations of mathematics are inconsistent, and the contradictions that are discovered in objects derived through abstraction cannot be resolved but only re-positioned, as it were, and, thus, that a contradictory moment necessarily remains in any abstraction (Priest (1995) hints at the same possibility), then the set-theoretic foundations of arithmetic cannot be formalized within a classical logic but will require (at the very least) a paraconsistent approach.

Russell's paradox reveals what appears to be a related inconsistency that, in Łukasiewicz' view, is "positioned within the logical foundations of mathematics" and "concerns the shared trunk from which all *a priori* sciences grow" (XVIII, 194). According to

Russell, the paradox emerged as an unintended result of his effort "to reconcile Cantor's proof that there can be no greatest ordinal number with the very plausible supposition that the class of all terms … has necessarily the greatest possible number of members" (Russell 1992 [1937], X, Sec.100, 101). It is the construction of sets with unrestricted comprehension terms, e.g., "the class of all terms" and similar, that is often identified as the item that is responsible for the contradiction. Consequently, one standard method that prevents the contradiction from arising is to disallow the construction of sets with unrestricted comprehension, as for example, in Zermelo-Fraenkel set theory. However, in Russell's opinion at the beginning of the twentieth century, as expressed in the *Principles of Mathematics*, the "class of all terms" is "essential to all formal propositions" (1903, Sec.101).

Łukasiewicz observes that in the case of Russell's paradox, each of the two possibilities, i.e., that the Russell set is a member of itself or that it is not a member of itself, leads to a contradictory conclusion. One solution is to accept the contradiction and deny the principle of contradiction. The set both is and is not a member of itself. However, as Łukasiewicz points out, there is an alternative solution, which is to deny the principle of excluded third and hold that the set neither is nor is not a member of itself. Thus, Łukasiewicz concludes, Russell's paradox presents not one but two equally unacceptable solutions: "either not to follow the principle of contradiction or to discard the principle of the excluded third" (XVIII, 197).

However, Łukasiewicz does not draw the conclusion that the various paradoxes offer sufficient reasons to hold that the foundations of mathematics and logic are inconsistent, i.e., that the Russell set is and is not a member of itself or that the set of natural numbers does have parts that are and are not equal to the whole. On the one hand, he admits that the paradoxes that arise from Dedekind and Cantor's work on number theory do not have a solution (at the time of his writing) and that the foundation of mathematics may be necessarily inconsistent, on the other hand, he expresses the opinion that it may be possible to find a solution to Russell's paradox that preserves both the principle of the excluded third and the principle of contradiction (XVIII, 197).

Łukasiewicz' conclusion to his investigation of objects that are constructed through *a priori* stipulations is skeptical and inconclusive. Regarding objects that appear to be consistent, he claims that it is impossible to know "with certainty whether apparently contradiction-free objects really are such" and, in the case of a constructed objects that do contain what appear to be intrinsic contradictions, he claims that it is impossible to know "whether it will be possible to remove it [the contradiction] once and for all" from such an object (XVIII, 197). However, Łukasiewicz does not explore the conclusion that could be drawn from the positive results of his investigation, namely that there are objects that are contradictory, for example, the Russell set, and that the theoretical constructions of Cantor's and Dedekind's number theory, which aim to describe the foundations of mathematics, do generate paradoxical statements. These findings suggest that contradictions are a fundamental feature that is part of the foundation of both mathematics and logic and, thus, that a theory that can accommodate these features into a unified account cannot be expressed within the framework of a classical, Aristotelian logic. The set theoretic paradoxes, carefully explicated by Łukasiewicz, offer the strongest support his call for a re-examination of the principle of contradiction and motivate the search for a Non-Aristotelian logic that allows for contradictions to be countenanced without logical explosion. Today, they are frequently invoked by modern dialetheists as examples of true contradictions.

Commentary – Chapter XIX
The Principle of Contradiction and Reality

- Motion and Contradiction
- Logical Multiplication and Temporal Simultaneity
- Moments in Time without Duration
- Experience and Negation
- The PC and the Principle of Causation

After his discussion of abstract objects, Łukasiewicz turns to the question "whether concrete objects, such as things, conditions, phenomena, events, do contain contradictory *properties* or not" (XIX, 199). In terms of Łukasiewicz' distinction between two conceptions of what constitutes an object, concrete objects certainly are objects in the first sense—they are something and not nothing. The question now is whether proof can be found that concrete, physical objects are objects in the second and more restricted sense, i.e., that they are objects that do not contain contradictions. *Prima facie*, experience seems to show that they do not. "If there is anything that cannot be doubted," Łukasiewicz notes, "then it is this fact: that the real existing phenomena, things and their qualities do not contain contradictory properties" (XIX, 199).

The Consistency of the Observable World

It is the experience of daily life that seems to provide strong support in favor of the principle of contradiction. Ordinary objects and situations, as they are experienced through the senses in everyday interactions, appear to conform without exception to the principle of contradiction and ordinarily do not exhibit any aspects that would raise doubts about principle.

However, as Łukasiewicz points out, it had been precisely the results obtained by "the analysis of the facts of experience" and not the results obtained by an analysis of abstract concepts or the logical principle as such, which historically had provided the source for the majority of arguments against the principle of contradiction (XIX, 200).[69] Long before Aristotle even formulated his defense of the principle of contradiction, Zeno's paradoxes aimed to show that the common place observation of movement and change engenders contradictory conclusions. These conclusions, according to Zeno, show that the sensible world of change and motion is an illusion and does not exist. Movement and change are impossible. Instead, all that truly exists is the One, the unchanging (and unchangeable) sphere of being, as Zeno's teacher Parmenides famously claimed.

However, the strongest arguments for the existence of real contradictions in the world emerged in the teachings associated with Protagoras and related sensualist theories. In these accounts, what is perceived by the senses is not at all illusionary but real. Sense perception not only provides access to what is real, the senses provide the only access point to reality that is available to man. It is the sensualist arguments associated with Protagoras and his followers that Aristotle himself considered to be the most important ones and, consequently, Aristotle responded to them in greater detail than to other objections to the principle of contradiction. Łukasiewicz, too, considers the ubiquitous observation and experience of motion and change as a potentially fertile ground for the discovery of real contradictions in the actual world and sets out to analyze the logical and ontological structures of physical motion.

It is interesting to note that in this very important part of his inquiry into the principle of contradiction, Łukasiewicz returns to Hegel's argument that the phenomenon of physical movement offers a prime example of concretely existing and real contradictory states of affairs. The phenomenon of motion is also appealed to by modern dialetheists, for example Priest (1985, 1989), among others. Łukasiewicz once more cites the passage from Hegel's *Science of Logic,* which he had introduced earlier (V, 109; cf. discussion of Hegel's analysis of motion, 38 ff.). In the passage, Hegel credits the ancient philosophers with being the first to demonstrate that the phenomenon of motion contains contradictions. Hegel, of course, rejects Zeno's conclusion that "motion does not exist" and, instead, argues that "motion is the *being-present* of contradiction" (Hegel 1834, IV, 69).

Łukasiewicz' first reference to this passage occurred in his discussion of the psychological formulation of the principle of contradiction. Now, Hegel's point serves to introduce the key question of Łukasiewicz' analysis of motion: does the experience of movement and change reveal the existence of real contradictions in the perceptible world? For Łukasiewicz, the phenomenon of ordinary, concrete objects in motion presents *prima facie* the most promising area of investigation into the possibility of existing, real contradictions. "If it is possible to cast doubt on the principle of contradiction at all," he notes, "then it is in the area of concrete objects, that is, in the area of facts of experience" (XIX, 201).

Time, Change, and Contradiction

According to Łukasiewicz, the "weakest point of the principle of contradiction" is contained in the condition of the *simultaneous* presence of two contradictory states or properties (XIX, 201). For abstract and, thus, extemporal objects, this condition is expressed by the concept of logical multiplication; for concrete objects and empirical phenomena, it is expressed by temporal coincidence, i.e., simultaneity. If a contradiction were to exist concretely in reality, something has to be and not be the case at one and the same instant in time.

Sense perception shows that an object may acquire or lose properties over time and, thus, that it may have different sets of properties at different points in time. Thus, an object may acquire contradictory or contrary properties. However, it acquires the properties at different moments in time. According to Łukasiewicz, this succession of incompatible (contrary or contradictory) properties suggests the view that "time exists only so that objects and phenomena can have contradictory properties—without detriment to the principle of contradiction" (XIX, 201).

Łukasiewicz' suggestion articulates a critical response to Kant's conception of time. In Kant's account, time and space are two pure forms of sensible intuition. They are the two necessary and *a priori* conditions of cognition (Kant, A22, B36)[70] and, among the two, time is the "formal condition *a priori* of all intuition whatsoever" (Kant, A34, B50).[71] One consequence of this privileged *a priori* status of time in Kant's account is that a presentation of time is the pre-condition for an understanding of change. "The concept of change and, with it, the concept of motion (as change of location) is possible only in and through a presentation of time" (Kant, A32, B48).[72]

However, whereas for Kant, time is an *a priori* form of intuition and, thus, a necessary condition for the intuition of any phenomenon (including change or motion), Łukasiewicz' point is that the dependence relation can be reversed so that movement or change becomes a necessary condition for the existence (and cognition) of time. All movement and every change, Łukasiewicz notes, "do not merely appear to be a *measure* of time but also its *condition*" (XIX, 201).

Łukasiewicz' remark suggests a view in which time is clearly a feature of reality. The reality of time is generated by and dependent upon movement and change, rather than movement and change requiring time as a pre-condition for their existence. In this interpretation of the two accounts, Łukasiewicz' analysis is characterized by its ontological and empirical orientation whereas Kant's analysis focuses on the epistemological conditions under which cognition becomes possible. For Kant, the perception of change—and its cognitive understanding—presupposes a "presentation of time". For Łukasiewicz, the ontological presence of time—its reality and the possibility of an experience of time through the experience of motion or change—presupposes and, thus, is subsequent to the existence of movement (and, thus, the existence of objects that move or undergo change).

Nevertheless, both Kant and Łukasiewicz construct their analysis of change by presenting change and motion within a series or sequence of successive but distinct moments. At any of the moments that belong to the period (series of moments) in which an object is changing, the object has at least one property that it did not possess in the next moment. Consequently, in this presentation of change, a contradiction would arise, if two succeeding and distinct moments in which the object respectively does and does not have a property were no longer distinct and separate moments, if they were to collapse into a single moment. In that case, a contradictory state would obtain at that single moment because the object would simultaneously have and not have a property.

For Kant, change consists in "the connection of contradictorily opposed predicates (i.e., the being at one location and the not-being of the same object at the same location)" (Kant, A32, B48) and the possibility of change in one and the same object is intelligible (that is, non-contradictory) only in the form of a presentation of successive and distinct moments in time. "Only in time can both contradictorily-opposed determination be met in a thing, precisely *one after the other*" (Kant, A32, B48-49).[73]

Łukasiewicz follows Kant in his analysis of an object undergoing change as a temporal succession that separates what otherwise would result in the simultaneous possession of contradictory attributes.

> The object that is changing loses properties that it did have, and takes on new ones that it did not have. A contradiction would result in the first and in the second case if different time determinations did not exist (XIX, 201).

In the case of a continuous movement, for example, that of an arrow in flight, the arrow is always at different locations at different moments in time. However, the crucial question is: what is the location of the arrow if the distance between time moments is "is reduced to zero, if we consider only *one* instant as a non-continuous point on the time line?" (XIX, 202)

The Presentation of Motion

A common representation of a moving object at a moment of zero duration depicts the objects as 'frozen' at one position in space. At a moment of zero duration, no movement is possible since time (as duration or interval) and motion are conditions of each other. The arrow, in this representation, would accordingly no longer be in motion but fixed at a single location in space.

Łukasiewicz illustrates this representation of a world frozen in time by evoking the imagery of European fairy tales, which include the figure of the entire world magically standing still with everything remaining motionless in its place. However, it is interesting to note that during the second half of the nineteenth century, this popular type of an imaginary representation of a world in which time and motion has ceased to exist, gained additional acceptance as a veridical depiction of the actual world at a moment of zero duration through the development of high-speed photography.

The work of Eadwaerd Muybridge (1830-1904) in the United States and Étienne-Jules Marey (1830-1904) in France produced the first photographic images of moving objects without the telltale blurry edges and shadowy streaks that used to indicate of a moving object. Instead, the objects now appeared in sharp focus, frozen in time and space, and without any of the familiar indicators of movement found in earlier photographic renderings. This technological extension of the visible beyond unaided human perceptual capacity opened a previously impossible glimpse into minute details of objects in motion. Muybridge and Marey's investigations of motion through high-speed photography (together with astronomical and microscopic photographic applications) presented a first glimpse of what today is often referred to as hyper-reality; technologically enhanced renderings of the real that significantly exceed the range of what is perceptible by unaided human senses. Muybridge and Marey's technological expansion of the visible engaged the imagination of the age and fascinated audiences in Europe and the United States. Distributed widely in print and popular exhibitions, the revolutionary new visions opened by the technological advances in what then was called "chronophotography" quickly became part of the visual lexicon of the late nineteenth and early twentieth century.

However, even though the images seem to present moving objects stopped in their motion and apparently frozen in time and space, they do not depict moving objects at a point in time with zero duration. The images are recordings of light over an interval of time, a much briefer interval than what is observable by unaided human visual perception, but the photographs nevertheless present a recording of electro-chemical events during a positive interval of time. They do not present a moment of zero duration. But, for Łukasiewicz and his investigation of the problem of contradiction and motion, the question is precisely about the situation that obtains in a moment of zero duration. Both the stop-motion photographic images and the imaginary scenes depicted in fairy tales suggest that at a single point in time a moving object is precisely at a single location in space. Łukasiewicz, however, questions the assumptions that underlie this presentation of a moving object.

> How do we know that it would have to be at only *one* location? As long as it was moving, it continuously changed its location in space and, consequently, it was present at many locations even within each smallest of time-moments. Why, then, could it not also be at least at *two* different places in the not extended time-point of the transverse section, why could it not *be* at one place and also

> *not be* at that same place at the same time? (XIX, 202)

For Łukasiewicz, these questions cannot be answered because neither *a priori* considerations nor empirical observation can provide a positive account of the situation. *A priori* considerations, Łukasiewicz claims, must rely on the PC and thus involve a *petitio principii* since it is the PC (as a principle that governs the features of observable objects and states of affairs) that the investigation tries to establish or refute. An empirical investigation of what takes place at a point in time that has no duration is impossible since the state of affairs that obtains at such a moment is not (and cannot be) empirically accessible. Consequently, that the assumption that everything would be frozen in a single place at such a moment is a mere hypothesis that cannot be verified (or refuted) through observation. Perception requires temporal duration. Any perceivable object *must* exist for some period of time to be perceived.[74] However, a point in time has no duration and whatever state of affairs obtains at that point is *eo ipso* not perceptible (if perception is limited to that point in time). Thus, Łukasiewicz concludes, "we do not know what takes place in a not extended time-moment" (XIX, 202).

But does the empirical inaccessibility of a moment of zero duration establish that contradictory states of affairs cannot be observed? Why should the meaning of "simultaneously" be restricted to a single, non-extended moment in time? Observable states of affairs obtain during the course of an interval of time. *Prima facie*, there is no reason why contradictory states of affairs could not obtain simultaneously during an interval of time of sufficient length so that the contradictory states are jointly perceivable. Łukasiewicz does not consider this possibility. His analysis focuses exclusively on an investigation of the state of affairs that obtains at a single, not-extended moment of time. Such a moment, which has no duration, is an ideal object but not an observable, concrete object. It is intelligible but not perceptible. But it is precisely the consistency of perceptible reality that Łukasiewicz aims to investigate. By restricting his analysis to the state of affairs that obtains at an ideal, not-extended moment, Łukasiewicz unnecessarily forecloses on his stated goal.

In terms of Łukasiewicz' own distinction between construction objects and reconstruction objects, the question arises whether the concept of a moment without duration—the instant—presents a reconstruction aiming to capture a concrete object or an ideal and abstract construction that is independent of any empirically observable objects? If it is a reconstruction object and employed to denote concrete, empirical objects or states of affairs, then it has no referent and generates a paradoxical consequence: the constitutive parts of an extended moment of time are moments of no duration that, as empirical objects, do not exist—thus, the whole exists but its ultimate constitutive parts do not.

In light of the young Łukasiewicz' interest and admiration for the work of Alexius Meinong, it is surprising that Łukasiewicz does not explicitly draw on the analysis of not-extended moments of time and perception that Meinong developed in his influential article "*Ueber Gegenstände höherer Ordnung und deren Verhältniß zur inneren Wahrnehmung*" (On higher order objects and their relation to inner perception), which was originally published in 1899 and subjected to careful review by Bertrand Russell only a few years later (Meinong 1899; Russell 1904).

In the article, Meinong considers the paradoxical consequences that spring from the application of the concept of an ideal, not-extended moment in time to the analysis of perception. In his discussion, Meinong notes that the paradoxical consequences of a conception of the present as constituted by a not-extended moment were previously articulated by Friedrich Schumann in an article titled "Zur Psychologie der Zeitanschauung" (On the psychology of the intuition of time). Schumann argues that in ordinary language-use, the psychological moment referred to by "now", the experienced psychological present, always has a positive duration. Thus, the psychological (and, thus empirically accessible) present is a time interval that has a minimal duration (Schumann, 126). However, the introduction of a mathematical interpretation of the present moment as an instance of no duration leads to confusing and paradoxical conclusions. In this conception, "the present is supposed to be a continuously moving point that generates the timeline" (Schumann, 127).[75] According to Schumann, the interpretation of the present as a not-extended instant or point on a timeline leads to a conception of time in which

> time consists of the past and the future, which are separated by the movable point of the "now". Since the past is no longer, and the future is not yet, time would be something real that consists of

> two halves, each of which is not real (Schumann, 127).[76]

Schumann concludes that this paradoxical result shows that the application of a mathematical conception of the present is not suitable for a reconstruction (!) of reality because the mathematical point is an ideal object that has no corresponding counterpart in the empirical world.

> The mathematical point is a limit that one can get arbitrarily close to but that one cannot reach. But if one defines the concept of the present in such a manner that nothing real corresponds to it any more, then one should not be surprised if this concept is unusable for a reconstruction of reality (Schumann, 127).[77]

In passing, it is interesting to note that McTaggart's argument for the unreality of time, published only a few years after Schumann, Meinong, and Russell's discussion, also relies on a conception of time in which the present corresponds to an ideal, not-extended and moving point (or position) on a timeline (A-series) that divides past and future (McTaggart 1908). However, whereas Schumann rejects the introduction of ideal—and, thus, non-empirical—objects into the analysis of real phenomena because they generate contradictions, McTaggart famously concludes that time is not real because of the contradiction that he derives in his analysis of the (ideal or *a priori*) relation between events and the temporal ranges indicated by the past, present, and future (taken as non-relational, singular predicates) in the A-series presentation of time. The outcome of McTaggart's analysis is that

> the application of the A series to reality involves a contradiction, and that consequently the A series cannot be true of reality. And, since time involves the A series, it follows that time cannot be true of reality (McTaggart, 470)

Thus, McTaggart's conclusion relies on the realization that the ideal construction of the A-series presentation of time does not afford an acceptable reconstruction of reality since its application to reality engenders a contradiction (or, at the very least, succumbs to an infinite and vicious regress, if the contradiction is to be avoided). The underlying assumption is that anything that is contradictory cannot exist. Thus, in a move reminiscent of Zeno's rejection of the reality of motion and change, McTaggart rejects the reality of time.

Schumann, on the other hand, rejects the introduction of an ideal object, the not-extended point in time, as the reconstruction (or presentation) of an empirical object because the properties of the ideal object generate contradiction and paradox if applied to empirical phenomena. It would go beyond the scope of this discussion to pursue the details of Schumann and McTaggart's analyses of time, but the rough sketch provided gives an indication of some of the potential difficulties that arise through the use of ideal objects and, in particular, of ideal objects that denote a limit, as reconstructions of concrete objects in the analysis of concrete phenomena.

Meinong, in his response to Schumann's rejection of a not-extended moment in time, argues that Schumann goes too far in denying the existence of not-extended moments just because they are ideal objects. After all, Meinong points out, extended moments of time do exist, intervals of a certain duration, and surely they can be represented as series of non-extended moments. In Meinong's view, it is the *isolated* point, which is an ideal object that does not have concrete existence. The solution, Meinong argues, becomes clear if the distinction between being (existence) and being-so (subsistence) is brought into the analysis. "A point by itself cannot exist, but only subsist; but where a point is, something may exist, only not restricted to the point alone" (Meinong 1899, 260).[78]

Russell offers a rebuttal to Meinong's account in which he argues from the existence of time to the existence of un-extended moments of time. If the existence of time is admitted, Russell points out, then "it may be enough to argue that instants are the ultimate constituents of time, and that a whole cannot exist if none of its parts exist" (Russell 1904, 213). Meinong's argument collapses if the reality of non-extended moments of time is admitted. What can be salvaged, however, is the assumption in Meinong's argument that existent things can only be perceived "if they exist through a finite time", which, according to Russell, "is doubtless in some sense true" (Russell 1904).

In his analysis, Łukasiewicz does not give any indications that he harbors any doubts about the existence of time or the existence of un-extended moments of time. In fact, it is precisely a single, un-extended moment of time that denotes the crucial and concrete referent in his analysis of the PC:

> it is exactly this moment that concerns the principle of contradiction, because if we say that the arrow cannot *simultaneously* be and not be at the same location, then the little word 'simultaneously' refers to the *same*, that is, only *one* not extended moment (XIX, 202).

However, even if the existence of non-extended moments in time is granted, it is not obvious that Łukasiewicz' claim that nothing can be known about its content constitutes the ultimate endpoint of an investigation into the potential inconsistencies contained in and exhibited by the phenomenon of motion. Rather, the introduction of a non-extended moment as a real, concrete object introduces its own inherently contradictory aspects into the analysis.

The ideal object denoted by the term "a moment of zero duration" presents a reconstruction of contradictory object that denotes a moment of time without duration. But a moment without duration is not a moment of time at all—it is a duration of time that—by definition—is not a duration.

From a dialethic position, this is not surprising. A moment of zero duration denotes a limit.[79] Limits, as argued by Priest (1987, Ch.II), tend to be dialethic, that is, limit areas generate contradictions. The concept of a point in time with zero duration is no exception. Furthermore, this is so whether the concept of zero duration is considered as a purely abstract and theoretical concept or as a re-constructive concept in Łukasiewicz' sense, that is, as a concept that is constructed as a model of certain aspects of concrete, empirically accessible reality.

Still, Łukasiewicz concludes that since a zero time moment is neither accessible on empirical nor on theoretical, *a priori* grounds, the question of real contradictions in the phenomenon of motion is unanswerable. Just as in the case of abstract objects, there is no guarantee or demonstration that concrete objects do not contain contradictions. However, there also are no conclusive considerations that they do, just as there was no conclusive evidence that abstract objects do contain contradictions. Thus, for Łukasiewicz, the principle of contradiction is shown to have a similar cognitive ranking as the principle of sufficient reason. Its truth is not observable as an empirical fact. It is not demonstrable as a theoretical truth. But there also are no decisive reasons and considerations to deny its validity.

Finally, as a consequence of his analysis, Łukasiewicz rejects Kant's critical account of the conditions and principles of cognition. For Łukasiewicz, the determination of both the form and content of sensible experiences is exclusively a matter of *a posteriori* considerations. "There are no *a priori* and thus necessary and certain laws of experience" (XIX, 203).

Commentary – Chapter XX
The Significance of the Principle of Contradiction

Łukasiewicz considers the broader philosophical implications of the results of his analysis of the principle of contradiction. His examination has shown that the principle does not permit objective proof; Łukasiewicz' formal *a priori* proof restricts the validity of the principle to objects that are consistent by definition. Because of this feature, the formal proof does not answer the deep ontological and metaphysical questions associated with the principle. Instead, it shifts the question to the nature of objects. But, according to Łukasiewicz' analysis, no conclusive demonstration that would establish the consistency of objects is available for abstract or concrete objects. Most of Łukasiewicz' results are critical challenges to established and accepted traditional assumptions and beliefs surrounding the principle.

There is no proof that the principle of contradiction articulates the highest and most complete ontological principle. Łukasiewicz allows the possibility that the PC does express the ultimate principle of being. However, the investigation of being is primarily a matter of empirical and, therefore, *a posteriori* investigation. In this effort, *a priori* principles merely serve as tools to enable and secure knowledge about the world; they do not and cannot generate such knowledge by themselves.

In the preceding chapter, Łukasiewicz argued that even though it is not possible to prove that the PC governs empirical reality, there also is are no empirically grounded reasons to believe that it does not hold. In this sense, the PC is like the principle of causation and should be accepted as a principle that correctly describes a fundamental feature of empirically observable, concrete objects. However, it is no longer an *a priori* principle but an inductively derived *a posteriori* principle. Thus, it is defeasible. Inconsistent objects may be discovered at any moment and would have to be recognized as exception to this otherwise intact principle.

In short, the PC has no value as a fundamental logical principle (in the propositional calculus introduced in the appendix, it is a derived theorem and not an axiom). Further, it is not an ultimate object-theoretical principle. Apparently consistent abstract objects have been shown to generate contradictions and paradoxes. Observable, concrete objects appear to be universally consistent in their properties, but this is—at best—an empirical fact and, in principle, defeasible by a future observation of an object that has contradictory properties. Thus, the PC is not a secure *a priori* principle. It is also not secured with certainty (and cannot be so) as a metaphysical principle, that is, as a principle that describes a universally true feature of all empirical objects (even if it is merely an inductively justified principle).

In Łukasiewicz' view, the value of the principle of contradiction is relative to its utility in the domain to which it is applied. In the domain of logic, truth is a principal value. But without proof, the logical value of the principle of contradiction is null since it is neither demonstrably true nor demonstrably false. It has no logical value. Furthermore, with respect to statements about the actual, empirically observed world and with respect to statements about ideal and abstract obejcts, the principle of contradiction is equally valueless. As Łukasiewicz puts it:

> Those statements about which we do not know whether they are true or false do not contain any logical value as long as their truth cannot be determined. They are logically *valueless* statements. The principle of contradiction belongs to these statements insofar as we apply it to being in general, and actual being in particular. (XX, 208)

Furthermore, the principle of contradiction does not have value as an inductive generalization and scientific hypothesis. In the pursuit of scientific knowledge, the principle is without use and, thus, without value. According to Łukasiewicz,

> the principle of contradiction does not join diverse phenomena and laws into a whole nor does it order any facts at all. And we have never used it with the aim of predicting future events based on it (XX, 208).

However, the situation is dramatically different with resepect to the detection of error and lies in a domain that is part of the social world of men. In this domain, Łukasiewicz argues, the principle of contradiction is of tremendous value and significance.

Łukasiewicz notes that this result may present the "most important idea" of his investigation into the principle of contradiction:

> *the value of the principle of contradiction is not of a logical but of a practical-ethical nature: this practical-ethical value, however, is so great that the lack of logical value does not count in comparison* (XX, 209)

The great practical and ethical value of the PC is generated by the utility of the principle in the detection of errors and deceptions. This utility of the principle is especially important in cases where the determination of facts relies exclusively on witness testimony. Statements that some individual asserts to be true but for which no corroborating physical or material evidence is available, are problematic since

> it is impossible to prove such statements; only memory and the truthfulness of the speaker serve us as guarantees for them (XX, 209).

However, Łukasiewicz argues, the principle of contradiction permits the rejection of contradictory statements in practical and ethical considerations and, thus, its application is most valuable in the detection of errors or lies. Even further, Łukasiewicz argues, the principle of contradiction "is the only weapon against mistakes and lies" (XX, 210). Without the principle, errors or deliberate misrepresentations in conflicting witness statements could no longer be identified, because

> if contradictory statements were to be *reconcilable* with each other, if affirmation were *not to nullify* denial, but if the one were to be able to meaningfully co-exist next to the other, then we would have no means at our disposal to discredit falsity and unmask lies (XX, 210).

Considering Łukasiewicz' extensive and careful critical analysis of the principle of contradiction, his attempt to vindicate the principle of contradiction in the ethical domain introduces a rather unexpected turn in his exposition. But even more suprizing is the uncharacteristic weakness of his argument in support of this claim. Łukasiewicz commits the same error that he attributed to Protagoras and other opponents of the principle of contradiction in his earlier discussion (XII, 149; see also Commentary, 356). A rejection of the principle does not require a commitment to the view that all contradictory statements are reconcilable or that all affirmations nullify their corresponding denials—all that is required is the admission that there are *some* true contradictions. In that case, the principle of contradiction remains intact for sentences that have simple truth-values (i.e., that are true or false simpliciter and nothing in addition) and fails for sentences that do not.

As unsatisfactory and puzzling as it may be, Łukasiewicz' defense of the ethical and practical value of the principle of contradiction sheds light on an interesting aspect in the understanding of the principle. Without secure and independent foundations, whether *a priori* or empirically grounded, the recognition of principle's utility for ethical and practical matters is contingent on historical and social factors—a point Łukasiewicz himself acknowledges when he notes that "the practical and ethical need to recognize this principle" makes it "apparent how very relative the acceptance of this principle is" (XX, 210).

Two decades later, Conze (1932; 1934, 1937) attempts to show that historical and social conditions not only inform the adoption of ethical and moral principles but that they form important conditions for the articulation and acceptance of *a priori* claims in general, including the principle of contradiction in all its formulations.

However, Łukasiewicz' historical thesis that Aristotle—aware of the logical and ontological weakness of his account of the principle—defended the principle as a dogma to create a foundation that would provide him and his allies with an advantage in the social and political struggles of the day, remains hopelessly dependent on auxiliary hypotheses that are difficult to substantiate. Again, Łukasiewicz disregards an argument that he presented and endorsed in an earlier part of the book. He strongly objected to attempts to re-interpret Hegel's writings with the aid of auxiliary hypotheses (V, 109), but he does not hesitate to attribute sociopolitical motives to Aristotle's attempt to solidify a broad acceptance of the principle of contradiction. Łukasiewicz defends his claim by placing greater importance on the social and political turmoil of Aristotle's days than on the complexities and difficulties of Aristotle's pioneering attempt to develop a science that investigates being *qua* being. Given the careful attention and effort that Aristotle dedicates to his discussion and defense of the principle of contradiction in the *Metaphysics*, it remains doubtful, if not altogether unlikely, that Aristotle actually saw no other options than "to declare the principle of contradiction a *dogma*, and to set authoritarian limits to any destructive works" (XX, 213).

While Aristotle's principle of contradiction undoubtedly evolved into one of the most persistent dogmas in the Western tradition, the transformation of Aristotle's theory into a dogma was almost certainly not the result of Aristotle's efforts as a philosopher. Rather, it was the result of the work of later generations of philosophers and interpreters, which created and enshrined the figure and authority of Aristotle as "the philosopher" over centuries and millennia to come.

What does emerge from the text of the *Metaphysics* and other writings is that Aristotle thought that the principle of contradiction presents the first and ultimate, unprovable and most secure *arche* of a newly conceived science—the science that investigates being *qua* being. Aristotle believed that there is no contradictory being.

Being *qua* being, in all its modalities, is consistent, or it is not being. And he tried to demonstrate that a denial of this truth about the nature of being leads to utterly unacceptable consequence. In this effort, Aristotle employed all his skill and ability to convince his followers, students, sympathizers, critics, and opponents alike, that this is the case. What he does not do, however, is to simply assert the truth of his arche as a dogma to be accepted on his authority alone. That was the work of later generations of philosophers, who created and fostered dogmatic belief in Aristotle's teachings.

Aristotle's arguments and reasons in support of his metaphysical principle of being *qua* being may not succeed in convincing his opponents or skeptics, but they present the philosopher's attempt to unravel the mysteries of being. At times, Aristotle may be struggling with the complexity of his subject matter on one hand and the eristic sophistries of his oppenents on the other, but his struggles with the subject matter of being are first and foremost those of a philosopher—his personal concerns about the political and social fabric of the Hellenic world may or may not be part of the subtext of the *Metaphysics*, but they are hardly part of the issues that Aristotle is trying to address and solve in this work.

The strength and accomplishment of Łukasiewicz' analysis emerges from his analytic approach to the questions surrounding the principle of contradiction. In Łukasiewicz' critique, analytic precision and mathematical rigor combine with a deep reading of Aristotle's original attempt. The result is a pathbreaking effort to end the blind acceptance of a "scientific dogma" and to open up a first glimpse at "the strange construction of this principle in complete and truthful illumination" (XX, 213).

But, perhaps, Łukasiewicz' greatest achievement in his 1910 work springs from Łukasiewicz' genius in the combination of historical and analytic insight: his prediction of a "third moment" (Introduction, 80) in the understanding of the principle of contradiction—an understanding that combines and completes the achievements of both Aristotle and Hegel. An understanding that builds on the realization that both Aristotle and Hegel's contributions contain the building blocks of a more comprehensive, subtle, and penetrating theory of the principle of contradiction.

Bibliography

Albertazzi, Liliana 1993. Brentano, Twardowski, and Polish Scientific Philosophy. In *Polish Scientific Philosophy: The Lvov-Warsaw School. Edited by Francesco Coniglione, Roberto Poli, and Jan Woleński.* . Amsterdam: Rodopi.

Andreas, Antonius. 1481. *Quaestiones subtilissimae super duodecim libris metaphysicae Aristotelis*. Venice.

----------. 1523. *Questiones Antonij Andree super XII libros metaphysice : nouissime diligenti examine recognite ; ac nouis additionibus textuum ; alijsque quampluribus postillis in margine decorate ; addita tabula alphabetica, que omnes principales quamomnes, et incidentes propositiones recto ordine monstrat.* Venetijs: F. Pauli Nicolai Serrani.

Anscombe, G.E.M.. 1961. Aristotle. In *Three Philosophers*, edited by P. T. Geach. Oxford: Basil Blackwell.

Aristotle. 1933-35. *The Metaphysics*. Translated by H. Tredennick. 2 vols, *Loeb Classical Library*. London: William Heinemann, Ltd.

----------. 1992. Categories. Translated by J. L. Ackrill. In *Aristotle: The Complete Works. Electronic edition of The Complete Works of Aristotle. BOLLINGEN SERIES LXXI · Volume I*: InteLex Corporation.

----------. 1992. De Anima. Translated by J.A. Smith. In *Aristotle: The Complete Works. Electronic edition of The Complete Works of Aristotle. BOLLINGEN SERIES LXXI · Volume II*: InteLex Corporation.

----------. 1992. De Interpretatione. Translated by J. L. Ackrill. In *Aristotle: The Complete Works. Electronic edition of The Complete Works of Aristotle. BOLLINGEN SERIES LXXI · Volume I*: InteLex Corporation.

----------. 1992. Metaphysics. Translated by D. Ross. In *Aristotle: The Complete Works. Electronic edition of The Complete Works of Aristotle. BOLLINGEN SERIES LXXI · Volume*

II: InteLex Corporation.
----------. 1992. Posterior Analytics. Translated by Jonathan Barnes. In *Aristotle: The Complete Works. Electronic edition of The Complete Works of Aristotle. BOLLINGEN SERIES LXXI · Volume I*: InteLex Corporation.
----------. 1992. Prior Analytics. Translated by A. J. Jenkinson. In *Aristotle: The Complete Works. Electronic edition of The Complete Works of Aristotle. BOLLINGEN SERIES LXXI · Volume I*: InteLex Corporation.
Arruda, Ayda I. 1989. Aspects of the Historical Development of Paraconsistent Logic. In *Paraconsistent Logic : Essays on the Inconsistent*, edited by G. Priest, Richard Routley, Jean Norman. München: Philosophia.
Austin, J.L. 1975 [1955]. *How to do things with words*. 2nd ed, *William James Lectures; 1955*. Oxford: Clarendon Press.
Bach, Kent, and Robert M. Harnish. 1979. *Linguistic communication and speech acts*. Cambridge, MS: MIT Press.
Bain, Alexander. 1870. *Logic. Parts First and Second: Deduction and Induction*. 1st ed. London: Longmans, Green, Reader and Dyer.
Barnes, Jonathan 1969. The Law of Contradiction. *The Philosophical Quarterly* 19 (77):302-309.
Bazhanov, Valentine A. 1990. The Fate of One Forgotten Idea: N.A. Vasil'év and His Imaginary Logic. *Studies in Soviet Thought* 39 (3/4):333-341.
Betti, Arianna 2010. The Incomplete Story of Łukasiewicz and Bivalence. http://segrdid2.fmag.unict.it/~polphil/PolPhil/Lukas/LukasBival.pdf.
Betti, Arianna, Maria van der Schaar. 2004. The Road from Vienna to Lvov. Twardowski's Theory of Judgment between 1894 and 1897. *Grazer Philosophische Studien* 67:1-20.
Bizoń, M. 1942. *Der Ursprung der Logik. Für Ingenieure, Techniker und andere Berufe in 10 Lektionen, die von Prof. Jan Łukasiewicz in Warschau in der Zeit vom 1. bis 20. Juli 1942 gehalten wurden*. Katowice: Biuro Handlowo-Montażowe.
Brandis, Christian August. 1836. *Scholia in Aristotelem*. Berolini: Reimer.
Brentano, Franz. 1956. *Die Lehre vom richtigen Urteil*. Edited by

F. Mayer-Hillebrand. Bern: Francke Verlag.

----------. 1995 [1874]. *Psychology from an Empirical Standpoint* Translated by A. C. Rancurello, D. B. Terrell and Linda L. McAlister. Edited by L. L. McAlister. London: Routledge. Original edition, *Psychologie vom Empirischen Standpunkt*, Leibzig: Meiner, 1924-25.

Brockhaus, Richard R. 1991. Realism and Psychologism in 19th Century Logic. *Philosophy and Phenomenological Research* 51 (3):493-524.

Burge, Tyler. 1978. Self-Reference and Translation. In *Meaning and Translation. Philosophical and Linguistic Approaches.*, edited by F. Guenthner, and M. Guenthner-Reutter. New York: New York University Press.

Calvert, Brian. 1976. Aristotle and the Megarians on the Potentiality-Actuality Distinction. *Apeiron: A Journal for Ancient Philosophy and Science* 10 (1):34-41.

Case, Thomas. 2008. *Article on Logic, Encyclopedia Britannica, 1911* [Web Page]. Edward Buckner 2005 [1911] [cited August 16 2008]. Available from http://uk.geocities.com/frege@btinternet.com/cantor/Logic1911.htm.

Cocchiarella, Nino B. 1987. *Logical Studies in Early Analytic Philosophy*. Columbus, OH: Ohio State University Press.

Conze, Eberhard 1932. *Der Satz vom Widerspruch. Zur Theorie des dialektischen Materialismus*. Hamburg.

Conze, Edward. 1934. Social Implications of Logical Thinking. *Proceedings of the Aristotelean Society* XXXV (1934-5):23-44.

----------. 1937. Social Origins of Nominalism. *Marxist Quarterly* 1 (1):115-124.

----------. 2016 [1932]. *The Principle of Contradiction. On the Theory of Dialetical Materialism*. Translated by H. Heine. Langham, MD: Lexington Books. Original edition, Der Satz vom Widerspruch (1932).

Couturat, Louis. 1905. *L'algèbre de la logique*, *Scientia, Phys. Math. 24*. Paris: Gauthiers-Villars.

----------. 1914. *The Algebra of Logic*. Translated by L. G. Robinson. Chicago: Open Court Publishing Company. Original edition, *L'algèbre de la logique.* Paris: Scientia, 1905.

Cresswell, M J. 2003. Non-Contradiction and Substantial

Predication. *Theoria: A Swedish Journal of Philosophy* 69 (3):166-183.

Dancy, R. M. . 1975. *Sense and Contradiction: A Study in Aristotle*. Dordrecht, Holland: D. Reidel Publishing Company.

Davis, Paul K. 1999. *100 Decisive Battles from Ancient Times to the Present: The World's Major Battles and How They Shaped History* Oxford: Oxford University Press.

de Morgan, Augustus. 1868. Review of a book on geometry. *Athenaeum* 2:71.

Dedekind, Richard. 1888. *Was sind und was sollen die Zahlen?* Braunschweig: Vieweg.

----------. 1995. *What Are Numbers and What Should They Be?* Translated by H. Pogorzelski, W. Ryan & W. Snyder. Orono, ME: Research Institute for Mathematics. Original edition, Dedekind (1888). *Was sind und sollen die Zahlen?*

Denyer, Nicholas. 1991. *Language, thought, and falsehood in ancient Greek philosophy*. London ; New York: Routledge.

Descartes, René. 1968 [1641]. *Discourse on method ; and the Meditations / Descartes ; translated with an introduction by F.E. Sutcliffe.* Harmondsworth, England: Penguin Books.

Diels, Hermann ed. 1901. *Fragmente : Griechisch und deutsch / Herakleites von Ephesos.* Berlin: Weidmann.

Ferreirós, José 2001. The Road to Modern Logic-An Interpretation. *The Bulletin of Symbolic Logic* 7 (4):441-484.

Frege, Gottlob. 1879. *Begriffsschrift: eine der arithmetischen nachgebildete Formelsprache des reinen Denkens*. Halle: L. Nebert.

----------. 1966 [1892]. On sense and reference. In *Translations from the Philosophical Writings of Gottlob Frege*, edited by P. Geach, and Max Black. Oxford: Basil Blackwell. Original edition, *Zeitschrift für Philosophie und philosophische Kritik*, Vol.100 (1892), 25-50.

Fries, Jakob Friedrich. 1811. *Grundriss der Logik*. Heidelberg: Mohr und Zimmer.

Gabryl, Franciszek. 1903. *Metafizyka ogólna czyli Nauka o bycie.* Kraków: Księgarnia Spółki Wydawniczej Polskiej.

Goethe, Johann Wolfgang von. 1990 [1828-29]. *Faust : eine*

Tragödie. Erster Teil. Edited by O. Pnowier. Berlin: Fischer.

Grim, Patrick. 2004. What is a Contradiction? In *The Law of Non-Contradiction. New Philosophical Essays*, edited by G. Priest, J.C. Beall and Bradley Armour-Garb. Oxford and New York Oxford University Press.

Guthrie, William Keith Chambers 1979. *A History of Greek Philosophy 3: The Fifth-Century enlightenment.* Cambridge: Cambridge University Press.

Haack, Susan. 1974. *Deviant Logic. Some philosophical issues.* Cambridge: Cambridge University Press.

Halper, Edward. 1984. Aristotle on the Extension of Non-Contradiction. *History of Philosophy Quarterly* 1 (4):369-380.

Hart, W. D. 1970. On self-reference. *Philosophical Review* 79:523-528.

Hegel, Georg Wilhelm Friedrich. 1833. *Wissenschaft der Logik. Erster Theil: Die objektive Logik.* Edited by L. v. Henning, *Werke.* Berlin: Duncker und Humblot.

----------. 1834. *Wissenschaft der Logik.* Edited by L. v. Henning. Vol. 4, *Georg Wilhelm Friedrich Hegel's Werke / Vollständige Ausgabe durch einen Verein von Freunden des Verewigten: Ph. Marheineke, J. Schulze, Ed. Gans, Lp. v. Henning, H. Hotho, K. Michelet, F. Förster.* Berlin Duncker und Humblot.

----------. 1892. *The Logic of Hegel. Translated from the Encyclopaedia of the Philosophical Sciences.* Translated by W. Wallace. 2nd ed. Oxford: Oxford University Press. Original edition, 1873.

Heine, Holger. 2016. Aristotle, Marx, Buddha: Edward Conze's Critique of the Principle of Contradiction. In Conze (2016), *The Principle of Contradiction.* Lanham, MD: Lexington Books.

Höfler, Alois, Alexius Meinong. 1890. *Logik, Philosophische Propaedeutik.* Prag: Tempsky.

Horae diurnae Breviarii romani. 1886. Mechliniae.

Husik, Isaac. 1906. Aristotle on the Law of Contradiction and the Basis of the Syllogism. *Mind* 15 (58):215-222.

Husserl, Edmund. 1900. *Logische Untersuchungen : Theil 1, Prolegomena zur reinen Logik.* Halle a.S.: Niemeyer.

Kant, Immanuel. 1976 [1787]. *Kritik der reinen Vernunft. Nach der ersten und zweiten Original-Ausgabe neu herausgegeben von Raymund Schmidt.* Durchgesehener Nachdruck der 14. Auflage (1930) ed, *Philosophische Bibliothek Band 37a.* Hamburg: Felix Meiner.

Kirwan, Christopher. 1993. *Aristotle. Metaphysics. Books Γ, Δ, and E. Translated with Notes by Christopher Kirwan.* Translated by C. Kirwan. 2nd ed. Oxford: Clarendon Press. Original edition, 1971.

Kleinpeter, Hans 1905. *Die Erkenntnistheorie der Naturforschung der Gegenwart.* Leipzig: Barth.

Kneale, W. C., and Martha Kneale. 1962. *The Development of Logic.* Oxford: Oxford University Press.

Kusch, Martin. *Psychologism* [Website] 2007 [cited July 23, 2008. Available from http://plato.stanford.edu/entries/psychologism/.

Laertius, Diogenes. 1925. *Lives of eminent philosophers.* Translated by R. D. Hicks. London: Heinemann.

Lear, Jonathan. 1980. *Aristotle and logical theory.* Cambridge: Cambridge University Press.

Long, Herbert S. 1972. Introduction. In *Diogenes Laertius. Lives of eminent philosophers.* Cambridge, MA: Harvard University Press.

Łukasiewicz, Jan. 1903. O indukcji jako inwersji dedukcji (On Induction as Inversion of Deduction); repr. in Łukasiewicz 1998, pp. 203–227. *Przegląd Filozoficzny* 6:9-24, 138-152.

----------. 1910. O zasadie wyłączonego środka. *Przegląd Filozoficzny* 8:372-373.

----------. 1910. *O zasadzie sprezeczności u Arystotelesa. Studium krytyczne. (On the Principle of Contradiction in Aristotle. A Critical Study).* Kraków: Polska Akademia Umiejętności.

----------. 1910. Über den Satz des Widerspruchs bei Aristoteles. *Bulletin International de l'Académie de Sciences de Cracovie, Cl. d'histoire et de philosophie.*

----------. 1912. O twórczości w nauce. *Księga pamiątkowa ku uczczeniu 250 rocznicy założenia Uniwersytetu Lwowskiego, Lwów:*1-15.

----------. 1934. Z historii logiki zdań. *Przegląd Filozoficzny* 37:417-437.

----------. 1935. Zur Geschichte der Aussagenlogik. *Erkenntnis*

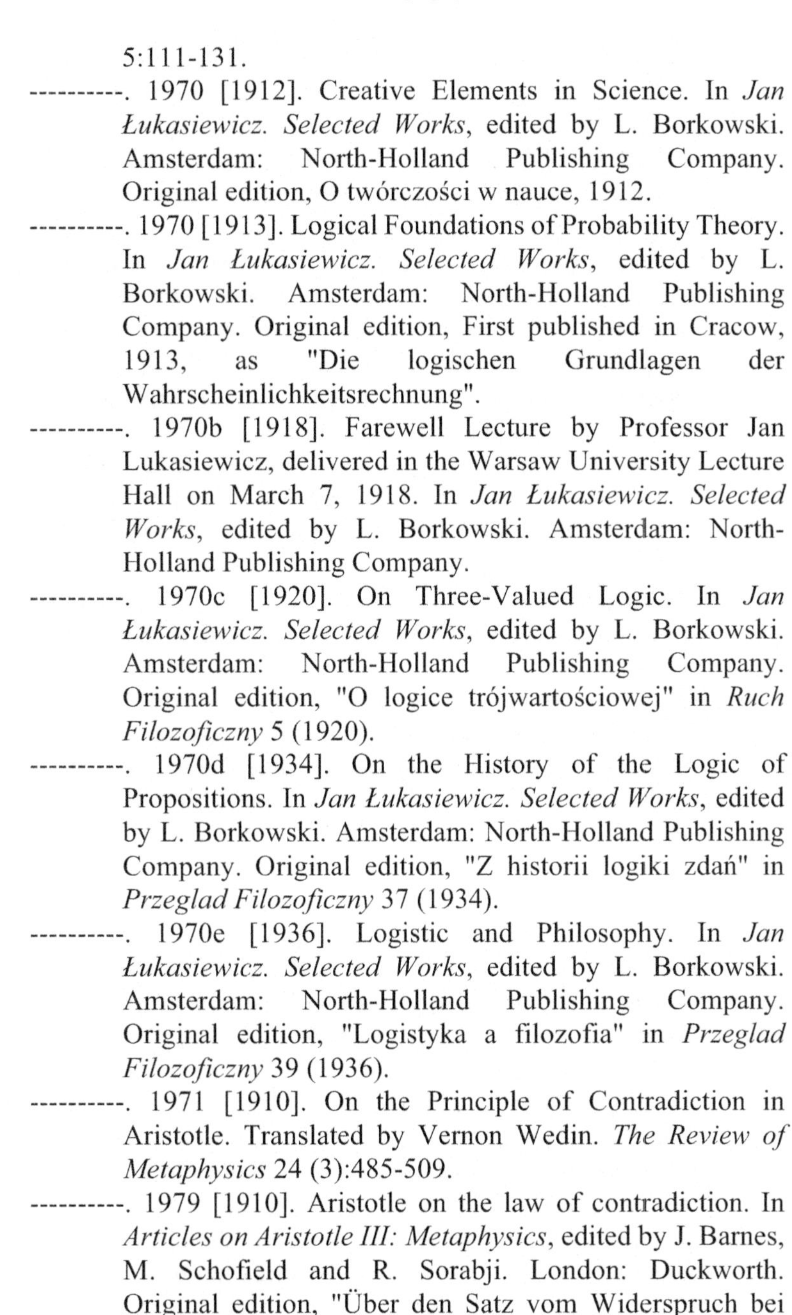

5:111-131.

----------. 1970 [1912]. Creative Elements in Science. In *Jan Łukasiewicz. Selected Works*, edited by L. Borkowski. Amsterdam: North-Holland Publishing Company. Original edition, O twórczości w nauce, 1912.

----------. 1970 [1913]. Logical Foundations of Probability Theory. In *Jan Łukasiewicz. Selected Works*, edited by L. Borkowski. Amsterdam: North-Holland Publishing Company. Original edition, First published in Cracow, 1913, as "Die logischen Grundlagen der Wahrscheinlichkeitsrechnung".

----------. 1970b [1918]. Farewell Lecture by Professor Jan Lukasiewicz, delivered in the Warsaw University Lecture Hall on March 7, 1918. In *Jan Łukasiewicz. Selected Works*, edited by L. Borkowski. Amsterdam: North-Holland Publishing Company.

----------. 1970c [1920]. On Three-Valued Logic. In *Jan Łukasiewicz. Selected Works*, edited by L. Borkowski. Amsterdam: North-Holland Publishing Company. Original edition, "O logice trójwartościowej" in *Ruch Filozoficzny* 5 (1920).

----------. 1970d [1934]. On the History of the Logic of Propositions. In *Jan Łukasiewicz. Selected Works*, edited by L. Borkowski. Amsterdam: North-Holland Publishing Company. Original edition, "Z historii logiki zdań" in *Przeglad Filozoficzny* 37 (1934).

----------. 1970e [1936]. Logistic and Philosophy. In *Jan Łukasiewicz. Selected Works*, edited by L. Borkowski. Amsterdam: North-Holland Publishing Company. Original edition, "Logistyka a filozofia" in *Przeglad Filozoficzny* 39 (1936).

----------. 1971 [1910]. On the Principle of Contradiction in Aristotle. Translated by Vernon Wedin. *The Review of Metaphysics* 24 (3):485-509.

----------. 1979 [1910]. Aristotle on the law of contradiction. In *Articles on Aristotle III: Metaphysics*, edited by J. Barnes, M. Schofield and R. Sorabji. London: Duckworth. Original edition, "Über den Satz vom Widerspruch bei Aristoteles", *Bulletin international de l'Académie des Sciences*, Cracovie (1910).

----------. 1987. *O zasadzie sprezeczności u Arystotelesa. Studium krytyczne. (On the Principle of Contradiction in Aristotle. A Critical Study)*. Edited by J. Woleński. 2nd ed. Warsaw: PWN.

----------. 1987 [1910]. On the Principle of the Excluded Middle. Translated by Jan Woleński and Peter Simons. *History and Philosophy of Logic* 8 (1):67-69.

----------. 1993. *Über den Satz des Widerspruchs bei Aristoteles. Aus dem Polnischen übersetzt von Jacek Barski. Mit einem Vorwort zur Neuausgabe von J. M. Bocheński.* Translated by J. Barski. Edited by N. Öffenberger. Vol. Band V, *Zur modernen Deutung derAristotelischen Logik*. Hildesheim: Georg Olms Verlag. Original edition, 1910.

----------. 2000. *Du principe de contradiction chez Aristote. Traduit du polonais par Dorota Sikora. Préface de Roger Pouivet.* Translated by D. Sikora. Paris: Éditions de L'Éclat. Original edition, 1910.

Mahoney, Edward P. 1988. Aristotle as "The Worst Natural Philosopher" (*pessimus naturalis*) and "The Worst Metaphysician" (*pessimus metaphysicus*): His Reputation among Some Franciscan Philosophers (Bonaventure, Francis of Meyronnes, Antonius Andreas, and Joannes Canonicus) and Later Reactions. In *Die Philosophie im 14. und 15. Jahrhundert*, edited by K. Michalski, Olaf Pluta, Oël Biard. Amsterdam: John Benjamins Publishing Company.

Maier, Heinrich. 1896. *Die Syllogistik des Aristoteles*. (3 Theile) 2 vols. Tübingen: Laupp.

----------. 1969. *Die Syllogistik des Aristoteles*. Reprographischer Nachdruck ed. (3 Teile) 2 vols. Hildesheim: Olms.

Mares, Edwin D. 2004. Semantic Dialetheism. In *The Law of Non-Contradiction. New Philosophical Essays*, edited by G. Priest, JC Beall, and Bradley Armour-Garb. Oxford: Clarendon Press.

McTaggart, John Ellis. 1908. The Unreality of Time. *Mind* 17 (68):456-473.

Meinong, Alexius. 1899. Ueber Gegenstände höherer Ordnung und deren Verhältnizur inneren Wahrnehmung. *Zeitschrift für Psychologie und Physiologie der Sinnesorgane* 21:182-272.

----------. 1902. *Über Annahmen, Zeitschrift für Psychologie und Physiologie der Sinnesorgane / Ergänzungsband ; 2.*

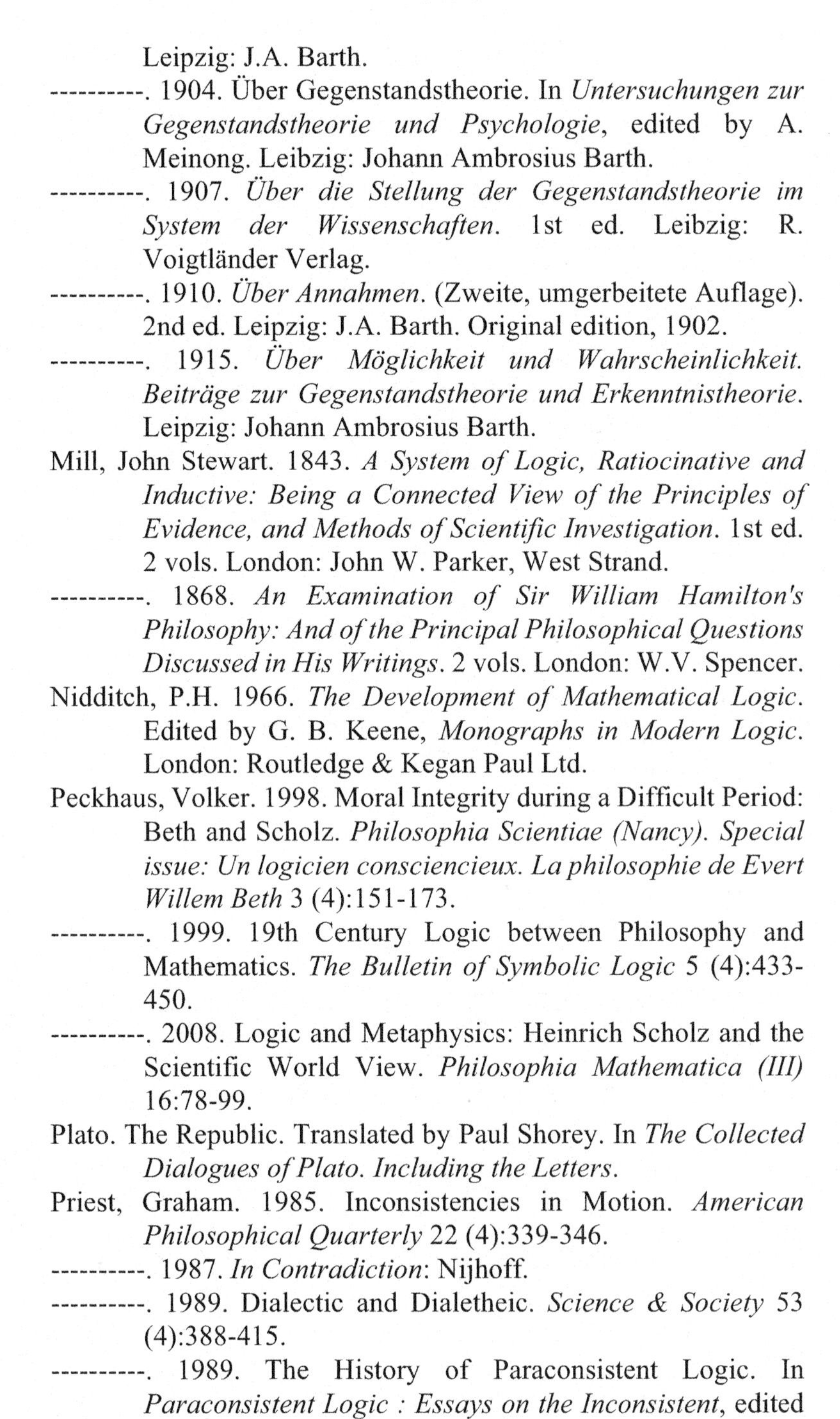

Leipzig: J.A. Barth.

----------. 1904. Über Gegenstandstheorie. In *Untersuchungen zur Gegenstandstheorie und Psychologie*, edited by A. Meinong. Leibzig: Johann Ambrosius Barth.

----------. 1907. *Über die Stellung der Gegenstandstheorie im System der Wissenschaften*. 1st ed. Leibzig: R. Voigtländer Verlag.

----------. 1910. *Über Annahmen*. (Zweite, umgerbeitete Auflage). 2nd ed. Leipzig: J.A. Barth. Original edition, 1902.

----------. 1915. *Über Möglichkeit und Wahrscheinlichkeit. Beiträge zur Gegenstandstheorie und Erkenntnistheorie*. Leipzig: Johann Ambrosius Barth.

Mill, John Stewart. 1843. *A System of Logic, Ratiocinative and Inductive: Being a Connected View of the Principles of Evidence, and Methods of Scientific Investigation*. 1st ed. 2 vols. London: John W. Parker, West Strand.

----------. 1868. *An Examination of Sir William Hamilton's Philosophy: And of the Principal Philosophical Questions Discussed in His Writings*. 2 vols. London: W.V. Spencer.

Nidditch, P.H. 1966. *The Development of Mathematical Logic*. Edited by G. B. Keene, *Monographs in Modern Logic*. London: Routledge & Kegan Paul Ltd.

Peckhaus, Volker. 1998. Moral Integrity during a Difficult Period: Beth and Scholz. *Philosophia Scientiae (Nancy). Special issue: Un logicien consciencieux. La philosophie de Evert Willem Beth* 3 (4):151-173.

----------. 1999. 19th Century Logic between Philosophy and Mathematics. *The Bulletin of Symbolic Logic* 5 (4):433-450.

----------. 2008. Logic and Metaphysics: Heinrich Scholz and the Scientific World View. *Philosophia Mathematica (III)* 16:78-99.

Plato. The Republic. Translated by Paul Shorey. In *The Collected Dialogues of Plato. Including the Letters*.

Priest, Graham. 1985. Inconsistencies in Motion. *American Philosophical Quarterly* 22 (4):339-346.

----------. 1987. *In Contradiction*: Nijhoff.

----------. 1989. Dialectic and Dialetheic. *Science & Society* 53 (4):388-415.

----------. 1989. The History of Paraconsistent Logic. In *Paraconsistent Logic : Essays on the Inconsistent*, edited by G. Priest, Richard Routley, Jean Norman. München: Philosophia.

----------. 1995. *Beyond the Limits of Thought*. Cambridge: Cambridge University Press.

----------. 2000. Truth and Contradiction. *The Philosophical Quarterly* 50 (200):305-319.

----------. 2000. Vasil'év and Imaginary Logic. *History and Philosophy of Logic* 21:135-146.

----------. 2001. *An Introduction to Non-Classical Logic / Graham Priest*. Cambridge: Cambridge University Press.

----------. 2006. *Doubt Truth to be a Liar*. First paperback, 2008 ed. Oxford: Clarendon Press.

----------. 2008 [2006]. *Doubt Truth to be a Liar*. First paperback, 2008 ed. Oxford: Clarendon Press.

Raspa, Venanzio. 1999. Lukasiewicz on the Principle of Contradiction. *Journal of Philosophical Research* XXIV:57-112.

Redding, Paul. 2007. *Analytic Philosophy and the Return of Hegelian Thought*. Cambridge: Cambridge University Press.

Richards, John. 1980. Boole and Mill: differing perspectives on logical psychologism. *History and Philosophy of Logic* 1 (1-2):19-36.

Ross, W. D. (William David). 1924. *Aristotle's Metaphysics : a revised text / with introduction and commentary by W.D. Ross*. 2 vols. Vol. 1. Oxford: Clarendon Press.

Ross, W.D. 1949. *Aristotle*. 5th ed. London: Methuen.

Russell, Bertrand. 1903. *The Principles of Mathematics*. Vol. 1. Cambridge: University Press.

----------. 1904. Meinong's Theory of Complexes and Assumptions (I.). *Mind* 13 (50):204-219.

----------. 1905. Review: Untersuchungen zur Gegenstandstheorie und Psychologie. *Mind* 14 (56):530-538.

----------. 1922. Introduction. In *Tractatus logico-philosophicus / by Ludwig Wittgenstein*. London: Kegan Paul, Trench, Trubner & Co.

----------. 1992 [1937]. *The Principles of Mathematics*. 2nd ed. London: Routledge. Original edition, 1903.

Schaff, Philip. 1877. *The creeds of Christendom : with a history and critical notes*. 2 vols. New York: Harper.

Schmidt am Busch, Hans-Christoph and Wehmeier, Kai F. 2007.

On the relations between Heinrich Scholz and Jan Łukasiewicz. *History and Philosophy of Logic* 28 (1):67-81.

Schröder, Ernst. 1890–1905. *Vorlesungen über die Algebra der Logik*. 3 vols. Leipzig: B.G. Teubner.

Schumann, Friedrich. 1898. Zur Psychologie der Zeitanschauung. *Zeitschrift für Psychologie und Physiologie der Sinnesorgane* 17:106-148.

Schwegler, Albert 1847. *Die Metaphysik des Aristoteles : Grundtext, Übersetzung und Kommentar nebst Anmerkungen*. 3 vols. Tübingen: Fues.

----------. 1960-1968. *Die Metaphysik des Aristoteles : Grundtext, Übersetzung und Kommentar nebst Anmerkungen*. Unveränderter Nachdruck ed. 2 vols. Frankfurt/Main: Minerva.

Seuren, Pieter A. M. 2005. Eubulides as a 20th-century semanticist. *Language Sciences* 27:75-95.

Sigwart, Christoph. 1873-78. *Logik*. 2 vols. Tübingen: Laupp.

----------. 1889. *Die Lehre vom Urteil, vom Begriff und vom Schluss*. 4th ed. 2 vols. Vol. 1, *Logik*. Tübingen: Mohr.

----------. 1895 [1873]. *Logic. Vol.1. The Judgment, Concept, and Inference*. Translated by H. Dendy. 2nd ed. London: Swan Sonnenschein & Co. Original edition, Logik, 1873.

----------. 2001 [1873]. *Logic*. Translated by H. Dendy. 2 vols, *reprinted from the 1895 edition*. Bristol: Thoemmes Press.

Simons, Peter M. 1989. Lukasiewicz, Meinong and many-valued logic. In *The Vienna Circle and the Lvov-Warsaw School*, edited by K. Szaniawski. Dortrecht: Kluwer.

----------. 2009. Twardowski on Truth. *The Baltic International Yearbook of Cognition, Logic and Communication* 4:1-14.

Słupeki, J. 1970. Foreword to Jan Łukasiewicz. Selected Works. In *Jan Łukasiewicz. Selected Works*, edited by L. Borkowski. Amsterdam: North-Holland Publishing Company.

Stcherbatsky, Theodore. 1930. *Buddhist Logic*. 2 vols. Vol. 1, *Bibliotheca Buddhica*. Leningrad: Akad. Nauk.

Trendelenburg, Friedrich Adolf. 1840. *Logische Untersuchungen*. 2 vols. Berlin: Bethge.

----------. 1842. Zur Geschichte von Hegel's Logik und dialektischer Methode. Die logische Frage in Hegel's System. Eine Aufforderung zu ihrer wissenschaftlichen

Erledigung. *Neue Jenaische Allgemeine Literaturzeitung* 1 (97 ff. April 1842):pp. 405-414.

----------. 1843. Zur Geschichte von Hegel's Logik und dialektischer Methode. Die logische Frage in Hegel's System. Eine Aufforderung zu ihrer wissenschaftlichen Erledigung. *Neue Jenaische Allgemeine Literaturzeitung* 1 (45 ff. February 1843).

----------. 1843a. *Die logische Frage in Hegel's System: zwei Streitschriften*. Leipzig: F.A. Brockhaus.

----------. 1870. *Logische Untersuchungen*. 3rd ed. 2 vols. Leipzig: Hirzel.

Twardowski, Kazimierz. 1894/5. Logik. Vienna: Vienna University Archive.

----------. 1977 [1894]. *On the Content and Object of Presentations*. Edited by R. Grossman. The Hague: Nijhoff. Original edition, *Lehre vom Inhalt und Gegenstand der Vorstellungen*, 1894. .

----------. 1999 [1900]. On So-Called Relative Truths. In *On Actions, Products and Other Topics in Philosophy*, edited by J. Brandl, Jan Wolenski. Amsterdam: Rodopi. Original edition, 1900.

Ueberweg, Friedrich. 1857. *System der Logik und Geschichte der logischen Lehren*. Bonn: Marcus.

----------. 1871. *System of Logic and History of Logical Doctrines*. Translated by T. M. Lindsay. London: Longmans, Green & Co.

----------. 1882. *System der Logik und Geschichte der logischen Lehren*. Edited by J. B. Meyer. 5th ed. Bonn: Marcus.

----------. 2001. *System of logic and history of logical doctrines*. Translated by T. M. Lindsay. Bristol: Thoemmes Press. Original edition, *System der Logik und Geschichte der logischen Lehren,* 1857.

Upton, Thomas V. 1983. Psychological and Metaphysical Dimensions of Non-Contradiction in Aristotle. *The Review of Metaphysics* 36 (3):591-606.

Vasil'év, Nicolas. 1910. On particular propositions, on the law of the excluded fourth, and on the triangle of opposites. *Scientific papers of Kazan University*: (As cited by Vasil'év 1993b).

----------. 1912. Imaginary (non-Axistotelian) logic. *Journal of the Ministry of Public Education, St. Petersbourg*: (As cited by Vasil'év 1993b).

----------. 1912-1913. Logica i Métalogica. *£ogos* 1912-1913 (Bd 1-2):53-81.

----------. 1993b. Imaginary (Non-Aristotelian) Logic. *Axiomathes* 4:353-55.

Venn, John. 1894. *Symbolic logic* 2nd, revised and rewritten ed. London: Macmillan.

Whitaker, C. W. A. . 1996. *Aristotle's De Interpretatione. Contradiction and Dialectic*. Edited by J. Annas, and Lindsay Judson, *Oxford Aristotle Studies*. Oxford: Clarendon Press.

Whitehead, Alfred North, and Russell, Bertrand. 1910-1913. *Principia mathematica*. 3 vols. Cambridge: University Press.

Wittgenstein, Ludwig. 1922. *Tractatus logico-philosophicus / by Ludwig Wittgenstein ; with an introduction by Bertrand Russell*. London: Kegan Paul, Trench, Trubner & Co.

Woleński, Jan. 1989. *Logic and philosophy in the Lvov-Warsaw school*. Edited by J. Hintikka. Vol. 198, *Synthese library*. Dordrecht: Kluwer.

----------. 2000. Jan Łukasiewicz und der Satz vom Widerspruch. In *Beiträge zum Satz vom Widerspruch und zur Aristotelischen Prädikationstheorie*, edited by N. Öffenberger. Hildesheim: Georg Olms Verlag.

----------. 2008. Mathematical Logic in Warsaw: 1918-1939. In *Andrzej Mostowski and foundational studies*, edited by A. Ehrenfeucht, Wiktor Marek, and Marian Srebrny. Amsterdam: IOS Press.

Woleński, Jan & Joseph Agassi. 2010. Łukasiewicz and Popper on Induction. *History & Philosophy of Logic* 31 (4):381-388.

Wundt, Wilhelm. 1893. *Erkenntnislehre*. 2nd, revised ed. 2 vols. Vol. 1, *Logik. Eine Untersuchung der Principien der Erkenntnis und der Methoden wissenschaftlicher Forschung* Stuttgart: Enke.

Contributors

Jan Łukasiewicz (1878–1956) was a Polish logician and philosopher. He produced pioneering works in mathematical logic, the history of logic, and the philosophy of logic. He was an innovative thinker who contributed to the understanding of traditional propositional logic, Aristotle's syllogistic, and foundational principles of logic like the principle of non-contradiction and the law of the excluded third. Among his greatest achievements was the development of one of the first formalized systems of many-valued logic. As a historian of logic, Łukasiewicz approached the history of logic from the standpoint of modern formal logic. He is regarded as one of the most important historians of logic of the twentieth century.

Graham Priest has held chairs of philosophy in Australia, the United Kingdom, and the United States, as well as many visiting positions at universities in Europe and Asia. He is currently Distinguished Professor of Philosophy at the Graduate Center, City University of New York, Boyce Gibson Professor Emeritus at the University of Melbourne, and International Research Fellow at the Ruhr University of Bochum.

Holger Heine is a philosopher and historian of philosophy specializing in the history of the principle of contradiction and the emergence of early conceptions of non-classical logic during the late nineteenth and early twentieth century. He is the author of a translation of Edward Conze's 1932 work *The Principle of Contradiction*, Lexington Books (2016).

Endnotes

[1] Łukasiewicz later pointed out that "Non-Chrysippian" would be the more apt term to describe the type of logic that he was trying to develop, since it was the Stoic logician Chrysippias and his followers who were among the staunchest defenders of the principle of bivalence.

[2] References to the translation of Łukasiewicz' monograph include chapter title or chapter number followed by page number in this document.

[3] Łukasiewicz (1910, 1910), Meinong (1904, 1907, 1910, 1915), Vasil'év (1910, 1912, 1912-1913).

[4] 1910 was a rather uneventful year in European history. The passing of Halley's Comet created great popular excitement; the 13th Dalai Lama, Thubten Gyatso, was driven out of Tibet by Chinese military forces and fled to the British-Indies; in England, miners went on strike for the eight-hour work day. However, 1910 is quite a remarkable year in the history of logic: To start, 1910 saw the publication of the first volume of *Principia Mathematica* (1910-1913) by Bertrand Russell and Alfred North Whitehead. It is also the year in which Jan Łukasiewicz published his work on *The Principle of Contradiction in Aristotle*. The revised second edition of Alexius Meinong's *Über Annahmen* (*On Assumptions*) appeared the same year (Meinong 1910). And it marks the year in which Alexander Vasil'év presented his initial lecture on his conception of an *Imaginary Logic*, that is, a non-Aristotelian logic at Kazan University (Bazhanov 1990; Vasil'év 1910, 1993b).

[5] Łukasiewicz raised similar issues and criticisms with regard to the validity of the principle of the excluded third in a talk to the Philosophical Society at the University of Lvów in 1910 (Łukasiewicz 1910, 1987 [1910]).

[6] A notable exception is Raspa (1999), who recognizes the importance of Hegel, Trendelenburg, Ueberweg and Sigwart to Łukasiewicz' work.

[7] Sigwart was also read with great interest by Vasil'év, who considered Sigwart's work revolutionary, as noted by Priest (2000, 145).

[8] "Die äußerliche sinnliche Bewegung selbst ist sein unmittelbares Daseyn. Es bewegt sich etwas nur, nicht indem es in diesem Jetzt hier

ist, und in einem andern Jetzt dort, sondern indem es in einem und demselben Jetzt hier und nicht hier, indem es in diesem Hier zugleich ist und nicht ist. Man muß den alten Dialektikern die Widersprüche zugeben, die sie in der Bewegung aufzeigen, aber daraus folgt nicht, daß darum die Bewegung nicht ist, sondern vielmehr daß die Bewegung der daseyende Widerspruch selbst ist" (Hegel 1833, IV, 69).

[9] The division of Łukasiewicz' work into an early, "philosophical" and a subsequent "logical" period is frequently introduced in the literature. While it marks a significant changes in Łukasiewicz' overall philosophical position, it also introduces a division and compartmentalization of Łukasiewicz' work that seizes on a single moment in the continuous succession of evolving philosophical and logical views that Łukasiewicz articulated during his lifetime. The arbitrariness of this division is particularly pronounced in light of Łukasiewicz' life-long interest and work in the history of philosophy and logic, which forms a strong and indisputable continuity in his work and which clearly contradicts the somewhat unhappy division into so-called philosophical and logical periods.

[10] An interesting distinction between varieties of dialetheist positions is developed by Mares (2004), who distinguishes between *semantic* and *metaphysical* dialetheism.

[11] Hegel's claim, on one reading at any rate, suggests a greater universality in its scope. Everything contains contradictions. The original *Ur*-contradiction, which is the generative condition of the Hegelian unity of being and nothing, is not only canceled but also preserved in its *Aufhebung*, it is contained and present in all forms of being (and not-being). Contradiction is a universal feature of anything that is "being" or "notbeing".

[12] "Es wurde ein Dogma der neurn Philosophie, dass das dialektische Verfahren die *absolute* Methode sei; und an dieser grossen Entdeckung, der grössten, die je auf dem Gebiete der Philosophie gemacht zu sein schien, hielten auch Solche fest, die der Ertrag nicht befriedigte" (Trendelenburg 1843a, 6).

[13] "Die Logik will nichts voraussetzen als das reine Denken, das keine äussere Anschauung, kein Bild, indem nur sich selbst besitzt, aber indem es aus sich schafft, die Begriffe und Bestimmungen des Seins hervorbringt" (Trendelenburg 1843a, 12).

[14] "Die Frage, die zur Entscheidung kommen muss, einfach diese: *Ist Hegel's dialektische Methode des reinen Denkens ein wissenschaftliches Verfahren?* ... Nach den geführten Untersuchungen müssen wir sie rein und rund *verneinen*" (Trendelenburg 1843a, 26).

[15] Ueberweg "will sogar den Satz des Widerspruchs aus den Begriffen der Wahrheit, des Urteils und der Bejahung und Verneinung beweisen" (Brentano 1956, 163).

[16] In a brief rebuttal, Brentano argues that Ueberweg's proof involves a confusion of presentations and judgments. Logical consequences, however, are derived from other judgments, not from presentations (Brentano 1956, 165).

[17] Łukasiewicz cites Ueberweg's *System of Logic* in a footnote to his discussion of the conceptual components of the principle of contradiction and the possibility of deriving it from simpler, more fundamental principles (Chapter VII, 126 n.50). But Łukasiewicz does not mention or discuss Ueberweg's attempt to prove the principle of contradiction and other fundamental principles of logic based on the concept of truth, the meaning of statements, and the distinction between affirmation and denial.

[18] "Der Skotist Antonius Andreä scheint der Erste gewesen zu sein, der dies Ursprünglichkeit und die Unmöglichkeit eines direkten Beweises in Abrede stellte und den Satz des Widerspruchs aus dem Satze: *ens est ens*, der als der positive der frühere sei, abzuleiten versuchte" (Ueberweg 1857, 195).

[19] Andreas' work *Quaestiones subtilissimae super duodecim libris metaphysicae Aristotelis* first came into print in Venice in 1481—more than a hundred years after his death (Andreas 1481; cf. Andreas 1523). His work, together with Duns Scotus' writings, quickly became the subject of considerable scholastic controversy (cf. Mahoney 1988, 268).

[20] "*Gegen ihn [Antonius Andreas] nahm später der Thomist Suarez die Aristotelische Lehre in Schutz, und erklärte die Formel: ens est ens, um ihrer Lehrheit und Unfruchtbarkeit willen für unberechtigt, als oberstes Prinzip und als Grund des Satzes vom Widerspruch zu gelten*" (Ueberweg 1857, 195).

[21] "Auch für uns ist das oberste logische Prinzip nicht der Satz des Widerspruchs, sondern vielmehr die Idee der Wahrheit, d.h. der Uebereinstimmung des Wahrnehmungs- und Denkinhalts mit dem Sein. Daß ein Beweis wünschenswert sei, kann heute wohl nicht mehr in Abrede gestellt warden, da nicht nur über die richtige Formel, sondern auch über die Gültigkeit des Satzes, über seine Voraussetzungen und die etwaigen Grenzen seiner Anwendung so manche Diskussionen schweben, die ohne einen Beweis, aus welchem zugleich die wahre Bedeutung des Satzes erhellen muß, wohl niemals eine allgemein anerkannte Erledigung finden warden" (Ueberweg 1857, 181).

[22] "Der Grundsatz des (zu vermeidenden) Widerspruchs (*principium contradictionis*) lautet: contradictorisch entgegengesetzte Urtheile (wie: A ist B, und: A ist nicht B) können nicht beide wahr, sondern das eine oder andere derselben muβ falsch sein; aus der Wahrheit des einen folgt die Falschheit des anderen. Oder: die Doppelantwort: ja und nein, auf ein und dieselbe in dem nämlichen Sinne verstandene Frage ist unzulässig" (Ueberweg, 178).

[23] In his discussion Aristotle's account in the *Metaphysics*, Ueberweg distinguishes between the *metaphysical* formulations of the principle at 1005b 19 and 1006a 2 and the *logical* formulation at 1011b 13-14 (Ueberweg 1857, 193).

[24] "Der Beweis dieses Satzes ist vermittelst der Definition der Wahrheit (§3), des Urtheils (§67) und der Bejahung und Verneinung (§69) zu führen. Diesen Definitionen gemäβ ist die Wahrheit der Bejahung gleichbedeutend mit der Uebereinstimmung der Vorstellungscombination mit der Wirklichkeit, folglich mit der Falschheit der Verneinung, und die Wahrheit der Verneinung gleichbedeutend mit der Abweichung der Vorstellungscombination von der Wirklichkeit, folglich mit der Falschheit der Bejahung, so daβ, wenn die Bejahung wahr, die Verneinung falsch, und wenn die Verneinung wahr, die Bejahung falsch ist, was zu beweisen war" (Ueberweg 1857, 178).

[25] Łukasiewicz takes Ueberweg's work into consideration in Chapters VII and VIII, where he discusses the possibility of a derivation of the PC based on the principle of identity (VII, 128 ff.), and in the next chapter the importance of the definition of a true statement (VIII, 134 ff.). The influence of Ueberweg's account on Łukasiewicz' analysis receives additional consideration in the Commentary to both chapters (*VIII, The Ultimate Principle*, 381 f.; *XVIII, Proof of the Principle of Contradiction*, 475 ff.).

[26] Łukasiewicz responds to two further positions attributed to Sigwart. He charges Sigwart with psychologism, agreeing with Husserl's criticism in the first volume of the *Logische Untersuchungen* (Husserl 1900; cf. Łukasiewicz, Chapter V, 110, n.40), and notes the carelessness in Sigwart's (as well as Trendelenburg's and Ueberweg's) formulations of the principles of identity, double negation, and contradiction (Chapter VII, 120, n.50).

[27] For an additional discussion of Łukasiewicz' critique and use of Sigwart's analysis of categorical statements, see Commentary on Chapter VII, 377.

[28] De Morgan himself had sight on only one eye.

[29] The landscape example is discussed in detail by Łukasiewicz' teacher, Twardowski, in his 1894 monograph *On the Content and Object of Presentations* (Twardowski 1977 [1894]).

[30] "Two kinds of judgements must be distinguished in science: some are supposed to *reproduce* facts given in experience, the others are *produced* by the human mind. The judgements of the first category are true, because truth consists in agreement between though and existence" (Łukasiewicz 1970 [1912], 13).

[31] Łukasiewicz himself commented on this fact in a letter to Czeslaw Lejewski, dated March 14, 1955 (Archive of the University of Warsaw): In the 1910 book, "I find new historical details, which I have completely forgotten. I not only encounter terms like 'metalogic' and

'metalogical', but I also discover that the determination of these terms agrees with their contemporary meaning since what is dealt with is the investigation of the independence of one logical principle from others" (my translation; as cited by Woleński 2000, 17 n.10).

[32] Łukasiewicz reports in a footnote that the initial research for the article was begun during his stay in Graz. The article was first published in German under the title "Die logischen Grundlagen der Wahrscheinlichkeitsrechnung" one(Łukasiewicz 1970 [1913], 16 n.1).

[33] Cf. Łukasiewicz' talk at the University of Lvow titled "O zasadie wyłączonego środka" (On the Principle of the Excluded Middle) *Przegląd Filozoficzny* (Łukasiewicz 1987 [1910]).

[34] "Was beweisbar ist, soll in der Wissenschaft nicht ohne Beweis geglaubt werden" (Dedekind 1888, vii).

[35] "Die Zahlen sind freie Schöpfungen des menschlichen Geistes, sie dienen als ein Mittel, um die Verschiedenheit der Dinge leichter und schärfer aufzufassen" (Dedekind 1888, vii-viii).

[36] Łukasiewicz takes up the question of free creativity and a priori reasoning in 1912 in his article on "Creative Elements in Science" (Łukasiewicz 1970 [1912]), which is discussed in the introduction to Łukasiewicz' monograph (57 ff.) .

[37] Die "Möglichkeit, solche Wahrheiten auf andere, einfachere zurückzuführen, mag die Reihe der Schlüsse noch so lang und scheinbar künstlich sein" (Dedekind 1888, ix).

[38] "einen überzeugenden Beweis dafür, daß ihr Besitz oder der Glaube an sie niemals unmittelbar durch innere Anschauung gegeben, sondern immer nur durch eine mehr oder weniger vollständige Wiederholung der einzelnen Schlüsse erworben ist" (Dedekind 1888, ix).

[39] For example, Edward Conze in his monograph *Der Satz vom Widerspruch* (Conze 1932). For more on Conze and his discussion of the principle of contradiction, see Commentary, 320 ff.

[40] This is most apparent in his discussion of Aristotle's concept of "opposed statements" immediately following the statement of Aristotle's logical formulation. Cf. I, 90 f.

[41] The first edition of Conze's substantial, 525-pages book, titled *Der Satz vom Widerspruch. Zur Theorie des dialektischen Materialismus* (*The Principle of Contradiction. On the Theory of Dialectical Materialism*) was almost completely destroyed just months after its publication during the Nazi book burning campaign in 1933. Only a handful copies survived and Conze's early work has remained virtually unavailable to contemporary scholarship despite the vast scope and breadth of its erudite treatment of the history of the principle from Aristotle's days to the beginning of the 20th century. My translation and introduction to the book, with a foreword by Graham Priest, was published by Lexington Books, MD, in 2016.

[42] For additional information on Scholz and Conze, see my introduction to Conze's 1932 book titled "Aristotle, Marx, Buddha: Edward Conze's critique of the principle of contradiction" (Heine 2016).

[43] This and subsequent translations of Meinong's work are my own. The corresponding original German passages are provided as notes. The original passage cited is:

"Jedenfalls wird künftigen Generationen viel unnütze Arbeit zu ersparen sein, wenn man sich ein für allemal entschliesst, das Wort Urteil nur mehr im Sinne des Erlebnisses zu gebrauchen und den durch das Urteil erfassten Gegenstand ihm unter einem besonderen Namen, etwa dem von mir vorgeschlagenen Terminus Objektiv ausdrücklich gegenüberzustellen" (Meinong 1907, 125).

[44] "Das Seiende, die 'Tatsache', ohne die kein Erkennen für Erkennen gelten dürfte, ist das durch den betreffenden Erkenntnisakt erfaßte Objektiv, dem ein Sein, genauer Bestand zukommt, mag es positiv oder negativ, mag es ein Sein oder ein Sosein sein." (Meinong 1904, 25)

[45] "Das alles ändert nichts an der Tatsache, daβ das Sosein eines Gegenstandes durch dessen Nichtsein sozusagen nicht mitbetroffen ist. Die Tatsache ist wichtig genug, um sie ausdrücklich als das Prinzip der Unabhängigkeit des Soseins vom Sein zn formulieren, und der Geltungsbereich dieses Prinzips erhellt am besten im Hinblick auf den Umstand, daβ diesem Prinzipe nicht nur Gegenstände unterstehen, die eben faktisch nicht existieren, sondern auch solche, die nicht existieren können, weil sie unmöglich sind. Nicht nur der vielberufene goldene Berg ist von Gold, sondern anch das runde Viereck ist so gewiβ rund als es viereckig ist" (Meinong 1904, 8).

[46] Wittgenstein, *Tractatus 4.21*: "The simplest kind of statement, an elementary statement, asserts the existence of a state of affairs" (Wittgenstein 1922). In his "Introduction to *Tractatus Logico-Philosophicus*", Russell defines an atomic statement as follows: "A statement (true or false) asserting an atomic fact is called an atomic statement" (Russell 1922).

[47] An exception to this fundamental principle occurs in the translation of certain self-referential sentences from one natural language to another where, as Tyler Burge put it in quasi-paradoxical terms, "self-reference is preserved by not preserving reference" (Burge 1978). The situation is even further complicated in the translation of sentences of the form 'This sentence is in English.' For details, see W.T. Hart (1970) and my "The Paradox of Translation" in *Fragments* (Heine 2021 – forthcoming).

[48] The meaning of the Polish word *"sąd"* most closely corresponds to the English word "judgment" or "opinion" (it also means "court of law"). The German translation renders it as "Urteil". However, given Łukasiewicz' technical use of the word, which corresponds more closely to the English "statement", it has been translated almost exclusively as

"statement" or "logical sentence". Read literally, Łukasiewicz' passage asserts that the two judgments express the same object. Thus, in light of the context in which the passage occurs, "object" is probably best understood as referring to statement or propositional content (cf. Notes on the Translation, 75).

[49] Łukasiewicz' translation is more careful and preserves Aristotle's distinction between convictions and statements: "convictions that have corresponding contradictory statement are opposed to each other" (18). Cf. Dancy: "the contrary of a belief is the belief in its contradictory" (Dancy, 156) and Kirwan: "the opinion contrary to an opinion is that of the contradictory" (Kirwan, 8).

[50] Łukasiewicz cites a sentence from *De Anima* (428a 20-21) where Aristotle seems to make exactly this point (III, 104).

[51] Aristotle considers a possible exception to this in the case of future contingents in Ch.9 of *De Interpretatione.*

[52] Twardowski's argument appeals to Aristotle's psychological PC. "No one will manage to get himself to believe that the same judgment could be a true judgment, yet simultaneously false" (Twardowski 1999 [1900], 163). According to Twardowski, it is because the principle of non-contradiction "can in no way be eliminated from human reasoning and thinking" (Twardowski 1999 [1900], 163).

[53] Kirwan translates the phrase as "the *firmest* of all principles," avoiding the psychological connotations of the notion of certainty (italics added). The phrase appears three times in close succession in the Greek passage (Ross' text) *βεβαιοτάτη δ' ἀρχὴ πασῶν* (1005b 11), *βεβαιοτάτη πασῶν ἀρχὴ* (1005b 18), *βεβαιοτάτη τῶν ἀρχῶν* (1005b 22). Dancy (1975, 156), in agreement with Kirwan, also translates *βεβαιοτάτη* as "firmest."

[54] Priest makes the same observation and concludes that "it is not at all obvious that no proof of the LNC (Law of Non-Contradiction) in Aristotle's sense is impossible" (Priest 2008 [2006], 13).

[55] In Chapter X, Łukasiewicz goes further and offers an argument to show that there is doubt that the three principles even are (logically) equivalent.

[56] Italics added for emphasis.

[57] A similar point is made by Bach and Harnish (1979), who argue against Austin that performativity can be explained inferentially and without any appeals to special meanings or conventions associated with performative expressions (cf. Bach 1979, Ch.10).

[58] Chapter 20 of *Prior Analytics II,* which Łukasiewicz cites in parts, reads as follows: "Since we know when a deduction can be formed and how its terms must be related, it is clear when refutation will be possible and when impossible. A refutation is possible whether everything is conceded, or the answers alternate (one, I mean, being affirmative, the other negative). For, as has been shown, a deduction is possible both in

the former and in the latter case: consequently, if what is laid down is contrary to the conclusion, a refutation must take place; for a refutation is a deduction which establishes the contradictory. But if nothing is conceded, a refutation is impossible; for no deduction is possible (as we saw) when all the terms are negative; therefore no refutation is possible. For if a refutation were possible, a deduction must be possible; although if a deduction is possible it does not follow that a refutation is possible. Similarly refutation is not possible if nothing is conceded universally; since refutation and deduction are defined in the same way" (Aristotle, , Pr.An. II 66b 4-17; Jenkinson translation).

[59] Ross: "contradictories cannot be predicated at the same time" (1007b 18).

[60] The inevitability of an appeal to the PC in these inference schemas becomes even clearer in consideration of the equivalence between the material conditional $A \rightarrow B$ and its formulation as a conjunction, $\sim(A \wedge \sim B)$. As mentioned in the commentary to Chapter VII and Łukasiewicz' discussion of the principle of identity, the propositional formulation of the PC, $\sim(A \wedge \sim A)$ follows directly from the conditional formulation of the principle of identity, $A \rightarrow A$.

[61] All citations from the *Categories* are from Ackrill's translation (Aristotle 1992).

[62] Priest, too, identifies the introduction of the claim that whatever is completely indefinite because it is exclusively determined by contradictory statements must be something that is potential and cannot be actual as the premise in Aristotle's argument that begs the question (Priest 2008 [2006], 34-35).

[63] Priest (2008 [2006], 36) points out that (iii) is an additional possibility, but remains inconclusive as to the reasons for its omission in Aristotle's account.

[64] In the *Phaedo*, Plato includes both Antisthenes and Euclid of Megara among those who were present at Socrates' death.

[65] For instance, in his *Examination of Sir William Hamilton's Philosophy*, Mill argues that"logic is not a science, separate from and coordinate to psychology. So far as it is a science at all, it is a part or branch, of psychology; differing from it, on the one hand, as a part differs from the whole, and on the other,as an art differs from a science" (Mill 1868, II, 146). Regarding the foundation of the principle of contradiction, Mill declares that he considers the principle to be "like other axioms, one of our first and most familiar generalizations from experience" (*A System of Logic,* 8th edition, 1891, 205; as cited in Richards 1980, 27).

[66] "Daher müssen wir auch den Satz des Widerspruchs als *das allgemeine und völlig zureichende Prinzipium aller analytischen Erkenntnis* gelten lassen" (A151/B191 – my Italics).

[67] See Introduction (69-71) for a more detailed discussion of Brentano's critique of Ueberweg in Brentano's posthumuously published lectures on logic (Brentano 1956, 163-167).

[68] Łukasiewicz reports that he was first introduced to Meinong's distinctions between objects in Meinong's lectures, which he attended during his visit to Graz in the winter of 1908-9 (XVIII, 203, n.123). A detailed account of Meinong's distinctions between complete and incomplete objects is found in Meinong's monograph on possibility and probability (Meinong 1915, Ch.2, 168 ff.).

[69] The Megarian challenges in general and the paradoxes attributed to Eubulides in particular may be an exception to this claim. Except for the Sorites paradox, Eubulides' paradoxes were discussed by Scholastic logicians during the middle ages. However, at the time of Łukasiewicz' writing, the importance of the paradoxes and their direct bearing on the semantic and logical theories that were just beginning to take shape in the work of Frege and Russell was not yet recognized. For a more detailed discussion of the Megarian challenges to the principle of contradiction, see Commentary to Chapter XIV, on the challenges of Eubulides' paradoxes to contemporary logic and semantics, see Seuren (2005).

[70] "Bei dieser Untersuchung wird sich finden, daβ es zwei reine Formen sinnlicher Anschauung, als Prinzipien der Erkenntnis a priori gebe, nämlich Raum und Zeit" (Kant 1976 [1787], A22, B36).

[71] "Die Zeit ist die formale Bedingung a priori aller Erscheinungen überhaupt" (Kant 1976 [1787], A34, B50).

[72] "Hier füge ich noch hinzu, daß der Begriff der Veränderung und, mit ihm, der Begriff der Bewegung (als Veränderung des Ortes) nur durch und in der Zeitvorstellung möglich ist" (Kant, A32, B48).

[73] "Wenn diese Vorstellung nicht Anschauung (innere) a priori wäre, kein Begriff, welcher es auch sei, die Möglichkeit einer Veränderung, d.i. einer Verbindung kontradiktorisch entgegengesetzter Prädikate (z.B. das Sein an einem Orte und das Nichtsein eben desselben Dinges an demselben Orte) in einem und demselben Objekte begreiflich machen könnte. Nur in der Zeit können beide kontradiktorisch-entgegengesetzte Bestimmungen in einem Dinge, nämlich *nacheinander*, anzutreffen sein" (Kant, A32, B48-49).

[74] Priest, in his discussion of the possibility of an empirical observation of a contradictory state of affairs, makes the same point: "one can perceive states only if they persist for some minimal time ... Hence, though a moving object may realize instantaneous contradictory states, these are not such as can be seen" (Priest 2008 [2006], 58).

[75] "Die Gegenwart soll ein in continuirlicher Bewegung befindlicher Punkt sein, welcher die Zeitlinie erzeugt" (Schumann 1898, 127).

[76] "Die Zeit besteht aus Vergangenheit und Zukunft, die durch den beweglichen Punkt des 'Jetzt' getrennt sind. Da die Vergangenheit

nicht mehr, und die Zukunft noch nicht ist, so wäre die Zeit ein Wirkliches, das aus zwei Hälften besteht, die beide nicht wirklich sind" (Schumann 1898, 127).

[77] "Der mathematische Punkt ist die Grenze, der man beliebig nahe kommen, die man aber nie erreichen kann. Definirt [sic] man aber den Begriff der Gegenwart in der Weise, daß ihm nichts Wirkliches mehr entspricht, daß er zu einer mathematischen Fictíon wird, so darf man sich auch nicht wundern, daß dieser Begriff zur Construction der Wirklichkeit nicht brauchbar ist" (Schumann 1898, 127).

[78] "Der Punkt selbst freilich kann nicht existieren, sondern nur bestehen; aber wo der Punkt ist, kann sehr wohl etwas existieren, nur nicht beschränkt auf den Punkt" (Meinong 1899, 260).

[79] A second limit of duration (time) is expressed by the concept of an infinite, that is, unbounded duration or time, whose contradictory aspects are generative components of Kant's first antinomy (cf. Kant 1976 [1787], B 454 ff.).